ASIAN ENERGY MARKETS
DYNAMICS AND TRENDS

ASIAN ENERGY MARKETS
DYNAMICS AND TRENDS

**THE EMIRATES CENTER FOR STRATEGIC
STUDIES AND RESEARCH**

THE EMIRATES CENTER FOR STRATEGIC STUDIES AND RESEARCH

The Emirates Center for Strategic Studies and Research (ECSSR) is an independent research institution dedicated to the promotion of professional studies and educational excellence in the UAE, the Gulf and the Arab world. Since its establishment in Abu Dhabi in 1994, ECSSR has served as a focal point for scholarship on political, economic and social matters. Indeed, ECSSR is at the forefront of analysis and commentary on Arab affairs.

The Center seeks to provide a forum for the scholarly exchange of ideas by hosting conferences and symposia, organizing workshops, sponsoring a lecture series and publishing original and translated books and research papers. ECSSR also has an active fellowship and grant program for the writing of scholarly books and for the translation into Arabic of work relevant to the Center's mission. Moreover, ECSSR has a large library including rare and specialized holdings, and a state-of-the-art technology center, which has developed an award-winning website that is a unique and comprehensive source of information on the Gulf.

Through these and other activities, ECSSR aspires to engage in mutually beneficial professional endeavors with comparable institutions worldwide, and to contribute to the general educational and academic development of the UAE.

The views expressed in this book do not necessarily reflect those of the ECSSR.

First published in 2004 by
The Emirates Center for Strategic Studies and Research
PO Box 4567, Abu Dhabi, United Arab Emirates

E-mail: pubdis@ecssr.ac.ae
pubdis@ecssr.com

Website: http://www.ecssr.ac.ae
http://www.ecssr.com

ISBN 9948-00-570-8 hardback edition

ISBN 9948-00-569-4 paperback edition

CONTENTS

Figures and Tables   ix

Abbreviations and Acronyms   xiv

Foreword   xix
Jamal S. Al-Suwaidi

INTRODUCTION

Asian Energy Markets: An Overview   3
John V. Mitchell

GENERAL OUTLOOK

1   The Asian Energy Market: A New Geopolitics?   21
    Robert A. Manning

2   Future Supply and Demand Trends in the Asian Energy Markets   55
    James P. Dorian

CORE ENERGY ISSUES

3   Energy Trade in Asia: An Overview   113
    Amy Myers Jaffe and Kenneth B. Medlock III

4   Regulation and Deregulation of Energy in the Asian Market:
    The Case of China   143
    Philip Andrews-Speed

MARKET STATUS AND PROSPECTS

5   The Present Status and Future Prospects of Energy
    Demand and Supply in East Asia   181
    David Von Hippel

6   The Electricity Supply Industry in East Asia
    and the Implications of Increasing World Energy Prices   241
    Romeo Pacudan

7   The Present Status and Future Prospects of Energy in China   275
     Kenneth B. Medlock III, Ronald Soligo and Amy Myers Jaffe

8   The Present Status and Future Prospects of Energy in India   311
     Leena Srivastava and Megha Shukla

     Concluding Observations   341
     John V. Mitchell

Contributors   347

Notes   357

Bibliography   379

Index   391

FIGURES AND TABLES

FIGURES

Figure 1.1	Middle East Oil Supplies (1995)	26
Figure 1.2	Middle East Oil Supplies (2015)	27
Figure 1.3	GDP Per Capita Vs Primary Energy Demand Per Capita in Selected Asian Economies (1995)	35
Figure 2.1	Oil Consumption in the Developing World (1970-2020)	65
Figure 2.2	Increases in Natural Gas Consumption by Region (1999-2020)	70
Figure 2.3	Present and Planned Natural Gas Pipelines of China	72
Figure 2.4	World Coal Consumption by Region (1980, 1990 and 2020)	74
Figure 2.5	Renewable Energy Consumption in Developing Asia (1999, 2010 and 2020)	80
Figure 2.6	Renewable Energy Consumption in Industrialized Asia (1999, 2010 and 2020)	81
Figure 2.7	Major Oilfields of Central Asia	84
Figure 2.8	Present Electric Industry Structure of the Philippines	98
Figure 3.1	Share of the World Total Primary Energy Supply (TPES) By Selected Regions (1980 and 2000)	116
Figure 3.2	Primary Energy in Asia (2000)	117
Figure 3.3	Primary Energy Per Capita in Asia (2000)	118
Figure 3.4	Structure of Primary Energy Consumption in Asia-Pacific Region (1980 and 2000)	120
Figure 3.5	Carbon Emissions in Asia and the World (2000) by Source	124
Figure 3.6	Potential for Asian Energy Demand Per Capita	128
Figure 3.7	IEA Incremental Oil Demand Projections by Sector (1997-2020)	133
Figure 4.1	Energy Supply and Demand (1980-1999)	156
Figure 4.2	China Oil Supply and Demand (1980-2001)	158
Figure 4.3	Schematic Summary of China's Energy Sector Structure Before and After the 1998 Reforms	163
Figure 5.1	Primary Fuels Demand in China	184

Figure 5.2   Crude Oil Exports, Imports and Net Imports in China   185

Figure 5.3   DPRK Energy Demand Indicators by Fuel and Sector
               (1990 and 1996)   187

Figure 5.4   DPRK Energy Supply Indicators (1990 and 1996)   190

Figure 5.5   Japan Energy End-Use Demand by Sector
               and Fuel Type (1998)   191

Figure 5.6   Fraction of Primary Energy Use in Japan by Fuel Type   192

Figure 5.7   Commercial Fuels Use in Mongolia   194

Figure 5.8   Primary Energy Demand in Mongolia by Fuel Type   195

Figure 5.9   ROK Gross Domestic Product   196

Figure 5.10   Total Energy Demand and Energy Imports
               in the ROK (1980-2000)   199

Figure 5.11   ROK Generating Capacity by Fuel Type   199

Figure 5.12   Estimated Energy Demand by Sector in China: BAU Scenario   206

Figure 5.13   Estimated Energy Demand by Sector in China:
               Alternative Scenario   206

Figure 5.14   End-Use Coal Demand in China: Scenario Comparison   207

Figure 5.15   Total Coal Requirements in China: Scenario Comparison   207

Figure 5.16   Total Oil and Oil Products Net Import Requirements in China:
               Scenario Comparison   208

Figure 5.17   Relative Electric Capacity and Operating and Maintenance
               (O&M) Costs: Scenario Comparison   209

Figure 5.18   DPRK Energy Demand Scenarios by Fuel Type (1990-2010)   210

Figure 5.19   DPRK Energy Demand Scenarios by Sector (1990-2010)   211

Figure 5.20   Energy Demand by Fuel Type   214

Figure 5.21   Energy Demand by Sector   215

Figure 5.22   Relative Benefits: Alternative Case Minus BAU Case   218

Figure 5.23   Final Energy Demand by Fuel in Mongolia: ALGAS Results   219

Figure 5.24   Final Energy Demand by Sector in Mongolia: ALGAS Results   220

Figure 5.25   ALGAS Estimates of Future Fuel Supply in Mongolia   220

Figure 5.26   Historical, Estimated and Projected Energy Demand
               in the Russian Far East by Sector   225

Figure 5.27   Historical, Estimated and Projected Energy Demand
               in the Russian Far East by Fuel   225

Figure 5.28   Historical and Projected Carbon Emissions in Northeast Asia
               and the Rest of the World   230

Figure 5.29   Global Warming Potential from All Fossils Use:
               Scenario Comparison   231

Figure 6.1   Proposed Gas Interconnection Routes in Northeast Asia   249

Figure 6.2   Northeast Asia Proposed Power Grid Interconnection   258

Figure 6.3   Power Grid Interconnection in Southeast Asia   260

Figure 6.4   Electricity Supply Industry Structural Models   263

Figure 6.5   Electricity Industry Structure and Ownership in Asia   267

Figure 7.1   Energy Intensity of Selected Nations (1995)   277

Figure 7.2   Vehicle Registrations for Selected Nations (1979-1995)   280

Figure 7.3   Energy Demand by End-Use Sector for a Hypothetical Country   282

Figure 7.4   Chinese Total Final Energy Consumption (1978-1999)   283

Figure 7.5   Chinese TFC by Sector (1980 and 1999)   283

Figure 7.6   Chinese TPES and Composition by Source (1980 and 1999)   285

Figure 7.7   Reference Case Energy Demand Forecast for China
               to the Year 2020   288

Figure 7.8   Reference Case Energy Demand Forecast for China to the
               Year 2020 with Adjustment to Global Average Tendencies   290

Figure 8.1   Comparative Trend in GDP and Total Primary
               Energy Consumption   312

Figure 8.2   Low Levels of Per Capita Consumption in India   314

Figure 8.3   Comparison among Countries with Respect to Per Capita
               Electricity Generation   315

Figure 8.4   Comparison among Countries with Respect to Per Capita
               Oil Consumption   315

Figure 8.5   Increasing Reliance on Oil Imports   316

Figure 8.6   Current and Projected Energy Mix for 2001 and 2025   317

Figure 8.7   Inter-Modal Share of Freight Traffic   321

Figure 8.8   Electricity Capacity Additions in Plan Periods   326

Figure 8.9   T&D Losses in Uttar Pradesh   330

TABLES

Table 2.1   Growth Rate of Asian GDP (2000-2020)   58

Table 2.2   World Petroleum Trade, 1998 and 2020 (a)   68

Table 2.3   World Net Electricity Consumption by Region (1990-2020)   76

Table 2.4   World Consumption of Hydroelectricity and Other
Renewables by Region   79

Table 2.5   Central Asia: Existing Energy Production by Country   83

Table 3.1   Countries Included in Asia   113

Table 3.2   Asian Production and Consumption of Energy by Source
(1980, 1990 and 2000)   121

Table 3.3   Carbon Emissions and Population (1980 and 2000)   123

Table 3.4   Asian Share of World Fossil Energy (2000)   129

Table 3.5   Asian Oil Demand and GDP Growth (1996-1999)   130

Table 3.6   Russian Far East: Recoverable Gas, Oil
and Condensate Reserves   139

Table 4.1   Structure of Primary Energy Consumption (1980-1999)   157

Table 5.1   Fuels Consumption in Northeast Asia and the World   182

Table 5.2   Summary of Energy Demand in the ROK
(1990-2000) by Fuel Type   197

Table 5.3   Summary of Primary Energy Supply in the ROK (1990-2000)   198

Table 5.4   Primary Energy Consumption and Share of Energy Imports
In the Russian Far East (1990 and 1996)   201

Table 5.5   Discovered Primary Energy Reserves of the Russian Far East   202

Table 5.6   Scenarios for Primary Energy Supplies by Fuel in the DPRK   212

Table 5.7   Growth of Overall Sectoral Energy Demand (1995-2020)   216

Table 5.8   Primary Supplies of Fuels and Resources by Balance Category   217

Table 5.9   Primary Energy Demand Forecast for the ROK (2001-2006)   222

Table 5.10   Final Energy Demand Forecast for the ROK (2001-2006)   223

Table 5.11   Annual Average Growth of Energy Use   224

Table 5.12   Estimated Emissions of Acid Gases in Northeast Asia in 1990   228

[xii]

Table 6.1	Electricity Capacity and Generation: Historical and Forecast Growth Rates	243
Table 6.2	Electricity Generation Mix	245
Table 6.3	Energy Reserves and Hydro Potential in East Asia	246
Table 6.4	Steam Coal Exports and Imports, Natural Gas Imports in Asia	247
Table 6.5	Existing and Planned LNG Infrastructures in East Asia	248
Table 6.6	Cross-Border Natural Gas Trade	250
Table 6.7	Price Trends of Asian Reference Fuels	251
Table 6.8	Technology Comparative Costs	254
Table 6.9	Renewable Energy Policies in Selected East Asian Countries	255
Table 6.10	Northeast Asian Power Grid Ring	258
Table 6.11	Southeast Asia Power Interconnection Projects	260
Table 6.12	Status of Reforms in Selected East Asian Countries	268
Table 7.1	Structure of Consumption	279
Table 7.2	Energy Demand Forecasts for China to the Year 2020	287
Table 7.3	Reference Case Energy Demand Forecasts for China to the Year 2020 with Adjustment to Global Tendencies	290
Table 7.4	Projected Chinese Crude Oil Requirements by Sector	293
Table 7.5	Projected Chinese Natural Gas Requirements by Sector	294
Table 7.6	China's Oil Production by Field	296
Table 7.7	Cost Estimates of Alternative Routes	302
Table 7.8	China Refinery Capacity by Crude Types	305
Table 8.1	Major Challenge—High Energy Intensities	312
Table 8.2	Increasing Share of Roads in Freight and Passenger Movement	320
Table 8.3	Proposed Renewable Energy Capacity Addition (2012)	324
Table 8.4	Capacity Additions per Annum in Plan Periods	328
Table 8.5	Potential and Achievement in Renewable Energy	336
Table 8.6	Current and Estimated Future Costs of Renewable Energy Technologies	337
Table 8.7	Potential for Improvement in Energy Efficiency	339

ABBREVIATIONS AND ACRONYMS

ADB	Asian Development Bank
AEO	Annual Energy Outlook
ALGAS	Asia Least-Cost Greenhouse Gas Abatement Strategy
ASEAN	Association of South East Asian Nations
APEC	Asia-Pacific Economic Cooperation
APEC	Asia Pacific Energy Consulting
APERC	Asia Pacific Energy Research Center
BAU	business as usual
BEE	Bureau of Energy Efficiency
BOT	build-operate-transfer
BP	British Petroleum
BTU	British thermal units
CNA	Center for Naval Analysis
CBM	coal bed methane
CCGT	combined cycle gas turbine
CEA	Central Electricity Authority
CEPMLP	Centre for Energy, Petroleum and Mineral Law and Policy
CERF	Civil Engineering Research Foundation
CFR	Council on Foreign Relations
CIF	cost, insurance and freight
CIS	Commonwealth of the Independent States
CMIE	Center for Monitoring Indian Economy
CNG	compressed natural gas
CNOOC	China National Offshore Oil Corporation
CNPC	Chinese National Petroleum Corporation
CNSPC	China National Star Petroleum Corporation
CPC	Caspian Pipeline Consortium
CSCAP	Council for Security Cooperation in the Asia Pacific
CTBT	Comprehensive Test Ban Treaty
CWC	Chemical Weapons Convention
DGH	Directorate General of Hydrocarbons
DPRK	Democratic People's Republic of Korea

DSM	demand side management
E&P	exploration and production
EdL	Electricite du Laos
EE	Eastern Europe
EGAT	Electricity Generating Authority of Thailand
EIA	Energy Information Administration
ESENA	Energy Security and the Environment in Northeast Asia
EU	European Union
EVN	Electricity of Vietnam
FDI	foreign direct investment
FSU	Former Soviet Union
GAIL	Gas Authority of India Limited
GATT	General Agreement on Tariffs and Trade
GDP	gross domestic product
GEF	Global Environmental Fund
GEF	Global Environment Facility
GHG	greenhouse gas
GJ	gigajoules
GMS	Greater Mekong Sub-Region
GWe	gigawatt electric
HVDC	high voltage direct current
IBRD	International Bank for Reconstruction and Development
IEA	International Energy Agency
IEEJ	Institute of Energy Economics, Japan
IIEC	International Institute for Energy Conservation
IEO	International Energy Outlook
IEPE	Institut d'Economie et de Politique de l'Energie
IMF	International Monetary Fund
INM	International Nuclear Model
IPCC	Intergovernmental Panel on Climate Change
IPP	independent power producer
IREDA	Indian Renewable Energy Development Agency
IRP	integrated resource planning
JI	joint implementation
JNOC	Japan National Oil Company
KEDO	Korean (Peninsula) Energy Development Organization

KEEI	Korean Energy Economics Institute
KEPCO	Korean Electric Power Company
kcal	kilo calories
kgoe	kilograms of oil equivalent
kv	kilovolt
kWh	kilowatt hours
LBNL	Lawrence Berkeley National Laboratory
LNG	liquified natural gas
MEA	Metropolitan Electricity Authority
METI	Ministry of Economy, Trade and Investment
MESITA	Malaysia Electricity Supply Industry Trust Account
MFN	most favored nation
MGMR	Ministry of Geology and Mineral Resources
MITI	Ministry of International Trade and Industry
MLNR	Ministry of Land and Natural Resources
MMSCMD	million metric standard cubic meters per day
MMT	million metric tons
MMTOE	million metric tons of oil equivalent
MNES	Ministry of Non-Conventional Energy Sources
MOEP	Ministry of Electric Power
MoF	Ministry of Finance
MoPNG	Ministry of Petroleum and Natural Gas
MoR	Ministry of Railways
MOU	memorandum of understanding
MOX	mixed oxide
MTCR	Missile Technology Control Regime
MTOE	million tons of oil equivalent
MW	megawatt
MWe	megawatt electric
NAFTA	North American Free Trade Area
NEB	National Electricity Board
NELP	New Exploration Licensing Policy
NEMS	National Energy Modeling System
NIE	newly industrialized economy
NPC	National Power Corporation
NPT	Non-Proliferation Treaty

NPV	net present value
OECD	Organization for Economic Cooperation and Development
O&M	operating and maintenance
OPEC	Organization of Petroleum Exporting Countries
OSW	ocean, solar and wind
PARES	Pacific Asian Regional Energy Security
PEA	Provincial Electricity Authority
PLA	People's Liberation Army
PLF	plant load factor
PLN	Perusahaan Listrik Negara
PPA	power purchase agreement
PPI	Progressive Policy Institute
PPP	purchasing power parity
PRC	People's Republic of China
PSC	production sharing contract
RARE	remote area renewable energy
RE	renewable energy
REAP	Renewable Energy Action Plan
REPPA	Renewable Energy Power Purchase Agreement
RET	renewable energy technology
RFE	Russian Far East
RIIA	Royal Institute of International Affairs
RIL	Reliance Industries Limited
ROK	Republic of Korea
RPS	renewable portfolio standard
SAFIR	South Asia Forum for Infrastructure Regulation
SDPC	State Development Planning Commission
SEB	State Electricity Board
SESCO	Sarawak Electricity Supply Corporation
SETC	State Economic and Trade Commission
SLOC	sea lanes of communication
SREP	small renewable energy power
SPC	State Planning Commission
SPCC	State Power Corporation of China
SPP	small power producers
SSTC	State Science and Technology Commission

tcf	trillion cubic feet
T&D	transmission and distribution
TEDDY	Tata Energy Data Directory and Yearbook
TEPCO	Tokyo Electric Power Company
TERI	The Energy and Resources Institute
TFC	total final consumption
TNB	Tenaga Nasional Berhad
TOE	tons of oil equivalent
TPES	total primary energy supply
UNDP	United Nations Development Program
USDOE	United States Department of Energy
UNEP	United Nations Environment Program
URC	UNEP Risoe Centre
VSREPP	very small renewable energy power producers
WEPS	World Energy Projection System
WTO	World Trade Organization
WWW	World Wide Web

The Asian region has been growing in importance in the world energy scenario, mainly because of its high levels of energy consumption. By 2020, Asian energy consumption is expected to exceed one-third of total world consumption. Consequently, energy imports to countries in the region have risen steadily, especially to emerging economic powerhouses like China and India. Other developing countries in the Asian region, with their rising income levels and high economic growth rates look set to follow this trend.

Additionally, many Asian countries have been undergoing significant economic and social changes. From the 1980s to the turn of the century, governments in the region have increasingly embraced global market liberalism as part of their developmental strategies, while seeking to maintain a high degree of state control. Various Asian countries have applied these apparently contradictory principles to differing extents in charting their economic success. All these factors are crucial in assessing particular Asian countries and their future potential as major energy consumers. Asia's burgeoning need for assured energy supplies is a powerful driver that shapes its economic development, impacts on political relations between Asian states, and influences bilateral relations with countries beyond the region, especially the oil-producing states of the Arabian Gulf.

The Seventh Annual Energy Conference of the Emirates Center for Strategic Studies and Research (ECSSR) on *The Energy Markets in Asia*, held from January 13-14, 2002, in Abu Dhabi, UAE, explored current and prospective energy issues connected with the economic and structural changes underway in the Asian continent, most notably in India, China, East Asia and South East Asia. The informative conference presentations compiled in this volume provide a comprehensive look at the key determinants governing energy supply and demand in the Asian countries, including world energy prices, regional geopolitics, national economic and regulatory policies, as well as energy consumption patterns in the region.

ECSSR would like to express its appreciation to the conference speakers for their collective insight and also to the panel of expert referees who offered constructive comments on the conference papers. The Center is grateful to Mr. John V. Mitchell, Associate Research Fellow of the Royal Institute of International Affairs (Chatham House) for his introductory chapter and concluding remarks, which present the main issues and trends from an illuminating perspective. A word of thanks is also due to ECSSR editor Mary Abraham for coordinating the publication of this book.

Jamal S. Al-Suwaidi, Ph.D.
Director General
ECSSR

INTRODUCTION

Asian Energy Markets:
An Overview

John V. Mitchell

A sia matters. Energy consumption has risen strongly, though unevenly, through the past thirty-five years to 2002. Energy consumption in Asia[1] is now almost one third of world energy consumption, up from just over fifteen per cent in 1965. This consumption occurs in Asia, including Southwest Asia (the "Middle East" in European terminology) and Australasia. By 2020, Asia's share of world energy consumption will be around thirty-seven per cent, according to the reference case projections of the US Energy Information Administration.[2] Asian energy consumption already exceeds that of North America and is one and a half times that of Europe.

Asia is different. Although it has grown in relative importance as an energy-consuming region, Asia differs considerably from other regions in ways that are significant for energy markets and businesses. Asia is a geographical, not a political entity. Its countries do not share institutions like the North American Free Trade Area (NAFTA) or the European Union (EU). The countries of North America and Europe also have similar political institutions—elected governments, open markets and essentially capitalist economies. Some Asian countries have long-held commitments to market economics, while others are moving in that

[3]

direction. Yet, the diversity of its economic and political systems continues to differentiate Asia from North America, Europe, and the region of the former Soviet Union, which spans both Asia and Europe.

North American and European governments are deeply involved in the institutions of international trade and finance such as the World Trade Organization (WTO), and the Organization for Economic Cooperation and Development (OECD). Some Asian countries have long participated in these institutions. For example, Japan and now South Korea are members of the OECD. Japan and several other Asian nations are members of the General Agreement on Tariffs and Trade (GATT), the predecessor to the WTO. In fact, China's accession to the WTO in 2002 marked a huge shift in the balance of commitment of the Asian continent to the international trading system, just as Chinese economic reforms implemented since 1995 marked the start of a massive extension of the principles of market economics.

The future of world energy markets and investment in energy will be strongly influenced by how these differences develop in Asia in the future, as its weight in the global energy scene continues to increase. Trade within Asia already forms a large segment of world energy trade. For instance, in 2001,[3] this trade comprised seventy percent of inter-regional trade in liquefied natural gas (LNG), half the world trade in coal and nearly forty percent of the world trade in oil. In the case of oil, Southwest Asia is the key, supplying the rest of Asia with seventy percent of its imported oil and fifty-five percent of its oil consumption. In comparison, Southwest Asia supplies the rest of the world with only twenty-eight percent of its oil imports and only fourteen percent of its oil consumption. The dependence of the rest of Asia on its southwest region is not one way. South West Asia needs the East Asian energy market. Sixty per cent of Southwest Asian exports, and almost all its LNG exports, go east, not west. Interdependence will increase. The increase in oil consumption in the rest of Asia accounts for seventy percent of the increase in oil consumption outside Southwest Asia projected by the Energy Information Administration (EIA) in their reference case for 2020.[4]

The Four Transitions

As the Asian numbers gain more importance on the world energy scene, so do the trends in Asian market structure and international cooperation. In this volume, the contributing authors address from different perspectives, what might be described as "the four transitions," which in one way or another are affecting most Asian countries of importance in the energy scene. How each country is affected depends on its starting position. Where each country goes depends partly on how its own economic and political structure develops, and partly on what happens elsewhere in the region. Trends may not necessarily converge but they have to avoid contradiction and evolve some degree of coherence if they are to work. What will the ultimate coherence look like? This is the tantalizing question, to which I will return in the final chapter.

1. Transition to Market Economics

The first transition, touching almost all countries, is to the practices and institutions of a market economy. The biggest change relates to China. The country is moving from a planned economy dominated by state enterprises to one in which private property is recognized, non-state enterprises are not only tolerated but encouraged, and market pricing finds its way into the energy sector as it has into many other markets. There are some similar moves underway in India and Indonesia, while in Japan the liberalization of energy markets is gradually being realized as a necessary step to restore the competitiveness of the economy.

2. Growth of Imports

The second transition is the growing importance of imports as a source of energy. Again, China is the prime example, changing its status from that of an exporter to an importer since 1994. India is following the same road and Indonesia, as far as oil is concerned, may join this category in the future.

3. Increasing Use of Gas

A third transition, linked to the others, is the growth of natural gas as a fuel not only for power generation but also for industrial and domestic use. Many factors combine to make natural gas an attractive form of energy consumption. In cities, burning gas generates less pollution than burning coal or oil. In power generation, the increased efficiency and flexibility of Combined Cycle Gas Turbine (CCGT) generation gives it economic as well as environmental advantages. The challenge is on the supply side. Long distance infrastructure such as LNG terminal pipelines and ships must be built. At the consumer level, distribution systems need to be developed. Investment and promotion of gas to final consumers is something of a novelty in many Asian countries. There are uncertainties about how rapidly these developments will occur and what market and investment conditions will be provided.

4. International Activities

The fourth transition, which is also linked to the others, is the inevitability of growing involvement by Asian countries in international energy markets and institutions. In the absence of any regional organizing principle (except for The Asia-Pacific Economic Cooperation forum, APEC) there is no continent-wide institution comparable to NAFTA, the OECD, or the EU. Within global markets and institutions, Asian countries will carry weight and have opportunities to pursue their interests. However, it might be a mistake for the rest of the world to assume that the present structures of international cooperation will simply be "extended" to embrace Asian countries without some changes either in formal structure, pragmatic agendas, or both.

The key question is whether Asian governments will participate more fully in the global institutions, or whether Asian regional bonds will be strengthened in some formal way through bilateral arrangements or sub-regional commitments, for example in the Association of South East Asian Nations (ASEAN) or treaties specifically concerned with cross-border infrastructure such as the proposed gas pipelines in northeast and central Asia.

An Overview

The Numbers

Projection of Asian energy demand numbers is not easy. All energy demand forecasts for rapidly developing countries are necessarily brave attempts to quantify the unknowable. They are the product of high rates of growth in projections for the economy, assumptions about energy productivity, the degree of electrification and the speed of penetration of private automobiles and trucks in the transport sector, to name but some factors. Many of the contributing authors of this book wrestle with this problem. Robert A. Manning discusses the ending of the "Asian miracle" in the economic upheavals of 1998. He concludes that most Asian developing countries will continue to enjoy economic growth rates above the world average. Kenneth B. Medlock III, Ronald Soligo, and Amy Myers Jaffe discuss the determinants of energy demand. They highlight the strong association between rising incomes and levels of intensity, and produce their own projections for final energy demand in China under high and low efficiency cases. Leena Srivastava and Megha Shukla reinforce the point out that the high energy intensities in the record of China and India show the scope for technical improvements in efficiency. Manning points to South Korea as an example of how very rapid growth in oil demand can occur at a certain stage in a country's economic development, as rising incomes support an explosion of private vehicle ownership and use.

James P. Dorian in the first part of his chapter illustrates some of the country contrasts within the Asian energy scene and explains in some detail the US Energy Information Administration (EIA) forecasting methodology and current forecasts. The EIA projections are broadly similar to those made by the International Energy Agency in 2000. These "reference cases" are disciplined summaries of the effect of current policies and trends both on the demand side and in current investment plans.

In this chapter, the figures of the US EIA *International Energy Outlook*, 2002 reference case have been used as a basis for discussion. A new International Energy Agency (IEA) *World Energy Outlook* was published in September 2002.

[7]

North-East Asia

Medlock, Soligo and Jaffe in their chapter "The Present Status and Future Prospects of Energy in China" point out some anomalies in the historic record. China had showed an unusually poor productivity in the use of energy (per unit of national output) despite the fact that the transportation element in Chinese demand has been comparatively low. More recent figures bear out some of the authors' conjectures that energy efficiencies can and have been improved. David Von Hippel illustrates how the productivity of energy use (the inverse of energy intensity) has improved dramatically in China in recent years. The country's energy consumption in 2000 and 2001 fell, while its GDP, even measured on a Purchasing Power Parity basis, grew. There are several explanations for this: the growth of light and service industries, closing down of inefficient capacity in state heavy industries, and closing down of small power stations that used unwashed and unsorted coal. Accordingly, in these chapters, the projections for Chinese energy demand are far below those predicted five years ago.[5]

Von Hippel reports the results of Nautilus Institute's "business as usual" and "alternative" (more efficient) scenarios for future demand in China, Japan and the Korean Energy Economics Institute (KEEI) projects for Korea. Von Hippel also provides analysis and projections for North Korea, Mongolia, and the Russian Far East region. These constitute small components of regional energy demand but are important in the context of possible northeast Asian energy cooperation on pipeline projects to bring Russian resources to East Asian markets.

Fuel Mix

The future division of demand between fuels is uncertain: it depends not only on consumer preferences but also on supply developments. The future fuel mix for power generation in Japan and Korea depends on the fulfilment of government policies to promote the continuing expansion of nuclear generating capacity, which accounts for thirty percent of Japan's, and thirty-six percent of Korea's electricity. However, government policies are not what they used to be in these countries. Both countries are

[8]

liberalizing electricity markets–to reduce the price of electricity through competition. Korea is also privatizing utility companies that could previously have been relied upon to fulfil government plans. In Japan, utilities are already privately owned. The nuclear projections that are based on government policies may not be realized in the face of lower electricity prices–and increasing environmental opposition to the location of new plants.

In the case of natural gas, the projections assume investment in distribution systems to develop new markets as well as in the infrastructure necessary to bring gas supplies from remote sources. Several authors point to the proliferation of pipeline and LNG proposals in northeast, southeast and central Asia. Romeo Pacudan also describes power grid connection schemes in northeast and southeast Asia. Demand-pull and supply-push are difficult to disentangle when fuels are changing their share of the energy market. There is unlikely to be room for all the projects, even if it were possible to carry them out during the next twenty years. The question of which projects are carried out first—pipelines from Russia or LNG from the Middle East, for example, will affect the patterns of energy trade and, depending on their economics, the evolution of the fuel mix in individual countries.

Liberalization

Most governments of Asian energy-importing countries are carrying out programs of economic reform that are being extended into the energy sector. These include the freeing of prices, the privatization of state industries, the reduction of government regulation (except environmental regulation) and the promotion of competition. In many cases the energy sector is among the last to be liberalized, and the degree of liberalization varies greatly. This variety corresponds to the different political and economic systems in use in Asian energy-importing countries, and to the wide range in the degree of development—from Japan, Singapore and Korea at one extreme to Bangladesh at the other. Philip Andrews-Speed sets out the general case for liberalization—to promote investment by using private sector sources, to improve technical performance and management efficiency, and simultaneously through the pricing mechanism and through competition to provide incentives to consumers to use energy productively. For many Asian countries, in contrast to Europe and Japan, these reforms would or could imply increases in energy prices to consumers that had been held down by price controls (as in India) or through the policies of state monopoly suppliers (as in China). As governments move away from a socialist approach to resource allocation, profits need to be established within the power industry, in refineries, and in gas and electricity distribution if investment is to be sustained and increased to match the demands of rapidly growing economies.

Liberalization does not generally reach upstream. In most energy exporting Asian countries – Australia being the main exception – the energy sector is dominated by government ownership or control. Where reforms have occurred, these have mainly resulted in increasing domestic energy prices towards export levels.

Andrews-Speed points out that energy has tended (not only in Asia) to be slow to attract reforms. Continuity of supply is critical for economic and national security; natural resources are either in public ownership or under special fiscal regimes, competition in the building and use of infrastructure is not easy to achieve without a high degree of regulation; there are environmental consequences of energy supply and use which market prices do not necessarily reflect. Andrews-Speed reviews the main arguments and outlines the risks of poorly planned or badly co-ordinated liberalization. State control and finance of an entire sector – such as power generation – may be difficult, but privatization regulation also presents difficulties. Even in developed countries with experienced bureaucrats and transparent regulations, the privatization of the energy sector has been vulnerable to political pressures and vested interests – including those of the industrial managers. There have also been simple mistakes of policy and strategy. Many Asian countries lack some or most of these conditions.

The transition to liberalized trade and investment in the energy sector cannot easily move faster than broader economic reform. Given the value of the prizes in terms of revenue and patronage that exist in the energy sector it is not surprising that it lags, rather than leads the reform process. In Japan, where the sector was in private ownership and in the context of an established market economy, liberalization has followed the track of increasing competition, opening the oil market to imports, removing price controls in oil products, and generally encouraging the combination of competition with spare capacity. With spare capacity in almost every sector of Japanese energy industries, competition is enough to drive down consumer prices and "squeeze out" inefficiencies within the sector. In this respect, the Japanese situation is more comparable to Continental Europe, for example, Germany, than to other large Asian countries where there has been a context of socialist planning and state ownership.

China

China is a special case because of its size, economic reform program, and interests both upstream and downstream. Andrews-Speed gives a clear and detailed account of the evolution of energy regulation and liberalization in China, alongside the general process of economic reform and the developments in the energy sector itself—notably the shift from being an oil exporter to an oil importer and the dramatic reduction in the use of poor quality coal, mostly burned (if that is not too high a term for what happened to the mixture of coal and dirt that was poured into the oldest of China's small and old power stations). For the oil industry, and China's participation in international oil trade and investment, the major development has been the evolution of two vertically integrated, partly privatized companies – the Chinese National Petroleum Corporation (CNPC) and the China National Star Petroleum Corporation (CNSPC) – and the increase of internal prices to track international prices. The Chinese electricity sector remains essentially decentralized, not privatized, with the State Power Corporation promoting a slow program of separating transmission from generation and the corporatization of provincial generation enterprises. Competition may come, but it is a long way off.

India

In India, by contrast, there has been an active, though continually changing program of reform in the power sector. This aspect is described by Srivastava and Shukla. Restructuring has been patchily implemented, giving a wide range of generally unsatisfactory experiences from which to learn. In future it seems that more attention will be paid to the distribution sector. This involves the highly controversial problem of tariffs, which at present often involve cross-subsidies between different classes of consumers. Low overall margins do not provide the cash to fund the investment necessary to expand the distribution system in line with economic growth. In the oil sector there has been some progress in dismantling the complex structure of licensing and control that existed at every stage. India now has large independent refining companies, which are investing aggressively in expanding and modernizing its refining capacity. However, privatization of the public sector oil companies has met political obstacles.

Romeo Pacudan reviews electricity restructuring across East Asia generally. The extent to which consumer and industrial electricity markets are "contestable" differs widely between countries, with Singapore being the most open to competition in some ways. Pacudan draws links between robust world energy prices and the incentives for electricity sector reform to sustain growth in power supplies at acceptable costs. He also points out some of the difficulties encountered when reforms are incomplete, as for example, when Independent Power Producers (IPPs) are established to attract foreign capital, technology and energy supplies but their power output is sold into a heavily politicized, unreformed domestic electricity sector. The second part of James Dorian's paper also addresses this question in detail for the Philippines power industry.

Key Questions

Uneven and diverse though it is, the progress of liberalization in domestic energy markets in importing countries raises questions for the shape of future international energy relations:

- Domestic competition and "market pricing' in competitive markets will be difficult to reconcile with hopes for bilateral or "special" relationships with producers who seek to achieve the guaranteeing of prices or supplies.

[12]

- Transferring investment and planning risks to private sector enterprises will tend to minimize investments in "spare capacity" in pipelines and generation. In countries such as Japan and Korea, there is an excess of power and refining capacity for various reasons. However, this will eventually be absorbed and consumers could face not only volatile prices but also tightness of supply in the short term. In countries with rapidly growing demand these risks, which are typical of a commodity cycle, will tend to be borne by consumers.
- There may be an imbalance of bargaining power between dispersed importing organizations and the small number of government-owned exporting organizations.

Imports

Projections of trade for 10-20 years ahead are very uncertain, since they are the result of combining uncertain projections of economic growth, energy intensity (and therefore energy demand), the share of fuels, and the development of domestic supplies of energy. Jaffe and Medlock illustrate the impact on Japanese oil imports of different degrees of fulfilment of Japan's official policy for the expansion of nuclear power generation and the dependence of the forecast on policy assumptions (efficiency of energy use and environment) and technology (efficiency of power stations and automobiles). Coal is also a very large component of the energy market in India, China and Japan and an important component of energy trade within Asia. The direction of environmental and technical developments is to restrain the future growth of coal, as Dorian and others point out. This may change in the longer term, if economic "clean coal" technologies are developed in the US or elsewhere and adopted in China and India.

In his chapter, Manning points out that projections of future Chinese oil and gas production are likely to be pessimistic for a country which has large unexplored sedimentary basins, and a large basis of known and developed oil reservoirs. As in the North Sea, improvements in technology may increase the amount of oil that can be recovered from producing fields and improve the economics of small, undeveloped reservoirs.

Key Questions

What is important for policy and strategy is not the exact (but unreliable) long-term numbers but the trends reflected by these numbers. Some trends reflect structural changes that are already beginning to take effect, such as the change in the position of China from an oil exporter to an oil and gas importer. Others are simply "more of the same," as in the relatively slow growth of Japanese imports. These may be important because the numbers involved are large – Japan is likely to remain the Asian country with the largest energy imports – but they are less challenging from the point of view of the structure of the Asian energy markets and of new policies of international co-operation. The "interesting points" that projection numbers illustrate even if they are very unreliable, are four trends, which are common to most forecasts and to all the chapters in this book:

- First, East and South Asian imports will increase. West Asian supplies of oil to Northeast and South Asia will therefore increase in volume and their share of the South and East Asian oil markets will increase. In the EIA projections for 2020, Asian importing countries import twenty-seven million barrels of oil daily, compared to twelve million in 2000. This increase accounts for eight per cent of the increase in exports from West Asia over the period (and nearly ninety per cent of the increase in East and South Asian consumption).
- Second, China will become Asia's principal oil importer. The EIA 2002 reference case projections are for Chinese imports of over seven million barrels per day of oil by 2020, compared to Japan at just over six million barrels. There is not much scope for large errors in the projection for Japan, which is based on low growth of oil consumption in a developed economy. The projection for China is much more uncertain. It assumes a combination of an average growth of over five per cent annually in oil consumption over twenty years, combined with a slight decline in oil production. Von Hippel has lower projections, even for a "business-as-usual" case.

- Third, all the authors (and most other analysts) expect an increase in natural gas trade within Asia to support an increase in consumption of the order of two hundred and eighty per cent in the EIA projection. This implies bringing consumption of the natural gas share of the energy market in gas importing countries towards those achieved in Europe (over twenty per cent).
- Fourth, the total of these new gas market shares would amount to the equivalent of around five million barrels of oil per day by 2020, in addition to the growth of existing gas markets of almost 4 million barrels per day oil equivalent.

Natural Gas

Up to now, domestic resources have limited natural gas consumption in Asia. Indonesia, Malaysia and Australia have significant domestic markets (not very liberalized) for indigenous natural gas. Japan and Korea have established natural gas consumption, from imports, of around 10% of total primary energy. This is concentrated in the power- generating sector and was achieved by slightly different routes. It is led in Korea by the state gas and power companies, with investment in a national gas grid. In Japan, it is led by private sector utility and trading companies. China has a small domestic usage of natural gas (mainly for fertilizer manufacture) but an official policy of major increases in natural gas consumption based on domestic supplies (through the "West-East pipeline project") and imports of LNG.

The increases in natural gas consumption and share of the Asian energy market depend on establishing natural gas markets in the power and other sectors in China and other gas-importing countries. There is also an assumption that the gas share of energy consumption grows as a result of the penetration by natural gas in the non-power markets in Japan and Korea. Increased market share accounts for half the increase in gas consumption projected by the EIA for Japan, sixty per cent of that projected by Korea and around three quarters of that projected for other Asian countries. In total, these new market shares amount to the equivalent of around five million barrels of oil per day by 2020, in addition to the growth of existing gas markets of almost 4 million barrels per day oil equivalent.

Discussion in the *IEA World Energy Outlook 2001-Insights* suggests there is potential for an increase in Asia-Pacific gas production of the order of seven million barrels per day, against the projected increase in demand in the EIA projection of around nine million barrels per day oil equivalent. This cannot be compared exactly with the EIA consumption figures. The point is not the exact size of the import market, which will be the outcome of many uncertain factors. What matters is whether structures are developed to attract the investment needed to produce, transport and distribute the gas. Distribution in the case of new markets depends on investment to create the demand and the expense of existing usage patterns of other fuels. The availability of gas reserves to supply such a growth in demand by domestic production or imports is not in question. However, the timing and selection of investments is. There is no doubt that actual and potential gas exporters of Southwest Asia such as UAE, Qatar, Yemen, Oman and Iran could provide this and more.

The authors who have contributed to this volume do not discuss in detail the full range of possibilities for expanding gas supplies to Asian importers. New discoveries in Western China reported in 2001 seem to have justified commitment to the "West–East" natural gas pipeline which may pre-empt imports from Central Asia for some years. One LNG import facility has been approved and there is no shortage of more LNG competing projects. China will be a factor in the Asian LNG market within a few years.

Jaffe and Von Hippel discuss the scope for pipeline gas export possibilities from Eastern Russia to Northeast Asia. Andrews-Speed discusses Chinese commitments to the use of gas, and to the growth of both pipeline and LNG imports. Two such pipelines (which the resources of Eastern Russia could probably support) would equate to roughly one million barrels of oil per day. Dorian discusses the economically less attractive possibilities of supplies to China from Central Asia, for which the same arithmetic applies—two pipelines if built against adverse economics and politics, might supply the equivalent of one million barrels per day. Pacudan describes the developing gas interconnections in Southeast Asia. The maps, lists of projects, and discussion in these chapters reflect a very wide range of possible supply options, with different economics and logistics.

Key Questions

Some of the conditions for an expansion of the gas share of Asian energy markets are already present—such as favorable government policies, environmental attractiveness and an abundance of gas reserves in various countries that could become suppliers. The large number of potential pipeline and LNG projects indicates the scope for competition between potential suppliers that could add to the economic security and attractiveness of new gas supplies. However, these conditions may not be sufficient. The problems are:

- Many exporting countries require state participation in the production stage, without necessarily undertaking the financial risks
- LNG projects and ships have in the past been financed on the basis of long term contracts with utilities. These may not be available, or may be less secure, as importing markets undergo liberalization.
- Rapid penetration of gas into new markets, as envisaged in China, requires investment in distribution and marketing for which appropriate local organizations do not exist.

Section 1

GENERAL OUTLOOK

1

The Asian Energy Market:
A New Geopolitics?

*Robert A. Manning**

One of the most critical factors shaping global energy markets is burgeoning Asian oil and gas demand, particularly for fossil fuels. It is also a fascinating test case of globalization as a factor in global politics. For most of the past quarter-century, Asian energy demand grew at nearly three times the global average. Even in the slow-growth world economy of 2001 – with Japan, Singapore and Taiwan tipping into recession – Asian demand is growing at 5.1 percent, more than twice the world average. Asian demand has been a key driver of world oil markets and that trend is only intensifying. Together, the nations of the Asia-Pacific[1] already consume significantly more oil than the United States—20.7 million barrels in 2000, which is roughly two million barrels more than the United States consumption.[2] Asia will be the world's largest consumer of primary energy by 2010, with upwards of 75 percent of its oil imports coming from the Middle East. In the year 2000, the Asia-Pacific imported roughly 12.5 million bpd out of the 20.7 million bpd of its oil consumption.[3]

---

* The author completed this paper while Director of Asian Studies and Senior Fellow at the Council on Foreign Relations in August 2001. He is currently Senior Counselor, Energy, Technology and Science Policy, US Department of State. The views expressed here are solely the personal views of the author and do not represent the views of either the US Department of State or any other US government agency.

For Middle East producers, more than 62 percent of Gulf production is already being exported to the Asia-Pacific. Thus, a burgeoning Middle East–Asia energy nexus is a central factor in shaping world oil markets as well as geopolitics for both Middle East suppliers and Asian consumers.[4] This trend will only increase over the coming two decades, with big emerging markets in Asia, most importantly India and China, where per capita consumption of oil and gas is lower than that of the United States by roughly twenty and ten times respectively. As the Chinese and Indian economies modernize and the middle classes (not to mention 500 million citizens in ASEAN states) continue to grow, the fast-growing transportation sector will drive substantially higher levels of consumption, an estimated 25-31 million bpd in imports by 2020.[5]

The looming question that has fueled enormous speculation and much hyperbole is: What are the geopolitical implications of this growing energy nexus? Historically, Asian governments have viewed energy as a fundamental national security matter of the highest strategic importance. Across Asia, governments remain deeply involved in the energy sector – from state-owned oil companies that dominate all facets of energy production and distribution, to price subsidies and import-export regulation. Yet market forces, rather than *dirigiste* policies have increasingly proven the key to addressing energy questions—by enhancing energy efficiency, by new oil and gas exploration and development and through alternative energy sources. Asia is the only region of the world where the use of nuclear energy – despite its proliferation risks – is expanding significantly as a source of electricity. Moreover, this strategic view of energy security has been a staple of the national security and foreign policy calculus of most Asian actors in a region where underlying suspicion, distrust and rivalry remain part of the pathology of inter-Asian and trans-Pacific relations, which are still in a state of incremental and protracted historic transition.

Yet these energy realities and traditional perceptions are unfolding against a backdrop of a globalizing economy, not least in the energy sector where multinational energy companies have been involved in one merger after another and where the working of energy markets have in the past two decades increasingly begun to resemble global financial markets. The Middle East–Asia energy dynamic also occurs at a time when it is increasingly evident that the oil question is principally one of prices rather than of adequate supply, since world oil supplies are plentiful and markets are global. Thus, it is unclear how Asian policy-makers will view the global politics of Asian energy markets. Will they view it through the lens of traditional geopolitics of real estate and sea-lane security? Or will they view it through the lens of geo-economics, where international investment, joint ventures and global cooperation rather than competition for resources and conflict is the prevalent means to satisfy energy security requirements?

The literature of strategic analysts in Japan, China, and India on energy security is laden with what might be termed the dominant conventional wisdom—a tendency towards a pessimistic vision of strategic competition. This is characterized in dire terms by one analyst as a "tightening embrace of necessity between East Asia and the Middle East that, over the next generation, could fundamentally challenge the Western-dominated global order."[6] In this view, Asia's thirst for oil is not only hastening the end of the oil age, but en route it is increasing the likelihood of conflict over territorial disputes in the competition for increasingly scarce hydrocarbon resources. One variation of this perspective, discussed below, views these trends – Middle East producers needing Asian markets and Asians safeguarding secure supplies – as possibly coalescing into the West's worst nightmare in the form of an arms-for-oil "Islamic-Confucian" coalition of Samuel Huntington's "Clash of Civilizations." This is a worst-case extrapolation of the traditional geopolitics-centered view of the consequences of Asia's growing energy needs, one of low probability if not unimaginable. Nonetheless, in the case of China, some military (and dual-use) supplier activity continues, although thus far, this has not been quantitatively or qualitatively increased in a substantial manner.[7]

Viewed through the lens of geo-economic or market-centered approaches, however, a very different vision emerges, one of energy needs met through privatization, deregulation, regional integration, cooperative ventures, foreign investment, and absorbing technological innovation in a globalized, information age economy. This approach is focused on the commodification of oil and gas markets, and the increasing role of technology in the energy sector. In this vision, as Daniel Yergin, a leading energy analyst and author of *The Prize* has argued, "stresses can be resolved not through massive armies and blue-water navies, but through markets and investment within the ever-denser web of international commerce."[8] In this view, mobilizing the massive finance needed for energy infrastructures (estimated at over $1 trillion over the next decade) and commercializing new sources of energy (e.g. gas-to-liquids, superconductivity, fuel cells) will overshadow competing claims for real estate with oil and gas potential on its territory or adjacent waters in terms of defining Asian views of energy security.

From this globalist perspective, commerce and market forces shape inter-state relations more than ideological or nationalist imperatives shape commerce and trade. Indeed, many argue that globalization is the dominant trend of our epoch, redefining or at least altering the calculus of national interests. This perspective sees the downside of the phenomenon of "globalization"—as a source of volatility and instability, as evidenced in the Asian financial crisis. That is certainly one aspect of globalization. Yet globalization can also be the driving force of stability and prosperity, making sufficient quantities of resources available at lower prices, and pressuring domestic industries to produce and/or refine and market energy more competitively. Elements of both perspectives – and the related policy choices – are competing in Asia, though the region seems to be gradually moving in the direction of market-centered trends.

In terms of Asia's future choices, the two perspectives on energy currently coexist uneasily. How Asian governments define energy security will largely determine whether their nations make choices that lead them in one or the other direction. Will Japan continue to invest in its plutonium reprocessing program though it lacks any economic rationale? Or will it scale back its nuclear power ambitions and increase investment in the infrastructure required to expand natural gas use? Will India deregulate its power industry and abandon its risky, expensive and unproductive nuclear power program? Lastly, will Beijing, Delhi and Tokyo embark on a naval arms race under the rubric of protecting sea-lane security? These highlight the possible directions in which differing visions might take Asian energy policies. Deeply ingrained Asian "scarcity" psychology and statist habits suggest that it may be a decade before clear evidence of major direction shifts in energy policy are incontrovertible. There is a third approach, with overlapping elements of both approaches – at least for the near to medium term – as Asia, to borrow Deng Xiao-peng's description of China's economic reform strategy, crosses the river [of energy challenges] by feeling for stones.

Asia's Rise: The Energy Dimension

Asia's phenomenal economic trajectory (prior to July 1997), its steadily rising energy needs (with 53% of the world's population) and its accumulating impact on world energy markets give a particular urgency to the question of how the region meets its energy challenges. As the "Asian miracle" unfolded and growth rocketed from just 4% of world GDP in 1960 to roughly 25% by 1995, its energy consumption grew by similar proportions. By 1994, Asia-Pacific oil consumption rivaled that of the United States.[9] From 1971 to 1994, total primary commercial energy demand in East Asia (excluding China and Japan) grew by an average annual rate of 6.8%, quadrupling in absolute terms. In China, Korea, Thailand and Indonesia, electricity demand grew even faster than GDP, averaging 11-12% in this period. From 1983-93, four Asian economies – Japan, China, Taiwan, and South Korea – accounted for 36% of the world growth in primary energy demand.[10]

A turning point occurred in 1993 when China, then the world's 6th largest oil producer, became a net oil importer. This led analysts to ponder the implications of another quarter-century of the Asian miracle. Asia-Pacific was projected to need some 26-31 million barrels of oil (40% of total 1998 world production) by 2020 (depending on reference case or high growth scenarios). Where would this oil come from? How would such demand affect world markets, energy security, and the environment? On the Asian side, how would the various actors respond to their plight of steadily increasing dependence on imports? Asia's weight in the world economy was dramatically illustrated when, after the financial crisis in mid-1997, the region's consumption fell to -2.7% in 1998 after averaging over 5.5% annual growth for the past two decades.[11] This development led to a rare state of near zero-growth (0.5%) in world consumption of oil, as prices fell to pre-1973 levels, hitting $8 per barrel and left producers with an excess of more than a million barrels.

Yet for all the profound questions posed by East Asia's breakneck economic development achievements until the mid-1990s, energy questions remained the domain of specialized analysts. Except in Japan, energy rarely occupied the center stage of debates over economics or security. Instead, they focused on the marvels of export-oriented growth strategies and the virtues of the "Asian model." And why not? The Asian economic machine was the marvel of the world—even through the oil shocks of 1979-1980.

Figure 1.1
Middle East Oil Supplies, 1995
(thousands of barrels per day)

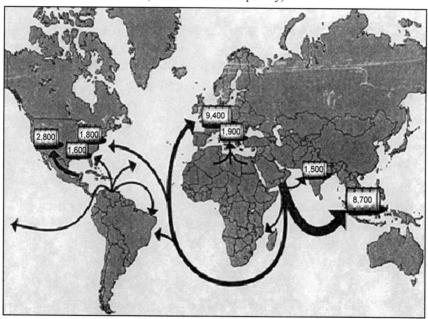

Source: *International Energy Outlook*, 1997 (See also Note 17).

[26]

Figure 1.2
Middle East Oil Supplies, 2015*

(thousands of barrels per day)

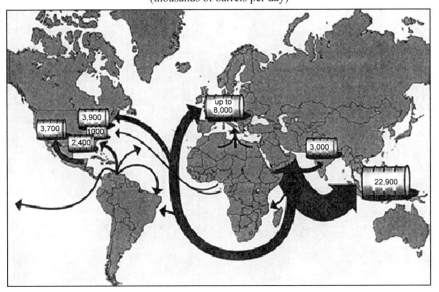

Note: *estimate.

Source: *International Energy Outlook*, 1997 (See also Note 17).

Similarly, until the mid-1990s, energy security did not figure prominently in the literature or the debates in the region about Asian security. Instead, Asian security debates tended to focus on military modernization, flashpoints such as the Korean Peninsula, the Taiwan Strait, Kashmir, the South China Sea and other territorial disputes, Japanese ambitions, and by the mid-1990s, concern over the significance of an emerging China. Apart from tensions over disputed (and alleged, but unproven, oil and gas rich) islands in the South China Sea, energy, prior to the mid-1990s, was not often on the Asian security radar screen at all, despite the region's negative energy balance. Gradually, however, the sheer volume of East Asia's real and projected energy needs – and their intersection with security issues – began to figure more prominently in the dialogue about the future of the Pacific. Thus, prominent regional specialists have suggested that energy is the "dark side to the explosive economic growth of East Asia, rooted in the region's profound energy

[27]

insecurities."[12] This view still is widely held among by many Asian security specialists, though most economists, and particularly energy specialists, dismiss such views as unwarranted.

However, assuming cool rationality as the basis of public policy (indeed, of any human behavior) can be a dangerous act. Nonetheless, on balance, recent Asian experience points more in the sunnier direction of the economists than the darker view of looming competition over scarce resources and conflict. Indeed, it is important to note here one of the most remarkable and under-appreciated facts about the "Asian miracle": all of the most dynamic and fastest growing "miracle" economies – Japan and the "four tigers" (South Korea, Taiwan, Singapore and Hong Kong) possess virtually no hydrocarbon resources! Yet this energy deficit was simply not a significant factor affecting the region's most remarkable economic success stories. To this, add the instructive experience of the West in coping with the 1970s oil shocks in order to get a sense of how energy issues might be managed. If the past is a prologue, it should provide reassurance, or at least give pause to those anxious about perceived energy vulnerabilities when contemplating Asia's future energy choices and alternatives.

Whither the "Miracle"?

Yet the first question about Asia's energy future must be the impact of the Asian crisis on expected economic growth, and consequently on likely energy requirements. Asian oil consumption decreased by some 500,000 barrels a day in 1998, though demand shot up again, growing by nearing one million bpd in 1999, and grew 2.9% in 2000. Does the current economic buoyancy present in much of East Asia signal a new phase—if more modest, of the Asian dynamism? Economic historians will no doubt continue to debate the relative weight of various causal factors of what was arguably the worst financial crisis since the Second World War for years.

The past six years have been a period of relative uncertainty about Asia's economic future. Nations that knew only robust growth for a generation suddenly faced deep recession in 1998. Yet in 1999, all showed growth in the positive column. Nonetheless, in 2001 amidst a global slowdown, the Asian economy appeared problematic. Singapore and Taiwan faced their first recession in more than a quarter century. Negative growth was projected for Japan. On the whole, China's continued official annual growth rate of nearly 8% helped the region to gain a 4.1% growth estimate by the International Monetary Fund (IMF) for the year 2001, and by the end of 2003, China, Korea, India and much of ASEAN appeared to be second only to the US as an engine of global growth. Even Japan's economy appeared on the upswing.

The realities that surfaced during the 1997-98 period, however, offer hints of continued economic vulnerabilities. In retrospect, it appears the negative synergy of certain key factors – excessive capital flows misallocated in the affected countries; fixed exchange rates; over-guaranteed, under-regulated and opaque domestic financial markets – served to precipitate the crisis. These elements sparked a fourth factor – contagion in international financial markets – that caused the rapidity and severity of the crisis.[13] Prior to the crisis, the region was a magnet for international lending, accumulating some $420 billion in net capital flows during the 1990s. Much of it was short term money, lent out, too often imprudently, in local currencies. This led to lavish real estate development, overvalued property and stock markets, as well as industrial overcapacity. Wild swings in the dollar–yen relationship – the dollar rising 60%, and the yen falling 60% – along with a 1994 Chinese devaluation, wreaked havoc on economic competitiveness, and heightened respective foreign debts. Devalued currencies meant that the price of oil imports (purchased in dollars) skyrocketed two or three times higher than before the crisis and affected Asian oil exporters such as Indonesia and Malaysia suffered declines in oil revenues.

Bad debt, both corporate and in the financial sector in Thailand and Korea has been in considerable measure worked out, and in Indonesia corporate debt has become far more manageable than many had forecast at the height of the financial crisis (bad loans at the end of 1999 accounted for 48% of total bank lending, 110% of GDP in Indonesia). Korea has made significant progress in addressing the weaknesses in its financial system and is at least beginning to change its business culture in a more market-based direction. Japan, the world's second largest economy remains flat, with fundamental, but slow motion restructuring of its corporate and financial sector unfolding amid declining stock and property prices, and debt at the local and national level deepening (gross debt is roughly 130% of GDP). The bulk of Japan's meager growth has been propelled by massive government stimulus packages (nearly US$1 trillion from the late 1980s to the end of the century) plus bank bailouts. Few analysts expect sustained Japanese growth to reach 2% before 2003-04.

Measured against numerous 1998 predictions of a 3-5 year crisis, the region has appeared to stabilize and achieved a relatively swift, albeit uneven, trajectory of renewed sustained growth. The downturn in the global information technology sector, upon which many Asian nations are heavily dependent, had dampened the region's economic prospects until 2002. However, for the longer term, it should be strongly emphasized that the fundamentals which led to the phenomenal Asian dynamism of the quarter-century preceding the crisis remain in place. High savings rates, strong emphasis on education, hard work, good macro-economic management, ability to absorb technology, and relatively open capital markets, remain important assets that have not abated. These underlying characteristics, the adjustments made by the affected countries such as delinking currencies from the US dollar, combined with the response of international financial institutions all help to explain the initial turnaround. The continued debt overhang plus the diminishing of the hi-tech economy, raises the question of whether the signs of recovery were ephemeral or the beginning of well-grounded, sustainable growth.[14] Yet the adjustments made by ASEAN and Korea, modernizing their respective financial systems and an increase in intra-Asian trade and investment seem to bode well for more dynamic growth through the latter part of this decade.

In terms of oil, by late 1999, demand had picked up from the previous year: 4.8% in Japan, 11.1% in South Korea, and 3% in China.[15] Sifting through International Monetary Fund (IMF), Asian Development Bank (ADB), revised International Energy Agency (IEA) forecasts, Energy

Information Administration (EIA), Goldman Sachs and other private analysts' projections gives some indicators of probable economic trends. For the whole region the most prudent forecast is for a moderate recovery in the near-term, in the 4.5% to 5.2% range, reflected in the IEA's "moderate" recovery scenario. In the 2004-2010 period, the higher end of that range is projected; while from 2011-2020, the lower end (+ or - .75) is a more likely outcome.[16]

Asian Energy Patterns

While the uncertainty factor (e.g. renewed recession, war, political turmoil in China, technological change) stalks all economic projections and cannot be discounted, even at what are likely to be far more modest growth rates than seen during the 1980s and early 1990s, oil demand – which generally lags, but closely tracks growth rates – is still projected to grow 2-3 times faster than the rest of the world. By 2020, according to the Energy Information Administration (EIA) of the US Department of Energy (DOE), Asian oil demand will still grow two to three times faster than that of the industrialized West.[17] This assessment assumes oil prices *averaging* $15-$17 a barrel range during this period. It should be noted that such a demand growth projection is similar to the pattern of the previous quarter century (1970-94): Asian energy demand grew by 274% while that of the rest of the world grew at 63% during that period.[18]

While the 1997-98 crisis altered the pace at which trends and patterns of energy use will unfold – and the time horizon in which energy investment decisions are made and implemented – the region's economic roller coaster ride does not change the basic circumstances of any nation in the region. Nor does it alter the current and looming Asian energy factor in world markets: the region has a large and growing oil deficit, already some 12 million barrels, or roughly 60% of its oil is imported, with limited capacity to expand production in the region. Already, China is the world's second largest consumer of energy and in 1997, India became the sixth largest. By 2020, the Asia-Pacific will consume more than one-third of the world's total energy and its oil imports will roughly double.[19]

Yet statistics can be deceiving in many ways. In the case of Asia, the aggregate numbers about the region's energy patterns can be deceptive, given the distorting effect of the volume and energy mix of China. The more developed Asian economies – Japan, South Korea, Taiwan, Hong Kong and Singapore – those in which energy demand growth will tend to be relatively slow over the coming two decades, account for only 7% of the Asian population, but consume nearly half the region's oil. These more mature economies depend on oil for about 55% of their primary energy needs (Thailand and the Philippines also rely on crude oil for more than half of their energy needs). However, in China, oil only accounts for 24% of its energy consumption, despite its pace-setting growth in oil demand. China's dependency on coal is around 70% of its energy needs (India's coal dependency being nearly 60% of its primary energy). This skews the fuel mix for the region, in which coal accounts for 46% of its total energy use. Similarly, the region as a whole uses slightly less oil (38% of total energy) than the world average; substantially less natural gas (8%) and less hydropower (1.4%).[20] This energy mix, with 84% of Asia's energy comprised of coal and oil, explains why the region is a leading source of greenhouse gas emissions.

More remarkable than the dimensions or even the growth of Asia-Pacific energy consumption is the fact that these energy realities occur at the same time that Asian per capita energy consumption is barely half the world average! The United States, for example, consumes nearly eleven times more energy per capita than China, and nearly twenty times more per capita than India. However, the more developed economies of the region – Japan and the "Four Tigers": South Korea, Taiwan, Singapore, Hong Kong – have per capita energy consumption levels closer to those of Europe and the United States. At the same time, the level of energy efficiency, measured in energy use per unit of Gross Domestic Product (GDP) is the inverse. China, for example, requires roughly four times the oil equivalent in energy consumption per thousand dollars of GDP of the United States, and nearly ten times that of Japan, an unusually energy efficient economy.[21] Moreover, China's per capita oil consumption is nearly 22 times less than that of the US, and 13 times smaller than that of

South Korea. Yet China's per capita oil consumption is nearly twice that of India's. The differences are of similar proportion in regard to electricity consumption, with per capita usage in China about 8% of the OECD average, and India just over 3%.[22] These patterns reflect respective levels of development and complexity of energy use.

As evidenced above, advanced industrial economies with higher living standards tend to have much higher energy use per capita than developing nations, but also tend to be relatively static in their consumption levels (which may even decline slightly). Energy intensity – the amount of energy needed per unit of GDP – tends to diminish in post-industrial societies that have moved to more services and knowledge-based economies. In contrast, developing countries with a large agricultural base, which are rapidly industrializing and urbanizing (such as China, India, Thailand) tend to have large non-commercial energy use (e.g. biomass) but move to a higher energy intensity, and toward oil products as they modernize agriculture and achieve greater levels of industrialization. This also includes different mixes of oil products (e.g. from kerosene to fuel oil) Much of this demand growth tends to come from the transport and residential use sectors as a country takes off and a large urban middle class is formed. In Asia, this has translated into rapid expansion of oil demand and projections of even higher increases in electricity demand with frequent fears of brownouts disrupting industry and private life.

The energy growth pattern of Korea, which reached OECD income levels of just over $10,000 per capita by 1996 (when it became the world's sixth largest consumer of oil) may help illuminate future demand growth elsewhere in Asia. From 1975 to 1992, South Korea tripled its per capita energy consumption. Its oil demand quadrupled from 1985-95, reflecting rapid structural change in the South Korean economy, one focused on rapid expansion with its booming steel, shipbuilding, petrochemical, auto and electronics industries, as it averaged nearly 8% annual growth. One intriguing question is why oil demand rose by only 2.7% annually from 1980-87, but averaged about 20% annually from 1987-95 though economic growth was about the same (7.8% and 7.9%, respectively in both periods).[23] No less intriguing is the fact that oil decreased as a share of South Korea's total energy mix in the first period, yet comprised 85% of the increase in total energy demand in the latter period. During this period, car ownership increased by 25% annually. From 1987-95, oil demand increased by 20% annually.[24]

There are several instructive points to be drawn from the Korean experience. First, the interaction of energy prices, government policies, and the pace and character of economic growth all influence the rate of demand growth. The Korean case is remarkable because by the mid-1980s it was already a relatively urbanized, industrializing economy, yet its oil consumption quadrupled in the decade before the economic crisis. Second, a phenomenon evident in dynamic ASEAN economies less developed and economically complex than Korea (e.g. Thailand, Malaysia, Indonesia), was that fledgling middle classes, clustered in major metropolitan areas – in the case of Thailand, largely around greater metropolitan Bangkok – rapidly moved to obtain motorized transport, as incomes roughly doubled. In Thailand, for example, personal automobile purchases increased by nearly 18% annually from 1985-92, and prior to 1997, Thailand and other booming economies in Southeast Asia were increasing automobile purchases by nearly 30% annually. Yet each of these economies have significantly less than half the automobiles per capita than Japan.[25]

In terms of probable growth in energy demand in the first two decades of the 21st century, such consumption trends allow one to begin to grasp the dimensions of demand growth in larger developing countries, particularly, China and India, and if the ten ASEAN states are added in, together they account for nearly half the world's population. For illustrative purposes, China, which accounts for roughly half of Asia's energy equation, offers a useful glimpse of the potential for future demand growth. Until mid-1980s, few Chinese had more appliances than televisions. Now, most urban Chinese (about 280 million) have televisions, stereos (about 300 million) and fans. About half of this number have refrigerators and washing machines. Since 1978, the total number of air conditioning units has grown more than fifty fold.[26] During the 1984-96 period, residential consumption of electricity more than quadrupled. Yet, as discussed above, China's per capita electricity consumption is barely 8%

of the OECD average.[27] And polls consistently point to the automobile as the next big item on the wish list of many Chinese families. In a scenario where China's per capita GDP growth averages 5% annually, by 2015, it is projected that automobile stocks in China could reach 42 million by 2015, or roughly 30 vehicles per 1000 people.[28]

Figure 1.3: GDP Per Capita Vs Primary Energy Demand Per Capita in Selected Asian Economies, 1995

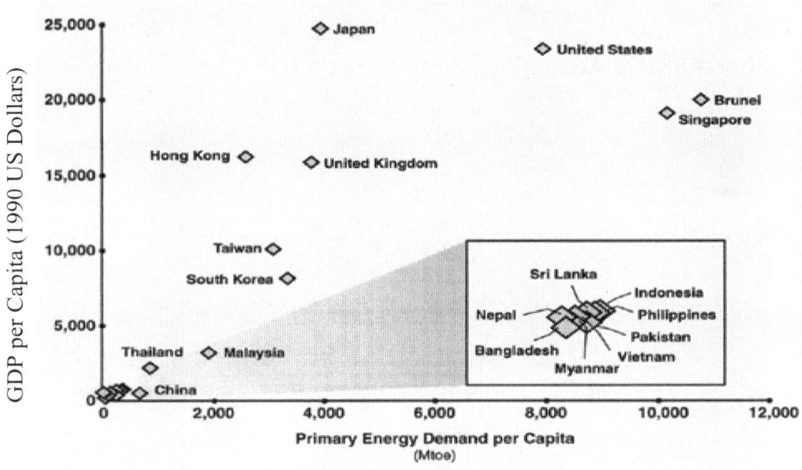

Source: Cambridge Energy Research Associates

Multiply this phenomenon of an emerging middle class, already in the case of China, roughly 100 million, by the perhaps 250 million more (of the 1.5 billion) in India and Southeast Asia, and the proportions of the consumer revolution in developing Asian states begins to register. Already, it is shifting the balance of oil consumption in the region. In the decade from 1988-98, Japan's share of total Asia-Pacific oil consumption shrunk from about 40% to 28%.[29] With regard to East Asia, a more economically integrated unit, Japan's share of oil imports has begun to sharply decline, from 77% in 1992, to about 56% in 1998, and is projected to decline to 36% of East Asian imports by 2010, while the imports of Greater China (China, Hong Kong, Taiwan) are projected to reach 28% by 2010.[30]

Asian Supply and Demand

The distribution of Asian energy demand, particularly oil will continue to shift towards China, India and Southeast Asia. Asian consumption will expand rapidly, if at a less frenetic pace than pre-1997 growth rates. Already, Asia has a substantial oil deficit. In 1998, the Asia-Pacific imported 11.5 million barrels per day (bpd) of the 19.1 million barrels it consumed daily, with imports rising to 12.5 million bpd in 2000.[31] This amounts to about 62% of the total petroleum products consumed. Asia-Pacific import needs are projected to approach 17-19 million bpd by 2010, and the EIA forecasts those import needs to rise to 24 million bpd by 2020. China's import needs alone are projected to grow to roughly 3 million bpd by 2010, and as much as 5-6 million bpd by 2020.[32] India's oil demand was 2 million bpd in 2000, nearly two-thirds imported. The EIA projects Indian demand to rise to 5.8 million bpd by 2020.

The composition of Asian energy demand is likely to change but only incrementally over the next decade. One important caveat, is growing environmental concern, the wild card in energy decision-making. Concerns about the human contribution to global warming and industrial pollution could alter energy consumption patterns more rapidly than "business as usual" projections suggest. In China, apart from horrendous pollution in major cities, acid rain from use of coal, particularly in the "rust belt" in Manchuria has become a problem across Northeast Asia. Nonetheless, the large coal reserves in China and India make it likely that coal will remain disproportionately large in their respective energy equations over the next two decades. Problems of public acceptance as well as management of nuclear waste are likely to limit the growth of nuclear energy in Asia, Japan, South Korea, and Taiwan. In the case of China, a larger impediment to expansion of nuclear energy is the cost. However, the effect is the same: major scaling-back of nuclear energy expansion plans over the coming decade.[33] Even the most optimistic projections regarding China's expanding use of natural gas, hydropower and/or nuclear energy to displace coal use do not envision a reduction of its coal reliance to lower than 60% by 2020.[34]

[36]

In any case, natural gas, which has been steadily growing at almost 18% annually, still only comprises less than 10% of Asia-Pacific primary energy consumption, far below OECD levels of about 26%. There is also large potential for the expansion of Asian production of gas, with Indonesia, Malaysia and Brunei already major exporters. Natural gas resources in China are under-explored and are likely to prove substantially larger than the current 48 trillion cubic feet of proven reserves (more than half the proven reserves of Indonesia).[35] Moreover, there are massive natural gas resources in the Russian Far East, roughly equivalent to world gas reserves as what Saudi Arabian resources are to world oil reserves. There are several pipeline schemes that have been under discussion in the region, particularly one seeking to link Russian gas in Irkutsk to China and Northeast Asia in an energy grid. However, this massive infrastructure project is at least 10-20 years away from being fully realized.

Since it is plentiful and a relatively clean fuel, natural gas is fast becoming the fuel of choice for much of the world. In Asia, expansion of liquified natural gas (LNG), currently imported largely by Japan, the world's largest LNG consumer, South Korea, and Taiwan, will accelerate in the decade ahead, particularly as southeastern China implements LNG plans already underway. Natural gas has been a significant, if largely unnoticed, integrative factor in East Asia, with more than half of Southeast Asian gas exported to the three Northeast Asian consumers. Pipeline gas, from within the region, of which there is currently very little, will gradually increase over the coming generation. Rapidly expanding use of natural gas will also add another dimension to the Asia-Middle East nexus. As both LNG and pipeline gas require substantial infrastructure investment, it will be a gradual process over the coming two decades, and will tend to substitute for coal and oil-fueled power generation. Gas will be increasingly important in avoiding one of the key strategic bottlenecks to economic growth – critical electricity demand in the region – as well as for residential use, but building the required infrastructure will be a protracted process over the next quarter century.[36] It must also be noted that in addition to their natural gas resources, Indonesia and Australia also have large reserves of low-sulfur coal, seeking export markets. However, natural gas is likely to be the fastest growing energy source in the 2001-2015 period.

About half of the growth in world oil demand over the next two decades, according to the EIA, will come from the transportation sector, and in the Asia-Pacific, the transport sector may well comprise an even larger portion of regional demand growth.[37] This raises the question of how much oil is likely to come from regional producers. Specifically, has Asian oil production peaked, or is it approaching its peak, or is there more room for growth? Many forecasters appear to have been unduly pessimistic about the prospects of Asian oil production. From 2000 to 2003, Asia-Pacific production held steady at just under 8 million bpd, just over 10% of world production. However, Asia possesses just under 5% of world reserves with a reserve/production ratio (how much proven oil remains if production continued at current rates) of 18 years, well below the 43 year world average reserve.[38] China, producing 3.2 million bpd, accounts for about 40% of Asian oil production. Indonesia produces 1.6 million bpd, half that of China. India, Malaysia, Brunei, Vietnam and Papua New Guinea account for the rest of the region's production. Indonesia, Malaysia, Brunei and Vietnam are the only net oil exporters in the region, and some forecasts suggest that they may be net importers by 2010.[39]

However, there is reason to believe, that most forecasts projecting that Asian production is near its peak and will begin to decline over the next decade may be overly pessimistic. This is not because of anticipated new finds of major fields. Indeed, the recent experience of oil exploration efforts in the East and South China Seas, and in western China's Tarim Basin – the most likely venues of new finds – has left Western oil firms rather skeptical about prospects of any such major commercial finds.[40] Rather, the reason pessimists may be wrong is in underestimating the potential of existing oil fields. A sampling of four prominent analysts ranges from declines of 1.1 million bpd to one of essentially maintaining current levels.[41] Comparing respective growth in Asian reserves to those of the North Sea from 1975-95, Paul Horsnell makes a cogent case that, just as the North Sea oil defied most predictions, Asian regional production may be able to rise to 9 million bpd or higher by 2010. The

[38]

obstacles to enhancing production in existing Asian oil fields, he argues, are principally government policies, not geology. This view was also conveyed to the author by a number of Western oil company officials.[42] Achieving higher production may be possible if Asian producers remove the policy impediments (price and tax regimes) to enhanced investment in technologies that can improve and prolong output.

The Asian-Middle East Energy Nexus

Nonetheless, in aggregate terms, what promises to be at best stable or moderately increased Asian production will only affect the Asia-Pacific regional oil deficit at the margins. Thus, it was emblematic of emerging oil politics when President Jiang Zemin made the first ever visit by a Chinese head of state to Saudi Arabia in November 1999, heading to Damman, the heart of Saudi oil country after a stop in Riyadh. That China, one of the world's largest oil producers, as well as other Asian countries are diligently cultivating energy ties to the Saudis and other major Gulf producers underscores a profound awareness of the limits of Asian oil production.

The dominant, and seemingly inexorable trend is one of growing Asian oil dependence on the Middle East and vice-versa. As mentioned above, over 60% of Middle East oil exports go to Asia, and nearly 75% of Asian oil imports come from Middle East producers. Moreover, the oil throughput for refineries in Singapore, Japan and South Korea, three major Asian refining centers is overwhelmingly from the Middle East: Singapore (84%) and Japan and South Korea (78%). New refineries elsewhere in the region have also begun to look to the Gulf/Middle East in making decisions about crude oil purchases. These trends are relatively recent. From 1975 to the early 1990s, OPEC Middle East exports to East Asia grew only by about 40%. This was the result of several factors: Middle East production cutbacks to maintain high prices in the early 1980s; Asian reduction in demand in response to the two oil shocks by diversifying away from oil, especially in the case of Japan; increased efficiency of industrialized Asian consumers; and growth in Asian production.[43]

However, the current burgeoning Middle East-Asian oil nexus that began to take shape in the 1990s appears a permanent structural feature of the new global, information age oil market that has changed dramatically over the past two decades. Gone are the days of exclusive, secretive fixed-contracts. Oil products have become fully commodified, mainly sold on a free market, floating price basis. International crude oil markets have become increasingly global and transparent, similar to the now familiar world financial markets that shuffles $1.5 trillion electronically around the world each day. In this new, more efficient oil market, oil export movements are driven mainly by transportation economics, as most sellers seek to maximize revenues by finding proximate end users.

As oil markets are now shaped more by transport costs than political relationships, the result, as discussed above, has been a largely bifurcated global market, with oil flows from the Middle East gravitating to Asia; while oil supplies from the western hemisphere (Mexico, Venezuela, Colombia, Canada), and the Atlantic Basin (North Sea, West Africa) have to a large degree, displaced Gulf oil from the US market. At present, only about 12% of total US oil consumed comes from the Middle East. According oil economist Fadhil Chalabi, a former senior OPEC official, by 2010, "the share of the Middle East's oil exports going to the Asia-Pacific region as a whole is expected to rise...to 66%...Interdependence between the Asia-Pacific and Gulf regions in the oil sector is firmly entrenched."[44] Indeed, the Asia-Pacific will likely be importing 20-24 million bpd from the Middle East by 2020, 95% of its total oil imports by 2010.[45] There may be some measure of uncertainty over the precise volume—whether Asian production increases, economic slowdowns weaken demand, or new technologies reduce oil demand (the latter may be a significant factor in the out years from 2015). Yet, even if such unanticipated developments reduce Asian oil imports by one-third, the basic phenomenon of Gulf/Middle East–Asian oil mutual dependence remains, whether it is 16 million bpd or 24 million bpd.

Yet if Gulf/Middle East–Asian energy interdependence is an emerging fact of life, its wider significance is a matter of much speculation and debate. The cosmic question is what this phenomenon of an energy

[40]

linkage between two potentially turbulent regions, the Gulf/Middle East and the Asia-Pacific, may mean in regard to the international system of relations. Is it principally a dynamic, complementary commercial relationship, or one that will radically alter the international order? Even if one views it less apocalyptically, what are the geopolitical implications of it for Gulf security, for Asian security, and for the US role in both Southwest and East Asia? The implications of the Middle East–Asian oil nexus may be initially divided into three related categories, the near-term (to 2010) and tangible and the long-term and intangible, and the potential nightmare scenarios.

Which Future: Geoeconomics or Geopolitics?

Both sides of the new oil equation have become increasingly animated by their respective imperatives: the need to ensure customers, on the part of Gulf/Middle East exporters; and the need to ensure oil supplies on the Asian side. "For the first time we are focusing on Asia," former Saudi Oil Minister and senior OPEC official Ahmed Zaki Yamani, reflecting fears at the time of the impact of the Asian crisis on OPEC, said in a keynote address to an annual London energy conference in 1998. "Asia," Yamani explained, "can play a crucial role in helping to improve OPEC's prospects."[46]

Thus, one central consequence of the Middle East–Asia oil link that has begun to unfold is a complex set of interlocking economic and financial relationships, a deepening commercial network weaving the two regions together: Asians investing in upstream oil and gas sectors in the Middle East; while OPEC Middle East exporters invest in downstream Asian activities. As OPEC Secretary General Rilwanu Lukman explained in a July 1998 speech at the Middle East Institute in Washington, "Asian investors, traders, operators and others are active in the energy sectors of the Gulf. On the other hand, Middle East companies and individuals have significant interests in the downstream energy industry in Asia."[47] Saudi officials have emphasized the importance of building the China market.

President Jiang's 1999 Saudi visit was one of the visible manifestations of this active trend. The Chinese leader interestingly proclaimed that

China is forming "a strategic oil partnership" with Riyadh. This was an intriguing choice of words, considering Beijing's penchant for declaring more generic "strategic partnerships" with Russia, South Korea, France and other countries. In 1995, Beijing decided to import 3.5 million tons of crude oil from Saudi Arabia annually (less than 1% of Saudi production). Jiang brought an entourage of Chinese business officials, signed oil cooperation agreements, and discussed a $1.5 billion refinery and petrochemical complex in Southern China that would use Saudi oil.[48]

There has been an accelerating pace in exploring and in many cases, concluding business deals between Asian and Gulf/Middle East officials in recent years. In addition to its efforts in Saudi Arabia, China has invested in oil fields in Sudan, Iraq and Iran since the mid-1990s.[49] Significantly, China has also forged energy links with Saudi Arabia on the other side of the Gulf, signing an open-ended supply contract, though at present it imports less than 70,000 bpd. As Saudi Arabia and other Gulf states open up to foreign investment in gas and oil exploration and production, CNPC and other Chinese oil companies are likely to increase their efforts to buy into these sectors. One conspicuous aspect of Chinese oil strategy has been to target countries sanctioned by the United States, where competition from major Western oil companies is less intense, such as the three states mentioned above as well as Libya. While Chinese state oil companies have been animated by the same desire as Japan – to diversify sources of oil – there are few illusions that dependence on the Middle East can be reduced except marginally.

Similarly Malaysia's state-run Petronas is in a joint venture with European companies to develop the South Pars gas fields in Iran as well as oil fields in Iran and Yemen. Both India and Indonesia have explored investing in the Tuba oil field in Iraq. Japan has steadily cultivated Gulf producers, with investment in Saudi Arabia, in Abu Dhabi, in oil and gas in Oman and along with South Korea, has invested in Qatar to produce LNG. Japan developed the Khafji oil field in the Neutral Zone, divided between Saudi Arabia and Kuwait in the 1960s. The Khafji field produces 300,000 bpd, 70% of it goes to Japan, part of nearly 1 million bpd Japan imports from Saudi Arabia and Kuwait. The lease on the Saudi portion of the field expired in 2000, and the Khafji lease expired in January 2003, though a Japanese firm reached an agreement to negotiate an extension of drilling rights beyond the current concession.[50] Japan has begun funding seismic analysis on Iran's giant Azadegan oilfield and is part of an international consortium developing the field with some 25 billion barrels of oil.[51]

In the other direction, OPEC Middle East producers have similarly been actively seeking to deepen their economic ties to Asia, with an emphasis on downstream activities, such as refining. The Saudis have been perhaps the most active in this area over the past decade, with the Saudi press covering visits of senior Saudi officials to China and other Asian nations with great fanfare. In 1991, Saudi Aramco bought a 35% stake in Ssangyong Oil Refining Co, the third largest refiner in South Korea, for $470 million and may increase its stake. Saudi Aramco also purchased a 40% stake in Petron, a major Philippines refiner in 1995, and in 1997, with Exxon in a large joint venture to expand a refinery in China's Fujian province from 80,000 bpd capacity to 240,000 bpd. At the same time, the state firm also formed an alliance with Royal/Dutch Shell to invest in Asian downstream ventures. Kuwait and Qatar have also cultivated Asian importers. In the case of Qatar, it is seeking to lock in long-term gas contracts with India, China and Japan. China has also been strengthening economic ties to Iran including agreements to increase oil imports and to build a joint refinery in China, as well as its oil investments in Iran.[52]

The effort on the part of some Asian states to diversify oil suppliers has led both Japan and China into new involvement in the Caspian Basin. Since the mid-1990s, Japan has embarked upon a "Eurasian strategy," articulated in 1998 by then Prime Minister Ryutaro Hashimoto. This Japanese initiative has seen a new approach to Russia in which oil and gas resources, particularly on and offshore Sakhalin Island has been a major component, and also has led to a new emphasis on aid and investment in pipelines as well as oil and gas fields in the former Soviet Republics in Central Asia.[53] Similarly, China entered the Central Asian energy game by outbidding Western firms for a major oil field in Kazakhstan in 1997, promising to build a pipeline, which has since been indefinitely postponed. Beijing's state oil companies are involved elsewhere in the Caspian region. Moreover, Beijing is actively exploring the feasibility of a 2400km pipeline to bring Russian gas from Irkutsk. It must be said, however, that the Caspian region is unlikely to account for more than roughly 3% of global oil production as its resources are gradually developed over the next decade or so.

It is important to note that this phenomenon of interlocking energy investments is only at an early stage, reflecting what is a fairly recent and still emerging reality. However, it appears an imperative, reflecting underlying anxieties about energy security on both sides. As the oil and gas relationship with Asia expands over the coming decade, there will be an enormous volume of capital flows into the OPEC Middle East producers. According to one estimate, by 2010, if Asia is importing 17 million bpd from the Middle East, at $20 a barrel, the result would be capital transfers to the Middle East of $124 billion annually.[54] Even in today's global financial markets, where some $1.5 trillion a day floats through cyberspace, that is real money. Such revenues could in part, be recycled into downstream investment in dynamic Asian economies. Yet, there are numerous other possibilities. Growing capital flows to the Middle East would go some distance in ameliorating a growing list of problems in major oil exporting countries such as Saudi Arabia, Kuwait, Iran and Iraq. Riyadh, for example has seen a significant decline in living standards over the past fifteen years, has a large demographic bulge of youth to absorb into its economy, and has accumulated $130 billion foreign debt. However, such capital flows could also accelerate efforts at obtaining a new cycle of modern weapons, including weapons of mass destruction.

The rough outlines of the anticipated economic and financial consequences of the Middle East–Asian energy relationship for the global economy are discernible in terms of orders of magnitude and economic patterns. However, the political/security implications enter the realm of the intangible and the speculative. In the 1930s, it was energy security that led Japan to occupy Indonesia and control its oil fields. Indeed, the US oil embargo was an important factor leading Tokyo to attack Pearl Harbor, which brought the US directly into the Second World War. Some analysts see China, as a rising power with a newfound energy dependence as a possible latter day version of that experience. "The problem for Asian stability, growing with each barrel of Chinese oil imports, is now clear," writes Kent Calder in an influential book on energy and security in Asia. "It is the danger," he argues, "that China's attempts to safeguard its oil supply lanes and defend its historical sovereignty in adjacent seas poses for other nations, especially Japan. China claims 80 per cent of the South China Sea as territorial water, 70 percent of Japan's oil supplies pass that way."

Thus, this chain of logic goes, "As Chinese imports steadily rise, defending the fragile sea lanes to the far-off...Gulf becomes a new security imperative for the PLA Navy."[55] This begins to move from the second category of intangible into the third, of nightmare scenarios: Chinese destroyers and aircraft carriers disrupting tanker traffic in a war over disputed islands in the South China Sea; or in a war with Japan over the virtually uninhabited Senkaku islands; or worse still, allying with Iraq or Iran in a future Gulf war. The US experience with such patron-client relationships in the Middle East should give China pause. It is also true that at present, China's refineries are not capable of processing more than about 240,000 bpd of sour crude from the Gulf, which would limit arms-for-oil barter. (Indeed, the difficulty and expense for China to alter its refineries to process more sour crude has led Beijing to import more sweet crude from Angola and other offshore Africa wells.) Moreover, China's oil relationship with Saudi Arabia would further argue against Beijing overtly taking sides in a Gulf conflict, lest it put those ties to the Saudis and their massive oil reserves at risk. Nonetheless, Chinese suppliers of military and dual-use equipment (e.g. fiber optic cable in Iraq) have continued activities, some of which bump up against PRC non-proliferation pledges. For the moment, it remains an open question whether China will pursue supplier relationships (on military and dual-use technology) with Gulf states on a strategic rather than largely commercial basis. Clearly, there is a desire to bolster political ties to oil producing states. Yet how that will be defined by Chinese behavior remains unclear.

To be sure, the number of oil tankers plying the waters of the Indian Ocean, through the straits of Malacca, and the South China seas for ports in Pusan, Yokohama and Shanghai in the two decades ahead will likely increase three-fold. Yet is there indeed, an ominous security threat as some fear? The scarcity notion can easily lead to a logic of: imports equals shortages equals resource competition equals territorial conflict. The 'looming conflict' model seems to be based on a sort of neo-mercantilist set of assumptions reminiscent of 19th century and pre-World War 2 interstate relations in Europe. Certainly, the Asia-Pacific has more than its share of bristling nationalism, historical grievance and ethnic antagonism. Yet, thus far it has not tended to manifest itself in a manner similar to the experience in Europe in the century leading to the Second World War.

Moreover, there does not appear any imminent shortage of oil, nor even if high end demand projections are realized, is a shortage likely over the next quarter century. A study by the Baker Institute at Rice University based on median assumptions of a cross-section of prominent industry consultant groups concluded that even assuming high end assumptions of Chinese demand of 7.1 million barrels per day (mbpd) by 2010, if non-OPEC production grew at 1%, a conservative forecast, the result would be a modest oil surplus of oil and prices under $20 barrel.[56]

To put Asian projected oil demand growth in historical perspective, it might be noted that US oil imports grew from 1.8 mbpd in 1960 to 8.8 mbpd in 1977 without creating crisis competition with other importers. Moreover, in the same time frame, oil demand for Europe and Asia rose from 4.5 mbpd to 19 mbpd, and by the mid-1980s world oil prices had gone into a downward spiral after the OPEC twin oil shocks of 1973-74 and 1979-80.[57] A rise in Asian oil imports from about 12 mbpd in 1999 to 25 mbpd by 2020 would be in a similar range, and it is not unreasonable to think it could be similarly accommodated in world oil markets. This is a projection that does not factor in any new technologies such as the mass-marketing of hybrid or fuel cell autos likely to occur well before 2020, which would dramatically reduce oil demand. And unlike the situation during the 1930s, foreign investment, long-term contracts and building strategic petroleum reserves are more efficient ways to safeguard supply than real estate grabs, and more likely to be the arena for resource competition.

China has not had a blue water Navy for nearly six centuries, since the days of Admiral Zhang He during the Ming Dynasty. Neither has it been dependent on foreign energy sources for the past six centuries. In any case, while Chinese military modernization continues apace, it is unlikely that China will obtain the air and sea force projection capabilities to challenge the United States in the Gulf or in the Pacific for at least the next two decades. Then there is the question of why import-dependent China would want to disrupt tanker traffic from the Gulf to East Asia. Some 40% of the world's trade passes through the straits of Malacca, and disrupting global trade would be the economic equivalent of using a nuclear weapon. Nonetheless, there has already been speculation about China seeking aircraft carriers, and announcements of Beijing's attempt to create a long range air force, as well, certainly indicate the ambition to eventually create a blue water navy, even if it remains a generation over the horizon.[58] Yet, such a move would be likely to spark a naval arms race with India and Japan, one that is unlikely to make China, India or Japan more secure.

Moreover, the Gulf is not an area where China has had historic ties nor compelling strategic interests apart from its general posture of countering "hegemony," Soviet influence during the Cold War, and to some degree, pre-eminent American superpower now. Yet the Middle East is fast becoming a significant trading partner for China, though Chinese exports –even after growing exponentially – are less than $5 billion to the entire Middle East. Beginning with the Iran-Iraq war, China developed an arms supplier role in the region, which continued into the 1990s, particularly in the form of missiles and other weapons of mass destruction to Iran. In one blatant 1997 episode, Beijing threatened to withhold support for continuing sanctions against Iraq if Kuwait did not agree to a major arms purchase, of self-propelled howitzers worth about $300 million.[59] At the same time, Beijing has developed a flourishing relationship with Israel and has supported the Middle East peace process. As was evident in its behavior during the 1990-1991 Gulf War, when Beijing went along with US-led efforts to reverse Iraq's invasion of Kuwait and with subsequent sanctions, China's top priority of economic modernization has been a dominant factor.[60]

Interestingly though, even as the specter of Middle East oil dependency has grown, China's arms sales, while not dissipating, have not significantly expanded, particularly the most troubling missile and nuclear technology to its most troubling client, Iran. Beijing had sold C802 missiles and other sophisticated military equipment to Iran and planned to build two nuclear plants and a hexafluoride plant, that could facilitate Iranian ambitions of joining the nuclear club. Some analysts suggest this has not occurred because economically troubled Iran was in arrears to China for some $900 million.[61] Another factor may have been Beijing's desire to improve relations with the United States. Yet, it also may be the case that China has reconsidered its dealings with Gulf-Middle East nations in light of its growing dependence on oil from the region. While China's behavior retains some ambiguity – selling technology and expertise rather than whole weapons systems, or in some cases all but complete systems – the trajectory of China's policies on missile and nuclear proliferation have been generally, though erratically and with some retreats, in the direction of international norms: the Non–Proliferation Treaty (NPT); the Chemical Weapons Convention (CWC); the Comprehensive Test Ban Treaty (CTBT); and pledges to adhere to Missile Technology Control Regime standards (MTCR).[62]

Certainly, highly dependent Asian energy importers are likely to have a new appreciation for stability in the Gulf. This can manifest itself in a varieties of ways, one of which might be the development of a new sense of common interests with the United States in the Gulf. This is a point US officials have repeatedly made to China in an effort to persuade Beijing that missile sales to Iran, for example, may not be in China's best interest. The geoeconomic argument views oil as a globalized commodity. Thus, a disruption anywhere is a price spike everywhere. The competition for resources is most likely one of determining the best price – who gets what long-term contract – rather than access to the strategic resource. There may well be problems of short term disruption, as occurred during the Iranian revolution in 1979. However, turbulence in Saudi Arabia or elsewhere in the Gulf would likely mean only short term interference and price hikes, not long-term competition for access to resources.

Yet that still leaves China and other Asian nations as free-riders, since the United States remains the guardian of stability in the Gulf. It is a legitimate question whether Beijing is comfortable remaining in such a position and for how long, as its Gulf oil imports increase to substantial volumes in the 2010-20 period. Yet such dependence – even if it grows from common interests – is almost certain to make China, with its pride and great power aspirations, rather uncomfortable. As in many areas, China's behavior is ambiguous. This ambiguity is reflected in a paper by a prominent Shanghai-based analyst, Ji Guoxing. In a paper on the security of Sea Lanes of Communication (SLOC), he writes, "China attaches much importance to SLOC security and would play a positive role in safeguarding of SLOC together with other regional countries." He adds that "the on-going naval build-up by regional countries would be another threat to SLOC security." Yet he also explains that in the mid-1980s, China changed its naval strategy from an emphasis on coastal defense to offshore defense. He cites the naval modernization plan of the then Chief of Naval Operations, Liu Huaqing as defining: "The outmost defense approaches of the Chinese navy will be spanned around the China seas: to the Korean Strait in the North, to Liuqiu Islands in the east, and to Nansha (Spratly) Islands in the south."[63]

China's policy calculus on the sea lane question will reflect in considerable measure on the character of Sino-American relations in the decades ahead. Arguably, given the alternative of naval arms races, it might be argued that Washington may want to encourage China's free-riding, or even consider sea lane security guarantee. In any case, China and India both envision building more capable maritime forces over the coming generation. How much of a premium either nation may place on maritime control of sea lanes far beyond the South China Sea, or the

[49]

Indian Ocean, respectively, remains to be seen. However, disrupting the flow of oil tanker traffic would cause equal opportunity damage, driving up the world price of oil. Given its dependence on Middle East imports, barring extreme circumstances such as a Third World War, it is difficult to see how China would benefit by interdicting oil shipping. Similarly, it is difficult to envision circumstances under which the US would interdict oil shipments to Asia short of a protracted global conflagration. Nevertheless, issues of nationalism and sovereignty rather than energy security may be more operative factors animating Asia-Pacific political/military decisions. The question is whether such limited ocean-going capacity would spark a Japanese or Indian naval arms race with China. In any case, while China's military modernization promises to begin limiting American freedom of action in the decades ahead—and could even do significant damage in a Taiwan conflict in the 2004-2010 period—there is no obvious candidate to displace American naval preeminence as the guardian of the major sea lanes of communication before the second quarter of this century if current trends continue.

Moreover, US Navy-funded studies of the SLOCs and the key chokepoints for shipping suggest that the likelihood of disruption is low, intentional disruptions are not likely to endure more than a matter of weeks, and alternative routes exist which, though they raise the cost of trade, are manageable, particularly if, as is highly likely, the time frame is limited.[64] A study published by the US Center for Naval Analysis (CNA), *Chokepoints,* examined the question of disruption of shipping through the straits of Southeast Asia – Malacca, Sundra, Lombok, (the most heavily trafficked) Phillip Channel and the Strait of Singapore. It concluded, "At present, events that could disrupt passage through the Southeast Asian sea lanes for an extended period of time are not likely to occur."[65] The study examined potential militarily-induced closures (as opposed to say, an accidental oil spill) as a result of conflict in the South China Sea, for example, or in the Taiwan Strait, closing the sea lanes. In these cases, closing the SLOC near the Spratly or the Taiwan Strait would mean diverting shipping to the Sunda and Lombok straits.

If all the straits were closed, nearly half the world's fleet, particularly oil tankers would have to divert to much longer and costlier routes, with shipping, insurance and freight rates significantly raised. However, the likelihood of them all being closed in the absence of a global conflict, is rather low. The CNA study concentrates on the economics of diverting shipping and suggests that a SLOC-closing scenario could be costly, but unlikely to be protracted in duration, and difficult but likely to be manageable economically. "Economic and political interests, and geography, on balance, should work to keep open strategic straits," the study argues.[66] Given the life-and-death common interests in sustaining the flow of goods to and from East Asia, overriding common interests of all concerned parties, "should work to maintain a consensus in favor of commercial freedom of navigation," the study concludes. For the foreseeable future, the US Navy is the only military power with the force projection capability to impose and sustain a closure, which underscores the US security guarantor role in the Asia-Pacific. It may also foreshadow the potential dangers of a naval arms race if China, Japan and India pursue large-scale blue water navies based on the SLOC safety rationale. As nearly half of the world's trade passes through the Straits of Malacca, it is difficult to envision scenarios where a major power would seek to shut down the Malacca or surrounding straits, outside of a Second World War type of protracted conflict.

Even so, there are several potential political questions raised by the Middle East/Asia energy connection that must be asked. One is the degree to which these burgeoning commercial relations acquire political weight. For example, during the 1990-1991 Gulf War, China abstained when the US mobilized a coalition to reverse Saddam Hussein's invasion and occupation of Kuwait. As Geoffrey Kemp has argued, if there is a future crisis in the region in which China or India, for instance, must chose between supporting directly or indirectly US actions that involve oil or gas suppliers to either Beijing or Delhi, the international political results might be very different.[67] More broadly, will the collective economic weight and shared interests of the Middle East–Asia economic nexus take on a political expression, if for example, there is a growing perception of the United States as a global bully, acting unilaterally to coerce or shape behavior that either or both do not view as being in their respective national interests? Or does the global nature of contemporary energy markets diminish the political import of the Middle East–Asia energy nexus?

The second political issue is that of burden-sharing. Given the growing Asian energy dependence on Gulf oil and gas, some observers suggest that major Asian powers should play a much larger political-military role in shoring up stability in the Gulf region. At some point in the medium to long range future it is possible that things may move in this direction. However, at present, such a displacement of the predominant US power is not only impossible in terms of military capabilities, but also would tend to be profoundly destabilizing and likely spark a regional arms race. For the forseeable future, the United States will remain a guarantor of stability in the Gulf. There is simply no other likely alternative on the horizon. Yet the resources that the US is protecting increasingly go elsewhere, largely to Asia, secondarily to Europe, but only marginally to the US. It can be argued that since oil is fungible the US does benefit from its role in the Gulf in any case. Yet there still remains the burden-sharing argument. US allies in Europe lack the capacity, and to some degree, the political will to assume more political-military responsibility. Japan is constitutionally prohibited from assuming a proactive military role, and certainly for the foreseeable future, is not likely to have a Japanese (not to mention regional) mandate to project force at great distance from the home islands. Will the American public and their elected representatives continue to support such a US military role in the region even if those directly benefiting from the US stabilizing role do not assume their fair share of responsibility?

Unfortunately, these necessarily remain unanswered questions. How they unfold will depend in large measure on how Asia-Pacific nations conceive of energy security, how the political environments both in East Asia and in the Gulf/Middle East evolve, and what the energy picture looks like a generation hence. Whether the uneven process of globalization trumps historic animosities in the Middle East and historic fears in Asia is an open question. It is the interaction between the two that is likely to determine the outcome of the larger impact of the Middle East–Asia energy linkage on the security of both regions. This emerging relationship between the two most prominent non-Western civilizations on the Eurasian landmass, a central fact in world energy markets, is emblematic of the historic shift in the center of gravity of the global economy toward the Pacific Rim that is certain to be one hallmark of the 21st century. It is a phenomenon that bears careful scrutiny over the next generation.

2

Future Supply and Demand Trends in the Asian Energy Markets

James P. Dorian

Given its huge population base and robust economic growth, the Asia-Pacific region is becoming the most critical influence on global energy markets. Continued dramatic growth to 2020 will further affect world energy conditions particularly in oil, LNG, and coal. Oil consumption levels in Asia are approaching that of North America and are significantly greater than in Europe. One-third of the world's coal reserves lie in Asia, more than any other region in the world, while two-thirds of global trade in LNG occurs within the region. Clearly, company strategists must monitor current energy developments in China, India, Japan, and other Asian countries plus newly emerging market areas such as the Central Asian republics to accurately forecast future world trends in prices, consumption and production.

This chapter therefore assesses future energy supply and demand trends in the Asia-Pacific region and highlights some of the important structural changes taking place in the oil, gas, coal and electricity sectors. A thorough understanding of the energy future of Asia is of huge importance to industry and government for strategic planning purposes. Trends in consumption are specifically highlighted given the rapidly increasing importance of Asia to world markets. While the region is considered in the aggregate for simplicity purposes, countries within Asia do sometimes vary considerably from each other. Thus the chapter analyzes specific areas and countries that are representative of important overall trends. Given the growing significance of energy efficiency and renewable energy within Asia, the chapter also highlights these emerging areas.

One group of countries within Asia that has the potential to noticeably affect future world oil and gas supplies is former Soviet Central Asia, which includes hydrocarbon-rich Kazakhstan, Turkmenistan, and Uzbekistan. An impressively large amount of untapped oil and natural gas may exist in Central Asia's vast fields, yet development prospects will remain dim until viable transport routes are established to bring these resources to lucrative markets in Europe, the Middle East and eventually, East Asia. While Central Asia is analyzed in order to shed light on important developments in oil and gas within Asia, the Philippines is also evaluated to illustrate dramatic changes taking place in the region's critical electricity sector. The Philippines is important to global energy markets because it is a growing consumer of energy, particularly electric power, and a significant potential market for foreign energy firms. In line with the country's economic policy for liberalization and privatization, the Philippines is geared towards full restructuring of the energy sector so as to encourage greater private sector participation and promote economic efficiency. Foremost among the structural reforms is the restructuring of the electric industry, which is discussed thoroughly in this chapter.

In addition to an examination of Central Asia's oil and gas sectors and the Philippines' electric power industry, this chapter highlights some of the key restructuring trends occurring regionally in Asia, including privatization, globalization and accountability, energy diversification, energy self-sufficiency, and attraction of foreign investment. Many governments in the Asia-Pacific region are seeking to modernize their energy industries to boost efficiencies, achieve economies of scale, and better protect their environments. Efforts are also underway to attract investment and technology as a means of promoting economic growth. While some Asian countries have been successful at attracting foreign capital to their energy industries, others are still in the early stages of revamping investment legislation to make climates more favorable. This chapter will examine the policy implications of recent restructuring trends.

Asia-Pacific Energy Supply and Demand

It is extremely difficult to project Asia-Pacific energy trends to 2020 with any degree of certainty, partly because the region is a complex mix of developed, developing, and newly industrialized economies and has the world's fastest economic growth. China, for example, can be characterized as having as many as 15 separate electricity markets, with some regions having a surplus of electricity, and others in deficit. Because of Asia's large and ever increasing dependence on imported crude oil, numerous external factors must be integrated into any analysis, including world oil prices and supply. Similarly, the issue of coal and gas substitution is a vital but uncertain factor, because of the great difficulties involved in projecting energy developments in China and the countries of the former Soviet Union or the impact of such developments on the region.

Macroeconomic Outlook

The Asia-Pacific region is economically and environmentally diverse. It occupies slightly less than a quarter of the world's land area but has more than half of the total world population. Rapid growth in the economy and population is putting pressure on the region's natural resources and environment. Asia is the fastest growing continent in the world in terms of energy and electricity consumption, economic growth and increased greenhouse gas emissions.

The projections made in this study are based on the underlying assumptions that the economies of the region will continue to expand, albeit at rates that will decline over time, and that no major disruption will occur in the economic development of China and the newly independent states of the former Soviet Union. Similarly, and most importantly, it is assumed that no major disruptions will occur in the global supply of crude oil. These assumptions will, almost certainly, have to be modified between now and 2020. Government policies are likewise expected to change during this period, in particular with respect to energy pricing, which will alter any price and demand–supply assumptions.

Table 2.1
Growth Rate of Asian GDP, 2000-2020
(% per year, unless otherwise noted)

Country	2000	2001	2002[a]	2003[a]	Average Annual Percent Change 1999-2020
Southeast Asia					
Cambodia	4.5	5.3	4.5	6.1	--
Indonesia	4.8	3.3	3.0	3.6	6.6[b]
Laos	5.5	5.5	5.8	6.1	--
Malaysia	8.5	0.4	4.2	5.8	7.0[b]
Myanmar	--	--	--	--	--
Philippines	3.9	3.4	4.0	4.5	7.0[b]
Thailand	4.2	1.8	2.5	3.0	6.3[b]
Vietnam	5.1	5.8	6.2	6.8	7.0[b]
East Asia					
Hong Kong	10.5	0.1	2.1	4.8	--
South Korea	8.8	3.0	4.8	6.0	4.5[c]
Singapore	9.9	-2.0	3.7	6.5	3.8[b]
Taiwan	6.0	-1.9	2.8	4.0	5.0[b]
China	8.0	7.3	7.0	7.4	7.0[c]
South Asia					
Bangladesh	5.5	5.2	4.5	5.7	--
Bhutan	6.1	6.5	6.5	6.5	--
India	6.0	5.4	6.0	6.8	5.7[c]
Maldives	4.2	2.1	2.0	0.0	--
Nepal	6.4	5.0	3.5	5.0	--
Pakistan	4.8	2.6	3.0	5.0	--
Sri Lanka	6.0	-1.3	3.5	5.5	--

Central Asia						
Kazakhstan	9.8	13.2	7.0	6.0	--	
Kyrgyzstan	5.4	5.3	4.5	4.5	--	
Tajikistan	8.3	10.0	6.0	5.0	--	
Turkmenistan	17.6	20.5	11.0	11.0	--	
Uzbekistan	4.0	4.5	4.0	5.0	--	

Notes: (a) Forecasts; (b) 1995-2020 GDP, reference case (moderate economic growth scenario), billion 1995 US dollars, estimated; (c) 1999-2020 GDP, reference case (moderate economic growth scenario), billion 1997 US dollars, estimated; (--) No estimate available.

Sources: (1) Energy Information Administration, March 2002, *International Energy Outlook 2002*, US Department of Energy, Washington, DC [1999-2020 projections]; (2) Asian Development Bank, 2002, *Asian Development Outlook 2002*, Tables 1.3 and A1, Manila, Philippines [2000-2003 figures]; (3) Asian Development Bank, May 7, 2001, Annual Meeting of the Board of Governors, Honolulu, Hawaii, USA [2000-2003 figures]; and (4) Parliament of Australia, March 3, 1998, *Background Paper 13 1997-98, An Asia Pacific Prognosis to 2020*, Commonwealth of Australia, Canberra, 29 pages [1995-2020 projections].

During the past thirty years, most Asia-Pacific countries have enjoyed spectacular economic growth.[1] Economic success not only has increased the region's share of the global economy, but also has exerted significant impacts on world energy markets, since the region is a net energy importer. In terms of economic performance, it will continue to be the most dynamic region in the world, both in the immediate and long-term (See Table 2.1).

Growth in developing Asia is expected to strengthen moderately in 2002, picking up further in 2003, as the region gradually returns to a more balanced and sustainable pace of development after a turbulent 1997-2001 period. Overall, aggregate growth for large developing countries in Asia will stay noticeably below its trend in the 1980s but within reach of its long-run (1951-2000) trend. Although economic growth has varied considerably from country to country, it is expected to be more uniform across Asia during the entire outlook period, 2000-2020. During that period growth rates of gross domestic product (GDP) will increase at an average annual rate of 5.5 percent for developing Asia under a moderate economic growth scenario compared to a 3.2 percent change for the total world.

The developed countries of the region, also referred to as the OECD countries, are Japan, Australia, and New Zealand. Their economies have been maturing, and their GDP growth rates during the outlook period will be considerably lower than those of the past.

The Asia-Pacific newly industrialized economies (NIEs) are Hong Kong, Singapore, South Korea and Taiwan. The NIEs have been able to sustain strong economic growth, although the growth rates in recent years have been lower than those achieved on average during the past two decades. The NIEs are in the process of a difficult transition from labor-intensive manufacturing to capital-intensive industries and services. International trade has a particularly strong influence on the economic performances of the NIEs, and during periods of slow growth in the United States and Japan, the NIEs' reliance on trade necessarily diminishes. Over the long term these economies will therefore require a concerted effort to improve productivity through technological innovations and enhance labor skill levels through human resource development to promote growth. The GDP growth of the NIEs will remain strong for the rest of this decade, but will become slower between 2005 and 2020 as their economies mature.

There are five major economies in Southeast Asia: Indonesia, Malaysia, the Philippines, Thailand, and Vietnam. These economies are more integrated than those of other Asia-Pacific countries and they have achieved remarkable growth, except for the Philippines. Sound macroeconomic policies and growth led by manufactured exports ensure that the rapid growth of the Indonesian, Malaysian and Thai economies will continue well into the first decade of the next century. Vietnam, as it implements economic reforms, is expected to have the highest economic growth rate in this group of countries during the outlook period. The economic growth rate in the Philippines is expected to increase, as the country's investment environment improves.

The three largest economies in South Asia are Bangladesh, India, and Pakistan. With the success of their ongoing economic reforms and the improvement of their infrastructure, they are expected to achieve higher growth rates during the rest of the outlook period. Bangladesh, with its limited natural resources, high population density, and vulnerability to natural disasters, can maintain no more than a moderate economic growth rate.

Although most of the other Asia-Pacific economies are relatively small, their economic growth is not necessarily slow. Taking into account the strong influence of their neighbors in the region, whose economies are growing rapidly, it is assumed that the other Asia-Pacific countries as a group will achieve a growth rate equivalent to the unweighted average rate of all the region's economies.

Asia-Pacific Realities: The Context

Developing Asia[2] includes the first, second, and fourth most populous countries in the world—China, India and Indonesia. As a region, Developing Asia accounts for more than 50 percent of the world's population, roughly 10 percent of its GDP, and about 7 percent of its natural gas consumption. Despite a two-year financial and currency crisis in Asia between 1997-1999, the region has successfully rebounded and strong economic growth is projected until 2020. According to Asian Development Bank officials, Developing Asia will enjoy aggregate growth of 4.9 percent in 2002, while Industrialized Asia will also enjoy robust growth. Developing Asia's economic growth rate is forecast to rise to 5.8 percent in 2003.

Long-term prosperity is predicted in Asia for several reasons, including a solid workforce, continued banking and financial sector reform, tremendous natural resources, and high education levels. Continued growth will require increased energy consumption, with much of the region's new sources of supply being met through oil and product imports from the Middle East. The Middle East remains the heart of the global oil industry, containing over two-thirds of the proven oil reserves and one-third of proven gas. Recent forecasts predict that the oil output of the Middle East would have to increase by over 50 percent in the next ten years to meet the expected rise in global oil demand.

The rapid growth in the Asian economies over the last two decades has been accompanied by rapid growth in energy demand and electricity demand, with resulting increases in oil imports and emissions of sulfur dioxide, nitrogen oxides, particulates, and carbon dioxide. This growth is expected to continue over the coming decades, with energy demand expected to grow 25 percent and electricity demand by 37 percent in Asia by 2010.[3] This demand growth, in turn, is projected to result in an increase of 25 percent or some 960 million tons per year in carbon dioxide emissions, as well as huge investment requirements for pollution control equipment.

Increased energy consumption in Asia is indeed leading to local and regional problems of air pollution, including transboundary air pollution. Ten out of 11 cities surveyed in the region have dangerous levels of suspended particulate matter that exceed World Health Organization guidelines by more than a factor of two. The main source of industrial energy in Asia is fossil fuel, which contributes substantially to air pollution.

Several observations on Asia's economy, energy industry and environment provide a context for the importance of the region to the rest of the world in terms of resource consumption and use. Some of these observations pertaining to economic, energy, and environmental issues are critical and worthy of mention here:

Economic Aspects

- Asia has 60 percent of the world's population today, numbering 3.5 billion people.
- By 2025, that number will grow to 5 billion, a 40 percent increase.
- Last century, when the world's population tripled, energy and natural resource consumption grew ten-fold (with much of that consumption based on the combustion of fossil fuel).
- By 2025, resource consumption, infrastructure development and service delivery in Asia will have to be increased by 40 percent simply to maintain the status quo.
- Asia will remain the world's fastest growing regional economy until 2020
- By 2020, 54 percent of Asians will live in urban areas.
- While there are 10 "megacities" in Asia today (with 10 million residents or more), this number may rise to 20 by 2025.

[62]

Energy Aspects

- The use of conventional energy like oil, coal, and electricity in Asian economies has increased enormously over the last 25 years. During the 1980s consumption more than doubled, with an average annual growth rate of 7 percent.
- A majority of the Asian economies are undergoing the industrialization phase, and this increases their energy intensity. The increased energy demand is largely covered by increasing fossil fuel consumption and hence leads to higher CO_2 intensity of the economies.
- In China, total energy consumption remains well below peak levels in 1996 due to dramatic declines in coal consumption and energy efficiency improvements in the national economy.

Environmental Aspects

- In most Asian economies the CO_2 emissions per capita are still quite low compared with most of the industrialized countries like the United States. However, of the 15 most polluted cities on earth, 13 are located in Asia.
- The development of energy sectors in Asia is to an increasing extent based on fossil energy use. There seems to be more fuel switching towards more carbon intensive production than to less carbon intensive production. (This type of development is mainly due to the fact that the Asian countries are industrializing economies and are following the Western pattern of development.)
- The CO_2 emissions will consequently increase due to the increased use of fossil fuels.
- Increased use of natural gas instead of oil and coal will however decrease the carbon intensity of energy production. Renewable energy sources such as hydro, wind and biomass based production provides another possibility towards a more sustainable energy future.

Forecasting Source and Methodology

Each year the Energy Information Administration (EIA) of the United States Department of Energy completes one of the most comprehensive energy trend forecasts found anywhere in the world. The EIA analyzes world energy consumption, world oil markets, natural gas, coal, nuclear power, hydroelectricity and other renewables, electricity, transportation energy use, and world environmental issues. For discussion purposes, the elaborate world energy forecasts for oil, gas, coal, electricity, and renewables compiled by the EIA are used in this paper, especially the *International Energy Outlook 2001 (IEO 2001).*[4] The EIA projections are based on a complex mathematical model and there is no attempt in this paper to modify these forecasts. Instead, the forecasts are used to highlight current energy trends in Asia and expected developments in key Asian countries. A summary of the World Energy Projection System (WEPS) employed by the EIA to complete the projections of world energy consumption is presented in the Appendix at the end of this chapter.[5]

For comparison, readers may refer to world energy forecasts of the Paris-based International Energy Agency (IEA), in *World Energy Outlook*, 2000. The IEA's central projections are derived from a "reference scenario," which assumes global economic growth of more than 3 percent per annum and a slowdown in population growth. In this chapter the primary energy forecasts are evaluated and interpreted by the author and original detailed analysis is provided on the energy futures of Central Asia, the Philippines, and China.

1-Oil

Oil prices averaged 58 percent higher in 2000 compared to the previous year, holding worldwide growth in consumption of that fuel to only 1.0 percent, effectively in line with its 1999-2000 average. Oil consumption rose by slightly less than 1 million barrels per day in 2000, with non-industrialized nations accounting for all the increase. Oil demand in the developing economies of the Pacific Rim and China was responsible for about 50 percent of the increase. Although the developing Asian economies are no longer in recession, their current growth is modest by comparison with the rapid economic expansion in the region during the early and mid-1990s.

Globally, the largest increase in oil demand is projected for the developing countries of Asia, where consumption is expected to increase by 3.9 percent per year between 1999 and 2020 (see Figure 2.1), or 220 percent. This region alone is expected to account for 37 percent of the increase in world oil demand in the forecast period, the highest regional growth in the world. Over the same two-decade period, US demand for energy is projected to increase by 32 percent.[6] Strong expected economic growth in developing Asia fuels the demand for additional oil consumption, both in terms of increasing demand for energy use in the transportation sector, electricity sector and for other industrial and building uses.

Figure 2.1

Oil Consumption in the Developing World, 1970-2020

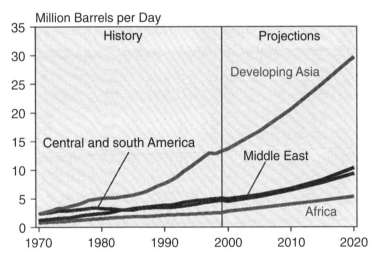

Sources: Energy Information Administration (EIA), Office of Energy Markets and End Use, International Statistics Database and *International Energy Annual, 1999*, DOE/EIA-0219(99) (Washington, DC: January 2001). Projections by EIA, World Energy Projection System (2001).

In the People's Republic of China, the biggest oil consuming nation within developing Asia, oil demand is forecasted to rise by 6.1 million barrels per day from 1999 to 2020, according to the US-based Energy Information Administration. A majority of the increase is expected in the transportation sector, where the need to transport people and goods will be increasingly critical for economic growth. Hydrocarbons remain a pillar of the Chinese economy and efforts are continuing to expand and modernize the industry. Today, China is the sixth largest producer of oil in the world and third biggest consumer.

In neighboring South Korea, during the past two decades oil consumption rose at an average rate that was among the highest in the world. The projected growth rate in energy use slows markedly over the 2000-2020 period as the transportation sector reaches saturation levels. Nonetheless, South Korea is expected to add 1.2 million barrels per day to world oil demand in the forecast period, only slightly less than Western Europe. South Korea's only significant indigenous source of energy is coal.

India's oil consumption in 2000 reached 2 million barrels per day, representing a 2.5 percent increase over the prior year. Demand in the country is expected to increase from 1.9 million barrels per day in 1999 to 5.8 million barrels per day in 2020. At 5.4 percent per year, the projected growth rate for oil use in India is the highest among the countries and regions in the forecast. The *IEO 2001* also predicts strong growth in petroleum consumption for the other developing countries in Asia, where oil demand is expected to rise from 5.0 million barrels per day in 1999 to 10.2 million barrels per day in 2020, at an average rate of 3 percent per year. The transportation sector's share of oil demand for this group as a whole is expected to remain just below 50 percent throughout the forecast period.

In the industrialized countries[7] of Asia, oil demand is expected to increase at an average annual rate of 0.5 percent over the forecast period, considerably less than the average increase of 1.4 percent per year from 1970 to 1999. Japan is the second largest oil-consuming country in the world, and its demand for petroleum products is projected to increase by about 350 thousand barrels per day from 1999 to 2020, at an average growth rate of 0.3 percent per year. The transportation sector's share of the oil market, at 3 percent, is the lowest among the industrialized countries. Japan energy sector is one of the most regulated in Asia, and the country's government has often been criticized for excessive protection of the industry. The country uses a much larger proportion of oil to power the industrial sector than does the United States or the OECD as a whole, mostly because Japan does not have easy access to natural gas or coal.

The region of Australasia – dominated by Australia but also including New Zealand and the US Territories – is projected to have a much higher growth rate in oil consumption than Japan. In spite of being an important producer of crude oil and condensates, Australia is a net importer in its international trade balance.

As for petroleum products, the Asia-Pacific region has experienced an unprecedented demand surge for these products in recent years, which has not been accompanied by adequate expansion of the region's refining capacity. Reliance on imported oil will increase in Asia particularly during the second decade of the forecast period, 2010-2020. The recent surge in petroleum product imports has resulted in greater dependence on Singapore as a refining center and has helped to create healthier refining margins in the region.

It may be noted also that the demand growth patterns are different for each product. As an example, diesel demand has grown more rapidly than the demand for other products, and diesel prices have thus grown faster than the prices of other products. In contrast, fuel oil has shown little demand growth, and therefore the price differential has increased between fuel oil and lighter products such as middle distillates and gasoline.

In terms of the petroleum trade, it is likely to increase noticeably in the region through the forecast period. In 1998, industrialized countries imported 16.9 million barrels of oil per day from the Organization of Petroleum Exporting Countries (OPEC) producers. Of that total, 10.3 million barrels per day came from the Gulf region (See Table 2.2). By the end of the forecast period, OPEC exports to industrialized countries are estimated to be about 5.7 million barrels per day higher than their 1998 level, and more than half the increase is expected to come from the Gulf region.

Table 2.2
World Petroleum Trade, 1998 and 2020(a)
(million barrels per day)

Exporting Region	Importing Region							
	Industrialized				Non-Industrialized			
	North America	Western Europe	Asia	Total	Pacific Rim	China	Rest of World	Total
Year 1998								
OPEC								
The Gulf	2.2	4.0	4.1	10.3	4.2	0.4	1.3	5.9
North Africa	0.4	2.0	0.0	2.4	0.0	0.0	0.1	0.1
West Africa	0.8	0.5	0.0	1.3	0.1	0.0	0.1	0.2
South America	1.8	0.2	0.0	2.0	0.1	0.0	0.9	1.0
Asia	0.1	0.0	0.8	0.9	0.1	0.0	0.0	0.1
Total OPEC	5.2	6.7	5.0	16.9	4.6	0.4	2.4	7.4
Non-OPEC								
North Sea	0.7	5.6	0.0	6.3	0.0	0.0	0.0	0.0
Caribbean Basin	2.4	0.5	0.0	3.0	0.2	0.0	2.1	2.3
FSU	0.0	2.6	0.0	2.7	0.1	0.0	0.1	0.2
Other Non-OPEC	2.7	2.0	0.5	5.2	7.7	0.5	1.3	9.5
Total Non-OPEC	5.8	10.7	0.6	17.1	8.0	0.5	3.5	12.0
Total Petroleum Imports	**11.0**	**17.4**	**5.5**	**34.0**	**12.6**	**0.9**	**5.9**	**19.3**
Year 2020								
OPEC								
The Gulf	4.7	3.7	4.8	13.2	8.2	5.3	8.3	21.8
North Africa	0.5	2.6	0.0	3.0	0.1	0.0	0.6	0.8
West Africa	0.9	1.2	0.3	2.4	0.1	0.0	1.1	1.2
South America	3.2	0.5	0.1	0.2	0.2	0.0	0.0	0.2
Asia	0.1	0.0	0.8	0.9	0.1	0.0	0.0	0.1
Total OPEC	9.4	7.9	5.4	22.6	8.9	5.3	11.9	26.0
Non-OPEC								
North Sea	0.7	5.1	0.0	5.8	0.1	0.0	0.0	0.1
Caribbean Basin	4.3	0.4	0.1	4.8	0.2	0.0	2.1	2.2
FSU	0.4	4.4	0.2	5.0	3.6	0.6	0.2	4.4
Other Non-OPEC	3.2	2.0	0.2	5.4	7.7	0.8	1.5	10.0
Total Non-OPEC	8.5	12.0	0.5	21.0	11.6	1.4	3.8	16.8
Total Petroleum Imports	**18.0**	**19.8**	**5.9**	**43.7**	**20.4**	**6.7**	**15.7**	**42.8**

Note: Totals may not equal sum of components due to independent rounding; (a) = Reference case.

Sources: **1998**: Energy Information Administration (EIA), Energy Markets and Contingency Information Division; **2020**: EIA, Office of Integrated Analysis and Forecasting, IEO 2001 WORLD Model run IEO01.B20 (2001).

From a supply perspective, Asia has a small amount of oil reserves, though the Central Asian states of the Former Soviet Union do have ample geological potential. Reserves amount to just more than 4 percent of the world's total. The biggest producers in the area are China, Indonesia, and Malaysia. As a region, production is approximately one-third that of the Middle East, and half that of North America. Output is expected to increase noticeably between 2000 and 2020 as a result of improved exploration and extraction technologies. India, in particular, is expected to show a modest supply increase this decade, with the Philippines holding promise for substantial new supplies of oil next decade. For Asia to realize its potential in new oil supplies to 2020, transportation infrastructure in China and other parts of the region will need to be expanded to bring the resources into the market.

2-Natural Gas

Natural gas was the most rapidly growing fossil fuel in 2000, experiencing a 4.8 percent growth. The projections for natural gas consumption in the industrialized countries of the world show more rapid growth and a larger share of the total expected increase in energy consumption than are projected for any other energy fuel. Gas use is projected to grow by 2.4 percent per year in the industrialized countries (compared with 1.1 percent for oil) and to account for 49 percent of the projected increase in their total energy use. Worldwide, gas use is projected to almost double, to 162 trillion cubic feet in 2020 from 84 trillion cubic feet in 1999. The world share of gas use for electricity generation is projected to rise to 26 percent over the same period, according to the *IEO 2001* reference case.

Within Asia, there are both gas producing and consuming economies, and economic policies toward natural gas development and use vary widely. Rapid growth in both GDP and gas use are expected for the region, which could account for about 13 percent of global gas use by 2020. The *IEO 2001* reference case projects that natural gas consumption in the whole of Asia (both industrialized and developing) will grow by an average of 5.0 percent per year, increasing Asia's consumption to 26.6 trillion cubic feet in 2020 from 9.6 trillion cubic feet in 1999. Much of this growth will be at the expense of coal and nuclear energy. The growth in developing Asia is expected to far outpace that in the industrialized countries of the region (Figure 2.2). Much of the gas that will be used in developing Asia is expected to cross international borders to reach markets, thus contributing to growing international trade. Japan is by far the largest consumer in Asia, accounting for 27.8 percent of total gas consumption in the region.

Figure 2.2
Increases in Natural Gas Consumption by Region, 1999-2020

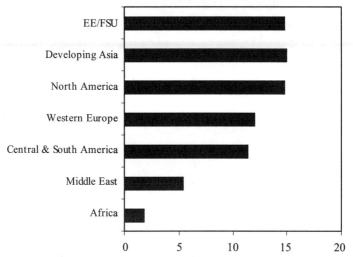

Source: **1999**: Energy Information Administration (EIA), International Energy Annual 1999, DOE/EIA-0219 (99) (Washington, DC: January 2001); **2020**: EIA, World Energy Projection System (2001).

In India, developing Asia's other giant, strong growth in gas consumption is projected to 2020. Many LNG import schemes are proposed for the country, and there are frequent announcements about them, but few are under construction or making concrete progress.

While both India and China are on the brink of becoming key LNG importers in Asia, Malaysia is proceeding in a unique manner with plans to build the country's third LNG plant (known as MLNG III or MLNG Tiga). In Malaysia and other parts of Southeast Asia, including Thailand, Indonesia and Singapore, plans continue to expand cross-border natural

[70]

gas pipelines. However, the timing of a proposed pipeline to deliver gas from a Malay–Thai joint development area (JDA) to both countries now seems to be in question.

For the countries of industrialized Asia, natural gas consumption is expected to rise from 3.6 trillion cubic feet in 1999 to 5.4 trillion cubic feet in 2020.[8] Australia – which has large, expanding gas reserves and further resource potential – continued to pursue supply projects during 2000, including a proposal for a gas-to-liquids project. Japan, with recent power sector deregulation, has not moved to fully renew LNG contracts that will be expiring in a few years. Japan remains the most critical LNG consumer throughout the world. As in Europe and the United States, in Japan deregulation is changing both the gas and power industries as gas companies move into the power sector and power companies pursue gas ventures.

In terms of natural gas trade, much of the trade in the Asia-Pacific region – unlike that of North America and Europe – has been, and will continue to be, in the form of LNG, since few international gas pipelines exist in this region. The nature of the LNG trade – which requires highly capital intensive supply trains, specialized marine transport carriers, and fixed receiving and degasification terminals – binds buyer and seller in a closer relationship than the pipeline gas trade does. Within Asia, many oil and gas importers were adversely affected by high oil prices in 2000, yet international trade in gas continued to grow. While LNG prices in the region are generally linked to crude oil prices, LNG trade is also dominated by long-term contracts, and high oil prices did not slow the LNG movements that currently dominate gas trade in the region.

Significant gas trade developments during the past year involved pipeline projects in Southeast Asia, prospects for LNG import terminals in China and India, and plans for additional LNG export facilities in Malaysia, Australia, and Indonesia. Liquefied natural gas transportation primarily to East Asia is expected to account for a growing share of the increase in international trade to 2020.

Worldwide natural gas reserves doubled during the past two decades and the same growth trend is expected to continue to 2020, with significant increases in reserves in developing Asia and the Former Soviet Union. As for supplies in Asia, countries with significant development of gas resources for domestic use include Australia, China, Malaysia, Pakistan, the Philippines, and Thailand. At the beginning of January 2000, the Chinese government formally approved its first plan to import LNG into Guangdong in the south. With a targeted startup date of 2005, the LNG project will involve China National Offshore Oil Corporation (CNOOC).

Toward increasing domestic gas supply, Shell, BP Amoco, and Enron all have agreements to develop gas resources and infrastructure in China.[9] Expansion and integration of pipeline infrastructure will be important to increasing gas use in China (See Figure 2.3). China also announced during 2000 the discovery of what it is calling the country's biggest natural gas field. Located in the northern part of the Tarim Basin in Xinjiang Province, the find is estimated by China to hold more than 7 trillion cubic feet of gas. Currently, Malaysia and Indonesia have the largest gas reserves in Asia, accounting for nearly half of the region's total.

Figure 2.3
Present and Planned Natural Gas Pipelines of China

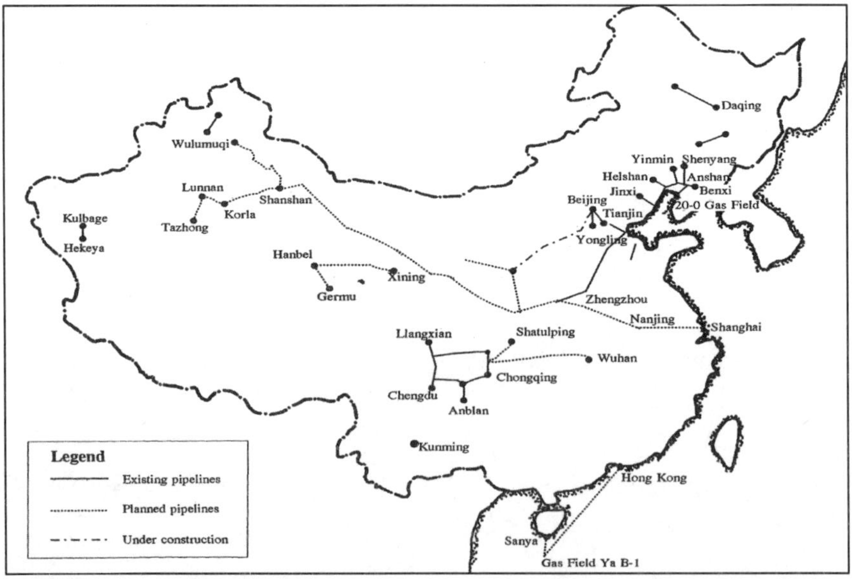

Sources: China OGP, China Petroleum Investment Guide, AP Energy Business Publications, Singapore, 1995; and author's files.

[72]

3-Coal

Coal consumption is heavily concentrated in the electricity generation sector, and significant amounts are also used for steel production. World coal consumption grew by 1.2 percent in 2000, the first increase since 1996. In the near future, coal use is expected to decline in Western Europe, Eastern Europe, and the former Soviet Union (FSU), but increases are expected in the United States, Japan, and developing Asia. An expected decline in coal's share of energy use would be even greater were it not for large increases in energy use projected for developing Asia, where coal continues to dominate many fuel markets, especially in China and India. As huge countries in terms of both population and landmass, China and India are projected to account for 29 percent of the world's total increase in energy consumption over the forecast period. The expected increases in coal use in China and India from 1999 to 2020 account for 92 percent of the total expected increase in coal use worldwide (on a BTU basis). Still, coal's share of energy use in developing Asia is projected to decline.

As a region, Asia accounted for 43.4 percent of the world's coal consumption in 2000. China, the world's largest consumer of coal, accounted for 22 percent of the global consumption that year. Currently, coal is the most important source of primary energy in China, providing about 75 percent of the country's total needs. The electricity sector accounted for roughly 30 percent of China's coal consumption in 1999 on a BTU basis. By 2020, coal use for electricity generation in China is expected to rise to 17.0 quadrillion BTU from 5.9 quadrillion BTU in 1999. With strong electricity demand-growth prospects, large increases in coal consumption are projected for China as well as for India (Figure 2.4), which also has sizable coal reserves and a favorable outlook for strong economic growth and increased demand for coal use in the industrial and power generating sectors.

Figure 2.4
World Coal Consumption by Region (1980, 1990 and 2020)

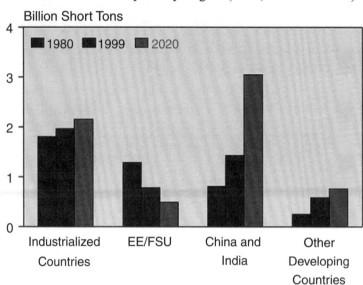

Sources: **1980 and 1999**: Energy Information Administration (EIA), Office of Energy Markets and End Use, International Statistics Database and *International Energy Annual 1999*, DOE/EIA-0219 (99) (Washington, DC, January 2001); **2020**: EIA, *World Energy Projection System* (2001).

Energy consumption in India is in fact dominated by coal, and more than two-thirds of the coal consumed is used in the power sector, where most growth in coal demand is projected to occur. The rest of developing Asia is a huge and diverse area, accounting for more than 15 percent of the world's current population and 11 percent of the increase in primary energy use projected in the *IEO 2001* reference case.

South Korea is a significant coal user in both the power and steel industries, although electricity generation there is also based on nuclear power and natural gas. Taiwan is the next largest coal user among other Developing Asia countries. Its electricity industry is similar to Korea's in that coal plays an important role together with nuclear power and imported natural gas. Indonesia is the third largest coal producer in Asia (after China and India), but with its smaller economy and power needs, it consumes less than half as much coal as Taiwan.

[74]

Among the Asian industrialized countries—Australia, New Zealand, and Japan—Australia is the world's largest coal exporter and Japan is a major importer. Japan, which is the third largest coal user in Asia and the fifth largest globally, imports basically all the coal it consumes, much of it from Australia. Japan continues to be the world's leading importer of coal and is projected to account for 24 percent of total world imports in 2020,[10] slightly less than its 1999 share of 27 percent.[11] As the leading importer of coal, Japan has been influential in the international coal market. Despite setbacks that resulted from the region's financial crisis in 1998, Asia's demand for imported coal remains poised for additional increases over the forecast period, based on strong growth in electricity demand in the region. Overall, there appears to be a shift occurring in the region away from contract purchases to the spot market.[12]

4- Electricity

According to the Energy Information Administration, in a reference case scenario worldwide electricity consumption is expected to grow at an average annual rate of 2.7 percent from 1999 to 2020 (Table 2.3). Coal will maintain its position as the world's primary single source of electricity generation. The most rapid growth in electricity use is projected for developing Asia—at 4.5 percent per year—and by 2020 developing Asia is expected to consume more than twice the electricity it did in 1999. In that year developing Asia accounted for 18 percent of worldwide electricity consumption. By 2020, it is expected to account for 26 percent.

Throughout Asia, the introduction of competition into electricity markets has been the means used by policymakers to increase economic efficiency in response to technology advances, globalization of industry, and marked growth of electric demand. Competition and restructuring have not slowed demand in China however, where electricity consumption is projected to triple, growing by an average of 5.5 percent per year from 1999 to 2020. The projections for electricity consumption in the developing world depend primarily on assumptions with regard to growth in population and per capita income. In countries where population is expected to remain stable, such as China, per capita income growth is the more important component of electricity demand growth. In nearby Japan, a decade-long economic slump continues to restrain that nation's electricity consumption growth.

Table 2.3

World Net Electricity Consumption by Region, 1990-2020

(Billion Kilowatt hours)

Region	History		Projections				
	1990	1999	2005	2010	2015	2020	Average Annual Percent Change (1999-2020)
Industrialized Countries	6,385	7,517	8,580	9,352	10,112	10,888	1.8
United States	2,817	3,236	3,761	4,147	4,484	4,804	1.9
EE/FSU	1,906	1,452	1,622	1,760	1,972	2,138	1.9
Developing Countries	2,258	3,863	4,988	6,191	7,615	9,203	4.2
Developing Asia	1,259	2,319	3,088	3,883	4,815	5,856	4.5
China	551	1,084	1,533	2,035	2,635	3,331	5.5
India	257	424	545	656	798	949	3.9
South Korea	93	233	294	333	386	437	3.0
Other Developing Asia Countries	357	578	716	858	996	1,139	3.3
Central and South America	449	684	844	1,035	1,268	1,552	4.0
Total World	**10, 549**	**12,883**	**15,190**	**17,303**	**19,699**	**22,230**	**2.7**

Note: EE/FSU = Eastern Europe and the former Soviet Union.

Sources: **1990, 1999**: Energy Information Administration (EIA), *International Energy Annual 1999*, DOE/EIA-0219 (99) (Washington, DC, January 2001); Projections: EIA, World Energy Projection System (2001).

Coal, which supplied 54 percent of the fuel used to generate electricity in developing Asia in 1999, is expected to maintain that level by and large, declining only slightly to 52 percent in 2020. In the rapidly growing Asian energy market, coal consumption in absolute terms is expected to more than double over the same period. Nuclear, renewables and oil are expected to lose market share. Natural gas is the only fuel that is expected to increase its share of the Asian electricity market, from 9 percent in 1999 to 11 percent in 2020.

[76]

Over the twenty-year outlook period, hundreds of billions of dollars will be needed to create new generating capacity in Asia, not including the costs of expanding the transmission and distribution network. Private investment in developing Asian power projects has however slowed considerably, after several years of rapid growth. Most of the investment now occurring is directed toward adding to the region's generation capacity. Among the developing nations, the decision to sell off complete electric utilities wholesale to private (including foreign) investors has largely been a South American phenomenon. Developing Asian nations have been much slower than the nations of South America to privatize national electricity assets. Privatization efforts in developing Asia have consisted largely of allowing private participation in new generation (green-field) investments.

Overall, China is expected to add more to its electricity generation capacity between 1999 and 2020 than any other nation in the world—for example, more than twice the capacity additions projected for the United States. The People's Republic of China is presently the world's third largest power producer, though several regions of the country suffer periodic capacity shortages, including Xinjiang province in the northwest. Coal currently accounts for 65 percent of China's electricity fuels market, and its share is expected to decline slightly through 2020. After coal, renewables account for the second largest share of China's electricity market, with a 26-percent overall share in 1999. China's consumption of renewable energy (mostly hydroelectricity) is expected to double between 1999 and 2010 and to increase its share of China's total electricity market. By the time it becomes fully operational in 2009 as planned, the US$30 billion Three Gorges Dam will have an installed capacity of 18,200 megawatts of power. Once completed, Three Gorges will be the largest dam in the world, five times wider than the Hoover Dam in the United States.[13] In the spring of 2002 plans were revealed to reorganize the Three Gorges project into the China Three Gorges Electric Power Corporation, which would seek capital through an offer to foreign investors, much like companies in China's petroleum industry.

During the late 1980s, China implemented electricity reforms aimed at reducing government's managerial role in electricity supply.[14] Price reforms were also introduced to boost the attractiveness of investments in China's electricity sector. Chinese government officials also have announced plans to promote an interconnection of the country's six regional grids between 2015 and 2020, in part to develop better capacity management and facilitate trade in surplus power where available. Other countries including Indonesia, South Korea, the Philippines, and Thailand have also announced similar plans to develop national electricity pools.

Just behind China among developing countries in terms of population and economic activity, India is expected to increase its consumption of electricity at a 3.9 percent annual rate over the forecast period. Heavy reliance on coal as an electricity fuel is expected to lessen somewhat, with coal's share of the market declining from 76 percent in 1999 to 65 percent in 2020. Natural gas and nuclear power will largely make up for coal's lost share.

5- Hydroelectricity and Other Renewables

With relatively high worldwide energy prices in 2000 and energy shortages in the US states of California and New York, Brazil, Armenia and other parts of the world, there is renewed interest in hydroelectricity and other renewables (including geothermal, solar, wind, biomass, and waste). Whether this will be a temporary or sustained interest will depend on the long-term outlook of energy prices, which are forecasted by most analysts to remain relatively low until 2020, which would constrain the expansion of renewables. Notwithstanding this, renewable energy use worldwide is expected to increase by 53 percent between 1999 and 2020, though the current 9 percent share of renewables in total energy consumption is projected to decline slightly, to 8 percent in 2020. Total renewable energy use is projected to rise from 33 quadrillion BTU in 1999 to 50 quadrillion BTU in 2020 (Table 2.4).

Table 2.4

World Consumption of Hydroelectricity and Other Renewables by Region[a]

Region/Country	History			Projections				Average Annual Percent Change, 1999-2020
	1990	1998	1999	2005	2010	2015	2020	
Industrialized Countries	9.3	10.8	11.1	12.5	13.6	14.1	14.5	1.3
United States[b]	5.8	7.0	7.0	7.7	8.1	8.4	8.5	1.0
Canada	3.1	3.5	3.6	4.3	4.9	5.0	5.2	1.8
Mexico	0.3	0.4	0.4	0.5	0.6	0.7	0.7	2.2
Western Europe	4.5	5.4	5.6	6.5	7.1	7.6	8.2	1.8
Industrialized Asia	1.6	1.7	1.7	1.8	1.9	2.1	2.3	1.4
Japan	1.1	1.2	1.2	1.2	1.3	1.5	1.6	1.5
Australasia	0.4	0.5	0.5	0.6	0.6	0.6	0.7	1.4
Total Industrialized	**15.4**	**18.0**	**18.3**	**20.8**	**22.6**	**23.7**	**24.9**	**1.5**
EE/FSU	2.8	3.0	3.0	3.2	3.5	4.0	4.5	2.1
Developing Countries								
Developing Asia	3.2	4.3	4.6	6.2	7.4	9.0	10.5	4.0
China	1.3	2.1	2.3	3.5	4.4	5.5	6.6	5.1
India	0.7	0.8	0.9	1.1	1.2	1.5	1.7	3.3
South Korea	0.0	0.0	0.0	0.1	0.1	0.2	0.2	7.9
Other Asia	1.1	1.3	1.4	1.6	1.7	1.9	2.0	1.8
Middle East	0.4	0.6	0.5	0.8	0.9	1.1	1.2	4.1
Turkey	0.2	0.4	0.4	0.4	0.4	0.5	0.5	2.0
Other Middle East	0.1	0.2	0.2	0.4	0.5	0.6	0.7	6.9
Africa	0.6	0.7	0.7	0.8	0.9	1.1	1.2	2.7
Central & South America	3.9	5.6	5.7	6.2	6.6	7.0	7.6	1.4
Total World	**26.3**	**32.0**	**32.7**	**38.1**	**41.9**	**45.9**	**50.0**	**2.0**

(a) Reference case; (b) Includes the 50 US states and the District of Columbia.

Notes: EE/FSU = Eastern Europe/Former Soviet Union. Totals may not equal sum of components due to independent rounding. US totals include net electricity imports, methanol, and liquid hydrogen.

Sources: **1990, 1998, 1999**: Energy Information Administration (EIA), *International Energy Annual 1999*, DOE/EIA-0219 (99) (Washington, DC, January 2001); **Projections**: EIA, *Annual Energy Outlook 2001*, DOE/EIA-0383(2001) (Washington, DC, December 2000), and World Energy Projection System (2001).

Since the Asia-Pacific region is projected to have the greatest need for new generating capacity over the 2000-2020 period and shows the greatest potential for economic growth, it is an attractive market for hydroelectricity, renewables, and energy efficiency. Indeed a substantial proportion of the growth in renewable energy use in the *IEO 2001* reference case is attributable to large-scale hydroelectric projects in the developing world, particularly in developing Asia, where China and India, as well as other developing Asian nations such as Nepal and Malaysia, are already building or planning to build hydroelectric projects that exceed 1,000 megawatts. Hydroelectricity and other renewable energy consumption is expected to grow by 4.0 percent per year in developing Asia over the projection period, with particularly strong growth projected for China (See Figures 2.5 and 2.6).

Figure 2.5
Renewable Energy Consumption in Developing Asia
(1999, 2010 and 2020)

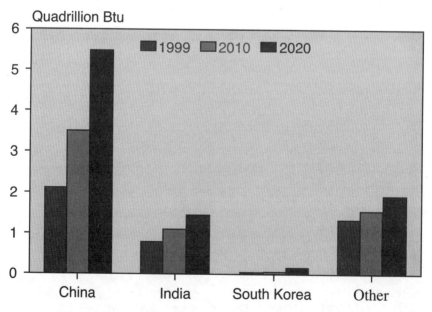

Sources: **1999**: Energy Information Administration (EIA), *International Energy Annual 1999*, DOE/EIA-0219 (99) (Washington, DC, January 2001); **2010 and 2020**: EIA, World Energy Projection System (2001).

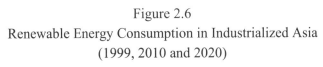

Figure 2.6
Renewable Energy Consumption in Industrialized Asia
(1999, 2010 and 2020)

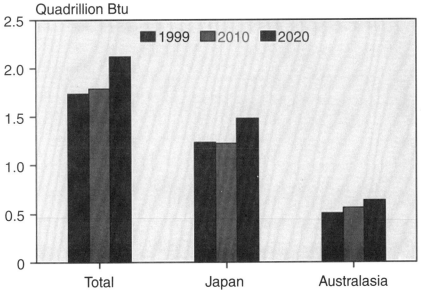

Sources: **1999**: Energy Information Administration (EIA), *International Energy Annual 1999*, DOE/EIA-0219 (99) (Washington, DC, January 2001); **2010 and 2020**: EIA, World Energy Projection System (2001).

For China alone, 5.1 percent annual growth in renewable energy use is projected between 1999 and 2020. The Chinese government would like to expand the amount of so-called "new" renewable energy sources and has set a target that 2 percent of the country's energy demand will be met by non-hydroelectric renewables by 2015.[15] To help China meet its goal, the World Bank's Global Environmental Fund (GEF) approved a US$12 million grant to install 98 megawatts of wind power in Dabancheng, Fujin and Xiwaizi.

Developing Asia is one of the only regions in the world that has plans to continue the development of large-scale hydroelectric projects over the *IEO 2001* projection period. In China, construction of the 18,200-megawatt Three Gorges Dam project continued despite charges of corruption that surfaced in 2000, including a charge of embezzlement of

US$1.4 million by an official who was subsequently found guilty and sentenced to death.[16] In India, the Supreme Court ruled that construction of the 1,450-megawatt Sadar Sarovar hydroelectric project could continue after being stalled by lawsuits for more than six years. In Malaysia, the government announced that it was considering increasing the capacity of its Bakun hydroelectric project from 500 megawatts to 2,500 megawatts, the scale of the original plans for Bakun. Laos signed a Memorandum of Understanding with Thailand for a 25-year power purchase agreement to take electricity from the proposed 920-megawatt Nam Theun 2 project.[17] Vietnam too is planning several hydroelectric projects to help meet growing electricity demand.[18]

In the Philippines, the government is trying to encourage the development of hydroelectricity and geothermal electricity resources, as well as renewable generation using solar, photovoltaic, hybrids, wind, and biomass.[19] Geothermal power is projected to contribute 558 MW to the present capacity mix during the 1999-2008 planning period.[20] Between 2005 and 2008, five new geothermal areas with a total potential capacity of 450 MW programmed are set for development in the Philippines.

The industrialized countries of Asia—Australia, Japan and New Zealand—have significantly different electricity energy mixes and thus different scenarios for renewable energy use. Japan, one of only three countries with a nuclear generation program, supplies one-third of its electricity from nuclear power plants. Hydroelectricity and other renewable energy sources supply only 12 percent of the country's electricity. The *IEO 2001* reference case projects that hydroelectricity and other renewable sources in Japan will grow by 1.5 percent per year between 1999 and 2020. Similarly, in Australia, renewables account for about 10 percent of the nation's electricity supply, and thermal generation (predominantly coal) accounts for nearly 90 percent. In contrast, renewable energy sources provide 73 percent of New Zealand's electricity supply.

Former Soviet Central Asia—An Energy Overview

Energy is the most abundant and valuable natural resource of Central Asia and northwest China and includes oil, gas, coal, and electricity (Table

[82]

2.5).[21] Kazakhstan has large reserves of oil and coal. Turkmenistan and Uzbekistan have significant reserves of gas. Kyrgyzstan produces significant amounts of hydroelectric power. Xinjiang, China has significant coal resources and an uncertain, although generally promising, potential for oil in the Tarim basin. These energy reserves form the basis for future economic growth and development, and energy exports promise to generate significant foreign exchange revenues. Central Asia is poised to become a major world supplier of energy, especially in the oil and gas sectors.

Table 2.5

Central Asia[i]: Existing Energy Production by Country

Commodity	Kazakhstan	Kyrgyzstan[ii]	Tajkistan[iii]	Turkmenistan	Uzbekistan	Xinjiang, China
Oil	High	--	--	Low	Low	Medium
Gas	Low	--	--	High	High	Low
Coal	High	--	--	--	Low	Medium[iv]
Electricity[v]	High	Low	Low	Low	Medium	Low
Solar	--	--	--	--	--	--
Wind	--	Low	--	--	--	Low
Hydro (water)	Low	High	High	--	Low	Low

Notes: Comparisons are relative to each other only.

--   Insignificant or non-existent.

i   For purposes of this paper, Central Asia refers to Kazakhstan, Kyrgyzstan, Tajikistan, Turkmenistan, Uzbekistan, and Xinjiang China.

ii   Kyrgyzstan's output of oil in 1998 amounted to an estimated 2,000 bbl/d. Consumption of gas was estimated at 68 bcf (all imported).

iii   In Tajikistan, oil produced in 1999 totaled 3,500 bbl/d, while consumption of gas amounted to 40 bcf.

iv   Output reached 20 million tons in 1996.

v   Total installed capacity on the Central Asian (excludes Xinjiang) interconnected electricity power grid in 1996 was 24,770 MW, including 11,280 MW Uzbekistan, 4,350 MW Tajikistan, 3,570 MW Kyrgyzstan, 3,040 MW southern Kazakhstan, and 2,530 MW Turkmenistan.

Sources: (1) James P. Dorian, *Oil and Gas in Central Asia and Northwest China*, The CWC Group, London, 2001, 176; and (2) James P. Dorian, Tojiev Utkur Abbasovich, Mikhail S. Tonkopy, Obozov Alaibek Jumabekovich, and Qiu Daxiong, "Energy in Central Asia and Northwest China: Major Trends and Opportunities for Regional Cooperation," *Energy Policy*, Vol. 27, No. 5, May 1999, Elsevier Science Ltd., 281-297.

Although Central Asia enjoys vast energy development potential, there are many obstacles to exploiting these resources, as in many parts of Asia. The most obvious is the limited infrastructure for transporting energy –

including oil and gas pipelines and electric transmission lines – in the region. Other obstacles include poor communications infrastructure, unstable government structures, political conflict, payment difficulties, and inadequate energy policies. Since Kazakhstan, Kyrgyzstan, Tajikistan, Turkmenistan, Uzbekistan and Xinjiang, China emphasize energy self-sufficiency at the expense of developing new trading linkages, the respective governments must first understand the benefits of regional cooperation before they are likely to commit to area-wide trade and other forms of cooperation.

Figure 2.7
Major Oil Fields of Central Asia

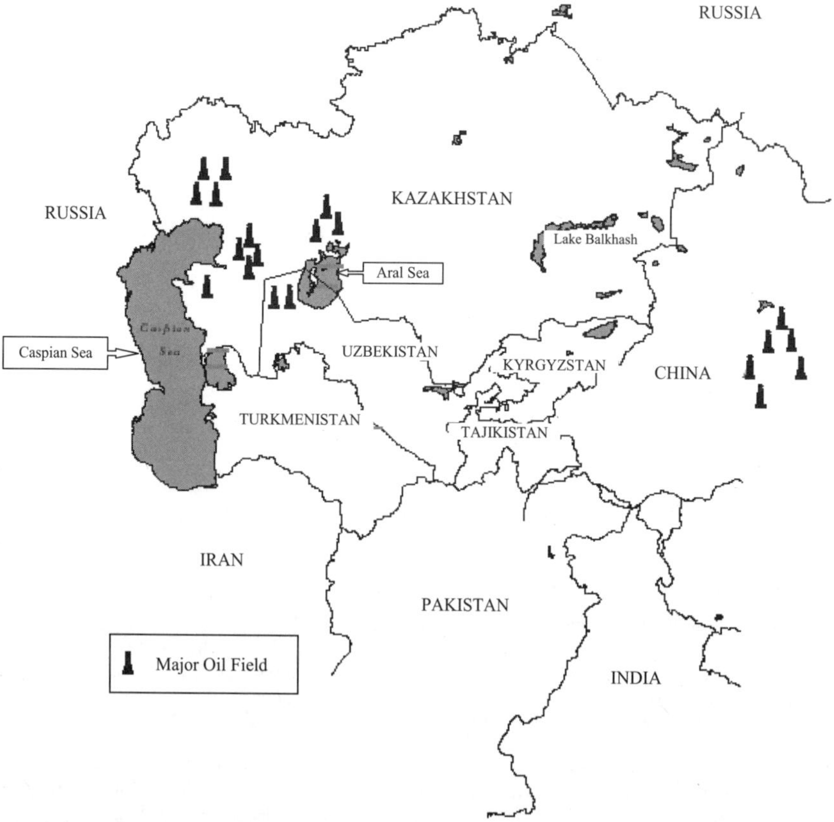

Source: James P. Dorian, *Oil and Gas in Central Asia and Northwest China*, The CWC Group (London, 2001): 176.

Several factors suggest that increased regional cooperation in oil, gas, coal, electricity and renewable energy in Central Asia is both possible and necessary:

First, economic growth in the region will generate increased energy demand — energy shortages are already occurring in Xinjiang, China, for example, where strong economic growth is outpacing energy supplies.

Second, an uneven geographic distribution of energy resources (See Figure 2.7) among the countries leaves each in need of energy forms that can be more efficiently supplied by other countries in the region. Kyrgyzstan has few proven gas and oil reserves and depends heavily on imports from Kazakhstan and Uzbekistan. Despite being well endowed with oil and gas resources, Kazakhstan depends on Kyrgyzstan and Uzbekistan for 60 percent of its electricity, and Kazakhstan purchases gas from Uzbekistan. Uzbekistan depends on electricity supplied by Kyrgyz hydroelectric power stations to meet seasonal electric needs. Xinjiang, China is actively seeking to import electricity and oil to meet chronic shortages.

Third, periodic energy shortages occur in the five former Soviet republics as a result of inadequate infrastructure, poor maintenance of facilities and management problems resulting from the breakdown of the former region-wide energy network of the Soviet period. Sustaining economic growth and development requires that these shortages be met by importing energy from neighboring countries.

Fourth, the large distances between energy-producing locations and the markets for that energy means that developing local markets within the region can lower transportation costs and increase the returns from energy development. These interdependencies highlight the potential, and perhaps even the imperative, for regional economic cooperation in the energy sector.

Oil and Natural Gas

Kazakhstan is the main producer of oil in the region, with proven reserves of 8 million barrels, or 1.1 billion metric tons. Its surplus has reached 500,000 barrels a day—an increase of almost 50 percent over 1995.

Kazakhstan's hydrocarbon reserves are contained in 153 occurrences, including 80 petroleum, 24 gas-petroleum, 21 petroleum-gas condensate, five gas condensate and 19 gas fields. The main hydrocarbon reserve base is concentrated in western Kazakhstan's Guryev, Mangistau, Uralsk and Aktubinsk regions. The hydrocarbon resources of these regions are almost equivalent to those of Western Siberia within Russia in terms of explored and extrapolated petroleum and gas reserves. Substantial oil reserves are also suspected in Kazakhstan's offshore Kashagan field, an 80km x 25km field reportedly capable of producing 2 mbpd in 15 years. This would make Kashagan the fifth-largest oil field in the world and the only one among the top five outside the Gulf.

The Tengiz deposit, discovered in 1981, is located in the northwestern Pre-Caspian area (Guryev District). Tengiz is a unique petroleum and gas deposit, unrivaled in the size of its reserves by any other known deposit in the world. Even though the deposit has been explored to a depth of only 5,500 meters, its potential reserves, estimated at 29-34 billion barrels of petroleum, suggest cost-efficient exploitation.[22] Extractable oil reserves are estimated at 11 billion barrels. However, some experts claim this figure should be raised to two billion tons, which implies that these reserves are valued at US$270-330 billion in current world prices. Kazakhstan presently produces 440,000 bpd of crude annually.

Kazakhstan operates three oil refineries – Pavlodar, Shymkent (formerly Chymkent), and Atyrau – with one each being located in the northern, southern, and western regions of Kazakhstan, respectively. The refineries have a combined total crude oil refining capacity of 427,093 bpd (20 million tons per year), and capacity utilization of 95 percent.[23] They are fed mostly by indigenous crudes or oil piped from Russia. More specifically, the Pavlodar refinery is supplied with crude oil from West Siberia by means of the Omsk-Pavlodar pipeline and the Shymkent refinery presently uses oil from Kazakh fields at Kumkol, Aktyubinsk and Makatinsk, but utilization is low because it is unable to process other oils. The Atyrau refinery is fully supplied with local Kazakh crude oil from the northwest.

Kazakhstan's natural gas reserves are estimated at 1.84 trillion cubic meters. Eighty-three deposits contain natural gas, though only 17 of those are exclusive gas reserves and the remaining are oil and associated gas reserves. Natural gas is unevenly distributed throughout the country. More than 40 percent of Kazakhstan's gas reserves are located in one field—the huge Karachagank field in the northwest part of the country.

The Kazakhstan gas processing industry consists of three plants – Kazak, Tengiz, Zhanazhol – with average capacity of 3.5 billion cubic meters per annum. The refinery capacity of these plants is not sufficient to process the increasing volumes of gas output expected because of the recent start up of the Karachaganak gas deposit. For this reason, as well as difficulties in processing gas at the nearby Russian Orenburg facility, a new US$600 million gas processing plant is slated to be built at Karachagnak by 2005 to process the condensates.[24] Gas output in Kazakhstan has been hampered because of insufficient infrastructure prompting proposals for the construction of an internal pipeline network costing more than US$1 billion. Gas products from the planned Karachagnak plant would be exported using the Caspian Pipeline Consortium (CPC) pipeline. Current gas output in Kazakhstan is around 9.2 billion cubic meters per year. The international consortium developing the Karachagnak gas field plans to invest an additional US$2.3 billion for a second phase of development to be finished this year, 2001. The consortium plans to invest more than US$4 billion in the Karachagnak field between 2002 and 2006 and US$11 billion in the period of 2007-2036.

Kazakhstan's primary oil pipelines, with a total length of 3, 384 km, were constructed at the end of 1960s and have now deteriorated. Kazakh crude is transported mainly to Russian refineries and exported via the Abut Volga and Black Sea pipelines. Two export pipelines transport the oil to refineries and export pipelines in Russia. Transportation of Kazakh oil also occurs by barge and rail to the Baltic, and by ship and rail to the Black Sea. The majority of Kazakh oil exports – 216,000 bpd – were shipped by pipeline, of which about 85 percent were transported by the Atyrau-Saransk-Samara pipeline through Russia.[25]

Turkmenistan, an important gas and oil producing republic of Central Asia, will play a critical role in future world energy markets, as it ranks eleventh in world reserves of gas, behind Iraq. Some analysts place reserve amounts at much higher levels. Remarkably, growth in gas production exceeded 50 percent in Turkmenistan last year. Yet, like its Central Asian neighboring states, transportation bottlenecks may, if not resolved, limit longer-term hydrocarbon development. The value of Turkmenistan's gas is determined in large measure by access to markets.

For this reason, a number of pipeline projects to carry Turkmenistan's resources are in planning or have been proposed. Three major pipeline projects are under serious consideration to provide an alternative export route outside of Russia for gas. One of the most ambitious of these projects now under consideration is a nearly 8,000 km trans-Asian Turkmenistan-China-Japan pipeline. The proposed pipeline is part of an overall trans-Asian pipeline network envisaged by Japanese industry and government officials for the twenty-first century. Turkmenistan was an integral part of the Soviet energy grid, and before 1991 the country's gas was shipped to all regions of the former Soviet Union and passed through to markets in Western Europe.

Uzbekistan is noted for being one of the few former Soviet republics that has increased oil output since becoming independent in 1991. State company Uzbekneftegaz boosted oil production to 7.6 million tons, or 175,000 bpd in 1996, achieving self-sufficiency that year. Consequently, the country stopped being a net importer that year. Since then, Uzbek output has stabilized at around 7.5 million metric tons, or 175,000 bpd (in 2000).

Uzbekistan has abundant oil and gas resources, with 60 percent of the country's land area showing oil and gas potential. Uzbekistan has modest oil reserves (0.6 billion barrels, or 0.1 billion metric tons) and produces 8 million metric tons of oil and condensates each year. It could increase output relatively easily if a viable external market were identified. In five of the republics's proven oil-and gas-bearing areas alone, potential (unexplored) resources are estimated at more than 5 billion metric tons of oil and condensate, and 5.5 trillion cubic meters of natural gas. By 2000, the Uzbekneftegaz National Oil and Gas Corporation had identified and explored 171 oil and gas fields, 51 of which were already producing oil, 27 producing gas, and 17 producing condensate. [26]

Unlike some of their Central Asian neighbors, Kyrgyzstan and Tajikistan produce only small quantities of oil. Tajikistan in particular has insignificant reserves of petroleum and natural gas and relies heavily on imports from other former Soviet republics, notably Uzbekistan and Turkmenistan. Kyrgyzstan contains seven developed oil fields and two oil/gas fields but due to difficult geological conditions, recovery rates are low. Exploration continues in the favorable Naryn *oblast* area of eastern Kyrgyzstan, situated just across the border from China's Tarim Basin. Current crude oil production levels in Kyrgyzstan are at around 100,000 tons (2,000 bpd); demand is 2.5 million metric tons per year (50,000 bpd).

In October 1996 Kyrgyzstan's first oil refinery, Jalalabad, opened with a capacity of 500,000 tons per year. Jalalabad remains mostly underused, however, with domestic output of crude at only 100,000 metric tons per year. Negotiations are also under way with Uzbekistan to import gas condensate for processing into gasoline at the refinery. Nearly all oil and gas products are imported into Kyrgyzstan from Kazakhstan and Russia.

The Chinese government has identified the autonomous region of Xinjiang, China in northwest China as a strategic base in the petrochemical and fertilizer industry in the country's next five-year plan (2001-2005). Yet the central government might have difficulty in balancing the petrochemical development initiated by different industry parties. Great expectations have been placed on oil beneath Xinjiang, China's major Tarim, Turpan-Hami, and Junggar basins, which could yield billions of tons of crude oil and billions of meters of natural gas. Four regional chemical bases are already established in Xinjiang, China. There are two bases in Urumqi, and one each in Tulufan and Hami. These bases are supported by three oil fields, four refineries, and rich mineral reserves.

Xinjiang contributes about 17 million tons from its three oil fields, a fraction of the national total. However, the annual rail capacity in

Xinjiang for the transportation of crude to the central network is only three million tons. After years of surveying, 42 oil and gas fields have been discovered in the three basins, with total proven reserves of 2.1 billion metric tons of oil. The Tarim Basin in southern Xinjiang covers an area of 560,000 square kilometers, with the oil and gas-rich Taklimakan Desert at the center. The Karamay oilfield in the Junggar Basin – the fourth largest in China – was established 45 years ago. The Xinjiang Petroleum Administration, which is in charge of developing oil and gas in the Junggar Basin, produced nearly 9 million tons of crude in 1999.

A significant breakthrough was made in onshore oil exploration in Xinjiang in 1984. The Tarim basin remains one of the largest and least explored inland basins in the world. The extent of the terrestrial Meso-Cenozoic upper basin is 560,000 square kilometers, and the Paleozoic platform covers an even larger area of about 7,000,000 square kilometers, incorporating the mountainous areas around the basin.[27] The interior of the basin mostly consists of the Taklimakan desert and is about 324,000 square kilometers in area. It is fringed by high mountains of Paleozoic foldbelts: the Tianshan mountains on the north, the Kunlun mountains on the south, the Altun mountains on the southeast, and the Pamir mountains on the west.

The Tarim basin has been the focus of special attention after exploration led to the discovery of a new oil and gas field in 1984. The Shacan well No. 2 from the Lower Paleozoic carbonates at 5,363 to 5,392 meters is on the Yakle structure, Tabei uplift. It was drilled in September 1984. This discovery, together with the discoveries of the Jurassic Ichklik (1958) and the Tertiary Kekey (1977) oil and gas fields, marked a breakthrough after decades of exploration, renewing interest in the basin.[28] Exploration in the past had suggested that both the basin's Meso-Cenozoic terrestrial fill and its Paleozoic platform cover contain substantial amounts of oil and gas.

Reserves in the Tarim Basin at 30 billion metric tons are more modest than previously thought. Geologists 10 or 15 years ago expected the reserves to be much larger.[29] This is one reason that China is looking to Kazakhstan as well as parts of the Middle East for additional oil supplies

[90]

to help sustain the country's tremendous economic growth rate. Annual output of crude in Xinjiang is expected to reach 24 million metric tons by 2005. Oil consumption is 15 million metric tons per year currently and is expected to rise to about 23 million metric tons by 2005. Although output predictions exceed these figures, national policies require Xinjiang, China to ship 50 percent of its crude oil production to other provinces in China, resulting in a deficit in Xinjiang itself. Therefore cooperation with other parts of Central Asia would be an important way for China to alleviate any future energy shortages.

To assess further the oil and gas reserves in the Tarim Basin, the China National Oil Development Corporation (CNODC) signed a geological survey agreement in 1997 with the Japan National Oil Corporation (JNOC). The two sides also signed an exploration contract with four other Japanese companies. The agreement and the contract focus on Tarim Basin's Misaray Block, a 7,397 square-kilometer block located on the north of Hetian Prefecture. Under the agreement, JNOC is completely funding geological exploration and drilling activities. If any commercial fields are found, Chinese and Japanese partners will co-develop the resources and share the revenues.

Coal

The two major coal producers in Central Asia are Kazakhstan and Xinjiang, China. Kazakhstan is estimated to contain 120 billion metric tons of coal in Karaganda and other areas, but the quality is generally poor,[30] and the deposits are distant from major industrial locations. Limited rail capacity for transporting coal is a structural bottleneck to expanding the exploitation and use of this resource. Xinjiang, China possesses large amounts of high-quality coal resources, with reserves of approximately 3.03 billion metric tons. [31] Kyrgyzstan is reported to have substantial coal reserves, but these are located in an inaccessible part of the country, with no railroad to transport the coal to market.

Kazakhstan has 37 primary coal deposits. Since coal is inexpensive, government officials are considering the possibility of constructing a plant for converting coal into synthetic oil to alleviate energy shortages in southeast Kazakhstan. Coal for this purpose is likely to come from the eastern half of the country. Oil prices are now at around US$80 per metric ton in eastern Kazakhstan, whereas coal prices average around US$7 per metric ton. According to preliminary engineering studies conducted by the Kazakhstan government, converting coal to synthetic oil would cost around US$65 per metric ton. The Kazakhstan government and US-based Varston and Marston company have reportedly discussed the possibility of constructing a new refinery to extract liquid fuel from coal at a cost of US$100 million.

Coal, including high-grade coal, is abundant in Xinjiang, China. Total coal reserves in Xinjiang, China are estimated at approximately 3.03 billion metric tons, or about 2 percent of the country's reserves. These are concentrated in the north Tian Shan mountains area. Output reached 20 million metric tons in 1996, fueling 70 to 80 percent of Xinjiang China's electrical power generation.

Notwithstanding limited coal reserves in Uzbekistan and Kyrgyzstan, and the low quality of Kazakhstan coal, this is an important energy source in Central Asia. Kazakhstan coal is regularly exchanged for Kyrgyz electricity. The coal industry is a major employer in Kazakhstan, and coal may play a more critical role in the longer-term energy industries of Kazakhstan and Xinjiang, China. Moreover, a dwindling supply of higher price coal from Russia has prompted increased reliance on local coal for power generation.

Transportation is the key problem for coal trade in the region, given that great distances separate markets from reserves. Coal is a high-volume, low-value commodity, ideally suited to rail transportation. At present, Kazakhstan transports coal by railroad to its own internal markets, and exports coal by rail to Russia, Ukraine, Kyrgyzstan and Uzbekistan. However, the infrastructure is limited and in poor condition. Negotiations are underway to sell coal to Turkey and Iran, but inadequate infrastructure is a stumbling block. In Xinjiang, China, transportation capacity also constrains the use of coal, with output largely dependent on very local demand. The completion of a rail line from Korla, in central Xinjiang, China, to Kashgar, in the south, will provide the capacity to ship coal from the northern coal fields to the newly industrializing southern part of the province. Kazakhstan faces capacity constraints in shipping coal by rail, and railroads do not currently penetrate to the coal-producing regions of Kyrgyzstan.

Pollution is the second key problem in the coal industry. Because the region's deposits have a high sulfur content, burning coal contributes to significant air pollution in urban areas. The introduction of modern technologies to reduce particle emission in coal-fired plants could relieve some of the problems but, given the economic and financial constraints facing the countries, these technologies are unlikely to be introduced in the near future.

Finally, accessibility is the major constraint to developing Kyrgyzstan's coal resources. These deposits are located in the mountainous central part of the country, which is unserved by railroads. Developing the deposits to reduce dependency on Kazakhstan coal has become a high priority, however, and building a railroad to the area is the major infrastructure development priority of the Kyrgyz government.

Electricity

Electric power is essential for economic development. The different countries of the region generate power by various means, depending on their own natural resource base. Kyrgyzstan, which has large hydro-electric potential, generates most of its electricity through hydroelectric power stations. Thermal power stations fueled by natural gas generate most of Uzbekistan's electricity, although hydro-powered electric plants do exist. The country also draws significantly on hydropower produced from power stations in neighboring Tajikistan and Kyrgyzstan. Kazakhstan and Xinjiang, China depend primarily on coal to generate electricity.

Electricity shortages are a major problem in the region, particularly in Kazakhstan and Xinjiang, China. Kazakhstan depended heavily on Russian coal imports and electricity from Uzbekistan and Kyrgyzstan to supply electric power and heat to its southern region, including the city of Almaty. Following the break-up of the Soviet Union, price increases in coal and transportation, and the financial crisis in Kazakhstan, these imports declined sharply, causing frequent power shortages. Kazakhstan's inability to pay resulted in considerable debt (estimated at US$350 million at the end of 1996) to the three countries and non-payments resulted in reduced shipments from those countries.[32] This electricity shortage in southern Kazakhstan continues, and is particularly troublesome. Although Kazakhstan has abundant oil and coal, it has not been able to overcome its deficit in electricity generation. Between September and November 1996, for example, major sectors of Almaty were without electricity for 8 to 10 hours on a nearly daily basis. Electric power imports, primarily from neighboring Uzbekistan, cost Kazakhstan at least US$150 million in 1996. To alleviate the power shortage the government recently implemented a privatization program aimed at rejuvenating the entire electric power industry.

According to the State Power Corporation of China, electric power shortages are serious in Xinjiang, China and neighboring provinces. This is partially because rapid industrial expansion in the province means that electricity demand is growing faster than supply. However, structural problems also contribute to the shortages. The northwest power network suffers from a serious lack of water, brought on by a severe drought in 1995, and coal shortages that resulted from price disputes and transport congestion. The lack of coal and water forced thermal power plants in the northwest to suspend operations in 1995 and again in 1996, slashing output by 2 GW.

A regional electricity grid serving Uzbekistan, Kyrgyzstan, Tajikistan, Turkmenistan and five districts in the southern territory of Kazakhstan,[33] was established in 1960. It is headquartered in Tashkent. This interconnected grid consists of 220-kv and 500-kv power transmission lines, with a primary 500-kv line connecting the five capital cities, and with an installed capacity of 24,779 MW. It provides power to an area of 2 million square kilometers and to a population of more than 35 million. Interconnecting the region's power system improved reliability and service quality under Soviet administration.

During the first years of independence there were relatively few problems with the region-wide system. Rainfall was abundant and Kyrgyzstan's Toktogul reservoir was full. However, between 1992-1997, rain amounts were less than average. Problems emerged in 1995 as hydroelectricity generation from Kyrgyzstan became less reliable. Shortages plaguing Central Asia's entire electric power system caused serious disagreements among the countries. The electric sector of Central Asia faces four major problems:

- Due to fiscal constraints, there has been little or no expansion of electric generating capacity in recent years. Even with the slowdown in economic activity in the three former Soviet republics, available power supplies are not keeping pace with development needs.
- The lack of funds for needed renovations and modernization has led to a deterioration of power generation stations (especially combined thermal power plants) and transmission lines.
- Problems with payments due to insolvency and disagreements over energy and water prices among the former Soviet republics has led to confrontations and supply cutoffs.
- Variability in rainfall has a significant impact on the stability of electricity in the interconnected grid, and on the availability of electricity for export.

Non-Traditional Energy Resources

Some of the countries in Central Asia have made substantial commitments to support development of non-traditional energy. In Kyrgyzstan, for example, the Kyun government agency is devoted entirely to examining alternative energy supplies, including solar, wind, geothermal and coal-bed methane gas. Kyun is one of four key energy agencies or ministries in Kyrgyzstan, directly under the Cabinet of Ministers and has the same level of authority and prestige as the other energy ministries.

In Kazakhstan, government officials have mapped alternative energy resources across the country to determine the feasibility of developing these resources. Kazakhstan's southern and northern tiers receive an abundance of sunshine annually and possess significant potential for solar energy. Potential wind and biogas resources have been identified in the west. Both southern and northeastern regions of Kazakhstan have the potential for geothermal energy.

Kyrgyzstan, Kazakhstan, and Uzbekistan have formed a joint venture to produce solar batteries and panel components for export to India and China.

In Xinjiang, China, wind and solar resources are abundant. Local government officials hope to augment local power plant capacity by attracting investment and joint-venture partners to develop wind and solar energy. In 1989, government authorities constructed a 2.05 MW wind power plant at Dabancheng near Urumqi.[34] This massive wind farm southeast of the capital city Urumqi is already operational, using Dutch and German-made equipment. It has been upgraded to an installed generating capacity of 17 MW, an insignificant fraction of the total Urumqi power grid. The plant, now being expanded with German financial assistance to generate an additional 10.7 MW, is expected to be expanded to 100 MW by 2000 and could produce approximately 3 percent of Urumqi's output at that time.

Today, 34 counties in Xinjiang, China are actively engaged in promoting and developing wind power. In China, only Tibet (Xizang) produces more solar-generated electricity than Xinjiang, China. More than two-dozen counties in Xinjiang, China now use solar-generated power for lighting and televisions for rural consumers, as well as for the fiber telecommunications relay stations outside Urumqi.

Despite the promise of non-traditional sources of energy in Central Asia, lack of financing and the high cost of experimental technologies prohibit serious development of this fledgling sector. Installation costs of large-scale wind and solar power facilities can also be prohibitive. Clearly, hydrocarbons and hydroelectric power are the preferred energy sources for baseload capacity. Solar and wind energy have generally been promoted for isolated areas requiring small systems. In the near term, energy conservation and efficiency measures in Xinjiang, China and other parts of Central Asia would probably yield the greatest benefits with the least costs. Restructuring power administrations can also be an effective means of improving productivity. If these two measures are adopted, governments in Central Asia could develop alternative sources of energy more effectively.

Republic of the Philippines: Electric Power Industry Restructuring

In line with the economic policy for liberalization and privatization, the Philippines is geared towards the full restructuring of the energy sector so as to encourage greater private sector participation and promote economic efficiency and consumer welfare. Foremost among the structural reforms is the restructuring of the electric power industry, which is serving as a model for similar restructuring in other parts of Asia. Huge capital requirements for new generation capacity and transmission and distribution system expansion during the planning horizon stress the increasing need for private sector involvement in the field of power generation. A successful private power program has been set in motion by the Government, largely through build-operate-transfer (BOT) agreements between the National Power Corporation (NPC) and independent power producers (IPPs). In spite of this, it is generally recognized that the basic inefficiencies associated with the still monopolistic industry structure and the high degree of political interference in the operations of the state-owned corporations constrain self-sustaining and efficient reforms.

Present Structure

The effective implementation of Executive Order No. 215, which allows the private sector to engage in the generation of power, has dismantled the NPC monopoly of power generation so much that today, independent power producers (IPPs) account for almost 50 percent of the country's total installed capacity.

Transmission, however, remains under the monopoly control of NPC, while distribution and retailing are undertaken by more than 140 privately-owned utilities, local government-owned or operated utilities, and electric cooperatives. NPC is likewise engaged in retail distribution, directly supplying more than 270 large industrial consumers.

The present set-up is heavily vertically integrated and governed by a monopolistic market structure in generation and customer sales (See Figure 2.8). This prevents competitive entry into the industry and offers little incentive for industry participants to operate in an efficient manner. The current market structure has resulted in a number of deficiencies, including the following:

- Retail rates that are the highest in Asia and non-transparent subsidies
- A pricing structure that does not reflect the true cost of electricity for every stage of delivery
- An absence of incentives to maximize allocative and productive efficiencies
- Inadequate accountability for reliability, cost and performance
- Supply reliability that is still a long term risk due to the massive financial requirements and overstrained infrastructure budget
- Continuing government responsibility and market-risk exposure despite the success of private power program.

Figure 2.8
Present Electric Industry Structure of the Philippines

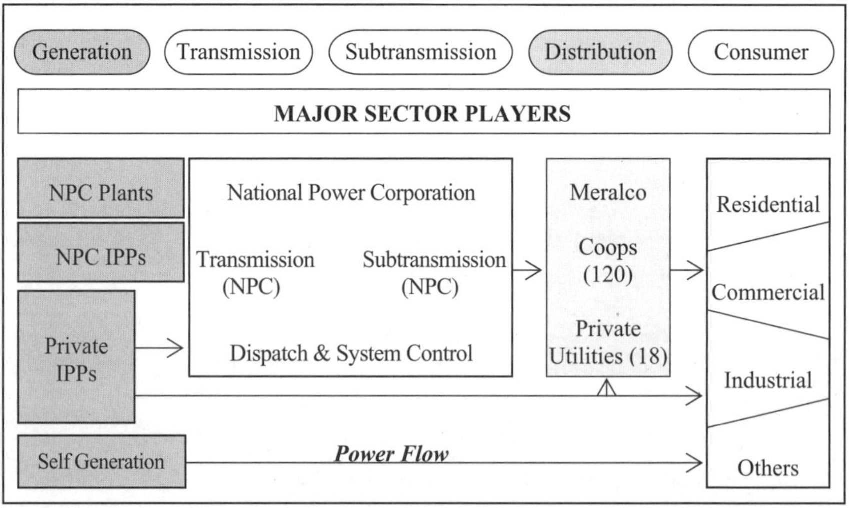

Sources: Ben-Hur Salcedo, James P. Dorian, Maurice H. Kaya, and John Tanlinger, "Restructuring of the Philippines Electric Power Industry and Future Power Development," *ASEAN Energy Bulletin*, vol. 4, no. 4, ASEAN Centre for Energy, Jakarta, Indonesia, December 2000).

Power Sector Restructuring: Objectives and Key Strategies

The restructuring program aims to achieve the following effects:

- ensure the availability and reliability of power supply with private sector investment support in building the energy infrastructure
- create an environment of competition and accountability to achieve greater operational and economic efficiency in the system
- rationalize electricity prices and provide transparent subsidies
- assure the development and operation of socially and environmentally compatible energy infrastructures.

Key strategies will be adopted to realize the desired objectives of the program. Strategies will include the separation or unbundling of generation from transmission, introduction of customers' choice in the distribution sub-sector, promotion of regulatory reforms to facilitate sustainable participation of the private sector in the industry, and adoption of necessary ancillary programs to maximize the socio-economic net benefit of the privatization activities.

The Proposed Industry Structure

The Department of Energy's (DOE) recommended industry structure is designed to meet all necessary conditions under a competitive market while taking into consideration the inherent limitation of the country's electricity industry. The proposed structure is characterized with unbundled functions, decentralized planning and inter-utility operations, and planning coordination. It will, therefore, consist of four separate functions: generation, transmission, distribution and supply.

Options in Meeting the Demand

The projected growth in electricity demand in the Philippines underscores the need to build additional generating capacities and expand the transmission and distribution networks. To meet the demand while ensuring the financial viability of the electricity industry, the government has four options as follows:

[99]

- finance the project itself
- increase power rates to generate the needed funds
- incur more loans
- encourage participation of private capital in the generating segment of the industry.

Considering the benefits that competition would bring to the industry and to the economy in general, the latter option seems to be the ideal approach, as it would provide benefits over the long term. In a truly functioning market, inefficient entities or activities will be forced out as market forces drive prices to their true economic levels of supply and demand.

The Omnibus Electric Power Bill

The DOE recently passed a law that will ultimately create a new structure of the entire electricity industry. The bill defines the organization of the industry, the transition from the present to the desired competitive structure, and the responsibilities of the various government agencies and the private entities during and after the restructuring process. Implementing rules and regulations will come by means of a grid code, distribution code, performance standards, procurement guidelines, licenses and franchises, and contractual arrangement.

The passing of the Omnibus Electric Power Bill in early 2001 after six years of negotiations marked an important turning point for President Gloria Arroyo's administration. Foreign investors as well as multinational lenders such as the Asian Development Bank consider the power bill as a critical step forward for the Philippines. The bill calls for the breakup and sale of the state-run National Power Corporation, which supplies just over half the country's electricity. Parts of the NPC could be sold as soon as the middle of 2002. Some critics do argue however that passage of the bill will simply lead to regional monopolies being created.

Forthcoming Changes

The Philippine energy industry is geared to change dramatically as it begins the new millennium. During this transformation the industry will continue to strive towards greater economic efficiency and competitiveness while also ensuring the protection and preservation of the environment. Changes occurring within the various energy sectors are serving as a framework for neighboring countries also interested in improving efficiencies of operations and bettering the environment. The pending new Omnibus Electric Power Bill, for example, is a model program on the restructuring of an electric industry to encourage necessary private sector participation while promoting consumer welfare. Some of the measures undertaken thus far in the Philippines have included the following:

- preparation of a comprehensive national energy plan covering a decade
- promotion of increased levels of energy efficiencies in operations and use
- deregulation and restructuring of the power and oil industries
- promotion and encouragement of international cooperation and business.

Major Asia-Pacific Energy Structural Trends

After decades of closed or shielded economies in Central Asia, China, Vietnam, and many other Asian nations, local government officials are now encouraging rapid development of their oil, gas, coal, and electricity sectors. This process has several implications for economic cooperation among the countries themselves as well as for countries outside the region. Additionally, liberalization of the Asian economies is prompting several structural changes in the region's energy industry, including reorganization, privatization, globalization, expanded efforts at attracting foreign investment, and efforts to achieve energy self-sufficiency.

Reorganization

To develop and restructure the energy sector in Asia, two key issues are being addressed by energy planners: overcoming periodic energy shortages, and reducing dependencies on unreliable sources of energy. All governments in the region are trying to develop new international markets that provide stable supplies of foreign exchange as they internationalize and develop ties with neighboring countries in the West and with their neighbors. They are therefore reorganizing and restructuring their oil and gas sectors to improve efficiencies, streamline operations, and internationalize. Four terms that are key to the process of restructuring include:

- privatization
- corporatization
- internationalization
- accountability.

Privatization versus Corporatization

Many government agencies and ministries involved in energy exploration, development and utilization are now being privatized (or more accurately, "corporatized") in Asia. Large state enterprises are being disaggregated and their component parts are adopting western managerial and accounting practices.

The term "privatization" as defined in the West does not always apply to the process that is occurring in Asia. Instead, a continuum of public, semi-public and private companies is emerging, with government ministries still heavily involved in ownership and operations of the newly created entities. A key issue to emerge from this process, which is perhaps better called "corporatization" relates to ownership and stability. Investors and lending agencies are uncertain about the responsibilities of the central and local governments. Frequent changes in structure, instability in management, and uncertain finances have increased the inherent risk of working with and investing in the new corporations.

Corporatization is being used in China, for example, in connection with the China National Petroleum Corporation (CNPC), which is adopting a much more corporate style and strategies in its development and exploration activities, and general business activities. This corporatization is bringing CNPC much more in tune with world market conditions. Even on a provincial level, energy agencies in China are increasingly operating on a corporate basis.

Globalization and Accountability

Globalization is another term being used throughout the worldwide energy industry and refers to an internationalization of the energy industries within individual countries, meaning that they are becoming more integrated into the global markets. The 'globalization' effect is occurring in Asia, particularly in those countries that are expanding efforts at attracting foreign investors to their energy sectors.

Accountability is another key issue affiliated with the structural changes taking place in Asia. Accountability means that companies have to look at what in the West would be referred to as "the bottom line." Are profits exceeding cost? Is the company losing money? Is the company making money? Are the decisions that are being made rational decisions? All decisions have to be justified. This is a particularly important factor to international lenders accustomed to making loans backed by national government guarantees. If newly privatized companies are independent of government, then loans to the companies will probably lack government guarantees and safeguards. This has been of concern to international donors in Central Asia, for example, where a few years ago privatization led to the cancellation of a major Asian Development Bank investment in Kazakhstan's utilities industry.

Attracting Foreign Investment

Virtually all Asian countries are actively seeking foreign investment and the region received international publicity in the early to mid-1990s because of the number of joint venture deals signed. Investor interest has slowed however since the financial crisis of 1997-1999. Much of the private foreign investment in Asia has focused on providing technology and expertise for developing the potential of the region's oil and gas fields, for example in Central Asia and China. Several multi-billion-dollar pipeline deals have already been agreed upon in Kazakhstan and Turkmenistan. This does not mean that these pipelines will be built, but they are being proposed, all parties have agreed on the economic sensibility of these pipelines, and the respective governments have signed agreements.

Substantial interest is also being paid to the electricity sector in Asia, as many nations are phasing in deregulation and, in the process, promoting independent power producers, or IPPs. Electricity-generation projects are particularly attractive in countries where programs are underway to streamline government regulations and improve operating efficiencies. Privatization of electricity in Asia has created numerous opportunities for international investors, including the following:

- construction of new power transmission lines
- renovation and expansion of existing electricity facilities
- improvement of energy efficiency rates at major power facilities
- introduction of energy-saving technologies
- advice on emergency energy planning.

Despite the abundance of investment and financing opportunities in the Asia electricity sector, it should be noted that essential foreign direct investment (FDI) in the region's power sector has dropped significantly from 1997 levels. According to *International Power Generation*,[35] FDI in the sector plummeted 90 percent from around US$5.4 billion in 1997 to only US$480 million in 2000. Reflecting these shortfalls, India's Power Ministry announced that new capacity during 1997-2002 was expected to total only 21GW against a 40GW target. In Southeast Asia, the domestic financial systems of South Korea, Thailand and Malaysia are still mired in the after-effects of the 1997-1999 crisis even while much needed capital does flow north to China. The established electricity sectors of the Philippines, Indonesia, Singapore, Taiwan and Pakistan seem less affected by the slump in FDI.

Some general efforts at attracting investment into the energy industries of Central Asia, China and the Philippines are highlighted below:[36]

Kazakhstan: The country's gas transmission system was sold to Tractebel of Belgium in 1997 as part of a privatization plan for the entire hydrocarbon industry. Tractebel agreed to build a 150km pipeline at an estimated cost of US$100 million. The Kazakhstan Government wants the new pipeline to supply some southern regions with Uzbekistan gas. Electricity generation projects are also beginning to attract foreign investors in Kazakhstan, where a comprehensive program is underway to streamline government regulations and improve operating efficiency.

Turkmenistan: Foreign investment in its potentially huge gas and oil industries is sought in order to alleviate problems of inadequate export infrastructure. Turkmenistan also aims to modernize and expand its oil refining industry using foreign financing and advanced technology.

Uzbekistan: As part of its strong effort to attract foreign capital and technology to its oil and gas sectors, Uzbekistan convened its Fifth International Oil and Gas Exhibition in Tashkent in May 2001.

Tajikistan: Depending on Uzbekistan for much of its oil product and gas imports, Tajikistan has a barter arrangement with Uzbek authorities under which gas is supplied in exchange for the use of rail transport across northern Tajikistan.

China: Foreign investment and participation in domestic oil activities is encouraged as part of the country's open-door policy and to facilitate the renovation of its energy industry. Government officials in Xinjiang, China have even more leeway to solicit foreign investment because of the autonomous status of the province and its remoteness. China announced that it was opening Tarim and other inland areas to foreign involvement in February 1993, at which time the country formally abandoned its historic energy self-sufficiency strategy. In 1999, China announced plans to further open the Tarim Basin for exploration by foreign companies, including blocs in the promising center of the area that had previously been barred to overseas firms.

Philippines: International cooperation involving the country's energy industry is an important means of acquiring advanced technology and policy assistance as well as project financing. Specifically, there are three areas where international cooperation is now underway: trade and investments, exchange of expertise to effect technology transfer, and the sharing of data and information. The Philippine electricity sector is particularly in need of foreign investment, given that the country's total electricity requirements will more than double from 46,262 gigawatt hour (GWh) in 2000 to 99,714 GWh in 2009, reflecting a yearly growth rate of 8.9 percent.

Energy Diversification

Diversification of energy sources and markets is a sound strategy and a number of countries within Asia are beginning to adopt and implement the approach. The Japanese government has long considered energy diversification as fundamental to economic security. In China, concerns over heavy dependence on the Middle East for imported oil and oil products led, in part, to the consideration of developing an alternative source of supply by importing Kazakhstan crude into Xinjiang. This option would only become viable if Middle East and world oil prices remained sufficiently high for a significant period. The United States pushed for diversification of its energy supplies after two unexpected oil price shocks in the 1970s, and greater emphasis was placed on developing alternative energy sources—notably, natural gas, solar, and wind. Although the United States failed in its attempt to become less reliant on Middle Eastern crudes and diversify its energy mix, many Asian nations are at a juncture where the adoption of appropriate strategies can reap tremendous future benefits.

Energy Self-Sufficiency

The energy crises of the 1970s awakened many countries, including the United States, to their vulnerabilities to imported energy products. Most governments realized that increasing the use of alternative fuels could be one means of strengthening national energy security and reducing the impact of any potential energy embargo.

As a result of Soviet domination for several decades and little control over their natural resources, most Central Asian nations still consider self sufficiency a necessary objective for long-term stability. Modern China too for much of its existence sought self-sufficiency in its resource industries with little regard to cost or efficiency. Vietnam, as well, is seeking to be energy sufficient to the extent possible.

Those countries that have the ability to do so are stressing energy self-sufficiency, even at the expense of energy cooperation and trade. Uzbekistan, for example, established a goal at independence in 1991 of achieving self-sufficiency in oil production by the year 2000. Kazakhstan has contemplated producing synthetic oil from Karaganda coal to avoid dependency on Uzbekistan for oil in southeastern Kazakhstan. In Xinjiang, China officials are still considering constructing a coal-fired power plant in Kashgar to avoid possible dependency on Kyrgyz-produced hydroelectricity across the border. In the immediate years ahead, it can be expected that many Asian nations will continue to strive for reduced reliance on external supplies of energy except where circumstances completely prohibit self-reliance.

Other Trends

In addition to these structural changes occurring within the Asian energy industry, other confirmed trends include a greater reliance on the oil and gas trade, a continued predominant use of fossil fuels in the energy mix, and an increase in CO_2 emissions led in part by growing power generation. Over the next two decades, trade in energy will occur more frequently on the World Wide Web, though the impact of e-commerce in oil, gas, and power on Asia will lag behind Europe, North America and the Middle East.

Summary and Conclusions

Worldwide energy consumption is expected to grow by 59 percent over the next two decades, or at an average annual growth rate of 2 percent, according to the *International Energy Outlook 2001*, published in April 2001 by the Energy Information Administration of the United States Department of Energy. One-half of the projected growth is forecast to occur in the developing countries of Asia (including China, India, and South Korea), owing to robust economic growth, which will spur growing demand for energy. With the increase in energy demand, CO_2 emissions will continue to increase steadily throughout the world. Fossil fuels will remain dominant in the global energy mix, accounting for about 90 percent in 2020.

While Asia-Pacific is as varied across countries as it is vast, combined, the region is fast becoming the critical player in world energy markets. Several countries including China and Indonesia are leading global producers of energy, while other nations are heavy consumers, such as Japan and South Korea. Natural gas and electricity demand are expected to grow particularly rapidly during the next two decades, although oil and coal will maintain large shares of Asia's total energy consumption. Trade involving the region will increase significantly, particularly after 2010. By 2020 many Asian countries and groups of countries may play an even greater role in energy markets than they do today. The Central Asian states of the former Soviet Union, for example, may as a bloc of nations become a formidable competitor for markets, capital and technology innovation with OPEC. The region is now creating its own Eurasian Economic Community, modeled after the European Union (EU).

Several structural trends are apparent in the Asia-Pacific energy industry today, which will affect the future impact of the industry on worldwide markets. These include restructuring, globalization and accountability, new efforts to attract foreign investment, and continuing strategies of energy diversification and self-sufficiency. Restructuring is perhaps most pronounced in the region's electricity sector, with more than half a dozen countries in Asia undergoing power sector deregulation. Developing Asia is also part of the world where electricity consumption is growing the fastest—4.5 percent a year, according to the US Energy Information Administration. Recent experiences in the US state of California are giving governments in Asia second thoughts about implementing deregulation at a fast pace, though the overall trend towards privatization and less government intervention will continue at some level.

APPENDIX
World Energy Projection System (WEPS)

The projections of world energy consumption published annually by the Energy Information Administration (EIA) in the *International Energy Outlook (IEO)* are derived from the World Energy Projection System (WEPS). WEPS is an integrated set of personal-computer-based spreadsheets containing data compilations, assumption specifications, descriptive analysis procedures, and projection models. The WEPS accounting framework incorporates projections from independently documented models and assumptions about the future energy intensity of economic activity (ratios of total energy consumption divided by gross domestic product, GDP) and about the rate of incremental energy requirements met by natural gas, coal and renewable energy sources (hydroelectricity, geothermal, solar, wind, biomass and other renewable sources).

WEPS provides projections of total world primary energy consumption, as well as projections of energy consumption by primary energy type (oil, natural gas, coal, nuclear, and hydroelectric and other renewable resources), and projections of net electricity consumption and energy use in the transportation sector. Projections of energy consumed by fuel type are also provided for electricity generation and for transportation. Carbon dioxide emissions resulting from fossil fuel use are derived from the energy consumption projections. All projections are computed in 5-year intervals through the year 2020. For both historical series and projection series, WEPS provides analytical computations of energy intensity and energy elasticity (the percentage change in energy consumption per percentage change in GDP).

WEPS projections are provided for regions and selected countries. Projections are made for 14 individual countries, 9 of which – United States, Canada, Mexico, Japan, United Kingdom, France, Germany, Italy, and Netherlands – are part of the designation "industrialized countries." Individual country projections are also made for China, India, South Korea, Turkey and Brazil, all of which are considered "developing countries." Beyond these individual countries, the rest of the world is

[109]

divided into regions. Industrialized regions include North America (Canada, Mexico and the United States), Western Europe (United Kingdom, France, Germany, Italy, Netherlands and Other Europe), and Pacific (Japan and Australasia, which consists of Australia, New Zealand and the US Territories). Developing regions include developing Asia (China, India, South Korea, and Other Asia), Middle East (Turkey and Other Middle East), Africa, and Central and South America (Brazil and Other Central and South America). The transitional economies, consisting of the countries in Eastern Europe (EE) and the former Soviet Union (FSU), are considered as a separate country grouping, neither industrialized nor developing. Within the EE/FSU, projections are made separately for nations designated as Annex I and Non-Annex I in the Kyoto Climate Change Protocol.

The process of creating the projections begins with the calculation of a reference case total energy consumption projection for each country or region for each 5-year interval in the forecast period. The total energy consumption projection for each forecast year is the product of an assumed GDP growth rate, an assumed energy elasticity, and the total energy consumption for the prior forecast year. For the first year of the forecast, the prior year consumption is based on historical data. Subsequent calculations are based on the energy consumption projections for the preceding years.

Projections of world oil supply are provided to WEPS from EIA's International Energy Module, which is a sub-module of the National Energy Modeling System (NEMS). Projections of world nuclear energy consumption are derived from nuclear power electricity generation projections from EIA's International Nuclear Model (INM), PC Version (PC-INM). All US projections are taken from EIA's *Annual Energy Outlook (AEO)*.

CORE ENERGY ISSUES

3

Energy Trade in Asia: An Overview

Amy Myers Jaffe and Kenneth B. Medlock III

Economic growth in Asia, which is defined here as including the Indian Subcontinent, Southeast Asia, East Asia, Australia and New Zealand but excluding the countries of the former Soviet Union and Middle East, will lead to significant expansion in energy use as the 21st century progresses.[1] (See Table 3.1 below) By 2020 energy use in all of Asia (including the industrialized nations of Japan, Australia and New Zealand) is projected to rival that in North America and Western Europe combined, accounting for about one-third of total global consumption.

The implications for global energy flows are substantial. Asia will become a major rival to Western Europe and North America for global energy supplies in the decades ahead, prompting geopolitical impacts and shifting alliances. Average annual growth in energy demand in Western Europe and North America is projected to remain around 1.4%, portending a possible intensifying of competition for energy supplies between the West and Asia. According to the Reference Case projections in the *International Energy Outlook 2002* (IEO) by the US Department of Energy (DOE), energy consumption in developing Asian countries alone could rise from about 18.5% of total global energy use in 1999 to 23.2% by 2010. This represents an average annual increase in energy demand of 4.0% per year, well above the projected global growth of 2.3%.

Table 3.1

Countries Included in Asia

Afghanistan	India	Niue
American Samoa	Indonesia	Pakistan
Australia	Japan	Papua New Guinea
Bangladesh	Kiribati	Philippines
Bhutan	Korea, North	Samoa
Brunei	Korea, South	Singapore
Burma	Laos	Solomon Islands
Cambodia	Macau	Sri Lanka
China	Malaysia	Taiwan
Cook Islands	Maldives	Thailand
Fiji	Mongolia	Tonga
French Polynesia	Nauru	US Pacific Islands
Guam	Nepal	Vanuatu
Hawaiian Trade Zone	New Caledonia	Vietnam
Hong Kong	New Zealand	Wake Island

Asia's rapid economic growth, explosive urbanization, dramatic expansion in the transportation sector, and politically important electrification programs, will have a dramatic effect on the dependence of Asian nations for imported energy. In the absence of significant growth in renewable energy supplies and/or new energy technologies, consumption of crude oil and natural gas will rise substantially. Given the inadequate resource endowment of the region, which is already dependent on imported oil supplies, Asia will exert an increasing pull on Middle Eastern and Russian hydrocarbon resources in the coming years. Asia's oil use, which already exceeds 20 million barrels per day (bpd), is larger than that of the United States.[2] As of 1999, about 60% of this amount must be imported. By 2010, total Asian oil consumption could reach 25 to 30 million bpd, the majority of which will have to be imported from outside the region.[3] China alone can be expected to see its oil imports rise from around 1.4 million bpd in 1999 to between 3 and 5 million bpd by 2010.[4] It is this latter eventuality that has awakened fears in Tokyo, Seoul and

[114]

New Delhi about competition or even confrontation over energy supplies and lines of transport.

Environmental concerns could exacerbate energy security fears. In particular, as countries such as China look to cleaner forms of energy, such as natural gas, there will be increased competition for supplies in the region. The potential costs of confrontation for energy supplies could push some Asian nations into developing new and more energy efficient technologies, or even alternative forms of energy. More likely in the immediate term, however, will be a move to diversify both the forms of energy used and the sources from which supplies come.

The quest for energy will create new economic and strategic challenges as well as alter geopolitical relations. The outcome of such trends will depend on the policy choices made by the key players in the region and by the United States. Issues of territory and nationalism remain defining issues in Asian interstate relations. This means that energy security for all concerned must be managed carefully lest other pathologies spread into deliberations in the energy area. Moreover, the diplomatic, strategic and trading focus of certain Asian states can be expected to shift in the light of growing energy import requirements, leading to a strengthening of economic and political ties between individual Asian states with major Middle Eastern oil exporting countries and African oil states.

The Energy Profile of Asia

Trends in Total Energy Use

Economic development and population growth are key drivers of any nation's energy needs. For the past two decades, Asian economic growth rates have been among the highest in the world. Developing Asia – defined here as China, India, South Korea, Pakistan, Taiwan, Thailand, Malaysia and Indonesia – logged an incredible 7.5% annual average growth rate in GDP from 1980 to 2000. During that same period, population has grown at an average annual rate of 1.65%.[5] This compares to world average economic and population growth rates of 3.0% and 1.6% respectively, for the same period.

[115]

Total primary energy supply (TPES) in the countries of Asia, in particular developing Asia, is growing relative to the rest of the world. Illustrating this point is Figure 3.1 which indicates the Share of World TPES in 1980 and 2000 for Developing Asia (exclusive of China), China, the Rest of Asia, the US, and the Rest of the World. In 2000, Developing Asia (with China) represented approximately 46% of the total world population, relatively unchanged since 1980. By contrast, Developing Asia's share of total world output (where output is measured as gross domestic product or GDP) has risen significantly, from just over 9% in 1980 to roughly 21% in 2000. During the same period (1980-2000), energy use in Developing Asia has risen from about 9.5% of the world total to about 18% in 2000. The rising share of total energy is a direct result of the tremendous economic progress made in these countries.

Figure 3.1
Share of World Total Primary Energy Supply (TPES)
by Selected Regions (1980 and 2000)

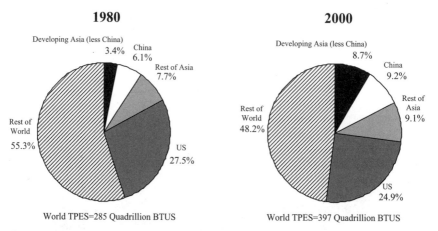

Source: EIA *International Energy Annual, 2002.*

The margin for expansion in energy use in Asia is tremendous given the size of the region's populations and the current low per capita income levels in many key countries. Figure 3.2 illustrates primary energy use in Asia by country in the year 2000. It is worth noting that about 82% of all energy consumption in Asia is by six countries: China, India, South

[116]

Korea, Indonesia, Australia and Japan. Moreover, and perhaps more importantly, more than half of the energy consumed in Asia occurs in the developing countries of China (34.2%), India (11.8%), South Korea (7.4%) and Indonesia (3.6%). This is important because, as shown by Medlock and Soligo, the income elasticity of energy demand is highest at low levels of per capita income.[6] As of 1999, GDP per capita in China, India, South Korea and Indonesia was $3,476, $2,171, $15,152, and $2,633 respectively, in terms of 1995 purchasing power parity dollars (PPP$). This compares to $23,401 in Japan and $24,680 in Australia. Thus, future economic growth in the developing Asian countries will result in larger increases in energy demand than future economic growth in the industrialized Asian nations of Japan and Australia. As a result, the share of energy use in Asia, *ceteris paribus*, will continue to shift toward these emerging countries. Moreover, since GDP per capita in most of Western Europe and the US rivals or exceeds that in Japan and Australia, economic growth in developing Asia, *ceteris paribus*, should lead to an increasing share of total world energy consumption in those nations.

Figure 3.2
Primary Energy in Asia, 2000

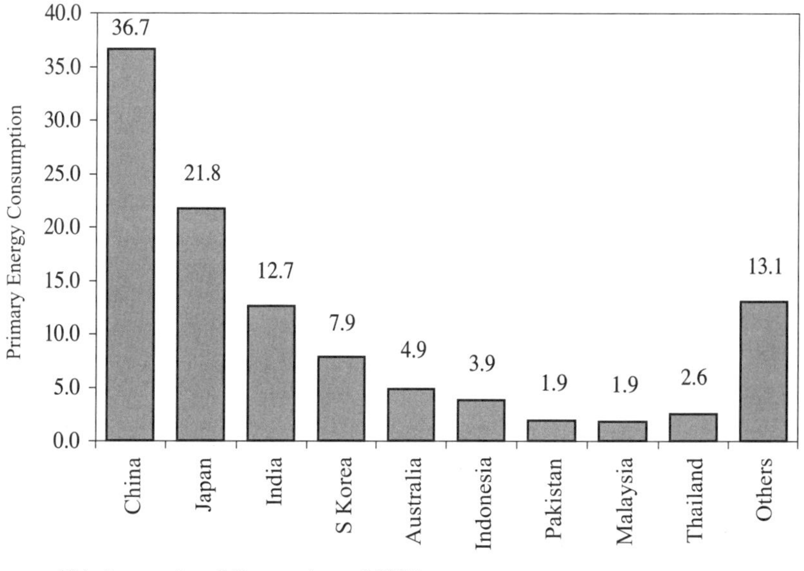

Source: EIA *International Energy Annual 2002*

The hypothesis of rising Asian prominence in world energy markets is reinforced when we consider energy consumption in Asia in per capita terms (see Figure 3.3). For example, as can be seen in Figure 3.2, China consumes almost 9 times the energy consumed in Australia and almost twice that in Japan. However, in terms of energy use per person, these ratios are considerably different. Australian energy use per person is almost 10 times that in China, and Japanese energy use per person is almost 7 times that of China. The primary differences between these countries that accounts for this disparity are population and GDP per capita. China's population is approximately 66 times that of Australia and 10 times that of Japan, while China's GDP per capita (in 1995 PPP$) is roughly 14% that of Australia and 15% that of Japan.

Figure 3.3
Primary Energy Per Capita in Asia, 2000

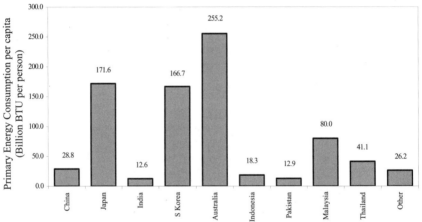

Source: EIA *International Energy Annual* and authors' own calculations.

Again noting the relatively low levels of per capita income in the developing countries of Asia, continued economic growth will push the per capita energy use in those countries toward that of the industrialized nations of Japan and Australia, which will considerably change the geopolitical landscape in Asia. For example, a 5% per capita GDP growth rate in China to 2020 (a rate of growth consistent with many projections) will lead to a Chinese per capita income of close to $10,000. Following Medlock and Soligo,[7] along this growth path, China's long run mid-point income elasticity of energy demand would be about 0.75, which would result in an increase in per capita energy use to about 61 billion BTU per person.[8] Assuming a population growth rate of 0.7% per year, and ignoring the effects of price and new technology, this translates into an energy consumption of about 88 quadrillion BTUs, or an increase of about 4.4% per year. A similar exercise can be performed for industrialized nations, but economic growth rates are typically lower (on the order of 2.5% to 3.0%), and, again following Medlock and Soligo,[9] the long run income elasticity of energy demand will be considerably lower (a mid-point elasticity of approximately 0.2 for Japan and Australia, and 0.16 for the United States). The end result is a smaller percentage increase in per capita energy use in these countries than in less developed countries.

Energy Use by Type

The composition of energy use in Asia is dictated, to a large extent, by domestic resources within individual countries. For example, in China, coal reserves are estimated to be over 126 billion short tons, which is about 40% of estimated coal reserves in Asia and about 12% of the world total. In turn, coal accounts for about 56% of TPES in China. Moreover, China accounts for over 70% of coal consumption in all of Asia. Likewise, in Indonesia, estimated crude oil reserves stand at over 30 billion barrels, representing over 50% of all oil reserves in Asia, and natural gas reserves are estimated at greater than 146.9 trillion cubic feet, which is just over one-third of all gas reserves in Asia. Accordingly, crude oil accounts for approximately 35% of TPES in Indonesia, and natural gas accounts for about 20% of TPES. In addition, as of 1999 Indonesian exports of crude oil exceeded domestic consumption (consumption of 963 thousand bpd vs. exports of 1,038 thousand bpd), and exports of natural gas also exceeded domestic consumption (consumption of 1,124 billion cubic feet vs. exports of 1,381 billion cubic feet).[10]

As indicated in Figure 3.4, coal and oil are, and have been, the predominant fuels consumed in the Asia-Pacific region, representing in 2000 about 41% and 40% respectively of total primary energy supply (TPES). However, the share of natural gas in Asia's energy mix has been

[119]

on the rise, expanding from 5.5% of total energy used to over 10% between 1980 and 2000, and is expected to continue to make significant gains. From 1990 to 2000, natural gas consumption has grown at an average annual rate of 6.7% in Asia, with demand growing fastest in South Korea (20.1% per year), Thailand (11.9% per year), and Malaysia (8.8% per year). Although the consumption of coal in Asia has increased from 1980 to 2000 (from 19.63 to 42.47 quadrillion BTUs), its share of total energy has remained relatively stable.

Figure 3.4
Structure of Primary Energy Consumption
in the Asia-Pacific Region (1980 and 2000)

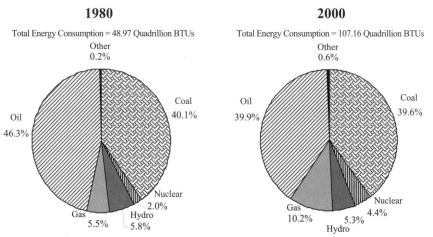

Source: EIA *International Energy Annual, 2002*

The share of hydroelectric energy has also increased steadily since 1980. Asian hydropower consumption increased at an average annual rate of 3.5% between 1980 and 2000. China is by far the largest consumer of hydroelectric energy in Asia, accounting for just over 40% of all hydroelectric consumption in the region, and has experienced an average annual growth rate of hydropower consumption of close to 7% since 1980. Japan, India, New Zealand and Pakistan are the next four largest users of hydropower, with both India and Pakistan having increased their usage over the past two decades at average annual rates of 2.5% and 4.8% respectively.

[120]

As of 2000, nuclear energy comprised about 4.4% of TPES, increasing from 2.0% in 1980. The increase in share has been primarily due to large commitments to nuclear energy development made by several countries in the region, most notably Japan. The consumption of nuclear energy has increased at an average annual rate of 8.3% in Asia from 1980 to 2000, but has occurred in only the handful of countries that have nuclear programs, namely Japan, South Korea, Taiwan, China, India, and Pakistan.

Table 3.2

Asian Production and Consumption of Energy

by Source (1980, 1990 and 2000)

		1980	1990	Annual Growth Rate (1980-1990)	2000	Annual Growth Rate (1990-2000)
Total Energy	Production	35.86	60.62	5.39%	76.69	2.38%
(Quadrillion BTUs)	Consumption	48.97	74.80	4.33%	107.16	3.66%
Coal	Production	1,029.35	1,825.27	5.90%	2,224.98	2.00%
(million short tons)	Consumption	1,072.50	1,820.74	5.44%	2,248.51	2.13%
Crude Oil	Production	4,848	6,468	2.92%	7,529	1.53%
(thousand b/d)	Consumption	10,729	13,595	2.40%	20,773	4.33%
Natural Gas	Production	2.44	5.44	8.35%	9.41	5.63%
(trillion cu. ft.)	Consumption	2.52	5.62	8.34%	10.27	6.21%
Nuclear	Production	92.7	279.9	11.68%	464.7	5.20%
(billion kWh)	Consumption	92.7	279.9	11.68%	464.7	5.20%
Hydro	Production	275.2	420.9	4.34%	543.2	2.58%
(billion kWh)	Consumption	275.2	420.9	4.34%	543.2	2.58%

Source: EIA *International Energy Annual, 2002*

The energy balance of Asia is increasingly turning to one of import dependence, characterized by the large deficit in local crude oil supply. The consumption of crude oil in Asia approximately doubled from 1980 to 2000, but production only increased by about 55%. Table 3.2 illustrates the consumption and production for total energy, crude oil and petroleum products, coal, natural gas, nuclear, and hydro in Asia in 1980, 1990 and 2000. Despite economic woes in Asia that have contributed to a slower rate of growth in the consumption of total energy during the late 1990s, the growth of oil consumption actually accelerated during the decade resulting in growing dependence on oil imports into the region.

As the economies of Asia continue to grow so will energy consumption, creating increased pressure on these economies to find new energy resources to fuel their growth. In effort to minimize energy security concerns and mitigate the environmental impact, many Asian nations will be forced to diversify their energy mix and/or turn to alternative forms of energy. This is already occurring in many nations, such as China, where the heavy use of coal has forced environmental concerns into the forefront of energy initiatives. In fact, air pollution in a majority of Asian urban centers remains a significant problem for the region, exceeding levels in most cities in North America and Europe and greatly surpassing World Health Organization guidelines. In China and India, in particular, urban air quality problems are extensive.

As economic development continues to gain momentum in Asia, increased concerns about global warming are likely to take hold in the region. Most Asian nations are not parties to the Kyoto Protocol—an agreement among industrialized nations to reduce the emissions of greenhouse gases, in particular carbon dioxide, in effort to curb global warming.[11] The Kyoto Protocol calls for a group of countries (referred to as Annex I countries in the Protocol parlance) to reduce carbon dioxide emissions by 8% to 12% of their 1990 levels by 2010. The Protocol does not include direct provisions for the reduction of emissions of less-developed and developing nations. Based on the principles of *the polluter pays* and *common but differentiated responsibilities*, the argument that industrialized nations should bear the costs of carbon abatement has been generally accepted. Less-developed and developing countries have argued that they lack the resources to abate carbon emissions while still preserving vital economic growth. In per capita terms, the carbon emissions of Developing Asia are well below the world average (see Table 3.3). However, the simple fact that such a massive portion of the world

[122]

population resides in these countries means that absolute total carbon emissions are considerable, and when considering the ramifications of carbon emissions for global warming it is the *total* rather than the *per capita* that matters.

Table 3.3

Carbon Emissions and Population (1980 and 2000)

	1980			2000			Annual Growth Rate	
	Per Capita	Gross	Population	Per Capita	Gross	Population	Per Capita	Gross
World	1.14	5075.21	4433	1.06	6443.38	6075	-0.38%	1.20%
Asia	0.40	973.06	2455	0.58	1970.22	3412	1.90%	3.59%
Developing Asia	0.29	581.02	2008	0.50	1386.43	2788	2.74%	4.44%

Units: *Per Capita* = metric tons of carbon, *Gross* = million metric tons of carbon, *Population* = millions

Source: EIA, *International Energy Annual, 2002*.

Carbon emissions in Asia are disproportionately high primarily due to the large share of coal in total energy consumption (see Figure 3.5). In fact, much of this consumption can be tied to two countries—China and India. In 2000, Chinese carbon emissions accounted for almost 40% (775 million metric tons) of total Asian emissions, and 76% of carbon emissions in China were from coal use. In 2000 carbon emissions in India accounted for about 13% (253 million metric tons) of total Asian emissions, 66% of which were from coal use. All told, China and India account for roughly 52% of all emissions in Asia, yet per capita emissions are far below the world average, standing at 0.61 metric tons per person in China and 0.25 metric tons of carbon per person in India. This is staggering when one considers that future economic growth in these countries will push these per capita numbers toward those of industrialized nations. In fact, Hartley, Medlock and Warby have shown that gross carbon emissions in China will most likely exceed those in the United States by 2010, making China the single largest emitter of carbon in the world.[12]

Eventually, international pressures on Asian countries to reduce carbon emissions will intensify, and already domestic pressures exist to reduce the emissions of sulfur and nitrous oxides, as well as other pollutants, associated with the burning of coal and other fossil fuels. Accordingly, Asian leaders are looking for ways to slow growth in the use of coal by encouraging investment in cleaner fuel sources. Developing additional nuclear and hydro generation is one means of reducing the consumption of coal and fossil fuels in general. However, the development of such options carries a host of problems, including a lack of appropriate geography and/or capital funding in the case of hydro, and, in the case of nuclear, uranium supply and waste disposal issues and negative public sentiment concerning the safety of facilities. Thus, increasing natural gas consumption may be the only real near term option available for reducing coal use, barring the development of new, more innovative technologies.

Figure 3.5

Carbon Emissions in Asia and the World (2000) by Source

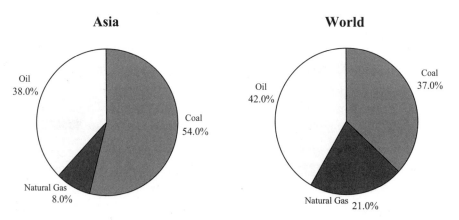

Source: EIA, *International Energy Annual, 2002*

Natural gas has tended to be underutilized in the Asia-Pacific region, despite its economic and environmental benefits. As of 2000, the share of natural gas in the region was only 10.2% of primary energy supply, compared to the world's share of 22.7%.[13] Natural gas market development in Asia has been delayed for a number of factors. To begin, prolific regional gas resources are distant from key end-user markets and are in

[124]

many cases separated by ocean or waterway. Liquefied natural gas (LNG) projects were organized to bring gas to consumers in Japan and South Korea, but these projects were initially costly and hard to organize. In countries such as Bangladesh and China, a lack of infrastructure to connect supplies to market, as well as a lack of capital necessary to develop infrastructure has hindered progress in the development of natural gas supplies. Subsidized and/or state controlled energy prices throughout the region have also discouraged investors. Finally, regional conflicts and territorial disputes have blocked the organization of cross-border projects.

At present, several major Asian countries are either investigating or have initiated programs to enhance natural gas use. Japan's Ministry of Economy, Trade and Investment (METI), for example, would like to see natural gas use in Japan rise from the 2000 levels of 13% of total energy to 20% by 2020.[14] China has targeted natural gas use to expand from 3% in 2000 to 10% by 2020.[15] In India, natural gas supplies constituted about 7% of India's total energy consumption in 2000, but this could double in the coming decade as gas use in the electricity sector rises rapidly.[16] Furthermore, new LNG terminal facilities and pipeline projects aimed at bringing international and disconnected domestic supplies to market are under consideration in Japan, China and India.

Nuclear power has the potential to ease air pollution and acid rain levels, and is being considered as a solution to environmental concerns in many countries. China, for example, has three nuclear reactors that account for just 1.3% of the country's total power output, but currently has another eight under construction. South Korea has 16 nuclear reactors that currently provide 36% of the country's electricity supplies, and four new nuclear reactors under construction. Japan, the regional leader in nuclear capacity, operates 52 reactors that provide roughly 30% of the country's electricity needs.

However, the Asian drive towards nuclear power is not without its problems. Many Asian countries must rely on imported uranium to operate their reactors and do not have the fabrication and enrichment services that are provided from the outside, raising a host of other questions that go beyond the energy security benefits of diversifying away from oil or the air quality benefits of moving away from heavy reliance on coal. South Korea, for instance, relies on Europe, Russia and the United States for its enriched uranium needs, while Korean firms provide nuclear power expertise and equipment to others, including China, Vietnam and Turkey.

Some Asian nations are working to expand the domestic content of their nuclear fuel cycles by building facilities for fuel enrichment, fabrication and reprocessing, as well as looking to invest in overseas uranium mines and locking up long-term enrichment contracts. For example, Tokyo's nuclear fuel cycle has been expanded to include fuel enrichment and fabrication facilities at the front end, and reprocessing and recycling facilities at the back end. While independent in plant operation, design and maintenance, Japan is reliant on uranium imports.

Public opposition also presents a hurdle for nuclear power development. For example, in the face of mounting public opposition in late 1999 the Japanese government cut back its goal of building 20 new nuclear reactors by 2010, reducing the number to 13. Indeed, a handful of accidents in the 1990s, most notably an incident on September 30, 1999 at the uranium reprocessing facility in Tokaimura, have undermined previously strong Japanese public confidence in atomic power. The accident at the Tokaimura facility was caused when workers ignored safety procedures and mixed several times the maximum safe amount of uranium in buckets, setting a nuclear chain reaction in motion. Two workers died as a result of serious radiation poisoning, while several hundred were exposed to abnormal radiation levels. Public opinion polls carried out in the months following the incident reflected an increasing loss of trust in the Japanese government's nuclear energy policy. On May 28, 2001, Japanese Prime Minister Junichiro Koizumi urged his government to redouble efforts to win public support for nuclear energy, one day after voters in the northern town of Kariwa rejected plans to use recycled plutonium – plutonium-based mixed oxide or (MOX) – in a large nuclear facility there. Koizumi stressed the need for Japan to develop its nuclear fuel-recycling program.

More recently, Japan's nuclear program suffered another setback when Tokyo Electric Power Company (TEPCO) in the summer of 2002 disclosed irregularities in maintenance and safety reporting for several of its 17 nuclear power plants in Japan. As a result of the scandal, nine of the company's plants (8,600 megawatts of generating capacity) have been shut down awaiting maintenance inspections, forcing the company to activate unused capacity at gas and oil-fired generating units.[17]

Total primary Japanese energy use is expected to rise from 480 million (metric) tons of oil equivalent (toe) in 1995 to between 673 and 717 million toe by 2015. Were Japan to shift away from increasing the share of nuclear power in its energy mix, the amount of incremental oil imports might rise from the 900,000 to 1.6 million bpd projected above to as much as 2.2 million bpd to 3.1 million bpd by 2015.[18] If incremental nuclear supplies were to be replaced with natural gas, Japan would have to increase imports by an additional 186.6 million cubic meters a day. A mix of 70% natural gas and 30% oil to substitute for nuclear power would equal an incremental 130.6 million cubic meters a day of gas and 350,000 bpd of oil. To summarize, without nuclear power development, Japan will be forced to increase its exposure to fluctuations in international oil and gas markets, which many policy makers inside Japan consider an undesirable outcome from an energy security policy perspective.

Asia's Growing Energy Dependence: Rising Imports

Referring to the work of Medlock and Soligo, we can discern the potential impact of future economic growth on energy demand per capita in Asia.[19] In their study, Medlock and Soligo used panel data for 28 countries at different levels of per capita income to identify patterns of total final consumption (TFC) of energy by end-use sector throughout the course of economic development (TFC is less than TPES by transmission and conversion losses incurred when converting raw resources into usable forms of energy). The curve in Figure 3.6 labeled 'Sample Average' is reproduced from that study, and represents the per capita TFC for the average country in the sample of countries used by Medlock and Soligo.[20] The curve labeled 'Asia' is constructed by adjusting the 'Sample Average' curve for actual TFC in Asia, a process that mimics a fixed effect for Asia since it captures the difference from the average constant term.[21]

According to the IEA, Asian per capita GDP in 2000 was $3,131 in 1995 purchasing power parity (PPP) terms. We have noted this position in Figure 3.6 after converting to 1985 PPP $ to be consistent with Medlock and Soligo's study. Also in Figure 3.6, we have illustrated the range of per capita incomes through which Asia will pass to the year 2020 assuming a 5.5% rate of GDP growth and 1.1% rate of population growth. It is apparent that Asian per capita TFC will grow appreciably in the coming years, in fact it is likely to more than double. When we consider the fact that population levels and population growth rates in Asia are higher than in the industrialized world, high growth rates in TFC *per capita* are magnified. Thus, it is most likely that Asia will exert a larger pull relative to the industrialized nations of the West on the world's energy resources.

Figure 3.6
Potential for Asian Energy Demand Per Capita

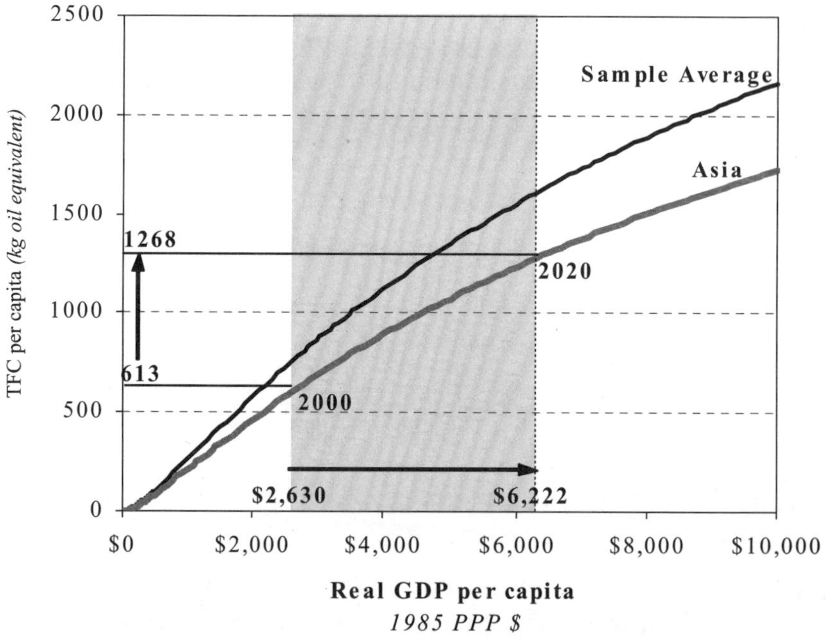

Note: Projected DOE Growth Rates for Asia: GDP=5.5% per year; Population=1.1% per year; GDP/cap=4.4% per year.

Source: Data obtained from Medlock and Soligo (2001). Simulated curves reproduced from that study. Range of Developing Asia outcomes based on authors' own estimates.

Historical growth in Asian countries has led to an increase in import dependence for energy resources from outside the region. This trend is likely to continue. Resources indigenous to Asia are not sufficient to supply growing demand. Already, Asia accounts for nearly half of world coal consumption, over one-fourth of world crude oil consumption, and just over one-tenth of world natural gas consumption (see Table 3.4). However, production already considerably falls short of these ratios for crude oil. While approximately 7% of the world's proven natural gas reserves are in Asia, many of which are unexploited to date, the massive energy requirements of the region and the uncertain status of capital availability for project development make it very likely that continued growth in natural gas consumption will push the region to increasing imports, most likely from the Middle East and/or Russia.

Table 3.4

Asian Share of World Fossil Energy (2000)

	Coal		Crude Oil		Natural Gas	
	million short tons	% of World	thousand bpd	% of World	trillion cubic feet	% of World
Reserves (Jan 1, 2001)	322394.0	29.8%	120547.9	4.3%	365.1	6.9%
Production (2000)	2225.0	44.0%	7529.0	11.1%	9.4	10.7%
Consumption (2000)	2248.5	43.7%	20773.0	27.3%	10.3	11.8%

Source: EIA *International Energy Annual, 2002*

Currently, the only significant fossil fuel import to Asia is crude oil, however, as natural gas use is encouraged, imports of it could rise significantly. To date, Asia has imported about 60% of its oil from outside the region, and this dependence could rise as high as 80-90% over the next decade or so as regional production fails to post major gains. Asian oil demand averaged around 19.6 million bpd in the first half of 2001 while local oil production totaled only around 5.9 million bpd, leaving a deficit of over 13.7 million bpd that was met by imports from the Middle East and Africa.[22] This is a rise from the 1998 deficit of over 11 million bpd.[23]

Rising demand for oil imports in Asia has implications for the energy security of all nations. There is a large body of research that links increases in energy prices to decreases in macroeconomic performance.[24] Indeed, since World War II every US recession except one has been preceded by a shock to the price of oil.[25] Energy is demanded to fuel industrialized economies. When energy prices increase, there is a negative demand response, and therefore a negative impact on macroeconomic output. Rapid growth in energy consumption in Asia, if not accompanied by commensurate increases in energy supplies, portends to drive world energy prices up, hindering economic growth rates.

The recent economic woes of Asian nations have delayed but not reversed the impact of Asian growth on world energy markets. From 1997 to 1998 Hong Kong, Indonesia, Japan, Malaysia, New Zealand, Philippines, South Korea and Thailand all posted negative GDP growth, and GDP growth in all of Asia was down year on year (see Table 3.5). Accordingly, Asian oil demand fell to 18.18 million bpd in 1998, down from 18.53 million bpd in 1997, a drop of 1.96%. This compared with an 8.1% rise in Asian oil demand between 1996 and 1997. However, from 1998 to 1999, all of the nations listed above posted positive growth, and GDP growth in all of Asia was up year on year. The result was an increase in Asian oil demand of 5.85%.

Table 3.5
Asian Oil Demand and GDP Growth (1996-1999)

	Growth Rate		
	1996-1997	*1997-1998*	*1998-1999*
GDP PPP *	6.30%	3.90%	5.86%
GDP XR **	5.94%	1.93%	5.40%
Oil Demand	8.08%	-1.96%	5.85%

Notes: * GDP PPP is the growth rate of GDP measured at 1995 prices and purchasing power parity.
    ** GDP XR is the growth rate of real GDP measured at 1995 prices and exchange rates.
Source: IEA *Energy Balances of Non-OECD Countries*

The slowdown from 1997 to 1998 in Asia contributed to a major change in the global oil supply-demand balance, limiting the growth in worldwide oil demand to only 0.5% compared to more typical annual growth rates of 2% to 3% in the mid-1990s. Oil markets responded to the decline in demand growth as prices dropped to levels not seen in over two decades. The turnaround in Asian oil demand the following year was accompanied by an increase in world oil prices. While other factors are important to the determination of world oil prices, the simple fact that recent swings in price are correlated so strongly with Asian demand cannot be ignored.

Despite recent economic setbacks, the potential for strong future growth in oil use in Asia remains high. As countries such as China, Thailand, India, and the Philippines achieve higher levels of economic development, the demand for oil in those countries will increase as well. More than half of the future growth in Asian energy demand is expected to come from the transportation sector where, barring a technological breakthrough, increased reliance on oil-related products will be unavoidable. Per capita income increases in countries such as China and India will encourage an increase in automobile ownership, and with it, a corresponding rise in gasoline demand.[26] In fact, oil demand in all of Asia is expected to grow two to three times faster than in the industrialized West, reaching around 29 million bpd by 2010, according to the "business as usual" scenario forecast by the International Energy Agency.[27] The US Department of Energy projects a similar growth path. This rapid growth rate is consistent with that seen during the period from 1970 to 1994 when Asian energy demand quadrupled in absolute terms and Asia's staggering economic growth promoted a 274% increase in the amount of oil used over the 24-year period versus an average for the rest of the world of 63%.[28] A potential mitigating factor is the meager level of energy efficiency in government regulated economies such as China and India, leaving room for improvements that could temper energy use increases, especially as government subsidized energy prices in countries like India are reformed and conservation rewarded by the marketplace.

Social preferences and environmental factors could push Asian oil use higher than most forecasts suggest for the coming decades. Popular opinion may press policy-makers to reduce heavy reliance on coal, and force them to abandon plans to expand nuclear power in favor of natural gas and other alternatives. Economic reforms may also bring changes in the composition of energy use.

For example, rational pricing might render coal as non-competitive with oil in Southern China due to the high cost of coal transportation. By the same token, political pressures in the wake of recent nuclear accidents and ongoing problems may force Japan to abandon plans to construct 20 new nuclear power plants to supply an additional 28 GWE of electricity.[29] Should Japan need to generate this amount of electricity using oil-fired plants, Japanese oil use would rise by an additional 1.17 million bpd, a contingency not reflected in current IEA or other forecasts for Asian oil demand.[30]

Beyond the 2010-2015 time frame, technological progress in the automobile industry could temper forecasts. In the IEA's "business as usual" forecast, 59% of the increase of the 41 million bpd increase in world oil demand to come between 1995 and 2020 will come from the transport sector (see Figure 3.7). However, Japanese automobile manufacturers are already introducing gas-electric hybrid engine vehicles, as well as developing fuel cell powered vehicles, each of which will get substantially better gasoline mileage than the conventional combustion engine vehicle. US automakers have also been introducing new technologies that will improve mileage standards by 25% in 2003, and it has been projected that by 2010 such technologies could represent 15-20% of new automobiles being sold. The Chinese government has embarked on programs to enhance the sale of vehicles run on LPG or compressed natural gas (CNG). To the extent that new automobile technologies replace existing traditional combustion engine systems, projections for large rises in oil use in Asia beyond 2010-2015 could be overstated.

Figure 3.7

IEA Incremental Oil Demand Projections by Sector (1997-2020)

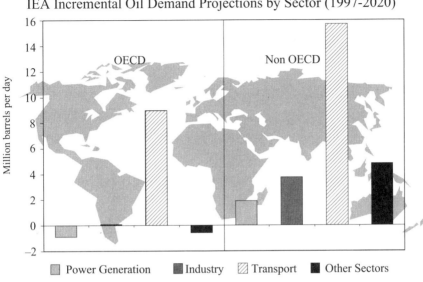

Power Generation ■ Industry ▨ Transport ■ Other Sectors

Source: Reproduced from the International Energy Agency's *World Energy Outlook*, 2000.

While Asian oil use could increase by between 6 to 12 million bpd in the coming decade, regional supplies are not expected to grow in any corresponding fashion. The IEA forecasts Asian oil production to fall to 6.4 million bpd by 2010 from 7.65 currently while other, more optimistic, analysts expect only modest gains of 1 million bpd or so.[31] Differences in forecasted production primarily reflects differing views about the future potential of production capacity in China, which represents almost half of the current regional output. In 2001, despite high international oil prices, Chinese oil production averaged 1.4% less in the first quarter of 2001, compared to the previous year. This trend is unlikely to be reversed given ineffective price reform, unfavorable geological factors and the general rigidity of state oil sector and capital constraints within China's major industries.[32]

Recently, there have been some exploration successes by foreign oil companies in China's offshore at Bohai Bay and the CACT consortium, comprised of Italy's Eni, Chevron and Texaco and China state-owned CNOOC, has announced a new oil find in the South China Sea.[33] China's

[133]

Western Tarim Basin is thought to hold some potential but its high cost, rugged terrain, and great distance from national infrastructure and coastal demand centers renders commercial exploitation among the most difficult and expensive in the world. According to Soligo and Jaffe,[34] Middle East oil prices must remain consistently above $15 a barrel before Tarim Basin shipments to the coast would be competitive with alternative world supplies.

The outlook for oil production increases elsewhere in Asia is not much more optimistic. Indonesia has seen proven reserves decline 14% since 1994.[35] However, much of the country remains unexplored, and it will be possible for Indonesia to boost production once more by inviting oil companies to explore for oil offshore and in the eastern section. Favorable investment terms will be needed to encourage use of advanced technology to forestall production declines in the main onshore production regions in Western Indonesia, just as such technology has arrested declines in oil fields in the North Sea. However, political instability hangs over efforts to enhance investment in the country's energy sector.

Other producers in the region such as Papua New Guinea and Vietnam are thought to have more modest potential for expansion while Malaysia's output is expected to begin declining by 2005. Several frontier areas with some exploration potential remain to be exploited in Asia, such as Eastern Indonesia, onshore India, coastal Vietnam, and Cambodia where until recently, land mines have thwarted activity. Despite some areas of limited promise, Asia's geology has not to date been conducive to many "elephant size" oil basin discoveries. In fact, over the last decade or more, over two-thirds of hydrocarbons found in Asia have been natural gas deposits. Some of these gas deposits, such as those in Natuna, Burma and Bangladesh have faced development hurdles due to technical problems (in Natuna's case, the field's high CO_2 content), political obstacles, lack of infrastructure, and lack of well-developed markets.

Geopolitics in Asia

The relatively pessimistic outlook for major expansion in local Asian oil and gas supply sources has led many large consuming countries in the region to bring import policies to greater prominence among national strategic concerns. Analysts are predicting an "inexorable trend" of "growing Asian oil dependence on the Middle East and visa versa."[36] Already, over 60% of Middle East oil exports go to Asia and nearly 70% of all Asian oil imports come from Middle East producers. Approximately 84% of all crude oil that is refined in Singapore and 78% of the crude processed in Japan is of Middle Eastern origin.[37] Moreover, the International Energy Agency projects that the Asia Pacific will be importing 20 to 24 million bpd from the Middle East by 2020.

The net result of such heavy oil dependence might be the development of a network of interlocking economic and political relations among Asian and Middle Eastern nations. In fact, such new, more complex relationships are already emerging, which include investments by Asian nations in upstream oil and gas sectors in the Gulf countries and investments by major Middle East oil producers in downstream facilities in Asia. These relationships also include cooperation in other spheres, such as military trade and diplomatic initiatives.

Several Asian entities have invested in oil and gas development activities in the Gulf. Japan has been very active in the Middle East oil sector over the past several decades, with investments in oil fields in Abu Dhabi and the Saudi-Kuwaiti Neutral Zone, as well as investments in LNG projects in Oman and Qatar.[38] Most recently, following the expiration of its upstream arrangement in Saudi Arabia's neutral zone, Japan has been seeking opportunities in Iran. As of mid-2001, the Silk Road Petroleum consortium, which is comprised of Japanese companies including Japex, JNOC, Inpex, and Tomen, is in the process of submitting proposals for the development of Iran's large Azadegan field.[39]

Japan is not the only Asian country investing in upstream activities in the Middle East. For example, Malaysia's Petronas, in a joint venture with European firms, is developing the South Pars gas field in Iran, as well as other oil fields in Iran and Yemen. Additionally, South Korea has invested in LNG projects in Qatar.

More recently, developing giants China and India are also seeking investment opportunities in the Middle East. Both countries have expressed interest in Iraqi and Iranian oil fields that might open to foreign investment—the former when UN economic sanctions have eased. Specifically, India has expressed interest in the Tuba oil field in Iraq, and China's state China National Petroleum Corporation (CNPC) has a $1.2 billion commitment to develop the Al-Ahdab oil field in southern Iraq. CNPC has also signed a memorandum of understanding with Iran's National Iranian Oil Company to explore for offshore reserves in Iran, China and elsewhere. To date, however, United Nations sanctions and lack of hard currency have together prevented CNPC from doing either. CNPC is also investigating the possibility of upstream investments in the Middle East countries outside the Gulf, such as Libya and elsewhere in Africa, in an effort to attain higher quality oil that is better suited for its refining system.[40]

As for downstream investments in Asia, several Middle East producers have sought refining assets in Asia in an effort to solidify relations and lock up markets for their oil. For instance, in 1991 Saudi Aramco acquired a 35% stake in Ssangyong Oil Refining Co., the third largest oil refiner in South Korea, for US$470 million. Saudi Aramco also purchased a 40% stake in Petron, a major Philippines refiner, in 1995, and has been recently negotiating with China about investment in a refinery in the Fujian province.[41]

The trend of cross-border investments is most evident in the new policies of China, where the government has encouraged its state oil companies to adopt a more outward-looking orientation to identify and obtain secure supplies of oil and gas in an effort to diversify its energy supply portfolio. In 1986, China's State Planning Commission, acknowledging that its domestic oil industry could not maintain oil self-sufficiency in light of the country's growing energy demand, gave the official approval allowing foreign crude oil imports.[42] However, it was not until 1993 that China became a net oil importer. Since then, import rates have risen slowly. Today, China's oil imports average around 1.5 to 1.7 million bpd, and are expected to grow to between 2 million bpd and 4 million bpd over the next ten years.[43]

In 1996, facing rising demand for oil and lagging domestic production, China unveiled a plan to attain around a third of its energy needs through international exploration and acquisition activities.[44] In 1997, CNPC outbid the international majors for oil fields and exploration acreage in Venezuela, Sudan, southern Iraq (on hold for the foreseeable future), Iran and Kazakhstan. In Kazakhstan, CNPC committed to spend $4.3 billion to buy a 60% stake in the Aktybinskmunai Production Association and the Uzen oil field.[45] The purchase was considered the most interesting of the CNPC investments since it opened the possibility that China could import oil over land by long distance pipeline as a means to hedge against disruptions of more distant Middle East oil supplies or against any upheaval in international sea lanes, particularly the choke points of South Asian sea lanes.

China recently allowed Gazprom and Shell to bid to build a 4,000-kilometer natural gas pipeline capable of carrying 20 billion cubic meters per year from the Xinjiang province in northwest China to Shanghai. Gazprom and Shell will be competing against a consortium comprising BP, Malaysia's state-owned Petronas and three Japanese firms as well as against an ExxonMobil-led group.[46] Analysts argue that the strategic energy cooperation of this sort will require a pragmatic and strong-willed joint effort as well as a clear means to overcome a shortage of capital.[47] Participation of international organizations and regional forums, such as the Asian Development Bank (ADB), IBRD, UNDP and APEC will be important for the implementation of these programs.[48]

China, as well as neighboring Japan, has looked to Russia as a possible means to diversify oil and gas supply, which could dramatically alter the relationships among world powers on the international stage. China has expressed interest in developing the Verkh-Chonskoye oil deposit of Russia Petroleum. Additionally, at a historic meeting between Chinese and Russian leaders in July 2001, Chinese leader Jiang Zemin spoke of an agreement to pursue an oil pipeline project to bring Siberian oil to Eastern China. Zemin and Russian Prime Minister Mikhail Kasanov signed an agreement for a feasibility study of a 400,000 bpd pipeline from Angarsk in Irkutsk to Eastern China. Eastern Siberia's Yurubcheno-Takhomskaya

[137]

zone is estimated to hold up to 11 billion barrels of crude and 36 trillion cubic feet of gas. Yukos and Slavneft have licenses there, and Slavneft's first well in the area flowed 3,700 bpd, boosting hopes for commercial development.[49] Russia's major developed resources, however, are located in Western Siberia, and, as such, are quite distant from consuming regions in China or Japan, making their economic viability as a supply option somewhat questionable.[50]

In Eastern Russia, the hydrocarbon reserves in the Sakhalin Islands area compare favorably with other substantial regional natural gas suppliers. Preliminary estimates indicate that proven and probable gas reserves in Sakhalin could be as high as 50 to 65 trillion cubic feet (tcf). By comparison, Indonesia, the world's largest LNG exporter, has proven reserves of around 82 tcf. The gas resources in other Eastern Russian areas are less prolific and more distant to markets. According to Washington, DC-based consultants Planecon, Inc., Yakutia is thought to hold an additional 35.3 tcf while the Kovyktinskoye field in Irkutsk is estimated to have possible reserves of 52 to 105 tcf.[51] Sakhalin's natural gas will become an increasingly attractive source of clean energy, especially if political and economic constraints stymie any expansion of Japan's nuclear power industry.[52]

The scattered natural gas resources of Irkutsk have been cited as a possible source of gas supply via pipeline to Northern China, but this project faces several commercial problems. These problems include high transport costs, questions of reservoir size, and quality of the targeted Kovyktinskoye field.[53] Table 3.6 outlines the resource potential of the Russian Far East. Indicated in Table 3.6 is the number of fields and the 2-P (proven and probable) and 3-P (proven, probable and possible) reserve estimates of recoverable gas, oil and condensate reserves of the region. The reserve estimates indicated in Table 3.6 seem to make the region very promising as a source of supply for Asia in the coming years. While the current political landscape presents barriers to expedient development of the region, the economic and social benefits that could be reaped by all parties involved should drive the winds of change. In addition, the entire world would feel less strain from Asia on existing supplies as these supplies are developed. In other words, Eastern Russia holds the potential to ease pressures on world energy markets by filling the supply-demand gap that would otherwise be created by future economic growth in Asia.

Table 3.6

Russian Far East: Recoverable Gas, Oil and Condensate Reserves

	No. of Fields	2-P Reserves	3-P Reserves
Natural Gas (*tcf*)	95	56.5	847.2
Condensate (NGL)			
(billion bpd)	95	3.0	11.6
Crude Oil (*billion bpd)*	60	2.6	66.6

Note: Proven and Probable reserves ("2P"); Proven, Probable and Possible reserves ("3-P"). The Russian system of classification uses A-E categories; A, B and C1 are roughly equal to the international classification of proven and probable reserves.

Sources: ICPBS/Gapmer; WoodMackensie Consultants; Asia Pacific Consulting and industry sources.

The export of Russian oil and gas resources to East Asia has several geopolitical advantages. Specifically, those regions that would be importing these supplies (China, Japan, and South Korea) would benefit from supply source diversification, and Russia would benefit from the revenues generated by the development of these resources. Japan seeks better relations with Russia in effort to balance China and to reduce its dependency on Middle East oil and gas. As energy diplomacy has improved, Tokyo has lowered the heat on the territorial dispute over the Kuril Islands, which were seized by Russia at the end of World War II. Russian Far East energy supplies also allow China to diversify its imports away from sea borne supplies from the Middle East that, as Beijing fears, could be blocked by the US Navy. These energy supplies are part of China's plans to forge a closer alliance with Russia to counterbalance US hegemony.[54] For Russia, development of resources and energy trade with Asia is an important engine of economic development of the country's Far East, a means to improve its relations with both China and Japan,[55] and an opportunity to invite foreign capital and technology for Russia's ailing oil and gas sector.[56]

Conclusion

Despite the promise of Russian and Central Asian supplies, growing Asian oil dependence on the Gulf will remain the prevailing trend in the coming decade. Moreover, as Asian economies continue to grow, natural gas import dependence will most likely increase as well. These trends could have important implications for the measures taken to maintain security in the Gulf and the parties involved in seeing those measures through. In addition, the role of the US Navy in Southwest and East Asia could become more prominent, depending on the security needs of the region.

Ironically, as Asian dependence on the Gulf expands in the coming years, the US should be able to increasingly rely on oil and gas from within the Western Hemisphere and Atlantic Basin. Globalization of energy markets has meant that oil, and increasingly gas (as LNG trade continues to develop) movements are linked more to transport economics than political relations. Increases in oil production in Venezuela, Colombia, Canada, Brazil, West Africa and the US deepwater Gulf have begun to crowd Gulf oil out of the US market. This development could raise burden-sharing issues regarding the defense of the Gulf, which is now protected almost single handedly by the United States.[57] China's rising import requirements will mean that it will become increasingly dependent on the same energy sources and sea borne lanes of transport as the United States, Europe, Japan, and other industrialized countries. This could tie its strategic interests in the Middle East more closely with those of the West. In 1990, China, which was then self-sufficient in its oil supplies, abstained when the United States mobilized an international coalition to drive Iraqi troops from Kuwait. Similar crises in the future that occur once China has become a major importer might have a very different reaction from Beijing—one that would put China and the US on the same side in conflict management.

While it is true that China will increasingly compete for similar energy supplies with Japan, South Korea and India, that this will lead to increased tensions and conflict is not a foregone conclusion. The pragmatic realities of interdependence in Asia suggest that the prospects for cooperation on energy could well be brighter than they are for conflict, a prospect borne out by the West's energy insecurity experiences of the 1970s. Rather than compete with each other to garner improved individual access to restrained Middle East oil supply, the members of the NATO alliance and Japan formed the International Energy Agency (IEA) to jointly fund alternative energy research and to develop joint strategies for conservation, stockpiling and research and development of alternative energy sources.[58] The West learned quickly – a lesson that served it well during the 1990 Gulf crisis – that it could minimize the impact of supply disruptions from the Middle East by sharing resources in a coordinated fashion rather than by acting alone, militarily or otherwise.

More generally, common regional activities in the energy arena could foster both the formal structures and informal norms that could lead to broader cooperation in the region. The European Union, for example, began as a relatively modest exercise in economic cooperation between Germany and France. This is not to suggest any similar drive towards economic, but much less political, union will occur in East Asia. However, on the margin, even limited cooperation, if successful, can help create, as it did in Europe, a network of personal relationships and an ethos of consultation among traditionally suspicious governments.

Areas for cooperation on the energy front are numerous. The key Asian consumers can mimic (or possibly join in some fashion) the IEA systems by creating their own joint stockpiling and research organizations to create "win-win" situations (Japan is already jointly pursuing clean coal technologies with China, for example). Additionally, there is room for Northeast Asia to link energy infrastructure to create synergies and market efficiencies, as well as improve access to foreign capital. While political obstacles might be great, the experience of the Western Hemisphere is instructive on the benefits of international natural gas and shared electricity grids in improving access to supplies and lowering energy costs to consumers. Several grids have been proposed in Asia, including natural gas grids linking ASEAN countries, one linking Burma, Bangladesh and India, and another more ambitious scheme that would carry Russian oil and gas to Japan, China and the Korean peninsula. Russia's Irkutsk region is also investigating exporting spare hydroelectric power to Mongolia and Northern China.

Finally, there are also areas of cooperation in the realm of security. Accident, terrorism and piracy in important sea-lanes constitute real threats to all the importing countries of the region[59] and, in addition to the direct financial costs they impose, each raises the specter of an environmental disaster that could affect the whole region.[60] An outright expansion of security responsibilities might create tensions among nations as naval capabilities are expanded, but joint agreements on capture and prosecutions of outlaws and on environmental clean-up and emergency procedures could provide opportunities for confidence-building among the regional powers and garner tangible benefits to the security of sea-lanes.

4

Regulation and Deregulation of Energy in the Asian Market: The Case of China

Philip Andrews-Speed

L iberalization continues to be presented as the most effective means of addressing the many problems and challenges facing energy sectors across the world. Liberalization, in its fullest sense, comprises four main reforms:

- A change in the structure of the energy industry
- A change in the ownership of the energy companies
- A change in the structure and function of government
- The development of energy markets

Whilst any one of these reforms may be implemented in isolation, the full benefits of liberalization can only be realized if all four are implemented in a well-structured manner, and if certain other pre-conditions are satisfied. For example, privatization alone will bring no benefits without competition, and competition cannot be introduced to power generation if the transmission infrastructure is poorly developed.

Even if the supposed benefits of liberalization are accepted in principle, Asian governments face a number of difficult questions: Will the long-term economic benefits of liberalization outweigh short-term potential political losses? How should liberalization be structured? When and how fast should liberalization be implemented?

The countries of Asia are too diverse for any single package of answers to be relevant, but the questions they face have certain similarities. The aim of this chapter is to examine the rationale behind energy liberalization, to identify the main risks and obstacles to successful implementation and then to explore these issues using the case of the People's Republic of China.

The Energy Sectors of Asian Countries

At the risk of gross oversimplification, a number of generalities may be made about the energy sectors of most Asian[1] countries today. These relate to the growing imbalance between energy supply and demand, the special nature of energy in policy making, the role of state-owned companies, and a range of short and long-term challenges facing the energy sectors.

The primary energy resources of Asian countries vary from very large, such as in Russia, China, Malaysia, Indonesia and Kazakhstan, to very small, such as Japan and Korea. One common feature is that the proven and probable commercially recoverable reserves of primary energy in most Asian countries are insufficient to satisfy growing domestic demand over the next twenty years.[2] Japan and Korea have long imported most of their energy requirements. China has recently become a net importer of energy. Indonesia is set to become a net importer of oil, though exports of coal and gas may compensate. Indeed the whole of South and East Asia will soon become a major focus for oil exports from the Middle East, whilst many countries in the region will be importing gas from Russia, Central Asia and the Middle East. Only a small number of countries will have a comfortable excess of primary energy supply, for example Russia, Kazakhstan, Azerbaijan and Turkmenistan.

This actual or potential shortage of domestic sources of primary energy may take three forms: an overall shortage of domestic energy resources; a shortage of energy resources useable in the transport sector (currently oil); and a shortage of clean forms of energy such as gas. In response to this perceived threat to the security of energy supply, governments have been taking a number of measures from promoting the development of domestic

[144]

energy resources, to building closer links with oil exporters and considering the substitution of domestic coal with imported natural gas.

Energy has been perceived as a special commodity by most Asian governments, whether they have been energy importers or exporters. Until recently most energy production, conversion, transmission, distribution and retailing of energy has been controlled by governments through their ownership of energy companies, and through the integration of corporate policy with government policy. Energy policy was dominated by political and social concerns rather than by economic concerns. Customers paid prices which were below long-run marginal cost or did not pay at all, state energy companies lost money and falling investment rendered the energy supply progressively less reliable.

The state-owned companies are a major economic and political force in most Asian countries, regardless of their economic performance. In most cases a single company controls the production and supply of oil and gas, coal and electricity respectively. They control vast revenues and assets, employ large numbers of people, and have the rest of the national economy dependent on them. Their ostensible role is to act in the interests of the people and on behalf of the government. In reality, state energy companies have their own interests, and have the power to wield undue influence over governments, thus distorting the policy-making and the policy implementation processes. Though most state energy companies are inefficient and lose money, a few have managed to attain a higher level of technical, managerial and financial performance. Their success may gain them even greater power to influence government policy.

A number of countries around the world have embarked on programs of reform in order to promote investment, to improve technical performance and the productive efficiency of energy companies, and to enhance end-use energy efficiency. These reforms have included variously the restructuring and privatization of state energy companies, the introduction of competition, the promotion of foreign investment, and the raising of energy prices to end-users.

Most Asian governments have been reluctant to rush headlong down the path of wholesale energy liberalization, for a number of reasons: a lack of ideological commitment; a fear of the consequences of inadequate liberalization; an unwillingness to lose control of a key sector of the economy; and the scale of resistance, especially from the state companies. As a result, substantial liberalization has taken place in few Asian countries.

In the petroleum sector, competition has been introduced in the retailing of petroleum products in a number of countries. However, the exploration and production of oil and gas remains firmly in the hands of state companies, though many countries have long-standing arrangements to permit foreign companies to exploit these resources in partnership with the state companies.

In recent years a number of Asian countries have allowed a limited amount of investment by foreign companies in electrical power generation. Many, but not all, of these investments have encountered severe problems with the stability of terms in the offtake agreements. The distribution and retailing of electricity and gas remains in the hands of monopolies, usually owned by local government. Governments of Asian countries face a number of challenges as they evaluate the need to reform their energy sectors:

- How can the use of domestic energy resources be maximized in a cost-effective manner?
- How can the efficiency of energy production, processing, transmission and consumption be improved?
- How can the level of investment in the energy industry be raised at the same time as reducing the need for government financing?
- How can the security of energy supply be enhanced?
- How can the local and regional environment be protected as energy supply and consumption rise?
- How can social equity concerns be addressed?

Governments have a choice. They can continue with state ownership and state control, and seek ways to raise the performance of the energy sector through incremental measures at the margin such as raising the quality of policy-making, improving the incentives for state companies, and allowing small amounts of private investment in selected projects.

Alternatively, they can embark on a program of progressive liberalization. The first approach carries few risks and may yield some short-term benefits. The second approach has many dangers, as Brazil and California have discovered recently, but it also holds the potential for substantial long-term benefits if the process is planned and implemented with case. Successful liberalization requires the government to have a clear understanding of a wide range of economic and technical issues, in order to develop a strategy that is appropriate to the political and economic structure of the country.

The Fundamentals of Energy Liberalization

The key components of the economic rationale behind liberalization of the energy sector vary little across the world. What does vary is the balance of emphasis between these components. Further, these economic imperatives are frequently clouded and overwhelmed by political motives.

This section addresses the fundamentals of energy liberalization whether in a developed, transition or developing state. First, it examines what features of the energy sector distinguish it from other industries. Second, it addresses the reasons why the energy sector should be liberalized, and third, it examines the risks inherent in any liberalization program.

Is Energy Special?

Before embarking on a discussion of the fundamentals of energy liberalization, it is worthwhile recalling why energy is distinct from most other industries in this context. From the point of view of the investor, energy projects are commonly characterized by higher capital investment, longer lead times and pay back periods, larger risks and greater market uncertainties than conventional manufacturing.[3]

From the point of view of government and society, four aspects of energy distinguish it from other sectors of the economy: the critical importance of energy to modern society; the ownership of primary energy resources in the ground by the nation; the negative externalities of many

[147]

forms of energy production and consumption; and the network-bound nature of much energy transportation.[4] The first two factors mean that most governments are bound to pay great deal of attention to domestic energy production and consumption. They are unlikely to be willing to liberalize the sector unless clear net benefits can be identified, and unless it is evident that the nation's security of energy supply will not be damaged. The range and scale of negative externalities associated with energy, particularly environmental, require governments to pay close attention to putting in place regulatory and fiscal measures to minimize or mitigate these externalities. Finally, the transportation of electricity and gas is largely constrained to fixed networks, which may be regarded as natural monopolies. This constrains how governments may liberalize these industries and provides regulators with substantial challenges as they seek to promote competition. As micropower and the spot LNG markets develop, the market power of these transmission monopolies should be dented.

For these reasons, energy is usually one of the last sectors to be liberalized in any economy, though oil, coal and the production of gas commonly precede electricity and gas distribution and retailing by several years. Even after liberalization, governments still retain the right and the willingness to control, regulate or influence the energy sector to a much greater degree than most other industries.

Why Liberalize the Energy Sector?

The question of why energy industries should be liberalized can be addressed by looking at two components of the question:

- What are the problems of government ownership and control of the energy sector?
- What are the intended advantages of liberalization?

The Problems of Government Ownership and Control

In a perfect world, an omniscient, prescient and benevolent government, holding only the interests of its citizens in mind, might indeed do a very good job of owning and managing the energy sector. The main reasons why this has not happened in practice, may be considered under three headings: political, managerial and economic.

Whether or not a government is democratically elected, it has a monopoly on power and has access to most or all of the tax revenues.[5] In order to maintain that power, most governments take decisions based on relatively short-term considerations in order to gain votes (in the case of democracies) or in order to placate key interest groups. Thus governments are unable or unwilling to identify and act in the true public interest, not least because of the amount of information and work which would be required to define this public interest. Thus government actions tend to be driven by the needs of the ruling party, the ambitions of the leading individuals in the government and by powerful vested interests. In this last group, energy producers are generally more powerful than energy consumers.

The managerial argument has two main features. First, energy industries and markets are too complex for any single organization to gather, analyze and understand all the information required to forecast, plan and manage in a timely manner. Second, and following on from this, most governments face great difficulties persuading state companies to act in the interests of the government, let alone in the interests of the country. This is the familiar 'principal-agent' problem, which is enhanced by the asymmetry between the relatively well informed energy companies and the significantly less well-informed government.[6]

Setting aside the theoretical economic arguments, we can readily identify a number of economic symptoms of inadequate government management of the state-controlled energy sectors. The one that drives many governments to privatization is the sheer cost of the energy companies.[7] This cost usually takes the form either of large government subsidies to the companies or of high energy prices to consumers. Government ownership and control of the energy sector may be justified by the need to enhance the security of energy supply for the country. In most cases the opposite is true. Over-dependence on a single supplier, mismanagement of policy and systems and barriers to entry by new investors have reduced the level of energy security.[8]

These and other considerations lay behind the ideological drive for privatization and market liberalization, based on a school of thought which declared that political, economic and social freedom are inseparable. As a result, the government's role in economic activity should be reduced to that of rule maker and referee.[9] These ideas formed the basis for the political drive to privatization, which first emerged in a sustained way in Britain in the 1980s. The government saw the privatization of the state monopolies as a critical step in removing the stranglehold the state held over business and domestic life in Britain. Further, it would reduce the power of the labor unions. By offering the companies for public sale the government intended and succeeded in creating a new class of shareholding voters.[10]

The Intended Advantages of Liberalization

Liberalization programs are necessarily launched by governments and, therefore, political objectives are likely to be inherent in nearly all cases. In any state, narrow political motives may include the desire on the part of the senior government ministers to seek personal financial benefits or to reward political allies at the time of asset sales, or to attack vested interests associated with the industry, such as unions or sate company officials. Especially in countries taking rapid strides from a planned to a market economy, liberalization, and associated privatization, are perceived as key steps in the process of introducing democracy, enhancing personal freedoms and property rights and explicitly reducing the role of government.[11]

Aside from these political drivers, the intended advantages of privatization of state industries and the liberalization of markets fall into three main categories: economic, managerial and financial.

The key economic motive for privatization and liberalization is to improve the productive and allocative efficiency of the industry concerned. In principle, if the privatization of a state monopoly is accompanied by the liberalization of the market, the privatized company will be forced to compete for business. In order to survive it has to improve its own productive efficiency and to keep prices close to market levels, thus improving allocative efficiency. At the same time, consumers will have to pay the full cost of energy. The new company should be freed from having purely social objectives, offer a higher quality of service and have greater incentives for innovation.[12]

Managerial motives are threefold. The first and most important is the need to stop the government interfering in the management of the company. The social and quota-driven goals should, in principle, be changed to economic ones.[13] Second, government decree and patronage would be replaced by market incentives for company management. The pressure for good performance should come from shareholders and from the threat of bankruptcy or take-over.[14] Finally, the privatization process may permit the break-up of large, unwieldy, over-centralized industrial empires. Peripheral components can be sold and the company can have the opportunity to focus on its core business.[15]

A successful privatization and liberalization program can improve the financial position of both the government and the company. In the short term the government is relieved of the need to subsidize a loss-making entity and should raise money from the sale.[16] However, if the state company is losing money, the proceeds from the sale are likely to be modest unless the fixed assets are of value in themselves. The government may face the choice of either investing money and effort itself to make the company profitable before selling it or disposing of it at a knock-down price. The company gains from privatization because, freed from social objectives, it should now find it easier to raise loans for financing capital projects. Before privatization the main source of funding was the government, which may have become unable or unwilling to invest the money itself.[17]

Other financial and economic benefits may accrue. The budget deficit should decline along with the need to subsidize loss-making enterprises, and thus the pressures on inflation are reduced.[18] If the privatized company increases its profitability, the government's tax revenue will increase. Successful liberalization should lead to increased level of investment in the energy sector from the newly privatized companies as well as from new entrants.[19] If foreign companies purchase part or all of the state entity, the foreign exchange reserves are boosted. Finally, public flotation can help the domestic stock markets develop.

Addressing the Risks of Liberalization

The liberalization of the energy sector in any country is accompanied by significant risks, because of the critical role of energy in the national economy and in daily life. The energy crises in California and Brazil during the year 2001 illustrated the consequences of poorly planned or executed liberalization. [20]

Markets are inherently unpredictable. Therefore governments must accept that it is not possible to predict the future development of the energy sector after it is privatized and liberalized.[21] The ownership and structure of the industry may evolve in just a few years to bear little resemblance to that of privatization, and deregulated energy prices will, by definition, be at the mercy of market forces, local, national and international. In addition, even those who propound the benefits of energy liberalization concede that it is very difficult to predict how the benefits are shared around the various parties.[22]

The uncertainty that follows liberalization is not the key risk. The main consideration for governments is whether the process of liberalization, the initial conditions for liberalization, and the policy and regulatory actions after liberalization allow the intended public gains to be realized.

The Risks

The risks that threaten the liberalization process in any country may be grouped into four types. If realized, any one of these risks would be sufficient to substantially reduce the success of the reform program. However, as each of the risks has a strong political element, they are likely to be interlinked and to materialize in association with the others.

The first is the risk that the process is deliberately distorted by vested interests. These interest groups may include politicians, the military, and managers and workers in the energy companies. Such parties stand to lose power, influence, revenue and even livelihoods. One or more of these can

[152]

conspire to manipulate the liberalization process either for short-term or long-term gain. Two common outcomes of privatization are that companies are sold at too low a price to favored parties, or that companies are being sold with their monopoly power intact in order to realize a high price or in order to pass that monopoly power to favored parties. The privatization of the UK gas industry is a prime example of a hasty, ill-conceived action. The state gas company was privatized a whole, as a vertically integrated company. Years of vigorous regulatory action were required to develop a competitive market.[23] In some countries, privatization has been entirely spontaneous and fundamentally illegal, with little or no payment for the assets.[24]

The second risk is that the legal framework and institutional structures of the country are inadequate to allow the newly formed energy markets to function effectively.[25] Under such conditions an old monopolist may retain or regain market power, or a new monopolist or an oligopoly may emerge. Consequently, the intended gains of higher productivity and downward pressure on prices are not realized.

A third risk concerns the policy framework of government at or after privatization. As discussed above, no government will leave the energy sector entirely to its own devices. The danger arises when governments seek to unduly interfere in the operation of energy markets either at the stage when the initial conditions are set or later after liberalization. For example, governments may regulate consumer prices so that they become detached from wholesale prices, as has happened in California, or they may fail to bring down barriers to entry for new investors. At a larger scale, governments commonly fail to develop a coherent approach to energy policy, particularly with respect to the links between different fuels and between energy and the environment. A good example of this deficiency has been the failure of successive UK governments to effectively address the challenges facing the nuclear industry.[26] Liberalization policies for the different energy industries (oil, gas, coal and power) have to be developed in a coordinated manner. If not, either the remaining state-controlled industry or the newly liberalized industry will suffer substantial financial losses. Likewise, over-ambitious environmental or planning regulations may prevent the necessary private capital being invested in new infrastructure, as has happened in California.

The final risk relates to the power and ability of the regulatory agency. No liberalization program can be perfectly designed and executed. Flaws will emerge for several years after the launch. It is absolutely critical that the regulatory agency or agencies have the political power, the will, the expertise and the manpower to recognize the flaws and to act promptly to remedy these flaws. An important lesson to draw from the experience of the United Kingdom is that a determined regulator can rescue a botched privatization.[27] However, at the time of the UK gas privatization it could not have been known that the regulator would have been successful in the introduction of competition. It was an implicit risk in the liberalization process.

The Key Elements and Pre-Conditions for Successful Liberalization

The government should formulate and publicize a clear plan for the liberalization of its energy industries, for three reasons. First, a coherent plan is needed for its own sake in order that the liberalization process can be structured in such a way as to minimize the risks and to maximize the public benefits. Second, confidence needs to be instilled in potential investors, especially foreign ones.[28] Third, the government can use the plan in its effort to promote public understanding and to reduce political opposition.[29]

Of paramount importance is the need for a clear and appropriate legal and institutional framework.[30] Where absent, laws on title, property rights, sanctity of contract, bankruptcy and competition should be put in place.[31] Within the government the roles of policy making and regulation should be separated, and the responsibility for economic regulation should be assigned to a regulatory agency. The main job of this agency will be to promote competition in the new market and to prevent the privatized industry committing a number of regulatory offences, both economic and social.[32] Of these the most important are high or predatory pricing, excessive profits, restricting access to facilities or resources, and providing poor service.

Much has been written about the prerequisites for effective regulation and on comparing the US and British systems of regulation. Despite differences of opinion, a number of common themes appear. The regulatory body must have the appropriate expertise, be independent of both the government and the industry, have the necessary authority and have access to the required commercial information. The regulator must take into account the interests of the government, the consumers and of the industry, and an appeal system must exist to prevent the regulatory agency abusing its powers.[33]

Effective regulation is, arguably, the most important prerequisite for energy liberalization. Yet all governments face the challenge of designing a regulatory system which is consistent with the existing institutional structure and behavioral norms of the country, which is suited to the structure of the liberalized industry, and which can be adequately staffed.[34]

Another challenging issue for developing countries is that of social equity. A large-scale program of privatization, or even just one of corporatization and commercialization, forces the government to take the responsibility for many aspects of social welfare that were previously shouldered by the companies. This may include unemployment payments, hospitals and schools. If the government has not established alternative means to deliver these services, which in a few cases may be provided by the private sector, then the resistance to reform and the social cost after reform will be great.

Finally, it should not be forgotten that energy is a highly technical industry. It is dependent on the application of appropriate technologies and on the construction of capital-intensive plant and networks. The capacity and capability of the plant and infrastructure is a key consideration in any energy reform program, especially if domestic energy demand is growing rapidly. The nature and state of the tangible assets will directly impact the sale value of any company on privatization. More importantly, it will effect the speed with which competition may be introduced, particularly for the network-bound industries of gas and electricity. In simple terms, competition cannot emerge if demand exceeds supply or if the transport infrastructure cannot deliver the available energy to the customers who are willing to pay for it.

The Case of the People's Republic of China

Recent Developments in the Energy Sector

China's Increasing Imbalance between Energy Supply and Demand

China's economic growth and industrialization has required a prodigious increase in energy supply. Since 1980 the consumption of commercial energy has risen by approximately 250% (see Figure 4.1). This rise in demand for energy provided the government with a major challenge. It responded by introducing measures to raise the output of coal—the form of primary energy that was most readily accessible in China. China has the world's third largest reserves of coal in the world and has been the largest producer of coal since 1991 when it overtook the USA.[35] From 1980 to 1990 the contribution of coal to China's energy sector rose from 72% to 76% (see Table 4.1). At the same time the government invested heavily in hydro-electricity and, to a lesser extent, in nuclear power. The output of crude oil and natural gas also rose, but their relative share of energy consumption declined. The balance between the supply and demand for primary energy stayed roughly in balance until the mid-1990s. Indeed China used to be a net exporter of both oil and coal.

Figure 4.1
Energy Supply and Demand, 1980-1999
(in million tons of oil equivalent)

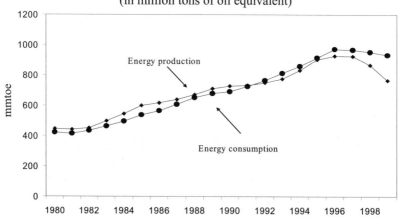

Source: Sinton and Fridley (2000).

Table 4.1

Structure of Primary Energy Consumption, 1980-1999

	1980	1985	1990	1995	1999
Coal	72.3 %	75.9 %	76.1 %	74.7 %	70.6 %
Oil	20.9 %	17.0 %	16.6 %	17.4 %	20.7 %
Natural gas	2.8 %	2.2 %	2.1 %	1.8 %	2.3 %
Primary electricity	4.0 %	4.9 %	5.2 %	6.0 %	6.4 %

Source: Sinton and Fridley (2000).

The ability of China to provide for most of its own energy requirements from domestic sources has depended as much on increasing the efficiency of energy use as on producing more energy. Though still high by the standards of developing countries, China's energy intensity has declined substantially during the last twenty years.[36] Two factors have contributed to this reduction of energy intensity. First, the structure of the economy has changed. The role of the service sector has grown, whilst the balance between heavy and light industry is generally shifting towards light industry. Second, the government has introduced a wide range of measures to increase the efficiency of energy end-use.

The middle and late 1990s saw two dramatic changes in the balance of energy supply and demand. The first change occurred in 1993 when China's consumption of oil exceeded its domestic production for the first time (see Figure 4.2). From being one of the world's major net exporters of oil, China was now a net importer, and the level of net imports has increased steadily since then. This situation has been caused by a substantial rise in the demand for oil products, mainly for transportation purposes, combined with a failure to raise significantly the level of domestic oil production.

[157]

Figure 4.2
China Oil Supply and Demand, 1980-2001
(in millions of tons)

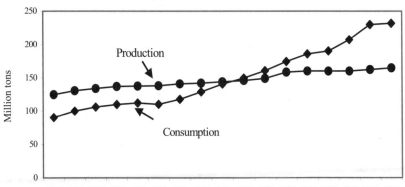

Source: *BP Statistical Review of World Energy* for various years.

The second hiatus occurred in 1998 and 1999 when energy consumption in China fell for two successive years (See Figure 4.1). At the same time, stocks of coal had built up to record levels as a result of years of overproduction. In 1998 the Chinese government embarked on a program to cut back on coal production which has been sustained through at least the year 2001. This fall in energy demand is best explained by a combination of general economic slowdown related to the Asian crisis, a decline in output from energy-intensive industries, closures of inefficient state factories and a general increase of end-use efficiency,[37] as well as some substitution of coal by gas. At the same time the demand for oil and electricity flattened temporarily before picking up again in the year 2000.

Any projection of future total energy demand in China depends on a number of factors such as the rate of economic growth, the structure of the economy and level of end-use energy efficiency, each one of which is difficult to forecast. This difficulty is enhanced in the case of China by the government's ability to dramatically and suddenly change policy, and thus influence energy consumption to a greater degree than is possible in a market economy. Most projections envisage that China's primary energy consumption will increase by at least 200% during the twenty years to 2020, to at least 2,000 million tons of oil equivalent per year.[38] The

[158]

critical issue is the future energy mix rather than the absolute level of energy consumption. Recent trends and analyses suggest that the coming twenty years will see a rise in the proportion of oil and gas consumption at the expense of coal.[39]

The Future Growth of Oil and Gas Imports

Forecasting the level of imports of oil and gas involves the integration of two parameters, supply and demand, which are themselves fraught with uncertainty. Added to which is the ability of the Chinese government to vary the level of imports and exports and yet keep the level of net imports the same.

Forecasts of net oil imports in the year 2010 made by non-Chinese specialists lie close to 150 million metric tons, which is similar to the predicted level of crude oil production in China at that time.[40] Thus China would be importing some 50% of its oil requirements, compared to 20% in 1999. Figures for 2020 suggest that net imports could exceed 250 million tons, which would be more than 60% of demand. Chinese estimates of net imports are substantially lower. This reflects more optimistic forecasts for both domestic production and the government's ability to constrain demand for oil products. The main uncertainty with respect to net oil imports is the level of demand, since most analysts are confident that China's oil production has nearly reached a peak.

The 1990s saw China making a strategic shift in its sources of oil imports. In the early 1990s more than half of this trade came from the Asia-Pacific region, mainly Indonesia and Malaysia. As China became a net importer of oil it deliberately sought to raise the proportion of imports from the Middle East and other regions such as Africa and Latin America. However its ability to take Middle Eastern crude oil was constrained by the need to upgrade its refineries to take the sour crude which typifies the Gulf. Since 1997 China has established long-term supply arrangements with Gulf states such as Saudi Arabia, Iran, Oman and Yemen. This provides both sides with a sense of security—for supplies in the case of China and for sales in the case of the Gulf states. At the same time the Gulf states have been actively pressing the Chinese government to allow

[159]

them to construct refineries in China. Thus it is reasonable to assume that an increasing share of China's oil imports will be in the form of crude oil from the Gulf.

The Chinese government has placed great emphasis on the development of domestic gas resources. Production is set to rise from about 25 billion cubic meters (bcm) in the year 2000 to 50-70 bcm by 2010 and to 100 bcm or more by 2020.[41] Despite this effort, the government's ambitions to provide the cities with clean energy will require a substantial import of gas. The level of future natural gas imports to China will be critically dependent on the rate at which the infrastructure for imports is constructed, whether that be in the form of pipelines or LNG terminals. The LNG project currently under construction in Guangdong has a planned capacity of 6.5 bcm by 2010. Current forecasts of total gas imports are consistent with one major import pipeline project being operational by 2010 and a second by 2020, producing aggregate imports of about 25 bcm and 50 bcm respectively.

China's Evolving Energy Policy

The Chinese government's policy priorities for the sector are enunciated in five-year plans and then repeated in a range of formal and informal documents from officials at different levels. The strategic priorities for the Ministry of Energy in the early 1990s included the following:[42]

- Giving equal emphasis to energy exploitation and energy conservation
- Improving the energy consumption structure by enhancing the use of oil and gas
- Recognizing that coal would remain a predominant source of primary energy, but realizing that China would need a much greater supply of electrical power if its modernization was to continue
- Rationalizing both consumer and producer prices
- Increasing the efficiency of energy production and utilization

The Ninth Five-Year Plan (1996-2000) showed a number of significant changes of emphasis. The importance of energy conservation seemed now to outweigh that of energy exploitation. In the petroleum industry the new line was to stabilize output in the east of China and to develop new fields in the west, and at the same time increase the emphasis on exploration and production of natural gas. China had become a net importer of oil and the exploitation of overseas oil and gas resources was explicitly promoted. Other priorities included large-scale hydro-electricity projects (laying the ground for the approval of the Three Gorges Dam), renewable energy and coal-bed methane.[43]

The same priorities were repeated during the subsequent years with increasing emphasis on overseas investment in oil and gas, the development of a domestic gas industry, the construction of mine-mouth power plants to reduce the need to transport coal, and opening up the domestic energy sector to foreign investment. At the same time, international and domestic pressure raised the level of debate on pollution abatement and energy conservation.

By the end of the decade, the future reliance of China on substantial imports of oil and gas had become a central theme in energy policy statements and accounts, and this was reflected in the Tenth Five-Year Plan announced in 2001.[44] Oil imports had to rise to satisfy the rising demand, mainly for the transportation sector. Domestic and international pressure for the reduction in the use of coal was driving the plans for a dramatic increase in the use of gas, much of which would have to be imported. However a determination to maximize the use of domestic resources, almost regardless of cost is clearly evident in the decision to build a gas pipeline from the Tarim basin in the far northwest of the country to Shanghai in the east.

Energy, particularly oil and gas, is clearly viewed as having strategic importance. The use of overseas resources was once again emphasized, along with a rather belated call for the construction of a strategic oil reserve. Researchers, rather than officials, have emphasized the need for a fundamental change in approach to energy policy, urging the government to introduce market mechanisms in the Chinese energy sector and to seek greater integration with the regional and international energy markets.[45]

The Ever Changing Structure of the Energy Sector

THE GOVERNMENT

China's energy sector has undergone a number of fundamental re-organizations since 1980, the last of which took place in 1998. The structure of the energy sector on the eve of the 1998 reforms had been in place since 1993, when the short-lived Ministry of Energy was abolished.

In the mid-1990s the structure of government for the energy sector, and indeed for many other industrial sectors, was very simple. The State Planning Commission (SPC), reporting to the State Council, stood at the pinnacle of the hierarchy and was effectively responsible for energy policy. The other two relevant Commissions, the State Economic and Trade Commission (SETC) and State Science and Technology Commission (SSTC), though nominally equal with the SPC, played relatively minor and subordinate roles in the energy sector (see Figure 4.3).

Each of the main energy industries was dominated by a single institution, which was either a state corporation or a Ministry: CNPC for petroleum exploration and production; Sinopec for oil refining and distribution; the Ministry of Electric Power; and the Ministry of Coal Industries.[46] These large institutions dominated their respective industries for two reasons: first, their sheer size and second, their dual role as government organ and commercial enterprise. These institutions were involved in policy formulation, regulation and enterprise management, though certain regulatory tasks such as investment approval and pricing were retained by the SPC.

The reforms of 1998 resulted in three major changes to the government structure in the energy sector.[47] First, the function of enterprise management was nominally removed from the government and assigned to the energy companies themselves. Second, the SETC, for the first time, was given an apparently important position in the energy sector. The previous Chief Executive of Sinopec was appointed Chairman of the SETC. Third, a new ministry was created, the Ministry of Land and Natural Resources (MLNR), to administer land use. The previous Chief Executive of CNPC was appointed Minister.

[162]

Figure 4.3
Schematic Summary of China's Energy Sector Structure
Before and After the 1998 Reforms

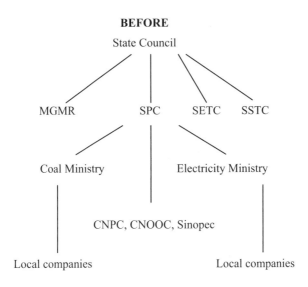

BEFORE

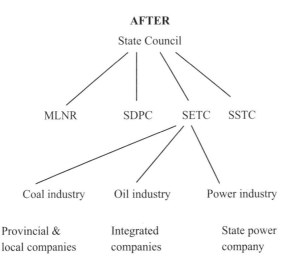

AFTER

Source: Author.

The petroleum industry was now regulated by at least four bodies: the Price Administrative Department of the SDPC; the Transport and Energy Department of the SDPC; the State Administration for Petroleum and Chemical Industries of the SETC; and the new Ministry of Land and Natural Resources (MLNR).

What was never satisfactorily resolved was the intended function of the SETC. Two new energy bureaus were created within the SETC, for petroleum and petrochemicals and for coal, and a new department for the power industry was set up. Each of these offices took responsibility for its particular industry. The precise scope of these responsibilities was never clear, though they appeared to include policy and regulatory tasks, as well as, possibly, enterprise management. The SPC (then renamed the State Development Planning Commission, SDPC) was clearly reluctant to relinquish some of its long held responsibilities and this led to an overlap of responsibilities and duties with the SETC.

The 'power struggle' between the SDPC and SETC took one step forward late in the year 2000 when a number of administrative bureaus of the SETC were abolished thus, presumably, confirming the predominant position of the SDPC in these sectors, including petroleum and coal.

THE PETROLEUM INDUSTRY

China's petroleum industry has been dominated in recent years by two state companies: CNPC which was responsible for onshore oil and gas exploration and production; and Sinopec which undertook much of the oil refining and distribution. Both organizations combined the roles of government and enterprise management. Other Chinese players have included: the Ministry of Chemical Industries; China National Offshore Oil Corporation (CNOOC); Sinochem the official international oil trader; two joint-venture trading companies, Unipec and China Oil; and the newly created China National Star Petroleum Corporation (CNSPC).[48]

The financial performance of China's oil companies depended to a great extent on the domestic price of oil, which was set at irregular intervals by the SPC. In the late 1980s and early 1990s the domestic prices for crude oil and oil products were raised from very low levels to rough equivalence to international prices. As a result, the profits of the upstream operator, CNPC, rose dramatically, while those of the downstream operator, Sinopec, stagnated.[49]

For the petroleum sector, the restructuring of 1998 involved two key components. First, as discussed above, the government functions were removed from the state companies and placed with the SETC. Second, the assets of CNPC and Sinopec were redistributed to create two regional, vertically integrated companies that spanned the full range of activities from exploration through refining to marketing. CNPC's assets now lie in the north and west of the country while Sinopec's assets lie in the south and east.

A further innovation was in the field of pricing. From now on domestic oil prices would be linked directly to international prices through a formula set by the SDPC. As international prices fluctuated, domestic prices would follow automatically. From the summer of 1998 domestic prices were only marginally above international levels.[50]

The nature of this restructuring appears to be based on three objectives specific to the oil industry: to remove the need for incessant lobbying by the upstream and downstream companies concerning the level of domestic oil price; to provide a stronger basis for China's oil companies to compete internationally; and to encourage competition within China.

The first of these objectives has clearly been achieved. Both CNPC and Sinopec now have upstream and downstream assets and are more able to cope with fluctuations in the international and domestic prices of oil.[51]

The ambition for China's two largest oil companies to become major players on the international stage is potentially realizable. However, size alone is not sufficient. A major improvement in technical, managerial and financial performance is required. The reforms to the national system for oil prices mark a significant step forward to provide incentives to the Chinese state oil companies to improve their performance.

The government's desire to develop a framework for domestic competition in the petroleum sector is laudable. Only with competition at home will CNPC and Sinopec develop the skills to compete overseas without subsidy. However, the government's vision of the nature of domestic competition is still far from clear. Certainly the two oil companies have to trade crude oil and oil products because of the geographical imbalance of oil reserves, refining capacity and markets in the country. The issue that does not seem to have been addressed is whether one oil company may invest and conduct exploration, production, refining or distribution in the other's territory. Competition in the retailing of oil products has emerged in the last three years, but not in other parts of the industry. Unless the government takes steps to promote such competition, also involving other oil companies, one possible outcome is that these two large oil companies will collude as a cartel rather than compete.

Further modifications to the structure of the three main players (CNPC, Sinopec and CNOOC) were implemented in preparation for their Initial Public Offerings (IPOs) in 2000 and 2001. It was necessary to separate productive assets, which could be included in the company to be offered, from unproductive or controversial assets that would remain with the holding company. In the case of CNPC productive assets in China were included in PetroChina, the vehicle for the IPO, whilst unproductive assets and the overseas investments were held in the hands of CNPC which remained the holding company. In July 2001 all three companies announced profits for the year 2000 which ranged from 150% to 400% of the previous year. The main contribution came from higher oil prices, but substantial cost-cutting measures also played an important role.

THE ELECTRICAL POWER INDUSTRY

Before 1997 the Ministry of Electric Power (MOEP) acted as policy-maker, regulator and enterprise manager for most of China's power industry. Under the MOEP the provincial power bureaus held monopoly power over transmission, distribution and supply within their respective areas. Some of these bureaus were consolidated into regional Power Groups for the purpose of inter-province transmission of power. In 1997, the State Power Corporation of China (SPCC) was established to take over the enterprise management functions from the MOEP. The provincial and lower level bureaus were renamed companies.

The reforms of 1998 resulted in little outward change except for the abolition of the Ministry of Electric Power and the transfer of its government functions to the SETC. Within the State Power Corporation a number of measures have been started such as the corporatization of provincial companies, the progressive separation of generation from transmission, and the corporatization of generation enterprises in selected provinces. In addition a number of experiments in "competition in generation" were introduced in six provinces during the year 2000. These trials involved only a small proportion of the total power sold, and seemed to be run in a fairly *ad hoc* manner.

Although these measures have led to some improvements in the performance of China's power sector, they do not amount to a sustained program of reform. Firstly there appears to be no overall long-term strategic plan for the reform, other than in very general terms. Second, the reforms appear to be driven more by the State Power Company than by the central government.

FOREIGN INVESTMENT

Foreign direct investors can play an important role in promoting competition and in raising the level of technical and financial performance of the domestic companies, regardless of the industry. To date, foreign investment in China's energy sector has been limited to the margins.

The greatest amount of activity has been in offshore oil and gas exploration and production, which commenced in the early 1980s. Foreign involvement in onshore exploration started slowly in the mdi-1980s and picked up slightly in the mid-1990s as more acreage became available. However, levels of interest have remained low because of the nature of the acreage on offer and the administrative obstacles.[52]

In the mid-1990s the Chinese government and foreign players saw great potential for foreign investment in power generation. Despite the rapid growth in the demand for power, the level of foreign investment has been substantially lower than expected, because of a range of policy, legal and regulatory concerns on the part of the potential investors.[53]

In other activities such as the retailing of oil products, oil refining and petrochemicals, and gas transportation, the first significant steps towards modest foreign involvement have only been taken in the last two or three years.

Challenges Facing China's Energy Sector

The over-riding energy challenge facing the government is that of energy security—securing an adequate supply of energy to sustain economic growth, but at a reasonable cost to the country and the consumers.[54] Five main categories of constraints may be identified:[55]

- *A shortage of domestic primary energy resources*: China's reserves of oil and gas are small relative to its likely future demand, as discussed above. Reserves of coal and hydro-electricity are large. However, exploitation of both has a substantial negative environmental impact.

- *A geographic mismatch between the location of primary energy resources and the main centers of demand*: Indeed, local shortages of energy have generally been caused by problems of inadequate transportation infrastructure rather than by an absolute shortage of energy resources.

- *Inefficient production and transformation of energy resources*: This fundamental weakness permeates all China's energy production industries, and relates to technological and skill deficiencies, poor management and regulatory systems, and a general lack of financial incentives to improve.

- *Inefficient end-use of energy*: Energy users can only improve the efficiency with which they consume energy if they have access to appropriate technologies and information and have financial and

[168]

regulatory incentives. Though China has taken great strides in this field, much remains to be done in order to sustain this improvement.

- *Pollution through the transformation and end-use of coal:* Coal will continue to provide more than 50% of China's primary energy supply for the foreseeable future. The use of clean-coal technology and the substitution of coal by natural gas and by primary electricity requires a sustained program of incentives and capital investment.

During the last ten to fifteen years the Chinese government has taken steps to address these challenges and substantial progress has been made on a number of fronts. Yet, a number of unresolved dilemmas remain.

A substantial mismatch exists between the energy consumers and the energy producers. The consumers increasingly lie in the unplanned, market-driven part of the economy, whilst the energy producers are still mainly in the hands of the state, either at central or provincial levels, and are subject to planning controls as well as structural inefficiencies which may be found in state companies anywhere in the world. Though steps have been taken to improve the technical, managerial and financial performance of these state enterprises, this improvement may not be sustainable without more radical restructuring of both the industry and the markets.[56]

This mismatch is further emphasized by the political power of the energy producers compared to the consumers. The reforms of 1998 which nominally separated enterprises from government, in fact passed a great deal of power to the state energy companies and left the government departments without the skills and the manpower to carry out their rightful functions.[57] Thus the state energy companies who are the producers, transformers and transporters of energy, would appear to have a greater role to play in the formation of energy policy than either the government or the energy users.

Despite the array of strategic objectives announced for the energy sector during the 1990s, there was no evidence of either coherence of these objectives or of well-considered means by which these objectives could be achieved.[58] Part of the cause for this may lie with the lack of real authority held by the Ministry of Energy during its short life, and the lack of any replacement institution once the Ministry was abolished in 1993. Again, the state companies have held the power, and objectives have been set largely on an individual industry-basis, rather than sector-wide. The vested interests of the state companies probably explains why steps to develop competition have been half-hearted at best.

Another dilemma facing the Chinese government is that of implementing energy policy. The problem of policy implementation affects most sectors of the economy. At least three causes may be identified. First, staffing levels in the civil service have been drastically reduced. The reform of the energy sector requires substantial government involvement, for which manpower and expertise is needed.[59] Second, the existence of multiple tiers of government in China (central, province, city, county) in the absence of a formal federal constitution provides ample scope for obstruction and obfuscation.[60] Finally, the power of the judiciary and other legal and regulatory institutions, though being gradually enhanced, is still insufficient for it to play a major role in a sector dominated by major state companies. These considerations raise two important questions:

- To what extent can the performance of the energy sector continue to be improved without radical reform and liberalization?
- What are the prospects for liberalization of the energy sector in China?

The Prospects for Liberalization of the Energy Sector in China

Given that China is not undergoing a radical political transformation, the political and ideological arguments in favor of liberalization of the energy sector are likely to be subordinate to the economic arguments. Most of the economic, managerial and financial motives for liberalization presented earlier in this chapter would accordingly be applicable to China's energy sector.

The most persuasive arguments are those which can be invoked to support the liberalization of any state enterprise in a developing or transition economy.[61] At the top of the list will come the need to remove government from the management of energy enterprises and to improve the productive efficiency and financial performance of the sector. The desire to reduce the financial burden on the government due to ailing state enterprises and to attract private investment will also rank high. Consumer concerns may not be at the forefront of the policy makers. Though enhanced investment should result in an improved quality of service, this may come at a higher rather than a lower price.

Obstacles to Liberalization

Despite the impatience of many and domestic external advisers to push ahead with a radical program of liberalization of China's energy sector, the spectrum of obstacles ranged against such a policy are formidable.

OUTRIGHT RESISTANCE

In China, as in many developing countries, the ideological drive for privatization is absent. Socialism and nationalism are too deeply ingrained in the population to be removed quickly. Political motivation is likely to be even less well developed. In a one-party state like China, the government will find it difficult to resist the urge to control as much economic activity as possible.

In such a situation, the ownership of major state enterprises, such as the energy companies, gives the government control over many aspects of life in China. Indeed, the political survival of the communist party may depend on maintaining such control. Complementing the lack of ideological drive is a very reasonable fear of the social and economic consequences of a poorly conceived and implemented liberalization program.

In society at large, resistance to wholesale privatization and liberalization may come from a number of quarters. The strongest and most open will be from the workers in these industries who fear for their livelihoods. Job security has been a central pillar of the communist state in China. The cracking of the "iron rice bowl" has not been welcomed in the large state enterprises.

POTENTIAL FOR ABUSE

The second type of obstacle to success comes in the form of forces that threaten to distort the process of liberalization. In a state with only one political party and lacking many key democratic institutions, the likelihood of manipulation for personal gain by those in power is significant. In China, the potential culprits probably lie in the central government, in the state companies and in the provincial governments.

In such a setting, a major program of privatization would have to be very carefully structured and monitored in order to prevent control of the privatized utilities from falling into the hands of one or the other component of the ruling elite.

LEGAL AND INSTITUTIONAL FRAMEWORKS

The most formidable and intractable obstacles to successful liberalization of the energy sector in China lie in the legal and institutional structures of the country. Despite substantial progress in the last two decades, there remains a long way to go on a number of points:

- China lacks an independent judiciary, and appropriate laws on competition and property rights. Contracts are unenforceable and the laws on bankruptcy are in their infancy. No system of monopoly regulation presently exists.
- The government presently lacks any single agency with substantial manpower and authority to formulate a coherent energy policy and a coherent strategy for reform of the energy sector.
- A multi-tiered system of government (Central, Provincial, City and County) is clearly necessary in such a populous country as China. But the lack of a constitutionally based division of powers between the tiers results in a continuous and destructive rivalry between them.
- Poor accountancy standards, combined with a culture of confidentiality and inaccurate reporting, would make a regulator's task nearly impossible.

- The lack of a free press, of parliamentary accountability to the people, and of independent consumer organizations would give any monopolist ample opportunity to abuse its power.

These weaknesses are deeply rooted in the political and economic structure of the country, and constrain China's ability to reform many aspects of the economy, not just the energy sector.

A further challenge is more specific to energy, or rather to sectors like energy in which competition is intrinsically difficult to introduce. Robust regulation is the single most important requirement for ensuring that privatization and liberalization does indeed lead to the development of effective markets. It would be critical to establish a regulatory agency that both has the authority to carry out its mandate and has the necessary independence from both government and the major energy companies. China has no history of independent regulation. Indeed, the structure of government does not provide any room for independence. The government is dependent on the Communist Party, and the parliament ("National People's Congress") has little real independence from the organs of government. How any regulatory agency would be fit into the existing institutional structure is a major unresolved question.

SHORTAGE OF SKILLS

A large program of privatization and liberalization is a difficult undertaking. A high level of skill and experience is required in the government administration and in the supporting consultants, accountants and banks. Among Chinese citizens, these skills are in short supply, though the level of understanding is increasing rapidly.

Managing a privatized company in a free or even partly liberalized market is quite different from running a state company driven by quotas and social goals. In developed countries, a supply of private sector managers is available to take on the challenge of managing newly privatized industries. If necessary, the skills are imported from other countries. In China, not only have these skills not been developed, but the government is also unlikely to invite foreign managers to occupy key positions in their energy industries.

INFRASTRUCTURE

The deficiencies in China's energy infrastructure severely constrain the rate and manner in which liberalization can take place, especially in the gas and electricity industries. Substantial investment is needed in transmission networks for both gas and electricity, and in distribution grids for natural gas. The ability of gas producers and power generators to compete is presently constrained by three aspects of the networks: first, the transmission grids lack the overall capacity to deliver energy from where it is produced to where it is in demand; second, in the case of electricity, the poor design of the network results in congestion points, and poorly-sited power plants will be unable to dispatch, despite the existence of demand; and, third, gas distribution networks are almost non-existent in most cities.

The Need for a Strategy

The previous analysis has shown that China's energy industry faces a number of major challenges if the country's future energy needs are to be met without a substantial cost. The numerous reforms to both government and state companies in the past fifteen years have led to a sustained improvement of technical and financial performance of the energy industry, but these changes have been incremental and have appeared to lack any long-term vision or strategy.

Despite this apparent success, it is questionable whether such improvements can be sustained for many more years without a far-reaching program of reform. The inherent limitations of government ownership and control were outlined earlier in the paper. In China, the great power of the state energy companies exacerbates the "principal-agent" problem. The common practice of promoting chief executives of state companies to ministerial positions reduces the efficacy of any financial incentives based on the economic performance of the companies.

The soft budgetary constraints and lack of a transparent framework for the embryonic competition in the energy sector reduce the pressures on companies to perform.

The government has three options. First, it can continue to maintain control and ownership over most of the energy sector, introducing reforms at the margin when it is expedient to do so. The short-term risk is low. In the longer term, one risk is that the cost to the government rises as it continues to be obliged to provide financial support to the state energy companies, either through direct subsidies or as loans through the state banks. Alternatively, some of these enterprises may become more profitable and gain access to more diverse sources of funding. In the absence of either competitive pressures or vigorous regulation, their economic and political power in China would continue to grow. The government's ability to develop and implement energy policy may decline in consequence. Europe and Asia are littered with countries in which energy policy lies in the hands of energy companies, be they private or state-owned. Without a coherent strategy for reform, the government may find that reform becomes progressively more difficult.

A second option is to embark on a rapid program of reform, involving the wholesale restructuring and privatization of the state energy companies and the liberalization of the markets. This might be possible for oil and gas exploration and production, and for the retail of petroleum products, as these industries are unfettered by the restrictions of transmission networks. However, for the downstream gas industry and for the electricity industry this would be a major mistake, because successful liberalization is so dependent on financial transparency and on the effective regulation of the transmission and distribution networks. The obstacles to liberalization in China are so substantial that any hastily conceived plan would be doomed to failure. The risk of crises, such as that experienced by California in 2001, would be high, and if these were repeated across the country, they might restrain the country's economic growth and development for a number of years.

The third option is to continue with the current range of measures, but at the same time to draw up a coherent strategy and plan for the

[175]

progressive liberalization of the energy sector. This approach would involve a substantial period of preparation for reform during which a wide range of measures would have to be undertaken in order to remove the obstacles to liberalization described above and to increase the chances of success. The most important issues to tackle will be those relating to the legal and institutional framework.

Conclusions: Implications for Asian Countries

Like China, most Asian countries face a range of challenges in their energy sectors, at the heart of which is the need to ensure an adequate supply of energy at a reasonable cost so that their economies continue to grow and the livelihoods of their people continue to improve. During the last ten to twenty years, some governments in Asia have been able to achieve improvements in the technical and financial performance of their energy industries through a range of minor adjustments and reforms which have rarely had any impact on the overall nature of the sector. Energy companies are still mainly or entirely owned by government, energy prices are set by government, little competition has been permitted, and foreign participation is limited and tightly controlled.

This lack of liberalization lies in stark contrast to other sectors of Asia's economies which, if not already so, have become progressively more liberalized in the last decade or so—though the record is still patchy in some countries. Governments face pressures, mainly from external parties but also from some domestic interests, to embark promptly on programs of liberalization of their energy sectors.

Consideration of the problems of government ownership and control of energy, and of the intended advantages of liberalization provide a strong argument for privatizing state energy companies and developing competitive energy markets. Yet, the risks inherent in any program of energy liberalization are sufficiently great that governments would be wise to deliberate the nature and timing of reforms with considerable care.

The case of China provides two key messages. First, the productive and allocative efficiency of the energy sector can be improved in a sustained manner without any dramatic or wholesale reforms. Second, the obstacles to successful liberalization of energy are so profound and wide-ranging that a long period of preparation and planning is required before major liberalization can be launched.

The energy sector of each Asian country has its own distinct characteristics, and the obstacles to wholesale liberalization will vary in scale and in nature. Governments would be well advised to proceed slowly on the road to energy liberalization, especially in the network-bound industries of gas and electricity. Substantial improvements are possible within a state-owned framework. That being said, Asian governments should recognize the long-term advantages of energy liberalization and begin to develop a strategy now. That strategy should include measures to address the wide range of obstacles to liberalization, some of which will go to the heart of the political and legal structure of these nations.

MARKET STATUS AND PROSPECTS

5

The Present Status and Future Prospects of Energy Demand and Supply in East Asia

David Von Hippel

R ecent economic growth in the Asia-Pacific region in general, and in many of the economies of Northeast Asia in particular, has been spectacular for most of the 1990s. This growth has brought a vast expansion in the need for energy services, and also in the demand for the fuels that help to supply these services. Future projections suggest that the growth of fossil fuel use in Northeast Asia, and in China in particular, is likely to have not just major consequences for local and regional financial and fuel markets, as well as local and regional pollution, but also global dimensions. Rapidly increasing growth of fossil fuel use in Northeast Asia will have ramifications for global energy and capital markets, and will have a profound impact on global greenhouse gas emissions.

Demand and Supply in Northeast Asia: Status and Trends

An Overview

Table 5.1 presents the current pattern of commercial fuel use in the countries of Northeast Asia by type of fuel.[1] The countries of Northeast Asia consumed slightly under 20 percent of the world's supply of commercial fuels in 1999, including about 18 percent of the petroleum

[181]

products, 5.5 percent of the natural gas, and about 33 percent (nearly a third) of the world's coal. Both North Korea and China consumed approximately 0.9 and 0.6 tons of oil equivalent (TOE) of primary commercial fuels per capita in 1996 and 1999 (respectively), while South Korea used 3.9 TOE per capita, and Japan used 4.0 TOE per capita.[2]

The major point here is that energy use in Asia—particularly in China and North Korea—would seem to have substantial "room to grow" before it reaches the levels currently maintained by Japan and other developed nations. The consumption of transport services, which Chinese and North Koreans currently use relatively lightly and very lightly, respectively, is one of the key areas that is bound to grow, and in all probability will result in a significant increase in transport energy use.

Table 5.1

Fuels Consumption in Northeast Asia and the World[*]

Primary Energy Use in Northeast Asia and the World, 1999**
(Unit: Million Tons of Oil Equivalent)

Country/Area	Oil	Natural Gas	Coal	Nuclear Energy	Hydro-electric	Total	Fraction of NE Asia	Fraction of World
China	207.2	19.3	512.7	3.8	16.8	759.8	47.6%	8.9%
Chinese Taipei (Taiwan)	39.9	5.6	24.9	9.9	0.8	81.1	5.1%	0.9%
DPRK (North Korea)	1.8	-	17.6	-	0.5	19.9	1.2%	0.2%
Hong Kong (China SAR)	9.3	2.4	3.9	-	-	15.6	1.0%	0.2%
Japan	257.3	67.1	91.5	82.0	8.0	505.9	31.7%	5.9%
Mongolia	0.5	-	1.2	-	-	1.8	0.1%	0.0
ROK (South Korea)	99.7	16.8	38.2	26.6	0.5	181.8	11.4%	2.1%
Russian Far East	10.5	2.6	13.5	2.1	0.1	29.5	1.8%	0.3%
Total Northeast Asia	**626.1**	**113.8**	**703.6**	**124.4**	**26.7**	**1,595.4**	**100.0%**	**18.6%**
NE Asia Fraction of World	**18.0%**	**5.5%**	**32.6%**	**19.1%**	**11.8%**	**18.6%**	–	–
Total Rest of World	**2,843.0**	**1,951.4**	**1,456.3**	**527.1**	**199.9**	**6,976.9**	–	**81.4%**
Total World	**3,469.1**	**2,065.2**	**2,159.9**	**651.5**	**226.6**	**8,572.3**	–	**100.0%**

Source: *Figures in this table are for 1999 for all countries except North Korea and for the Russian Far East region. 1999 fuels use in North Korea was probably somewhat less than the 1996 estimate shown in the table, and 1999 fuels use in the Russian Far East was probably somewhat greater than shown.

**1999 figures from *BP World Energy Statistics* (Excel workbook bp_global_ stats.xls) except for Mongolia, (figure from USDOE EIA), North Korea (1996 estimates from Von Hippel and Hayes, 1997), and the Russian Far East (1996 data from Kalashnikov, 1997). Mongolian and Russian Far East totals include some use of other fuels not reflected in individual fuel categories. See Notes and Bibliography for full references.

Editor's Note: Chinese Taipei, formally admitted to the World Trade Organization as its 144th member on January 1, 2002, covers the Separate Customs Territory of Taiwan, Penghu, Kinmen and Matsu.

Brief reviews of current and recent trends in the energy demand and supply in each of the countries of the region are provided below.

I-Energy Demand and Supply in China

As the world's most populous country (about 1.27 billion people by 1999), trends of energy use in China are one of the main drivers of overall energy use in the Northeast Asia region. End-use consumption of commercial fuels in China has grown remarkably over much of the past two decades with the growth and opening up of the Chinese economy. Growth in energy use, and particularly in coal use, appears to have slowed down in the last few years of the 1990s as the combined result of a regional and global economic slowdown and the impact of national policies to curb coal use in order to reduce coal-related air pollution.

The trend of primary energy consumption in China during the 1990s by fuel type is presented in Figure 5.1. Note that there is as yet some uncertainty as to the accuracy of the statistical figures (as published in China) that underlie the substantial reduction in coal use shown between 1997 and 1998, and particularly between 1998 and 1999. Still, it may be concluded that a shift toward reduced growth in overall fuels consumption, and particularly in coal consumption, seems to be underway.[3]

China has huge reserves/resources of coal (of the order of 100 to 1000 billion tons, depending on the definition) and about 3 billion tons of crude oil reserves. China's natural gas reserves are reportedly in the range of 1.7 to 2.7 trillion cubic meters. Some of China's major coal deposits and hydrocarbon basins are located in areas either offshore or in areas remote from major population centers, such as the Western areas of the country. China has substantial remaining untapped hydroelectric resources (of the order of 300 GW of installed capacity), with a significant fraction located in Southwest China.

[183]

Figure 5.1
Primary Fuels Demand in China

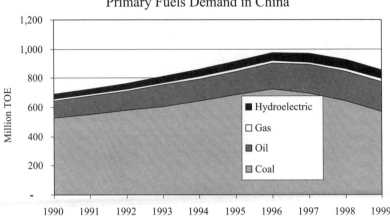

Source: Lawrence Berkeley National Laboratory, *China Energy Databook*, CD-ROM edition v. 5.0, May 2001, Table 4B.1 (Berkeley, CA: LBNL, 2001).

Oil production in China rose only modestly, from about 138 million to about 160 million tons per year, between the period 1990 to 1999, with production from many major oil fields either relatively constant or declining over the period.[4] In the year 1999, for the first time, crude oil inputs to Chinese refineries exceeded domestic crude oil production.

Figure 5.2 shows the trend of oil exports, imports, and net imports in China from the year 1980 through 1999.[5] Once a relatively large oil exporter, China became a net importer of crude oil in approximately 1995, and by the year 1999 the level of net imports had reached almost 30 million tons per year. Natural gas production in China rose from approximately 15 to about 25 billion cubic meters between the years 1990 and 1999.

Overall, the combination of growth in domestic demand for fuels in China and the country's increasing wealth, coupled with relatively restricted domestic supplies of oil and gas, plus the severe environmental effects of massive coal use, mean that the Chinese economy has increasingly looked toward imported fuels to meet its needs.

Figure 5.2
Crude Oil Exports, Imports and Net Imports in China

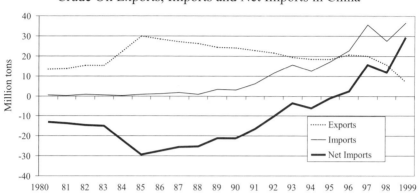

Source: Lawrence Berkeley National Laboratory, *China Energy Databook*, CD-ROM edition v. 5.0, May 2001, Table 7A.1.1. (Berkeley, CA: LBNL, 2001).

II-Energy Demand and Supply in North Korea

Overall energy use per capita in the Democratic People's Republic of Korea (DPRK, also referred to as North Korea) was relatively high as of 1990, primarily due to inefficient use of fuels and reliance on coal. Coal is more difficult to use with high efficiency than oil products or gas. Based on Nautilus Institute estimates, primary commercial energy[6] use in the DPRK in 1990 was approximately 71GJ per capita, approximately 3.1 times the per capita commercial energy use in China in 1990, and somewhat over 50 percent of the 1990 per capita energy consumption in Japan (in which 1990 GDP per capita was some ten to twenty times higher than the DPRK).

The DPRK energy sector has, however, changed drastically since 1990. The key changes in the energy sector between 1990 and 1996 were as follows:[7]

- A reduction in the supply of oil products due to the virtual cessation of crude oil supplies from the Former Soviet Union.
- A considerable reduction in industrial production, which has cut the demand for (and thus the production of) coal and electricity. Disentangling the causes of the decline in industrial output is difficult,

[185]

but the lack of oil products for industrial plants and goods transportation, the lack of foreign exchange capital to pay for spare parts to repair industrial and mining equipment, and the lack of international markets for DPRK goods are all contributing factors.

- A reduction in transport generally, and a reduction in the use of oil products in the transport and agricultural sectors, with biomass and human labor (respectively) serving as partial substitutes for gasoline and diesel fuel.

Most of the trends cited above appear to have continued between 1996 and 2000, based on the observations of those who have visited the DPRK during these years.

Energy Demand: Sectors, Fuels and Problems

The industrial sector was, as of 1990, the largest consumer of all commercial fuels, particularly coal, in the DPRK. The transport sector consumed a substantial fraction of the oil products used in the country. Most transport energy use is for freight transport as the use of personal transport in the DPRK is very limited. The residential sector is a large user of coal and in rural areas biomass fuels are used. The military sector (according to Nautilus Institute estimates) consumes an important share of the refined oil products used in the country. The public/commercial and services sectors in the DPRK consume much smaller shares of the fuel supplies in the DPRK than they do in industrialized countries, due primarily to the minimal development of the commercial sector in North Korea. Wood and crop wastes are used as fuels in the agricultural sector, and probably in some industrial sub-sectors as well. Figure 5.3 provides a summary of energy demand estimates in the DPRK by fuel and by sector in 1990 and 1996. Year 2000 figures for fuels consumption in the DPRK are even lower than the 1996 estimates shown here, based on an estimated DPRK energy balance for the year 2000 prepared by the author and colleagues from the Nautilus Institute.[8]

Figure 5.3

DPRK Energy Demand Indicators by Fuel and Sector (1990 and 1996)

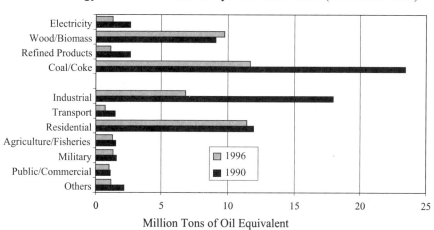

Source: D.F. Von Hippel and P. Hayes, *Demand for and Supply of Electricity and other Fuels in the Democratic People's Republic of Korea (DPRK): Results and Ramifications for 1990 through 2005* (Berkeley, CA: Nautilus Institute, 1997).

The estimated per-capita electricity demand in the DPRK in 1990 was about 1,400 kWh per capita. By comparison, the overall electricity demand in South Korea in the same year was about 2,200 kWh per capita.[9] Key energy-sector problems in the DPRK include:

- *Inefficient infrastructure*: Much of the energy-using infrastructure in the DPRK is reportedly antiquated and/or poorly maintained, including heating systems in residential and other buildings. Industrial facilities are either aging or based on outdated technology, and particularly in recent years are often operated at less-than-optimal capacities, from an energy efficiency perspective.

- *Suppressed and latent demand for energy services*: Lack of fuels in many sectors of the DPRK economy has apparently caused demand for energy services to remain unfulfilled. When and if supply constraints are removed, there is likely to be a surge in energy use (particularly in electricity), as residents, industries, and other consumers of fuels increase their use of energy services toward desired levels.

[187]

- *Lack of energy product markets*: Compounding the risk of a surge in the use of energy services is the virtual lack of energy product markets in the DPRK. Without fuel pricing reforms, there will be few incentives for households and other energy users to adopt energy efficiency measures or otherwise control their fuel consumption.

Energy Supply: Resources, Technologies and Processes

North Korea's major energy resource is coal. The DPRK has substantial reserves of both anthracite and brown coal, though the quality of its coal reserves varies substantially from area to area. There is little, if any, coal cleaning in the DPRK. There are no operating oil wells in North Korea, although oil resources reportedly have been located offshore in DPRK waters. All crude oil and some petroleum products were imported (as of 1990) from Russia, China, and Iran, along with some purchases on the Hong Kong spot market. Since 1990, crude oil imports have been restricted by a number of economic and political factors. Two operating oil refineries produced (as of 1990) the bulk of refined products used in the country. As of 1995 and 1996, only one of the two refineries was apparently operating, and imports of refined products had not expanded sufficiently to replace the lost production.

The total estimated supply of electricity (including electricity exports to China) decreased substantially between 1990 (46 terawatt-hours, or TWh[10]) and 1996 (24 TWh). As with coal, the bulk of the electricity demand in the DPRK has in the past been in the industrial sector, with the residential and military sectors (according to Nautilus Institute estimates) also accounting for significant fractions of electricity use. Electricity generation is primarily hydroelectric and coal-fired, in approximately equal proportions, with a small amount of oil-fired electricity generation capacity associated with the oil refinery at Sonbong. Much of the generation capacity was installed in the 1970s and 1980s, although a significant portion of generation facilities – particularly hydroelectric – date back to the Japanese occupation.

The DPRK has the coal resources necessary to expand its thermal power generation, but it not clear whether the coal mining or transport infrastructure is capable of supplying coal to power stations at a rate much greater than that prevailing in 1990—and coal supply infrastructure has been degraded very substantially since that time. Taking into account the prevailing weather patterns in the sub-region, North Korea probably has a significant wind power resource, as yet untapped (and largely unmapped). The DPRK also has some remaining undeveloped hydroelectric sites.

Power generation facilities are reported to be in generally poor condition and sometimes (because they are based on technologies adopted from China or the Former Soviet Union) not well adapted to the coal types with which they are fired. Consequently, the generation efficiency of the thermal power stations in the DPRK is reportedly low. Thermal power plants generally lack all but the most rudimentary pollution control equipment, and also, in almost all cases, lack any kind of computerized combustion control facilities. In-station use of power is reportedly fairly high, and "emergency losses" of power have been reported at major stations.

The system of electricity dispatching is inefficient, minimally or not at all automated, and prone to failure. Estimates of transmission and distribution (T&D) losses vary from an official 16 percent up to more than 50 percent, but any estimates of T&D losses are difficult to confirm, as there is minimal end-use metering in the DPRK.

Figure 5.4 provides indicators of the fuel supply situations in the DPRK in 1990 and 1996. Since 1996, electricity supplies have almost certainly continued to drop substantially, as have coal supplies. Imports of crude oil and oil products may not have changed as much.

Figure 5.4
DPRK Energy Supply Indicators (1990 and 1996)

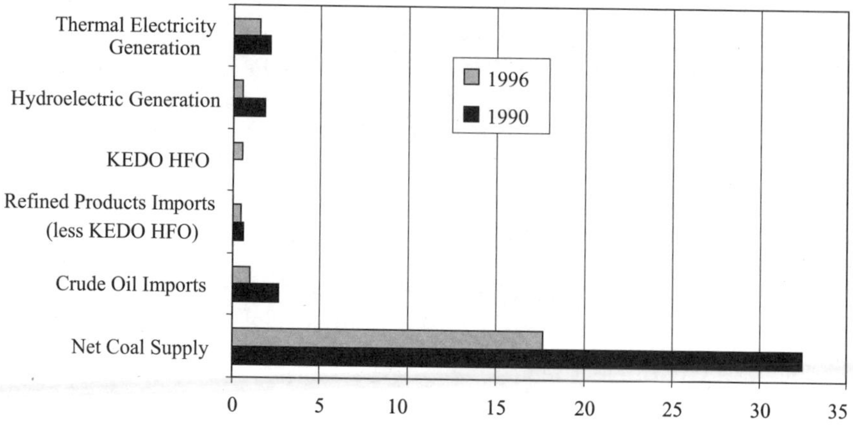

Million Tons of Oil Equivalent

Source: D.F. Von Hippel and P. Hayes, *Demand for and Supply of Electricity and Other Fuels in the Democratic People's Republic of Korea (DPRK): Results and Ramifications for 1990 through 2005* (Berkeley, CA: Nautilus Institute, 1997).

III-Energy Demand and Supply in Japan

Energy Demand by Sector

Figure 5.5 presents the division of 1998 final energy use by sector for each of the major fuels and for all fuel use.[11] Almost all of the coal used in Japan (apart from electricity generation) is used in the industrial sector, and over 90 percent of it is used in the iron and steel industry alone. The transport sector dominates the use of oil products, accounting for slightly over 40 percent of oil product usage. The residential and industrial sectors are currently the major end-users of gas, with 40 and 37 percent of demand, respectively. Industry also accounts for 44 percent of electricity use, with the residential and commercial sectors accounting for most of the balance of electricity demand. Overall, 43.3 percent of total final energy demand in Japan is by the industrial sector, 25.2 percent by the transport sector, 13.9 percent by the residential sector, 12.5 percent by the commercial sector, 3.1 percent by the agricultural, forestry and fisheries

[190]

sector and 2.1 percent is oil products used in non-energy applications. Over the last decade, the fraction of energy use in Japan accounted for by industry has declined somewhat, while the fractions accounted for by transport and the commercial sectors have risen.

Figure 5.5

Japan Energy End-Use Demand by Sector and Fuel Type (1998)

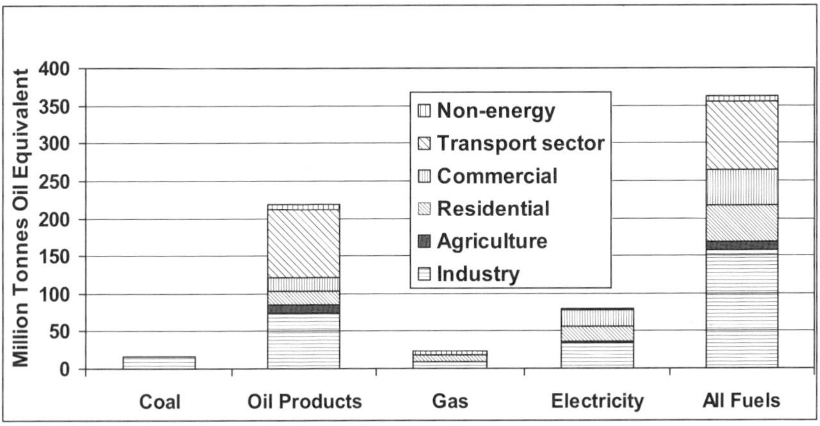

Source: Data from Statistics Bureau and Statistics Center, Ministry of Public Management, Home Affairs, Posts, and Telecommunications, Japan (Tokyo: Statistics Bureau and Statistics Center, 2001), *Japan Statistical Yearbook 2001.*

Energy Supply

As of fiscal year 1998, the structure of primary energy demand in Japan was as follows:[12]

- Oil 52.3%
- Coal 16.4%
- Nuclear 13.7%
- Natural Gas 12.3%
- Hydro 3.9%
- Geothermal 0.2%
- Others (including wood and biomass wastes, and solar/wind energy) 1.1%.

Overall primary energy demand in Japan showed minimal growth between 1995 and 1998, after growing at an average of 3.7 percent annually between 1985 and 1990, and at 2.4 percent per year between 1990 and 1995. Since 1990, the fraction of Japan's primary energy requirements supplied by crude oil and petroleum products has declined, while the proportions of requirements supplied by natural gas and nuclear sources have increased, and the supply fractions of other energy sources have changed only modestly. Figure 5.6 shows the changes in the patterns of primary fuel supply in Japan over the last few years.

Figure 5.6
Fraction of Primary Energy Use in Japan by Fuel Type

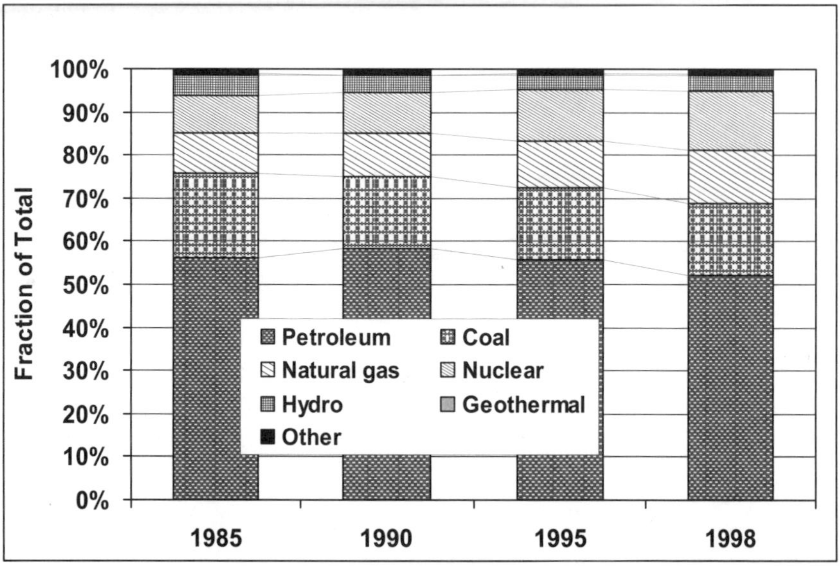

Source: Energy Data from Statistics Bureau and Statistics Center, Ministry of Public Management, Home Affairs, Posts, and Telecommunications, Japan (Tokyo, Japan: Statistics Bureau and Statistics Center, 2000), *Japan in Figures 2001.*

Virtually all (99.7 percent as of 1998[13]) of the total supply of crude oil in Japan is imported, and most of Japan's crude oil imports (78.8 percent in 2000[14]) come from the Middle East—principally from Saudi Arabia and the United Arab Emirates.[15] Most of the remainder of Japan's oil imports are from the Asia-Pacific region. Domestic coal production in

Japan accounted for about 2.8 percent of total 1998 net coal supplies, and domestic natural gas production accounted for a similar proportion of total gas supplies.[16] Japan is the world's largest importer of liquefied natural gas (LNG), consuming 53 percent of the world total. In 2000, about 20 percent of Japan's LNG imports came from the Middle East, with all but a small percentage of the rest originating in Southeast Asia and Australia.[17] Overall, domestic energy resources accounted for about 18 percent of total primary energy supply in 1998. If nuclear energy production—which primarily uses nuclear fuels imported into Japan—is considered as an imported rather than a domestic energy resource (and this distinction can be argued either way), the contribution of domestic resources to Japan's total primary energy use drops to about 4 percent.

IV-Energy Demand and Supply in Mongolia

Energy Demand in Mongolia

Mongolia, a country of about 2.6 million people, uses relatively little commercial fuels. According to the US Department of Energy (USDOE) statistics, demand for commercially-traded fuels in Mongolia in 1999 was about 25 GJ (or 0.6 TOE) per person.[18] Since 1990, as the economic support provided to Mongolia—including fuels provided at lower-than-market prices—from the former Soviet Union has eroded, Mongolia's consumption of commercial fuels has decreased markedly, falling by nearly 50 percent in terms of per-capita consumption. On a sectoral basis, as shown in Figure 5.7, the residential sector was the largest consumer of commercial fuels by 1995, with the industrial and transport sectors each consuming about 20 percent of the total.[19] Counting biomass fuels (fuelwood and dung) in the total adds another approximately 400 kTOE to total annual end-use energy consumption, probably largely in the households sector. Total demand for commercial fuels in Mongolia today is substantially constrained by economic problems – Mongolia is going through a period of restructuring to a market-oriented economy – and by simple lack of fuel supplies.

Figure 5.7
Commercial Fuels Use in Mongolia

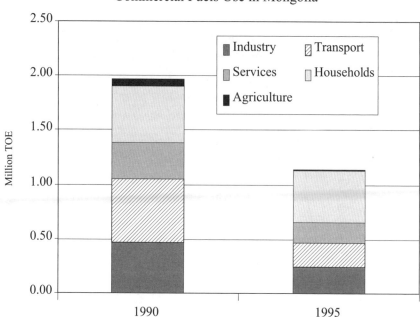

Source: Asian Development Bank (ADB), the Global Environment Facility, and the United Nations Development Program (Manila: ADB, 1998), *Asia Least-Cost Greenhouse Gas Abatement Strategy: Mongolia.* (Manila: ADB, October 1998) Table 3-5.

Fuel Supply in Mongolia

All of Mongolia's oil products are imported. Mongolia produces coal—principally lignite or brown coal—which is used in power generation, combined heat and power plants, and end-uses in all sectors except transport. Electricity generation is carried out at five mostly larger combined heat and power plants in major cities, plus 18 mostly smaller heat or heat and power plants at provincial centers. Additionally, Mongolia uses a very small amount of hydropower.

Figure 5.8 shows the trends in primary energy demand in Mongolia from 1980 through 1999.[20]

Figure 5.8
Primary Energy Demand in Mongolia by Fuel Type

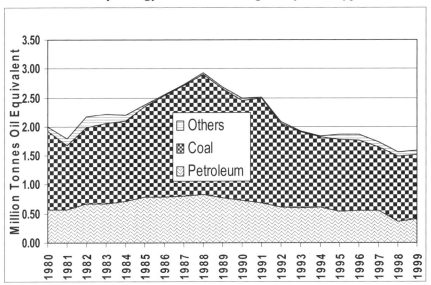

Source: Energy data used for these calculations are from USDOE Energy Information Administration International data files "table b1.XLS" and "table e1.XLS" (http://www. eia.doe.gov/emeu/iea/wecbtu.html). "Others" denotes the difference between total energy figures and the total of coal and petroleum products use.

V-Energy Demand and Supply in the Republic of Korea

The Republic of Korea (ROK, also referred to as "South Korea"), is a country of over 46 million people occupying a land area of just under 100,000 square kilometers. The economy of the ROK has been one of the most vibrant in the world in the last decade (See Figure 5.9[21]), producing growth in primary energy consumption of the order of 10 percent per year from 1990 until the Asian financial crisis in 1998.[22] Growth in energy consumption in the Republic of Korea has rebounded after a brief decline during the Asian financial crisis. Like Japan, the ROK has few fossil fuel resources of its own, and is thus nearly exclusively reliant on imports, including coal, oil and natural gas.

[195]

Figure 5.9
ROK Gross Domestic Product

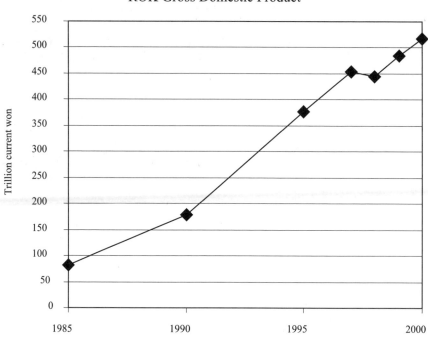

Source: Korea National Statistical Office, 2001. *Korea in Figures* (Seoul: National Statistics Office, 2001).

Energy Demand in the Republic of Korea

Table 5.2 shows the distribution of energy demand by fuel in the Republic of Korea from 1990 to 2000.[23] The consumption of coal in the end-use sectors changed very little between 1990 and 2000. Conversely, the use of town (piped) gas and electricity increased by factors of 12 and 2.5, respectively, and the use of district heat increased about 14-fold, all indicators of the desire to increase convenience and reduce pollutant emissions at the end-use level. Use of "non-fuel" oil, mostly naphtha used as an input to the petrochemical industry, also increased substantially during the 1990s.

[196]

Table 5.2
Summary of Energy Demand in the ROK by Fuel Type
(1990 to 2000, million toe)

	1990	1995	2000
Coal	19.86	17.76	19.47
Fuel Oil	34.99	59.10	53.72
LPG	3.37	5.45	8.25
Non-fuel Oil	6.89	18.33	32.10
Firewood/Other	0.80	1.05	2.13
Town Gas	1.01	5.59	12.56
Electricity	8.12	14.04	20.60
Heat	0.075	0.64	1.12
Total	**75.11**	**121.96**	**149.74**

Source: Korea National Statistical Office databases (http://www.nso.go.kr/cgi-bin).

Looking at the changes in the sectoral composition of energy demand by major fuel categories in the ROK between 1990 and 2000, the following aspects are noteworthy:

- Coal consumption in the industrial sector has risen by about 80 percent since 1990, but consumption in the residential and commercial sector has decreased by a factor of over 10.
- Consumption of fuel oils in the transport sector roughly doubled in the last decade, but most of that increase was between 1990 and 1995. Since 1995, the consumption of LPG in the transport sector has nearly doubled, as many urban motor vehicles, and especially taxis, have been converted to LPG to reduce air pollution. Consumption of fuel oils in the residential/commercial and public sectors increased by nearly two-fold between 1990 and 1995, but have declined considerably since. Overall industrial oil demand rose by a factor of about 2.6 between 1990 and 2000, but a 350 percent increase in the use of non-fuel oil products has meant that the use of fuel oil in industry grew relatively little during the decade, and actually declined between 1995 and 2000.

[197]

- Consumption of "town gas" increased more than ten-fold in both the industrial and residential/commercial sectors during the 1990s. In addition, the composition of town gas changed during the 1990s. In 1990, town gas was about 75 percent LPG and 25 percent LNG. The fraction of LNG in town gas was slightly higher by 1995, but by 2000 a marked change had taken place, with piped gas in the ROK being about 80 percent LNG.
- The use of electricity more than doubled in the industrial and public sectors between 1990 and 2000, but more than tripled in the residential/commercial sector.
- Increases in district heat use were concentrated in the residential/commercial sector.

Energy Supply in the Republic of Korea

Table 5.3 summarizes primary energy supply by fuel for the Republic of Korea for the years 1990, 1995, and 2000. Total primary energy supply approximately doubled during the decade, with supply of LNG growing fastest (over six-fold growth during the decade). Although the supply of petroleum products also doubled overall between 1990 and 2000, in the last five years consumption of fuel oils has declined overall, while coal use has grown.

Table 5.3
Summary of Primary Energy Supply in the ROK, 1990-2000
(million toe)

	1990	1995	2000
Coal	27.49	28.09	42.13
Fuel Oil	39.33	68.95	60.23
LPG	3.59	6.68	8.50
Non-fuel Oil	6.87	18.33	32.10
LNG	3.03	9.21	18.92
Hydro	1.59	1.37	1.40
Nuclear	13.22	16.76	27.24
Wood and Other	2.85	1.05	2.13
Total	**97.96**	**150.44**	**192.66**

Source: Derived from energy balance data from Korea National Statistical Office databases, as taken from http://www.nso.go.kr/cgi-bin.

Figure 5.10 shows the evolution of the share of imported energy in the overall ROK energy sector. By 2000, fuel imports supplied 97.2 percent of total fuels demand in the country, up from about 75 percent in 1980.

Figure 5.10

Total Energy Demand and Energy Imports in the ROK (1980-2000)

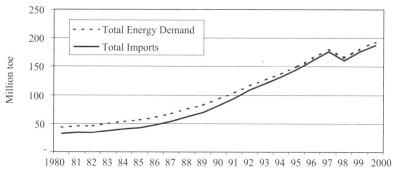

Source: Derived data from Korea National Statistical Office databases (http://www.nso.go.kr/cgi-bin).

Growth in the demand for electricity in the ROK has been rapid during the last decade, as noted above. A corresponding increase in electricity generation capacity has occurred, and a key development over the last five years, as shown in Figure 5.11,[24] has been the substitution of gas and, to some extent, coal for oil as a fuel for electricity generation.

Figure 5.11

ROK Generating Capacity by Fuel Type

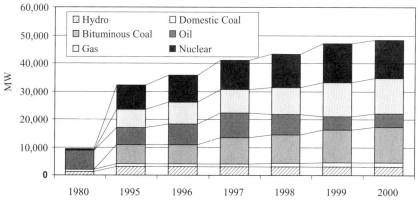

Source: Data for this figure from the Korean Electric Power Company (Seoul, ROK: KEPCO, 2001).

VI-Energy Demand and Supply in the Russian Far East

The area of Russia closest to the Pacific Ocean, and adjoining the other countries of Northeast Asia, is referred to as the Russian Far East. As a result of the breakup of the Soviet Union, the economy of the Russian Far East (RFE), which had been tuned principally toward producing raw materials and other goods for use in other areas of the USSR and affiliated states, declined markedly in the years from 1990 through about 1997, but has started to rebound somewhat since. The RFE is sparsely populated, with about 7,800,000 people in a territory of 6.2 million square kilometers (about 36.4 percent of the entire territory of Russia). Overall fuels demand in the RFE is modest, but the huge fuel resources of the area means that the RFE may well play a significant role in the energy markets of East Asia in the future.

Energy Demand in the Russian Far East

During the period between 1992 and 1998, the economic output of the RFE declined by about 50 percent, and the consumption of primary energy in the region declined by about a third. Since 1998, the economy of the region has recovered modestly, and the demand for electricity and other energy sources has been on the rise.[25] The industrial sector has historically dominated overall energy consumption in the RFE, but the fraction of total energy use accounted for by the residential and other sectors has been increasing since the early 1990s. During the 1990s, infrastructural problems with energy systems (including combined heat and power plants), the lack of investment capital for industry in general and for the energy industry in particular, and much higher tariffs for energy products have combined with the impact of economic restructuring to reduce energy demand in the region.

Energy Supply in the Russian Far East

The RFE is a region rich in primary resources, but constrained by both economic and geography in the degree to which those resources have been developed. Despite the RFE's resource endowment, a considerable fraction of the primary energy used in the RFE comes from other parts of Russia— its petroleum products in particular. Table 5.4 compares the primary energy use by fuel in the RFE in 1990 and 1996.[26] Coal and petroleum products (the latter largely for transport and some electricity production) have supplied the major shares of the energy requirements in the Russian Far East.

Table 5.4

Primary Energy Consumption and Share of Energy Imports
in the Russian Far East (1990 and 1996)

	Coal	Natural Gas	Petroleum	Hydro and Nuclear	Other Fuels	Total
Consumption in 1990 (MTOE)	**18.6**	**2.6**	**22.3**	**1.9**	**2.5**	**48**
Fraction of consumption by fuel	38.8%	5.4%	46.6%	3.9%	5.2%	100%
Fraction as Imports to RFE	14%	0%	91%	0%	0%	47.50%
Consumption in 1996 (MTOE)	**13.5**	**2.6**	**10.5**	**2.2**	**0.7**	**29.5**
Fraction of consumption by fuel	45.8%	8.8%	35.6%	7.5%	2.4%	100%
Import %	16%	0%	90%	0%	0%	39.50%

Source: Victor D. Kalashnikov, *Electric Power Industry of the Russian Far East: Status and Prerequisites for Cooperation in North-East Asia* (Honolulu, HI, USA: East-West Center, 1997). Khabarovsk Economic Research Institute Far Eastern Branch of Russian Academy of Sciences.

The energy resources of the Russian Far East include petroleum, natural gas, coal, and hydroelectric potential, as shown in Table 5.5.[27] The reserves shown in Table 5.5 are considerable by almost any standard. Many of these energy resources, however, are located in areas remote from population centers, and a concerted international financing and infrastructure development effort will likely be needed to create the infrastructure needed to develop these RFE energy resources and move them to markets elsewhere in East Asia.

Table 5.5

Discovered Primary Energy Reserves of the Russian Far East (MTOE)

Area	Coal	Oil	Natural Gas	Hydro	Total
Republic of Sakha	6,700	375	1,200	115.5	8,391
Magadan territory	710	14	13.3	33.0	770
Kamachatka territory	160	0	20.3	11.6	192
Amur territory	1,150	0	0	17.5	1,168
Khabarovsk territory	1,280	0	1.75	45.5	1,327
Primorskii territory	1,400	0	0	5.8	1,406
Sakhalin territory	1,080	620	850	1.1	2,551
The RFE as a Whole	**12,480**	**1,010**	**2,085.40**	**230**	**15,802**

Source: Victor D. Kalashnikov, *National Energy Futures Analysis and Energy Security Perspectives in the Russian Far East* (2000). Khabarovsk Economic Research Institute, Far Eastern Branch of Russian Academy of Sciences, paper prepared for The Nautilus Institute East Asia Energy Futures Project, June 2000.

Energy Demand and Supply in N.E. Asia: Projections and Scenarios

The countries of Northeast Asia include two of the world's fastest-growing economies (China and the ROK), three economies that can be considered developing or in transition (the DPRK, Mongolia, and the Russian Far East), and a major industrialized economy that has grown, in terms of economic output, relatively little over the past few years (Japan). Energy demand in this region can be expected to grow as fast as virtually anywhere in the world over the next decade or two. The future of energy demand in this region, including how (and whether) its economies evolve to make more extensive use of resources within the region, and the extent to which the region continues to increase its imports of energy products, can be expected to have a considerable influence on global energy markets and as discussed later, global capital markets and the global environment as well. It should be noted that although many of the country/region "scenarios" for energy sector development were developed using a similar end-use approach and modeling tool (China, the DPRK, Japan), scenarios for the other countries use different methods, models, and time horizons to develop projections for future energy supply and demand. As such, a sum of future regional energy supply or demand computed from these projections (and no such sum is attempted in this paper) would have to be used advisedly, and as only a rough approximation of the potential future situation in the region.

1-Future Energy Demand and Supply in China

Continued economic development in China will require a significant share of the world's resources—physical, financial and environmental. Different paths of energy-sector development in China will have different global, regional and local ramifications for the environment, energy trade with other regions, and, in all probability, the global political situation. The results of modeling two different medium-term energy futures for China (1990 to 2020, including historical data through 1998) on both the demand and supply-side, is summarized below. The focus here is on sketching two cases: a "Business-as-Usual" (BAU) Case, and an "Alternative" case that stresses the implementation of energy efficiency and renewable energy technologies, as well as some pollution reduction measures for the electricity generation sector. The relative impacts of the two scenarios on the supply and demand for different fuels in China are compared. This work has built upon on a number of past and ongoing Nautilus Institute initiatives.[28]

A demand-driven model with substantial sector, sub-sector, end-use and fuel detail was used to provide a methodologically simple, transparent, and convenient framework for assembly and testing of alternative energy futures.[29] Historical year data (for 1990, 1995 and 1998) from a variety of sources were used to create a data set that describes the flows and end-uses of fuels in the Chinese energy sector. Using a combination of analysis of recent trends and conjectures about changes in the consumption of energy services in China over the period through

2020, a Business-as-Usual scenario for energy demand was developed. The supply of resources, and the capacity to transform primary resources into fuels (including the stock of power generation facilities), was built up to meet final fuel demand.

The Business-as-Usual (BAU) demand scenario is an extrapolation of the performance of the Chinese economy over the last 15 years or so, tempered somewhat by consideration of the recent crisis in the Asian financial markets and its impacts, as well as by recent trends in China away from coal use. As such, the BAU scenario postulates relatively strong continued economic growth, with growth gradually slowing as the Chinese economy begins to mature. The commercial sector and lighter industries are assumed to show the strongest growth of the different sectors of the Chinese economy, with the growth in the output of heavy industries slowing down as recent trends already seem to show. Residential energy consumption is assumed to increase markedly, though household size declines and population growth slows. Personal travel is also assumed to expand markedly, with particularly rapid (continued) expansion in the stock and use of private vehicles. Energy intensities for demand-side devices continue to improve, but not at a rapid rate, as a combination of the desire to keep most production in-country and a lack of capital for high-efficiency investments tend to keep energy intensities higher than in the United States, Europe and Japan.

On the energy supply/transformation side in the BAU scenario, coal-fired generation facilities continue to provide the great bulk of power supplies, with most of the expansion of coal-fired capacity being domestically-produced units. Progressively larger fractions of coal-fired power plants have pollution control equipment. The share of total primary supplies provided by natural gas use expands as well, but remains relatively minor through 2020. The use of renewable energy sources for electricity and other uses continue to expand, but not aggressively.

The Alternative scenario demonstrates the production of the same (or very nearly the same) goods and services as in the BAU scenario, but does so in a different way, with different environmental consequences. As such, the Alternative scenario uses the same rates of growth of key variables such as population, households, urban migration, the use of energy services, and industrial production. The major differences between the Alternative and BAU scenarios lie in the degree to which energy efficiency improvements (in all sectors) and renewable energy devices, on both the demand- and supply-sides, are implemented. The energy-efficiency improvements were modeled assuming that improvements similar in magnitude to those available today (comparing high-efficiency versus standard appliances and equipment) could be phased in by 2020. Energy intensities in key end-uses in the Alternative scenario were thus modeled as decreasing, relative to BAU values, by an amount ranging from 10 to 30 percent by 2020. The Alternative scenario is intended as one example out of many possible outcomes, and it focuses on energy efficiency technologies primarily to illustrate the potential role that such technologies might play in changing the shape of China's energy future.

Figure 5.12 shows the changing sectoral pattern of energy demand under the BAU scenario. Although the industrial sector remains the largest consumer of energy through 2020, the fraction of energy used in the transportation and services sectors increase markedly. Residential energy demand increases less rapidly, primarily as a result of decreasing population growth and a trend toward more efficient use of fuels, including movement toward electric and gas home appliances.

Figure 5.13 presents the same sectoral pattern, but for the Alternative case. It may be noted from this figure that overall growth is substantially lower than in the BAU case, rising from about 900 Million TOE in 1998 to about 1,150 Million TOE in 2020, while energy demand in the BAU case rises to nearly 1500 million TOE by 2020. Please note that Figures 5.12 and 5.13 include end-use fuel demand only, but also account for use of non-commercial fuels (wood and other biomass).

Figure 5.12

Estimated Energy Demand by Sector in China: BAU Scenario

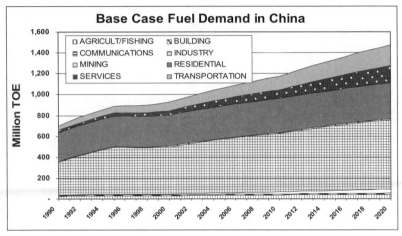

Source: Nautilus Institute Report. See Note 28.

Figure 5.13

Estimated Energy Demand by Sector in China: Alternative Scenario

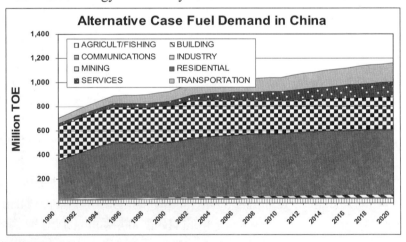

Source: Nautilus Institute Report. See Note 28.

Figures 5.14 and 5.15 present comparisons of the BAU and Alternative Scenarios with regard to end-use and total coal demand respectively. The difference in coal demand between the cases is significant – over 25 percent reduction in the Alternative case relative to the BAU case by 2020

– with important ramifications both for the environmental performance of the Chinese energy sector and for the need for other (largely imported), cleaner fuels.

Figure 5.14

End-Use Coal Demand in China: Scenario Comparison

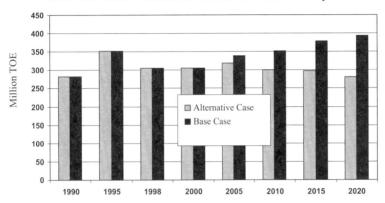

Source: Nautilus Institute Report. See Note 28.

Figure 5.15

Total Coal Requirements in China: Scenario Comparison

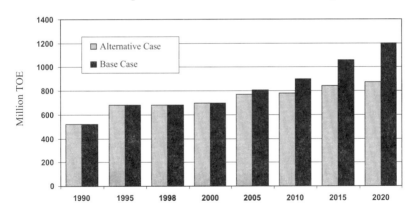

Source: Nautilus Institute Report. See Note 28.

The Alternative scenario includes significant energy-efficiency improvements in the Chinese transport sector, notably a much more efficient fleet of private vehicles. Transport sector and other improvements in efficiency in the Alternative scenario produce a dramatic difference in total crude oil and oil product imports, as shown in Figure 5.16. Year 2020 oil and oil product imports in China are nearly 40 percent (some 92 million TOE) less in the Alternative case than in the BAU case. Gas imports, assumed to be a combination of LNG and overland gas imports via pipeline from Russia, are somewhat higher in the Alternative case (26.9 MTOE) than in the BAU case (21.5 MTOE).[30]

Figure 5.16
Total Oil and Oil Products Net Import Requirements
in China: Scenario Comparison

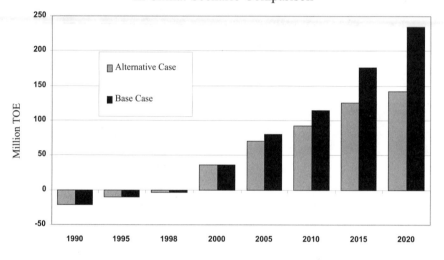

Source: See Note 29.

The analysis of the relative cost implications of the two scenarios is not yet complete at the time of writing. Figure 5.17, however, provides a partial indication of the benefits of the Alternative scenario in showing a comparison of the relative capital and (non-fuel) operating costs for electricity generation under the two scenarios. By 2020, savings in annual payments on capital costs for electricity generation, plus avoided operating and maintenance costs, total almost US$ 10 billion annually in the Alternative case, relative to the BAU case.

Figure 5.17
Relative Electric Capacity and Operating
and Maintenance (O&M) Costs: Scenario Comparison

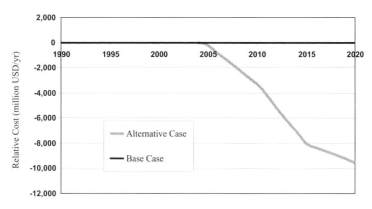

Source: See Note 29.

II-Future Energy Demand and Supply in the DPRK

To say that the future energy demand and supply situation in the DPRK is uncertain is a vast understatement. As noted above, energy consumption in the DPRK has been contracting virtually throughout the 1990s. In this section, the author presents an updated version of two scenarios ("Continued Decline" and "Rebuilding") for the DPRK energy sector, based on work done previously by the author and colleagues at Nautilus Institute.[31] These scenarios are indicative only, should be considered only initial indicators of the results of work in progress. The "Continued Decline" scenario assumes that the economy of the DPRK is not materially rebuilt over the next decade, but largely continues its stagnation, with only the most modest economic reforms and with international aid and austerity the main factors in maintaining the DPRK economy near its current levels. The "Rebuilding" scenario implicitly assumes a major breakthrough in relations with the ROK (and probably the United States as well), resulting in some investment in the industrial and energy infrastructure in the DPRK from outside the country and much increased foreign development aid. The "Rebuilding" scenario also assumes, however, that the DPRK government essentially maintains its integrity. If the current DPRK government loses power (and it is difficult to see signs of such a process at present), rapid reunification of North and South Korea may result, which probably means very large, very fast changes for the DPRK energy sector, providing that the unified Korea can obtain internal and external financing for infrastructure reconstruction in the North.

Future Energy Demand in the DPRK

Figure 5.18 shows estimated final energy demand by fuel type in the DPRK for the two scenarios described above. In Figures 5.18 and 5.19, and in Table 5.6, "D" (Continued Decline) and "R" (Rebuilding) refer to the two scenarios for the years 2005 and 2010. The rebuilding scenario shows much greater use of fossil fuels and electricity than the decline scenario, with the highest growth being in the highest quality fuels— petroleum products and electricity.

Figure 5.18

DPRK Energy Demand Scenarios by Fuel Type (1990-2010)

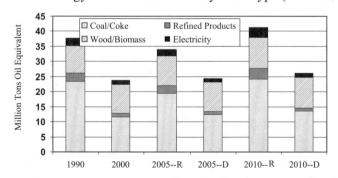

Note: D = Continued decline scenario and R = Rebuilding scenario for the years 2005 and 2010 respectively.
Source: Documented in D.F. Von Hippel and P. Hayes (Berkeley, CA USA: Nautilus Institute, 1997), *Demand for and Supply of Electricity and Other Fuels in the Democratic People's Republic of Korea (DPRK): Results and Ramifications for 1990 through 2005.* Nautilus Institute report prepared for the Northeast Asia Economic Forum/East-West Center.

Energy demand by sector under the two scenarios in the DPRK, as illustrated in Figure 5.19, is different for all sectors by 2005 and 2010, but the major difference between the two scenarios is resurgence in the industrial and transport sectors. There is some resurgence in the public/commercial sector as well. Rebuilding of the industrial sector in the DPRK will, however, mean more than just restarting existing industries, as those industries were initially designed to serve markets that do not now exist. Probably the first industries to be rebuilt in the DPRK will be those that produce raw materials with international markets, such as production of the refractory mineral magnesite, of which the DPRK has considerable reserves.

Figure 5.19

DPRK Energy Demand Scenarios by Sector (1990-2010)

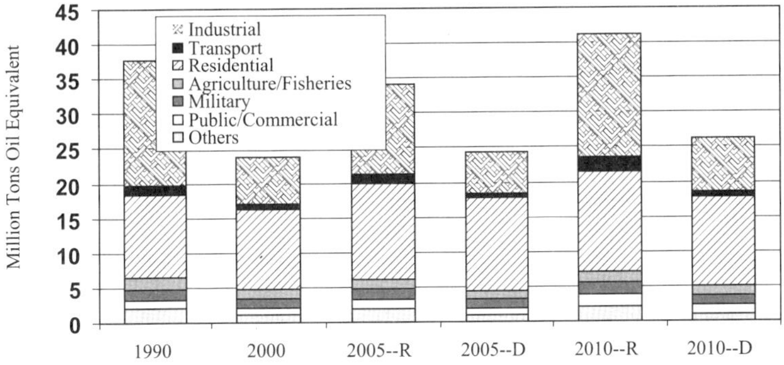

Note: D = Continued decline scenario and R = Rebuilding scenario for the years 2005 and 2010 respectively.

Source: Documented in D.F.Von Hippel and P. Hayes (Berkeley, CA USA: Nautilus Institute, 1997), *Demand for and Supply of Electricity and Other Fuels in the Democratic People's Republic of Korea (DPRK): Results and Ramifications for 1990 through 2005.* Nautilus Institute report prepared for the Northeast Asia Economic Forum/East-West Center.

Future Fuels Supply in the DPRK

The pattern of energy supply by fuel under the two scenarios for development of the DPRK energy sector is shown in Table 5.6. Coal will probably continue to be produced primarily domestically under both

[211]

scenarios, and crude oil and refined products will continue to be imported. In the "Rebuilding" scenario, imports for oil are likely to continue to come from China, augmented by imports from Russia and perhaps from the Middle East or elsewhere. The higher value for primary energy supplies from "Hydro/Nuclear" in the 2010–R and 2010–D columns reflects the start-up, possibly sometime around 2007 to 2009, of the nuclear reactors being built by KEDO in the DPRK.

Table 5.6

Scenarios for Primary Energy Supplies by Fuel in the DPRK (MTOE)

	1990	2000	2005–R	2005–D	2010–R	2010–D
Coal/Coke	32.41	17.66	27.45	16.86	32.28	18.10
Crude Oil	2.65	1.02	2.64	0.91	5.16	1.12
Refined Products	0.64	0.76	1.00	0.75	(0.32)	0.33
Hydro/Nuclear	1.83	0.51	1.26	0.75	3.22	2.24
Wood/Biomass	9.24	9.85	10.04	9.87	10.40	10.29
Total	**47**	**30**	**42**	**29**	**51**	**32**

Source: Documented in D.F. Von Hippel and P. Hayes (Berkeley, CA: Nautilus Institute, 1997), *Demand for and Supply of Electricity and other Fuels in the Democratic People's Republic of Korea (DPRK): Results and Ramifications for 1990 through 2005.* Nautilus Institute report for the Northeast Asia Economic Forum/East-West Center.

III-Future Energy Demand and Supply in Japan

As a part of a Japan case study of the concept of energy security in the Pacific Asian region, a team of researchers from the Nautilus Institute, collaborating with colleagues from Japan, assembled two medium-range (1990 to 2020) energy scenarios that describe the evolution of energy demand and supply in Japan.[32] As with the China energy scenarios summarized above, the case study scenarios for Japan were designed to produce similar levels of energy services, but in different ways.[33] The general outlines of the two paths are as follows:

1. *Business-As-Usual:* The BAU scenario largely follows and extrapolates recent trends in energy demand, energy supply investment, and environmental emissions control, with continued emphasis on fossil

fuel use and only modest increases in energy efficiency and in the use of renewable energy. In effect, the business-as-usual case includes nuclear power as an approximately constant fraction of total generation, increasing use of oil for transport, and continuing substitution of natural gas for other fuels in end-use sectors.

2. *Alternative:* This scenario includes increased emphasis on substitution of natural gas for coal and oil in both end-use demand sectors and electric power generation, plus aggressive application of end-use efficiency improvement and renewable fuels in all sectors. This path keeps the fraction of power supplied by nuclear energy roughly the same as at present, but the generation and capacity required is reduced due to efficiency improvements.

Japan Energy Sector Model: Base Year Values/Common Assumptions

Both the BAU and Alternative cases begin with a description of the status of Japanese energy demand and supply in 1990 and 1995. The main source that we used for recent Japanese energy data has been a set of very detailed (41 fuel categories by 45 rows) Japanese-language energy balances complied by the Institute of Energy Economics, Japan (IEEJ) and the Energy Conservation Center, and published by the MITI (Ministry of International Trade and Industry) Research Institute. This information was augmented by data from the USDOE EIA (the US Department of Energy's Energy Information Administration), the IEA (International Energy Agency), United Nations documents, a statistical compendium of Japanese energy and economic statistics, Japanese government statistics, World-Wide Web (WWW) sites, and other sources. Nautilus Institute was also fortunate to obtain a set of very detailed spreadsheets that provided historical energy and related data by end-use for each of the major sectors of the Japanese economy. These spreadsheets, developed by the International Energy Studies Group of Lawrence Berkeley National Laboratory, were used to provide additional end-use detail in many sectors.[34]

Future Energy Demand and Supply in Japan: Overall Results

The BAU and Alternative scenarios were designed to highlight different strategies for meeting Japan's needs for energy services over the period from 1995 to 2020. As such, it is not surprising that the future patterns of fuel demand and supply under the two paths are considerably different. The BAU case, for example, shows steady growth in overall fuel use, while energy use in the Alternative scenario actually declines after the year 2000.

Figure 5.20 shows future end-use energy demand estimates for the two scenarios by fuel category. Between 1995 and 2020, energy use in Japan in the BAU case grows at an average rate of 1.2 percent per year. In the Alternative case, on the other hand, overall energy use actually declines, as a result of energy efficiency and other "demand-side" measures, from 14.9 billion gigajoules (GJ) in 1995 to 14.5 billion GJ in 2020, an average rate of decline of about 0.1 percent per year. Key differences between the cases in the relative fractions of fuel use include a much greater use of co-generated heat and fuel gases in the Alternative scenario, as well as significantly less petroleum products use (50 percent of demand versus 60 percent in the BAU scenario). The fraction of final fuels demand provided by electricity is about the same in both cases in 2010 and 2020.

Figure 5.20
Energy Demand by Fuel Type

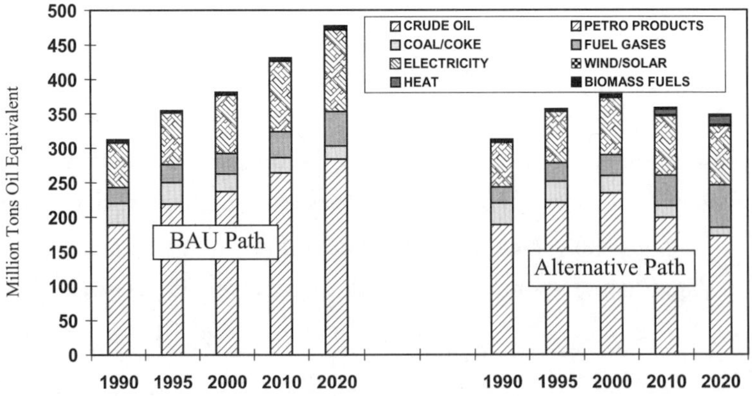

Source: See Note 32.

The change in energy demand by sector in the two different paths is shown in Figure 5.21. Here the most obvious difference between the two scenarios is the relative share of total energy demand accounted for by the transport sector by 2010 and 2020. In 2010, the BAU-case share of total energy accounted for by the transport sector is 28.2 percent, falling slightly to 27.8 percent by 2020.

However, in the Alternative path scenario, the transport-sector fraction of total energy demand is 22.4 percent in 2010, falling to less than 20 percent by 2020. This change in the relative importance of the transport sector between the two paths is due primarily, as in the China scenarios summarized above, to the assumptions about the use of high-efficiency road vehicles in the Alternative path.

Figure 5.21
Energy Demand by Sector

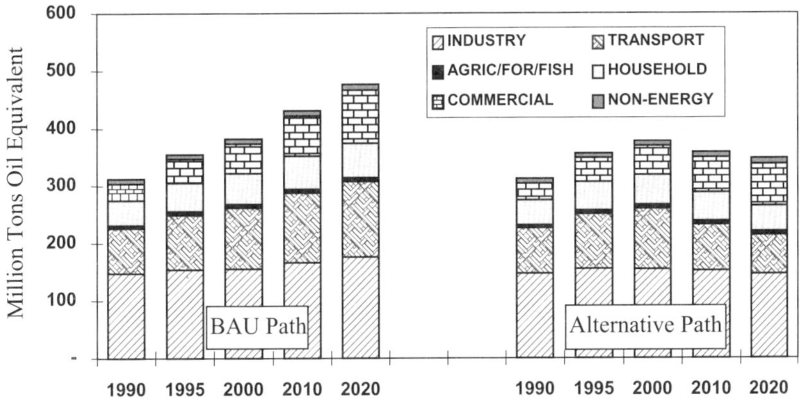

Source: See Note 32.

Table 5.7 summarizes the growth rates of energy demand by sector, for the two paths. In both cases, the commercial sector (including services and public institutions) shows the strongest growth in energy consumption (as per recent trends in Japan). For all other major sectors, overall energy use grows slowly in the BAU path, but declines in the Alternative path.

[215]

Table 5.7
Growth of Overall Sectoral Energy Demand, 1995-2020
(Average Annual Growth)

Sector	BAU Path	Alternative Path
Industry	0.5%	-0.2%
Transport	1.3%	-1.3%
Agric/Forestry/Fisheries	0.2%	0.0%
Household	0.8%	-0.5%
Commercial	3.2%	2.2%
Non-Energy	1.2%	1.2%
Total	**1.2%**	**-0.1%**

Source: See Note 32.

Turning to the overall fuel resource use implied by the two energy scenarios for Japan, Table 5.8 presents the total primary fuel supplies used in 1995 and, under the two different scenarios, in 2010 and 2020. The primary differences between the paths are:

- Overall primary fuel use in 2020 is nearly 25 percent lower in the Alternative case than in the BAU case, and, in fact, is only modestly higher than in 1995.
- The use of biomass fuels and, especially, wind and solar energy is much higher in the Alternative case than in the BAU case.
- Under the Alternative case, Japan becomes a net exporter of petroleum products by 2010, with exports of (principally) gasoline and heavy oil more than offsetting imports of LPG and naphtha. (Exports are reflected by the negative values for petroleum products in Table 5.8.)
- Crude oil imports to Japan under the Alternative scenario are about 15 percent less by 2020, than in the BAU case.
- By 2020, about half as much coal is used in the Alternative case as in the BAU case.
- Fuel gases – mostly natural gas/LNG – constitute a larger share of the energy mix by 2020 in the Alternative case than in the BAU case. The absolute amount of fuel gases used in the Alternative case, however,

[216]

is slightly lower, as a result of (mostly) energy efficiency measures and cogeneration, than in the BAU case.

• Fossil fuel use in the BAU case in 2020 is about 24.9 billion GJ, versus 16.3 billion GJ (about 65 percent of the BAU level) in the Alternative scenario.

Table 5.8
Primary Supplies of Fuels and Resources
by Balance Category (million toe)

Fuel/Resource	1995	BAU Path		Alternative Path	
		2010	2020	2010	2020
Crude oil	262.43	269.84	270.79	260.28	230.88
Petro Products	16.49	76.48	108.51	(3.82)	(6.69)
Coal/coke	81.50	81.74	90.34	58.08	46.61
Fuel Gases	53.30	87.48	124.76	94.17	119.02
Hydro/Geotherm	10.52	10.52	10.52	10.52	10.52
Wind/Solar	0.96	1.20	1.20	14.34	51.63
Nuclear	76.00	92.73	73.14	84.85	60.47
Biomass Fuels	6.69	6.93	6.93	8.37	9.32
Total	**507.89**	**626.91**	**686.19**	**526.77**	**521.75**

Fraction of Total Primary Fuel Supply

Fuel/Resource	1995	BAU Path		Alternative Path	
		2010	2020	2010	2020
Crude oil	51.7%	43.0%	39.5%	49.4%	44.3%
Petro Products	3.2%	12.2%	15.8%	-0.7%	-1.3%
Coal/coke	16.0%	13.0%	13.2%	11.0%	8.9%
Fuel Gases	10.5%	14.0%	18.2%	17.9%	22.8%
Hydro/Geotherm	2.1%	1.7%	1.5%	2.0%	2.0%
Wind/Solar	0.2%	0.2%	0.2%	2.7%	9.9%
Nuclear	15.0%	14.8%	10.7%	16.1%	11.6%
Biomass Fuels	1.3%	1.1%	1.0%	1.6%	1.8%
Total	**100%**	**100%**	**100%**	**100%**	**100%**

Source: See Note 32.

Fuel and resource imports under the two scenarios show similar patterns to overall primary energy use, as most fuels consumed in Japan are imported. Overall fuel imports in the Alternative scenario by 2020 are about 75 percent of those in the BAU scenario, with petroleum products and coal imports in the Alternative case approximately half of those in the BAU case.

Relative Cost of Alternative Scenarios in Japan

Figure 5.22 provides a summary of the relative benefits, by major cost/benefit category, of moving from the Business-as-Usual case to the Alternative case. The total net present value (NPV) difference – using a real discount rate of 2 percent per year – in net benefits (including demand costs, supply infrastructure costs, and resource costs) between the two cases is about 27 trillion 1990 yen (200 billion US$). As indicated in Figure 5.22, fuel costs in the Alternative case, summed over 1990 to 2020, are nearly 32 Trillion Yen less than in the BAU path. The bulk of these costs are import costs.[35] If one assumes an additional environmental benefit of (for example) 6750 yen per ton of carbon dioxide emissions avoided (about 50 US$ per ton of CO_2, or about 14 US$ per ton of carbon), an additional benefit of about 27 trillion yen accrues in moving from the BAU to the Alternative scenario.

Figure 5.22

Relative Benefits: Alternative Case minus BAU Case

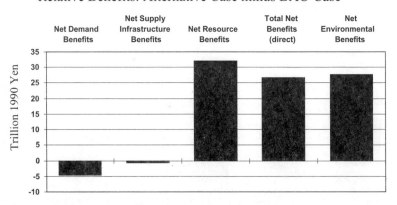

Source: See Note 32.

IV-Future Energy Use in Mongolia

To the author's knowledge, there are few projections of future energy use for the country of Mongolia. One such projection was, however, compiled as part of the ALGAS (Asia Least-Cost Greenhouse Gas Abatement Strategy) project, administered by the Asian Development Bank for the Global Environment Facility and the United Nations Development Program.[36] Figures 5.23, 5.24 and 5.25 summarize results of the Mongolia ALGAS study completed in 1997, and show, respectively, projected final energy demand by fuel, final energy demand by sector, and key energy supply statistics, for the years 1993 through 2020. In the ALGAS study, demand for commercial fuels increases rapidly, particularly in the years between 2010 and 2020. Sectoral fuel demand also increases in all end-use sectors, but growth in the industrial, transport and services sectors (with annual average 2000 to 2020 growth rates ranging from 9 to over 14 percent annually), particularly in the 2010 to 2020 period, is much higher than the growth in household or agricultural energy use (with annual average 2000 to 2020 growth rates of 1.8 and 3.8 percent, respectively). Between 1993 and 2020, coal extraction is estimated to increase by a factor of nine, petroleum imports and heat production are each projected to increase by a factor of 7.4, and electricity production is estimated to increase by a factor of 9.5.

Figure 5.23

Final Energy Demand by Fuel in Mongolia: ALGAS Results

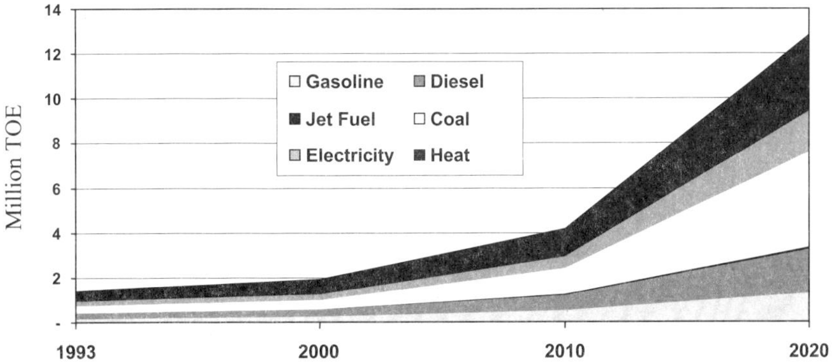

Source: Asian Development Bank (ADB), the Global Environment Facility, and the United Nations Development Program (Manila, Philippines: Asian Development Bank, 1998), *Asia Least-Cost Greenhouse Gas Abatement Strategy: Mongolia* (ADB, October 1998). Mongolia ALGAS report, 46-47.

Figure 5.24

Final Energy Demand by Sector in Mongolia: ALGAS Results

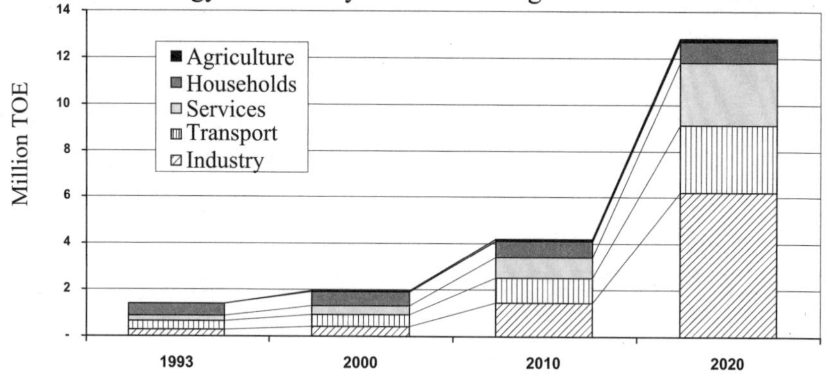

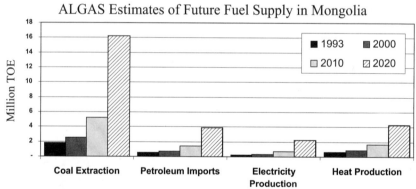

Source: Asian Development Bank (ADB), the Global Environment Facility, and the United Nations Development Program (Manila, Philippines: Asian Development Bank, 1998), *Asia Least-Cost Greenhouse Gas Abatement Strategy: Mongolia* (ADB, October 1998). Mongolia ALGAS report, 46-47.

Figure 5.25

ALGAS Estimates of Future Fuel Supply in Mongolia

Source: Asian Development Bank (ADB), the Global Environment Facility, and the United Nations Development Program (Manila, Philippines: Asian Development Bank, 1998), *Asia Least-Cost Greenhouse Gas Abatement Strategy: Mongolia* (ADB, October 1998). Mongolia ALGAS report, 46-47.

Given that demand for commercial forms of energy has continued to decline between 1993 and 2000, as indicated above, it is unlikely, in the author's view, that fuels demand or supply in Mongolia will expand to nearly the degree that the ALGAS projections suggest. Even if strong

[220]

economic growth in Mongolia were to start immediately, the author's guess is that an increase in demand by 2020 to the levels estimated by the ALGAS project for the year 2010 is still likely to be optimistic, though not impossible. Mongolia will continue, in any scenario, to consume a very small portion of the overall energy use in Northeast Asia. Mongolia may however, over the next two decades, become more important as a transit corridor used to move oil, gas, and/or electricity from Eastern Russia to China and other Northeast Asian countries. Mongolia's participation in these resource-sharing schemes may both boost its own economy (and fuel consumption) and affect the overall need for imports of energy, particularly oil and gas, in the region as a whole.

V-Future Energy Use in the Republic of Korea

The ROK economy, as noted above, rebounded relatively quickly from the financial crisis of several years ago, and strong growth in energy consumption in the ROK is likely to continue, with growth declining somewhat (particularly in the industrial and transport sectors) as the economy continues to mature. The sections below briefly summarize the results of two projections of energy demand and supply in the ROK as developed by the Korea Energy Economics Institute (KEEI). The first of the two projections is a short-term (2001 to 2005) estimate compiled recently, and the second is an older, longer-term projection of energy supply and demand to 2030.[37]

Table 5.9 shows the short-term forecast for primary energy use in the ROK. Coal consumption is forecast to increase moderately, particularly in 2002, while oil consumption, though continuing to increase, does so at a declining rate, increasing by just over 2 percent annually between 2004 and 2006. The use of LNG is forecast to continue increasing strongly through 2006, continuing the pattern of 1995 to 2006, but growth in the use of LNG is also forecast to taper off somewhat by 2006. Average total growth in primary energy use in the ROK from 2001 through 2006 is 4.1 percent annually. KEEI offers three scenarios ("Best Case," "Baseline,"

[221]

and "Worst Case") for the evolution of primary energy demand through 2006, with annual average growth rates ranging from 3.3 to 4.6 percent annually for the period from 2000 to 2006.

Table 5.9

Primary Energy Demand Forecast for the ROK (2001-2006)

Total consumption	2001	2002	2003	2004	2005	2006
Coal (million tons)	68.8	73.3	76.1	78	803	82.5
Oil (million bbl)	744.1	766.9	785.9	803.3	820.5	837
LNG (million tons)	16.8	19.0	21.2	23.1	25.1	27.1
Total (million TOE)	**198.6**	**209.3**	**218.5**	**226.8**	**234.8**	**242.6**
Change from Previous Year						
Coal	3.4%	6.6%	3.7%	2.5%	3.0%	27%
Oil	0.2%	3.1%	2.5%	2.2%	2.1%	2.0%
LNG	15.2%	13.1%	11.7%	9.2%	8.5%	7.7%
Total	**3.0%**	**5.4%**	**4.4%**	**3.8%**	**3.5%**	**3.3%**

Source: In-Gang Na, Yongduk Pak, Tae Heon Kim, Do Young Choi, *Mid-Term Energy Outlook, 2001-2005* (Seoul: Korea Energy Economics Institute, 2001).

The forecast structure of final fuels demand for the ROK for the period 2001 to 2006 is presented in Table 5.10.[38] Notable trends shown in Table 5.10 include the decreasing growth rate of energy demand in the industrial sector, as well as in the faster-growing transport sector, and an even steeper decline in the growth in energy use in the Residential/Commercial/Public sector as the ROK completes its transition to the status of an "industrialized nation." Of the individual fuels, oil product demand increases at less than 2.5 percent annually after 2002, as fuel use continues to shift to electricity and piped gas for many applications.

[222]

Table 5.10

Final Energy Demand Forecast for the ROK (2001-2006)

Demand by Sector (MTOE)	2001	2002	2003	2004	2005	2006
Industry	85.1	88.6	91.7	94.7	97.5	100.2
Transport	32.0	33.9	35.6	37.2	38.9	40.5
Residential/Commercial/Public	35.9	37.8	39.3	40.4	41.5	42.5
Total Final Demand	**153.9**	**161.2**	**167.5**	**173.2**	**178.8**	**184.1**
Demand by Fuel Type						
Oil (million bbl)	697.7	718.0	735.2	751.6	767.9	784.2
Antracite (domestic) Coal (Mte)	4.0	4.1	4.2	4.2	4.1	4.1
Bituminous Coal (Mte)	27.5	28.5	29.2	29.8	30.4	30.9
Electricity (GWh)	256.5	277.1	295.0	312.8	329.7	345.2
City (Piped) Gas	12.9	14.5	16.1	17.4	18.5	19.6
Change from Previous Year						
Industry	1.50%	4.10%	3.50%	3.20%	3.00%	2.80%
Transport	3.40%	6.00%	4.90%	4.70%	4.40%	4.20%
Residential/Commercial/Public	2.70%	5.20%	3.90%	2.90%	2.60%	2.40%
Total Final Demand	**2.50%**	**4.80%**	**3.90%**	**3.40%**	**3.20%**	**3.00%**
Oil	-0.1%	2.9%	2.4%	2.2%$	2.2%	2.1%
Antracite (domestic) Coal	18.4%	4.6%	0.9%	-0.5%	-0.9%	-1.5%
Bituminous Coal	1.8%	3.7%	2.3%	2.2%	2.0%	1.7%
Electricity	7.1%	8.1%	6.4%	6.0%	5.4%	4.7%
City (Piped) Gas	8.0%	12.6%	11.1%	7.6%	6.5%	5.9%

Source: In-Gang Na, Yongduk Pak, Tae Heon Kim, Do Young Choi, *Mid-Term Energy Outlook, 2001-2005* (Seoul, ROK: Korea Energy Economics Institute, dated October, 2001).

Table 5.11 summarizes KEEI's 1994 long-range forecast of energy use. Although the overall rate of growth forecast for energy use in the ROK has decreased somewhat between the time when this long-range forecast and the short-term projection summarized above were prepared, the overall patterns remain. Forecast growth is strongest for electricity and gas, with growth in use of oil products and coal declining, in relative terms, over the next three decades.

Table 5.11

Annual Average Growth of Energy Use

(from 1994 KEEI Long-term Forecast)

Fuel	1992-1997	1997-2000	2001-2010	2011-2020	2021-2030	2001-2030
Total	**8.8%**	**7.0%**	**4.1%**	**3.0%**	**2.4%**	**3.2%**
Oil Products	8.2%	4.7%	3.0%	2.0%	1.4%	2.1%
Electricity	11.7%	8.8%	5.7%	4.4%	3.4%	4.5%
LNG	21.3%	13.3%	6.6%	4.5%	3.5%	4.9%
Bituminous Coal	13.6%	7.8%	3.9%	3.1%	2.5%	3.2%

Sources: In-Gang Na, Yongduk Pak, Tae Heon Kim, Do Young Choi, *Mid-Term Energy Outlook, 2001-2005* (Seoul, ROK: Korea Energy Economics Institute, dated October, 2001). *Korean Energy to 2030*, document in Korean dated November 1994 (www.keei.re.kr). Korea Energy Economics Institute, Seoul, 1994.

VI-Future Energy Use in the Russian Far East

Energy demand in the Russian Far East (RFE) is projected to continue its relatively modest growth of recent years, though this growth assumes continued improvement of the supply of capital for investments in industrial and energy infrastructure, as well as continued economic restructuring. Figure 5.26 shows one estimate of future final energy demand by sector in the Russian Far East through 2010.[39] In this projection, overall energy use in the RFE exceeds 1990 energy use by less than 10 percent by 2010. Hidden in this relatively modest increase, however, may be a host of factors related to structural adjustment in the RFE economy and improved energy efficiency as the infrastructure in the region is modernized.

Figure 5.27 shows the same estimate of future energy demand in the RFE, this time disaggregated by end-use fuel. Here, use of electricity and natural gas show the most significant growth between 1995 and 2010, with growth in the use of petroleum products, coal, and heat totaling only a few to 10 percent over the same 15-year period.

Figure 5.26
Historical, Estimated and Projected Energy Demand in the Russian Far East by Sector

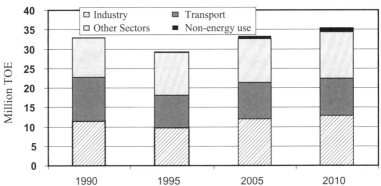

Source: Victor D. Kalashnikov, *National Energy Futures Analysis and Energy Security Perspectives in the Russian Far East*, Khabarovsk Economic Research Institute, Far Eastern Branch of Russian Academy of Sciences. Paper Prepared for The Nautilus Institute East Asia Energy Futures Project, June 2000.

Figure 5.27
Historical, Estimated and Projected Energy Demand in the Russian Far East by Fuel

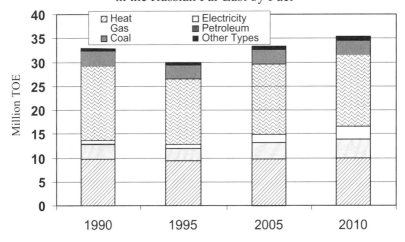

Source: Victor D. Kalashnikov, *National Energy Futures Analysis and Energy Security Perspectives in the Russian Far East*, Khabarovsk Economic Research Institute, Far Eastern Branch of Russian Academy of Sciences. Paper prepared for The Nautilus Institute East Asia Energy Futures Project, June 2000.

Environmental Implications of Growth in Energy Use

The countries of Northeast Asia currently produce somewhat under 20 percent of total world carbon dioxide (CO_2) emissions from energy-sector activities. This fraction has been projected to rise to 23 percent by 2010, meaning that, if the projections prove correct, about one-third of the global growth in CO_2 emissions will be in the Northeast Asia region. This projected growth in emissions will be brought by explosive growth in fuels use, particularly in China and the Koreas. In addition, the limits to domestic oil resources in China and the rest of the region means that imports of oil from outside Asia, principally from the Middle East, will grow substantially in the near future.

The combination of these issues present potentially massive environmental problems for the globe, the region, and the countries of the region. Growth in greenhouse gas emissions will eventually lead to a changed climate, which could have a variety of ecological, economic, and social impacts. Increased shipping of crude oil and refined products will make already crowded sea lanes in the region even more crowded, will increase the magnitude of accidental and routine spills, and may spur additional conflict over maritime resources.

Acid Rain in Northeast Asia

Of the many environmental concerns currently facing the nations of Northeast Asia, the problem of "acid rain" or "acid precipitation" presents perhaps the most potent combination of immediate and ongoing impact and regional scope.[40] "Acid rain" is a general, though not entirely accurate, term used to describe a complex set of processes. "Acid gases"—principally oxides of sulfur (SO_x) and nitrogen (NO_x) are emitted into the air during the combustion of fossil fuels, as well as from some natural processes. In the atmosphere, acid gases can combine with water vapor or water droplets to form sulfuric and nitric acids. These acids are transported by prevailing winds, and eventually fall back to earth (or to the ocean) as rain or snow. Acid gases can also be absorbed into particles in the atmosphere, and fall as to the ground as "dry deposition" with particles or as ions, becoming acidic when wetted.

[226]

The effects of acid rain vary considerably with the vegetation, soil types, and weather conditions in a given area. Under some conditions, the addition of sulfate and nitrate to the soil helps replace lost nutrients, and aids plant growth. In other instances, however, acid deposition can cause lakes and streams to become acid, damage trees and other plants, damage man-made structures, and help to mobilize toxic compounds naturally present in soil and rocks. The countries of Northeast Asia have already begun to experience some important impacts of acid rain. Forest health in some areas of the Koreas, China, and Japan has already revealed evidence of degradation that points to acid rain.[41] Man-made materials such as zinc-plated steel have drastically shorter-than-normal lifetimes in south China, and irreplaceable cultural landmarks made of limestone and other substances are being degraded at an accelerating rate.[42]

While natural sources account for a significant, though uncertain, fraction of the atmospheric sulfur and nitrogen oxides, human sources appear to be the major cause of recent declining trends in the pH[43] of rainfall. While some industrial sources of emissions, particularly the smelting of metal, can be important sources of sulfur oxides, the energy sector accounts for a large fraction of these emissions. Sulfur oxides are produced during combustion of coal, which in Northeast Asia contains varying amounts (0.5 to 5 or more percent) of sulfur, and during combustion of oil products, particularly the heavier grades. These fuels are commonly used in large industrial facilities and in electric power generation in all of the countries of the region, and coal is also a very common domestic fuel in North Korea (DPRK), China, and Mongolia. Nitrogen oxides are produced at varying rates by all types of fossil and biomass fuel combustion. The nitrogen in the NO_x produced during combustion is derived both from nitrogen in the fuel and from the molecular nitrogen (N_2) that makes up nearly four-fifths of the air we breathe. Gasoline-powered autos, trucks, and buses are major emitters of NO_x, as are many utility and industrial combustion devices.

Though acid deposition can be a local phenomenon, particularly in urban areas and in areas near a large point source of emissions, the extent to which acid gases are carried by prevailing weather patterns makes acid rain a truly regional issue, one that frequently crosses national boundaries.

Although, for example, a large fraction of the emissions in Northeast Asia both originate and fall to earth in China, there is substantial inter-country transport of acid gases. As the majority of the growth in emissions in the next two decades will likely be in China, a substantial regional, if not international, cooperative effort will be required to reduce emissions before the level of environmental damage becomes overwhelming.

Table 5.12[44] provides estimates of the emissions of both sulfur and nitrogen oxides for five of the countries of Northeast Asia for 1990. Emissions from China, particularly from area sources,[45] dominate the regional picture of SO_x emissions. For nitrogen oxide emissions, China's emissions still dominate, but Japan and South Korea produce a much larger portion of the total. RAINS-Asia reference-case projections, in which no improvement in emissions controls is assumed, show SO_x emissions from all countries of the region with the exception of Japan nearly tripling between 1990 and 2020, yielding total regional emissions in 2020 of almost 71 million tons. Zero values in the "Large Point Sources" column for Mongolia and (particularly) for North Korea probably reflects a lack of information about the sources of sulfur oxides in those countries, rather than the actual lack of large point sources.[46]

Table 5.12
Estimated Emissions of Acid Gases in Northeast Asia in 1990
(thousand tons)

Country	Sulfur Oxides			Nitrogen Oxides
	Area Sources	Large Point Sources	Total	
China	18,548	3,360	21,908	9,926
Hong Kong	31	108	139	391
Chinese Taipei	478	21	499	671
Japan	818	17	835	2,575
Mongolia	78	0	78	31
North Korea	343	0	343	518
South Korea	1542	98	1,640	1,045
TOTAL	**21,838**	**3,604**	**25,442**	**15,157**

Source: P. Hayes and L. Zarsky, "Acid Rain in a Regional Context," in Science and Technology Policy Institute and the United Nations University's Joint Seminar on "The Role of Science and Technology in Promoting Environmentally Sustainable Development." Science and Technology Policy Institute and The United Nations University, Seoul, June 1995; Table provided by David Streets, Argonne National Laboratory, Argonne, Illinois.

Indications from the current pattern of SO_x transport are that while virtually all of the sulfur oxides falling to earth in China originate in China, emissions from other countries constitute from 15 percent (South Korea) to over 60 percent (DPRK) of the total deposition in some of the other countries of the region.[47] A review of the soil types in the region most subject to acidification shows that key agricultural areas in Southern and Eastern China, in North and South Korea, and in Japan are at risk.[48]

The potential huge growth in regional emissions, coupled with the regional nature of atmospheric transport of acid gases and the sensitivity of key ecosystems to acidification, makes acid rain in Northeast Asia a major problem. First, this issue must be responded to forcefully and quickly, and second, it must be addressed at the regional level, as well as nationally and locally.

Increased Fuels Use and Greenhouse Gas Emissions

The current and projected growth in energy use in Northeast Asia, particularly in a "Business-as-Usual" world, means that the region will play an extremely important role in either exacerbating or reducing the impact of global climate change.[49] Scientific consensus is that increasing concentrations of greenhouse gases in the atmosphere, prominently including carbon dioxide and methane emitted by fossil fuels combustion, will cause global climate to change in the next several decades, if such changes have not already occurred.[50] The impact of climate change will vary widely across the globe, but those countries with the largest, least affluent populations per unit land area will likely be among the most vulnerable. China and North Korea (and Mongolia), therefore, face a dilemma. Development is necessary in both human and political terms, but one of the effects of development is likely to be increased greenhouse gas emissions, which puts those countries (and the globe) at risk from the impact of climate change.

Figure 5.28 shows a comparison of one set of greenhouse gas emissions projections for Northeast Asia as compared with projections for the rest of the world. In 1980, the countries of Northeast Asia accounted for just under 15 percent of the world's total carbon emissions. By 1992, the fraction had grown to nearly 20 percent. By 2010, based on projections by K. Fujime, carbon dioxide emissions from the region will be 23 percent of the global total, reaching a level nearly double that of 1992. This means that the region will have contributed nearly one-third of the total growth in global carbon emissions between 1980 and 2010.[51]

Figure 5.28

Historical and Projected Carbon Emissions in Northeast Asia and the Rest of the World

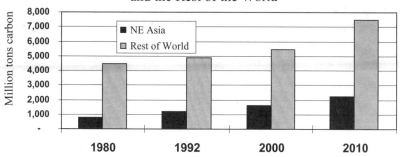

Source: K. Fujime, "Long-Term Energy Supply/Demand Outlook for Asia APEC Nations," *Energy in Japan*, Bimonthly Report No. 137, January 1996.

Although the process of climate stabilization is one that will, of necessity, take the better part of a century if not more, an increase like that shown above in only the next two decades will make stabilization that much harder to achieve. Managing the growth in fossil fuel use in Northeast Asia is therefore one of the keys in reaching GHG stabilization targets as soon as possible.

Figure 5.29 illustrates the possibilities for managing growth in fossil fuel use in Northeast Asia—in this case for China. Figure 5.29 compares the global warming potential (a measure of overall greenhouse gas emissions) under the "reference" (BAU) and "alternative" scenarios for future energy sector development discussed earlier in this paper. By 2020, the "Alternative" scenario yields a nearly a 20 percent reduction in greenhouse gas emissions relative to the BAU scenario, a huge savings for both China and for the globe as a whole.

Figure 5.29
Global Warming Potential from All Fossil Fuels Use:
Scenario Comparison

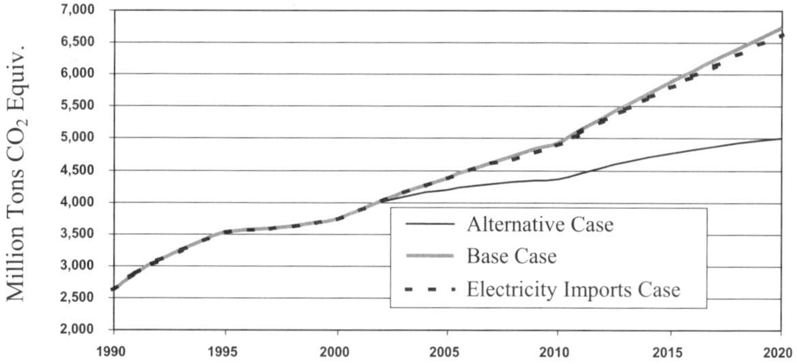

Source: See endnote 32.

Fossil Fuels Use and the Marine Environment

Increased use of fuels in Northeast Asia and Asia generally is likely to affect the global marine environment. As noted above, net oil imports by China alone are projected to reach about 120 million tons of oil equivalent (MTOE) per year by 2010, and under one projection, net imports to the Asian APEC region as a whole are expected to rise from about 75 MTOE in 1992 to 432 MTOE in 2010, an increase of nearly 500 percent. What this means is that much more oil will be on the high seas, traveling to Asian countries from exporting nations that are increasingly in the Middle East. Fesharaki et al [52] estimate that 95 percent of crude oil imports to Asia and the Pacific will come from the Middle East by 2010, as compared with 70 percent in 1993. This vast potential increase in tanker traffic brings with it potential for increased marine oil pollution from both routine and accidental spills. A contributing factor to the increased risk of oil spills in the Asian region in general, and in Northeast Asia in particular, is that the additional tankers carrying oil from the Middle East and elsewhere to China and other nations add to congestion in the relatively few major sea lanes in the region.[53] These sea lanes are already crowded by tanker and freighter traffic serving the booming economies of the area.

[231]

Impact of Energy Demand Growth on Capital Markets

Meeting the increased demand for fuels in Northeast Asia will require huge capital investments in a number of different sectors, including the following:

- Electricity generation, particularly to meet high growth in demand in China
- Coal mine expansion, and especially, coal transport facilities in China
- Oil exploration and production facilities, including offshore platforms
- Oil tanker docking facilities, especially in China
- Oil refining—including both new refineries and equipment to allow existing refineries to use high-sulfur (sour) crude oil from the Middle East
- Natural gas pipelines—virtually all of the proposals for bringing gas to Northeast Asia involve costs of US$10-20 billion or more, even before accounting for the costs of local distribution networks[54]
- Liquefied natural gas (LNG) terminals (up to $1 billion each) and transport vessels (in the region of $250 million each).

These potential investments will compete among themselves for scarce foreign and domestic capital. They may also compete for capital with environmental investments such as pollution control equipment, coal-mine safety investments, and energy efficiency investments. To the extent that the investments are (or can be made to be) attractive to the international private financial institutions, this competition may not be of great importance in the long run. If, however, investments in Northeast Asian countries are seen as too risky by bankers from Europe, North America, Japan, or the Middle East, energy-sector investments will have to rely on domestic financing and/or financing from multilateral development banks, both of which are in short supply. Further, energy-sector investments may reduce the availability of capital for important social investments, such as education, improvements in medical care, housing or other needs. The potential constraints on the capital markets that can supply the region have not been quantitatively examined in a thorough fashion as yet, but availability of capital remains a consideration that will determine, in part, the evolution of energy infrastructure in the region.

Conclusions and Key Issues for the Future

As noted in earlier sections of this paper, Northeast Asia will continue to be a major and fast-growing center of energy demand in the near future, but along with this demand will come increasing environmental concerns, and perhaps also concerns for regional capital markets. Some of the key features of the current and evolving energy future in Northeast Asia can be summarized as follows:

- Growth in fuels consumption, and especially gas and petroleum products, will continue at a fairly rapid pace in China and the Republic of Korea for the next decade, with growth slowing, first in the ROK, and somewhat later in China, as both economies mature.

- China is already a net importer of oil, and it will become an increasingly important consumer of oil imports, including imports from the Middle East, over the next two decades. This trend toward higher imports seems in recent years to have been increased by Chinese policies that have somewhat de-emphasized, for environmental reasons, the use of domestic coal, meaning more use of imported oil and gas.

- Future growth in fuels consumption in Mongolia and the DPRK are highly uncertain, and (particularly in the DPRK) very much at the mercy of both internal economic and political decisions, and of cooperation from abroad.

- Japanese energy consumption seems destined to grow relatively little in the near future. Despite the Japanese government's stated goal of reducing dependence on foreign sources of energy, the major potential source of increased "domestic" energy supply, nuclear power, seems for social and political reasons unlikely to actually increase its share of the nation's energy output—and a decline in nuclear power's share of primary energy in Japan is a real possibility over the next two decades. This means that Japan is likely to be reliant on imported oil and gas for the next two decades and beyond.

- Significantly increasing quantities of imported LNG are likely to be used in the region in the future, driven by a combination of overall increases in energy needs, the increasing availability and declining

[233]

prices of high-efficiency gas-fired electricity generation equipment (such as combined-cycle plants), and local, regional and global environmental concerns (for which cleaner-burning gas provides at least a partial solution). Major centers of demand will continue to be Japan and the ROK, but China will also develop considerable capacity for LNG use. Much of the additional LNG needed in Northeast Asia is likely to be shipped from the Middle East.

- The Russian Far East has massive energy resources, and the Russian government and local and regional governments and companies within Russia are highly motivated to make use of those resources by selling oil, gas and electricity to the RFE's neighbor nations. Officials and energy analysts in the Russian Far East see exports of energy and other resources as a key future driver of economic growth in the RFE. Harnessing these resources is, however, hampered by the remote and forbidding locations of these resources, by the high cost of extracting or harnessing these resources and bringing them to markets, and by a lack of capital to support the necessary infrastructure investments.

- Although several pacts on international energy infrastructure cooperation between Russia, Japan, China, and the ROK have been discussed, cooperation in this area has moved forward relatively slowly. The historical antagonisms between the countries of the region are partly to blame for the slow pace of cooperation in this area, as are the massive scale and technical complexity of the infrastructure projects being contemplated. Another key factor is that in Japan, the country with the most to offer by way of financing and technology for these projects, incentives to participate are mixed, at best. Local gas and electric utility companies in Japan, powerful both economically and politically, enjoy protected markets for their services, and are very reluctant to accept changes that (from their perspectives) would adversely affect those markets. This, for example, is a key reason why Japan lacks a national gas pipeline system, while the ROK has established a national gas transmission system that would allow it to take advantage of lower-priced gas imports from Russia, should such become available.

- Though the DPRK's demand for fuels, and particularly for oil and gas, will likely continue to be a very minor part of regional energy demand during the next two decades, the DPRK will play a pivotal role in spurring or retarding intra-regional cooperation on energy issues in Northeast Asia. Geographically, the major practical route for gas pipelines or electric transmission lines between Russia and the markets of the ROK pass through DPRK territory (in fact, would traverse most of the length of the DPRK). The DPRK has historical economic ties with Russia that would likely – in the event of political rapprochement between the DPRK and the ROK, or if reunification of the Korean peninsula occurs in the near future – result in enhanced chances for the use of Russian oil, gas, and/or electricity in both the DPRK and ROK. In addition, the nuclear reactors now under construction in the DPRK by the Korean (Peninsula) Energy Development Organization (KEDO) and its partners will require a source of back-up power that, in the short run, can only (practically speaking) come via a transmission link with the ROK, Russia, and/or China.[55] Therefore the receptiveness of the DPRK to energy trading on the Korean Peninsula (and the desire of regional and international partners to engage the DPRK on energy issues), plus the technical and political demands associated with the KEDO reactors, may be a major force toward major energy trading in Northeast Asia. Alternatively, if the relationship between the ROK and the DPRK (or the relationship between the United States and the DPRK) turns sour, regional electricity and gas grids could take much longer to come to fruition.

- To a much less uncertain extent, Mongolia could serve as a host to natural gas pipelines or electric lines from the RFE, Siberia or other parts of Russia. Mongolian energy demand is small, so use of transferred power or gas inside Mongolia is likely to be minimal, and the Mongolian government, eager for foreign exchange earnings, would likely be receptive to hosting these types of international energy infrastructure.

- Even if resource and energy transport infrastructure development in Russia were to start immediately on a relatively large scale, the impact of exports from Russia on the need for imports of oil and gas from outside Northeast Asia (mostly to China, Japan, and the ROK) is unlikely to be large, in terms of percentage of net imports, over the next two decades.

- Energy efficiency, and to a lesser extent, the development of renewable energy resources, offers, in the author's opinion, the greatest promise as a means for reducing demand for fuels and the associated environmental impacts of fuel demand in Northeast Asia. The combination of aggressive energy efficiency improvement, plus aggressive development of Russian resources and of domestic renewable sources of energy, could together significantly reduce – from reference case levels – the need for imported energy resources. This does not, however, mean that the need for imported oil and gas in Northeast Asia is likely to fall below year 2000 levels within the next two decades. The potential impact on imports of different energy scenarios in the different countries of the region should, however, be explored more fully and quantitatively than has been possible to date.

- The development of the efficiency of private motor vehicles in Northeast Asia could have an extremely profound impact on the overall use of oil products (and gas) in the region, and, by extension, on the need for imports of oil (and gas) from outside the region. Technologies arguably exist that could triple or quadruple the efficiency of the private car relative to today's average new vehicles. In China, where the number of new vehicles is growing explosively, the difference between adopting high-efficiency or standard automotive technologies and its impact on year 2020 oil demand is very large indeed.

International Cooperation in the N.E. Asia Energy Sector

There are a number of areas where international cooperation in the Northeast Asia energy sector, from both within and outside of Northeast Asia, could be very beneficial to the economies of the region, to the regional environment, and to the global environment. Most of the generic opportunities listed below pertain to the involvement of industrialized countries in general in the Northeast Asia energy sector; many of the Arab states, particularly those with technology and financing to offer, could be among the participants in these cooperative activities. The applicable approaches to cooperation in the Northeast Asian energy sector include:

- *Promote Joint Ventures and Licensing Agreements*: Fuel-switching and energy-efficiency equipment could be met by domestic production through joint ventures and licensing agreements between governmental or private organizations in China and North Korea and foreign firms with the necessary expertise to produce the needed equipment.

- *Provide Information and General Training to Government Officials*: Getting initiatives such as fuel-switching (particularly renewable resources) and energy efficiency programs off the ground in the developing countries of the region will require the understanding and support of top government officials. Consequently, the advantages and local/international opportunities provided by the measures and technologies covered here must be impressed upon top officials, via study tours, workshops and briefings.

- *Provide Specific Information and Training to Local Actors*: Training of a very specific and practical nature must be provided to personnel at the local level. Specific training will also be needed to allow local personnel to install and maintain new technologies transferred from other countries.

- *Provide Funding for Demonstration Projects:* As part of encouraging joint ventures and local manufacture, regional cooperation in the setting up and funding of key demonstration projects would help to catalyze the uptake of key technologies. Here, governments with sufficient financial resources could provide seed money and serve as liaisons between developing-country institutions and private actors (for both financing and technology transfer).

- *Assist in Forging Agreements on Development and Sharing of Energy Transport Facilities and Infrastructure*: As imports of energy products to the region—particularly oil and oil products—expand, competition among fuel purchasers in the region for fuel contracts and transport facilities are likely to tighten. This means that regional coordination and trade agreements will likely need to be fashioned to assure the orderly sharing of resources such as sea lanes, and to ensure that all of the countries of the region have equal and open access to markets for imported fuels. Actors and governments from outside the region can also lend their experience, expertise and their money toward the development of gas and oil pipelines and of electricity grids, which allow the resources of Russia to be tapped for use in China, the Koreas and possibly Japan.

- *Lead by Example*: Developing countries in the region are unlikely to adopt stringent and advanced energy-efficiency measures or invest in a substantial portfolio of renewable energy technologies unless industrialized countries – most notably, the United States, Japan, and the countries of Western Europe – do the same. Promptly deciding on and successfully achieving their own stringent, enforceable national goals for emissions reduction would be one of the best levers that other nations can use in encouraging the developing countries of Northeast Asia to put a maximum effort into continuing their development in an environmentally sustainable manner.

- *Promote and Assist in Applications that Demonstrate Promising Technologies*: This could include (but should not be limited to) participation in Joint Implementation (JI) projects, and in providing the equipment and expertise necessary to corroborate the net emissions reduction or carbon sequestration impacts of JI and GEF (Global Environment Facility) projects.

- *Strengthen Support for Basic and Applied Research on Energy Efficiency and Renewable Technologies*: Industrialized nations should increase funding for research and development on the most attractive/ promising methods for GHG emissions reduction, including collaborative research activities that involve (and train scientists from) other countries in the region.

The incentives of Arab states to participate in many of the cooperative activities above probably appear, in many cases, to be modest at best, as most of the activities are geared to results in a reduction of energy use in Northeast Asia. In the author's opinion, however, there are likely to be

[238]

substantial long-term benefits to the economies of the Arab states. These benefits may include:

- Participation in development of (and subsequent adoption of) energy efficiency technologies would help the Middle East nations to stretch their own oil and gas resources and thus prolong and increase foreign exchange earnings. To the extent that overall output of petroleum in some countries of the region is limited by international quotas, reducing consumption of oil domestically provides a way of increasing exports and export earnings.

- Arab states and companies may have technologies to offer to help extract and transport oil and gas resources in Russia, thus assisting with such infrastructure development may be an income-generating opportunity for Middle Eastern nations. Building relationships with Russian agencies and companies will take time, however, and many other international companies are also interested in helping to move Russian resources to markets elsewhere in Asia.

- Participating in and observing international resource sharing within Northeast Asia may provide experience that helps Middle Eastern countries to develop their own infrastructure and protocols for resource sharing and trade. Assisting Northeast Asia with the development of pipelines and possibly electricity interconnections, for example, will help Middle Eastern firms and governments learn some of the approaches and constraints to sharing resources among the countries of their home region.

- As rich as the Middle East is in oil and gas resources, it also has world class solar energy, and in some areas, wind power resources. Global oil supplies are, more than arguably, becoming increasingly scarce, and greenhouse gas concerns continue to become increasingly important. One way for the countries of the Middle East to improve their long-term economic future is to learn as much as possible about the cost-effective development of solar and wind resources, to invest in development of solar and wind resources within their borders, and to develop ways to export wind and solar energy to Europe and beyond.

[239]

6

The Electricity Supply Industry in East Asia and the Implications of Increasing World Energy Prices

Romeo Pacudan

The development of the electricity supply industry in East Asia has been influenced by economic and global events during the past decades. The rapid economic growth rates that characterized most countries in the past resulted in massive investments in the electricity supply infrastructure development in the region. Except in Japan, where utilities are private sector-owned, these investments were public sector expenditures.

The oil crises in the 1970s had an important impact on the development of the fuel supply industry. Fuel diversification policies and reduction of dependence from imported crude oil both in the overall economy and in power generation have become an important energy security policy in most East Asian countries. This created opportunities for the development of other indigenous conventional energy resources as well as opportunities to trade electricity and other energy sources.

Since the late 1980s, many, if not most Asian governments embraced the electricity supply industry liberalization and privatization that swept across several developed countries. While each country has its own rationale for such changes, the common reasons are to reduce electricity prices, improve the productive efficiency of the industry and reduce the financial burden incurred by the public sector in expanding electricity supply infrastructure. Several East Asian countries have already implemented reforms while others have drawn up plans to reform the industry.

The financial crisis that hit the region in 1997 slowed down the development of the electricity industry. Electricity demand fell and several supply-side projects including those in the fuel supply industry have been delayed or cancelled. Structural flaws of the current stage of reform have been exposed and governments have been urged to hasten the pace of the reform process.

Barely had the East Asian economies recovered from the crisis when the world oil prices increased due to controls in the global oil production imposed by the oil producing countries. This chapter reviews the implications of the upward movement of oil prices for the electricity supply industry, more particularly on the fuel supply market, electricity trade and industry reforms. The East Asian countries being focused upon in this study are the seven Southeast Asian countries (Brunei, Indonesia, Malaysia, Philippines, Singapore, Thailand and Vietnam) and five Northeast Asian economies (Japan, China, Republic of Korea, Hong Kong and Chinese Taipei).

Electricity Supply Market

The electricity demand in East Asia reached more than 3,100 TWh in 2000, of which roughly 88 percent were consumed in the countries of Northeast Asia and the remaining in Southeast Asia. The total installed capacity registered around 704 GW with Northeast Asia accounting for 91 percent and Southeast Asia accounting for 9 percent. The figures are shown in Table 6.1.

Table 6.1

Electricity Capacity and Generation: Historical and Forecast Growth Rates

Country	Electrification Rate[1] (% of villages connected to the grid) 1998	Per Capita Electricity Consumption (KWh/person) 2000	Installed Capacity[2] (MW) 2000	Net Power Generation[2] (TWh) 2000	Electricity Demand Growth[3] (%) 1980-1999	Electricity Demand Forecast[3] (%) 1999-2020
Southeast Asia			**61,817**	**379.2**		
Brunei	100	8359	705	2.5	11.6	3.1
Indonesia	55	584	20,762	112.0	13.5	6.6
Malaysia		2974	14,110	69.4	10.3	6.1
Peninsula	99					
Sabah/Sarawak	75					
Philippines	80	695	11,017	40.2	3.7	6.0
Singapore	100	7603	6,750	31.7	8.6	4.7
Thailand	82	1580	21,074	96.8	10.1	5.5
Vietnam	71	339	6,173	26.6	13.6	8.2
Northeast Asia			**642,133**	**2,726.7**		
China	95	1074	319,320	1,326.0	7.3	5.6
Hong Kong	100	4607	11,568	31.3	6.3	4.7
Republic of Korea	100	5634	47,876	266.4	11.1	4.7
Japan	100	8464	228,596	918.1	3.3	1.4
Chinese Taipei	100	8319	34,773	184.9	7.5	4.0

Sources: 1: *APERC*, 2001; 2: *Energy Argus -a, 2003*; 3: APERC, 2002b.

Electricity demand forecast for East Asia is relatively optimistic. In Southeast Asia, electricity growth rates in the past decades were relatively high, at double-digit growth rates. One has to recall that these countries experienced rapid economic growth rates in the past decades. In Northeast Asia, electricity demand growth rates were mixed with Japan experiencing moderate growth rates, China, Hong Kong, and Chinese Taipei at relatively high rates, and Republic of Korea at a very high rate of around 11 percent. Forecast of electricity demand growth rates range from slightly above 1 percent in Japan to more than 7 percent in China and Chinese Taipei.

Following the same trend in the past decade, Southeast Asian electricity demand is forecast to grow relatively faster than in Northeast Asia. Considering that most of the countries have lower electrification rates and electricity consumption per capita than its Northeast Asian counterparts (except China), the potential for growth in Southeast Asia is generally high.

The electricity generation mix is influenced partly by the availability of energy resources either as indigenous energy resource or imported commodity. Indigenous natural gas resources are abundant in Brunei, Indonesia, Malaysia, Thailand and Vietnam. Indonesia and Thailand have substantial coal resources.

The Philippines is the world's second producer of geothermal energy. Singapore and to some extent the Philippines, are dependent on imported energy which explains the high utilization of fuel oil in power generation. The electricity generation mix for Southeast and Northeast Asia is shown in Table 6.2.

With the exception of China, which is endowed with significant coal resources, most of the Northeast Asian countries are energy resource-poor countries. This explains the higher penetration of nuclear energy in power generation. Moreover, the availability of coal and natural gas in the Asian market enables these fuels to account for higher shares in the electricity generation mix.

Decreasing dependence on oil is a common trend in the East Asian region. Oil share in power generation is forecast to decline in the medium term. Coal and natural gas appear to be the fuels of choice in most countries in Southeast Asia. In Indonesia and the Republic of Korea coal is preferred to natural gas. Coal and gas shares also increase in Chinese Taipei and Japan. Gas is preferred in Hong Kong, while coal share is declining in China. Nuclear energy remains the mainstay fuel in Japan and Republic of Korea.

Table 6.2
Electricity Generation Mix (in percentages)

Country	Coal		Oil		Gas		Hydro		Nuclear		NRE	
	1995	2010	1995	2010	1995	2010	1995	2010	1995	2010	1995	2010
Southeast Asia												
Brunei	-	-	-		100	100	-	5	-		-	
Indonesia	26	65	18	7	38	15	7	5	-	-	12	9
Malaysia	10	14	23	16	63	64	5	3	-	-	-	-
Philippines	6	32	38	8	-	14	5	-	-	-	51	44
Singapore	-	-	74	50	26	50	-	2	-	-	-	-
Thailand	20	39	33	9	44	49	4	7	-	-	-	1
Northeast Asia												
China	86	80	6	6	-	-	6	-	1	6	-	1
Hong Kong	97	82	3	8	-	10	-	-	-	-	-	-
Republic of Korea	24	36	23	7	10	8	1	4	42	48	-	-
Japan	17	21	22	15	19	21	5	2	37	36	2	2
Chinese Taipei	34	43	24	6	5	21	3		35	29	-	-

Source: *APERC*, 1998.

Fuel Supply Market

Energy Reserves

As mentioned earlier, the fuel choice for power generation is partly influenced by the availability of energy as an indigenous resource. In Northeast Asia, only China is richly endowed with coal and hydro resources while most of the countries are energy resource-poor. In Southeast Asia, some countries are richly endowed with energy resources. Huge reserves of coal are found in Indonesia and Thailand; natural gas in Indonesia, Malaysia and Brunei, hydro resources in Indonesia and the Greater Mekong Sub-Region (GMS). Energy reserves in East Asia are shown in Table 6.3.

Table 6.3
Energy Reserves and Hydro Potential in East Asia

Country	Coal[1] Proven Reserves (in million tons)	Natural Gas Proven Reserves[1] (in Tcf)	Oil Proven Reserves[1] (in million barrels)	Hydro Technical Potential[2] (in TWh/y)
Southeast Asia				
Brunei	-	13.8 (2001)	1350 (2001)	-
Cambodia	-	-	-	83
Indonesia	5.75 (1996)	92.5 (2002)	5000 (2001)	402
Lao PDR	-	-	-	63
Malaysia	4 (1996)	75 (2002)	3000 (2002)	72
Myanmar	-	-	-	130
Philippines	366 (2000)	3.693 (2002)	178 (2002)	20
Singapore	-	-	-	-
Thailand	2200 (1996)	12.7 (2002)	515.7 (2002)	19
Vietnam	165 (1996)	6.8 (2001)	600 (2001)	90
Northeast Asia				
China	126200 (1996)	48.3 (2002)	24000 (2002)	1923
Japan	865 (1996)	1.4 (2002)	59 (2002)	64.9
Republic of Korea	86 (2000)	-	-	7.6

Notes: 1: http://www.eia.doe.gov/emeu/cabs/; 2: APERC, 2001.

Energy Trade

China and Indonesia are key coal exporters in East Asia. Major coal importers are Japan, Republic of Korea, Hong Kong and Chinese Taipei. Thailand and the Philippines are also importing coal. Natural gas exporters in the form of LNG are Brunei, Malaysia and Indonesia. LNG importers are Japan, Republic of Korea and Chinese Taipei. The Philippines has plans to import LNG in the near future while Singapore recently indicated that it will consider LNG imports. Energy exports and imports in East Asia are summarized in Table 6.4. LNG infrastructures in exporting Asian countries are shown in Table 6.5.

[246]

Table 6.4
Steam Coal Exports and Imports and Natural Gas Imports
in Asia (million tons)

Coal Exports	1996	1997	1998	1999p	2000e	2001f	2002f
Indonesia	33.4	37.9	41.8	47.3	45.0	48.5	50.5
China	24.4	26.1	27.2	30.5	48.0	52.0	56.0
Coal Imports	1996	1997	1998	1999p	2000e	2001f	2002f
Japan	60.8	64.1	68.9	74.1	80.6	81.3	87.8
Republic of Korea	28.6	32.3	34.2	35.4	45.3	48.9	47.2
Other Asia	56.9	62.0	66.1	72.5	82	85.3	92.4
LNG Imports	1996	1997	1998	1999	2000	2001	2002
Japan	46.4	–	–	–	53.6	53.0	50.3
South Korea	9.6	–	–	–	14.6	16.2	17.8
Taiwan	3.1	–	–	–	4.6	5.0	5.4

Source: Coal Imports and Exports (http://www.ame.com.au); LNG Imports, *Energy Argus –b, 2003.*

Natural Gas Grid Interconnection

Natural gas is used in the power, industry and commercial/residential sectors. In Northeast Asia, 55.35 percent of the total natural gas consumption is used for power generation while the figure is higher in Southeast Asia at 73.72 percent.

With the huge demand for electricity in China, Japan and Republic of Korea, and with the significant natural gas reserves in Russia, several alternatives to bring Russian natural gas to Japan through pipelines were proposed. Natural gas from Sakhalin (Sakhalin-1, recoverable reserves of 190 Bcm; Sakhalin-2, recoverable reserves of 336 Bcm; Sakhalin-3,-4,-5,-6, recoverable reserves of 4,000 Bcm) can be connected to the Japanese network which could then be linked to Republic of Korea. Natural gas from Sakha (recoverable reserves of 1,024 Bcm) was studied to meet Korean demand through the Korean Peninsula. Natural gas from

Irkutsk (proven reserves of 1,415 Bcm) could be connected to meet Chinese demand through Mongolia. The Chinese government has recently approved the development of the West-East Gas Pipeline project connecting western China (Tarim) to eastern China (Shanghai). This is shown in Figure 6.1.

Table 6.5
Existing and Planned LNG Infrastructures in East Asia

Country	Terminal	Train	Capacity (million tons)	Commissioning
Existing				
Brunei	Lumut	5	6.6	1972
Indonesia	Bontang A,B	2	5.2	1977
	Bontang C,D	2	5.2	1983
	Bontang E	1	2.6	1989
	Bontang F	1	2.6	1993
	Bontang G	1	2.7	1997
	Bontang H	1	2.7	1999
	Arun 1	3	6.0	1978
	Arun 2	2	4.0	1983, 1984
	Arun 3	1	2.0	1986
Malaysia	MLNG	3	8.1	1983
	MLNG	3	7.8	1995,1996
Under construction				
Malaysia	Tiga		6.8	2003
Under consideration				
Brunei		6th train	4.0	2008 (feasibility study completed in 2003, investment decision in 2005)
Indonesia	Tangguh		6.0	
	Undan		3.0	2003
	Natuna		15.0	2007

Source: APERC, 2001

Figure 6.1
Proposed Gas Interconnection Routes in Northeast Asia

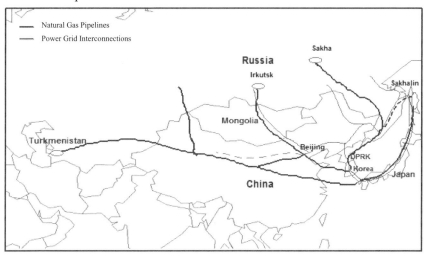

Source: APERC, 2001

In Southeast Asia, some countries such as Indonesia and Malaysia are richly endowed with natural gas resources, while Brunei, Myanmar, Philippines and Thailand have fair amounts of reserves. Aside from LNG exports to Northeast Asia, the rapidly expanding gas markets in Malaysia, Thailand and Singapore offer another opportunity for the gas producing countries in Southeast Asia. The first cross-border natural gas trade through pipelines was constructed between Malaysia and Singapore in 1992, followed by Myanmar and Thailand in 1998. Other cross-border trades have followed and are summarized in Table 6.6.

A broader vision to regionally interconnect natural gas was endorsed in 1997 by the Association of Southeast Asian Nations (ASEAN) composed of 10 countries of Southeast Asia, when it launched Vision 2020, the long-term energy development and cooperation program among the countries in the region. The concept is to interconnect the natural gas market centers to the supply points in the region with the objective of enhancing greater security of energy/natural gas supply for the ASEAN. The ASEAN countries have identified 7 gas pipeline interconnection projects with a total investment of around US$7 billion.

Table 6.6
Cross-border Natural Gas Trade

Pipeline	Economies Connected	Distance (km)	Flow Capacity (MMCMD)	Year of Completion
PGU II – Singapore	Malaysia, Singapore	714	4.2	1992
Yadana – Ratchaburi	Myanmar, Thailand	649	14.7	1998
Yetagun – Ratchaburi		170	5.6	2001
West Natuna – Singapore	Indonesia, Singapore	656	9.1	2000
Trans Thai – Malaysia	Thailand, Malaysia	423	11.05	2004
West Natuna – Malaysia	Indonesia, Malaysia	-	2.8	2002
Sumatra – Singapore	Indonesia, Singapore	500	4.2	2003

Source: Amin, 2001.

Crude Oil, Coal and LNG Prices

The upsurge of world oil prices could have an important impact on the electricity fuel supply industry. This impact is linked to the influence of the world energy prices on the prices of competing fuels in electricity generation. Most Northeast Asian countries are heavily dependent on imported fuels. In Southeast Asia, some countries are richly endowed with energy resources while others are partly dependent on imported energy supply.

While the regional prices of oil are interlinked through a well functioning global oil market, the market for other energy commodities is not as transparent and developed as the oil market. Coal trade in Asia is through long-term contracts with prices being reviewed annually. Price negotiations by large Japanese customers and suppliers provide a "benchmark" for regional price negotiations. Spot market for steam coal also exists but these are for small cargoes and on short-term basis. Most Southeast Asian countries source their coal in this market. When the Japanese government recently introduced competition in electricity generation, several Japanese electric utilities abandoned benchmark pricing and moved to the spot market in order to stay competitive (since spot prices were lower than the benchmark price in the recent past). The benchmark price is also considered to be inefficient since it represents the average cost of the coal producers. At present, however, the Japanese benchmark prices remain an important reference for coal pricing in Asia.

Natural gas prices for LNG in the Asian market, on the other hand, are determined through formula prices. These formula prices normally index LNG prices to the international crude oil price plus other parameters. During the period of depressed crude oil prices, the LNG industry of Asia was greatly affected. LNG infrastructure projects are capital intensive and need to be assured of sufficient revenues.

As shown in Table 6.7, LNG prices in the Asian market are clearly linked with crude oil prices. Though the coal prices are not directly connected with crude oil prices, coal price movements appear to follow the medium term pattern of crude oil prices. The increase in the price of crude oil also drives up the price of other conventional energy resources in the regional market.

Table 6.7
Price Trends of Asian Reference Fuels

| Year | Crude Oil (Dubai) | | LNG (Japan) CIF | | Steam Coal (Japan) CIF | |
	US$ per barrel	% change	US$ per million Btu	% change	US$ per ton	% change
1987	16.91		3.35		41.28	
1988	13.20	-0.22	3.34	0.00	42.47	+0.03
1989	15.68	+0.19	3.28	-0.02	48.86	+0.15
1990	20.50	+0.31	3.64	+0.11	50.81	+0.04
1991	16.56	-0.19	3.99	+0.10	50.30	-0.01
1992	17.21	+0.04	3.62	-0.09	48.45	-0.04
1993	14.90	-0.13	3.52	-0.03	45.71	-0.06
1994	14.76	-0.01	3.18	-0.10	43.66	-0.04
1995	16.09	+0.09	3.46	+0.09	47.58	+0.09
1996	18.56	+0.15	3.66	+0.06	49.54	+0.04
1997	18.13	-0.02	3.91	+0.07	45.53	-0.08
1998	12.16	-0.33	3.05	-0.22	40.51	-0.11
1999	17.30	+0.42	3.14	+0.03	35.74	-0.12
2000	26.24	+0.52	4.72	+0.50	34.58	-0.03
2001	22.80	-0.13	4.64	-0.02	37.96	+0.10
2002	23.85	+4.40	4.27	-0.09	37.04	-0.02

Note: CIF = cost+insurance+freight.
Source of data: http://www.bp.com

Fuel Supply Market and World Energy Prices

The highly volatile prices of oil in the international market have prompted most of the Asian governments to reduce oil dependence and move away from oil in electricity generation. Diversification of fuel sources and origin of supply has been one of the important energy security policies in Asia. The recent price movement of crude oil could strengthen these policies.

Coal remains the fuel choice for electricity generation in many coal-importing countries such as Japan, Republic of Korea, Chinese Taipei, the Philippines and Thailand because it is price competitive. As shown earlier steam coal imports in East Asia have been increasing in the past years. For countries with coal resources, its development is supported by policies related to energy security, protection of local coal industry, and stimulation of economic growth. One of the main objectives of China's coal resource development is to boost the economic growth of its coal-rich Western region. The development in coal resource-rich Indonesia and Vietnam is to promote industry development (consequently its contribution to economic development), sustain domestic demand, and support fuel diversification policies. Malaysia promotes the development of its coal industry as part of its five-fuel diversification policy. Developments in the Republic of Korea, Thailand and to some extent the Philippines are to sustain domestic demand and support the development of the domestic coal industries.

Associated with the utilization of coal is environmental pollution. China and Thailand had in the past experienced acute environmental pollution related to coal utilization and these two countries have active programs to promote the adoption of clean coal technologies. Most of the East Asian countries also have stringent environmental laws that necessitate clean technologies for its compliance. Despite these environmental requirements, coal remains competitive in power generation.

Nuclear power development remains an important energy diversification policy in Japan, Republic of Korea and Chinese Taipei. Also, Japan is obliged under the Kyoto Protocol to stabilize its greenhouse gas emissions and the promotion of nuclear energy is part of its national strategy to mitigate greenhouse gas emissions. Japan is currently focusing its research and

[252]

development on fast breeder reactor (FBR) technologies, which consume less uranium than conventional nuclear power technologies. Tokyo Electric is preparing two new 1380 MW nuclear power units; Taiwan started construction in 1997 of two 1300 MW units of nuclear power and the Republic of Korea planned to commission two 1000 MW units in 2003 and 2004. Among the Southeast Asian countries, only Vietnam has maintained a nuclear power policy. A plant capacity between 1 and 4.2 GW is being considered in various long-term electricity supply-demand scenarios.

Natural gas is being promoted in East Asia for both energy security and environmental reasons. Natural gas in the form of LNG for power generation would continue to grow in Northeast Asia. Moreover, the current nuclear energy supply constraints in Japan have resulted in an increased demand for natural gas. Russia is undertaking a study of an LNG export terminal in Sakhalin for the Japanese market. Japan and Republic of Korea are expanding their LNG storage facilities by 3.8 and 3.7 million cubic meters in 2006 and 2007 respectively. China is preparing for the development of LNG import terminals to supply its eastern seaboard market: one in Guandong with 3 million tons capacity per year and one in Fujian with two million tons capacity. The Philippines is also planning to build a LNG import terminal. Expansion of the LNG trains to increase LNG import to Japan is also planned in Brunei. Moreover, Brunei Gas Carriers (BCG) commissioned a new A-class 137,000 cubic meter capacity LNG tanker in July 2002.

Piped gas for power generation would continue to increase in Southeast Asia. The Camago-Malampaya Gas Pipeline Project in the Philippines was completed in October 2001. The project developers have firm contracts to supply fuel for 20 years to three power plants with combined capacity of 2,760 MW. Two Southeast Asian gas pipeline projects were also completed recently: West Natuna (Indonesia)-Duyong (Malaysia) in October 2002; South Sumatra (Indonesia) – Singapore in August 2003. Both the Northeast and the Southeast Asian gas grids would be incrementally developed, depending on the development of the power industry, the increase in the utilization of gas in other economic

[253]

sectors, the new discovery of other gas deposits, and the economics of the project.

Another important implication of the upward trend of energy prices is to improve the competitiveness of renewable energy in electricity generation. As shown in Table 6.8, most of the technologies are still not competitive with conventional energy, but costs for some technologies have started to fall in the past years. The utilization of renewable energy for power generation such as wind, solar, micro-hydro, biomass and municipal solid wastes, is relatively small in East Asia. There is, however, an increased interest in the utilization of these resources as part of the overall energy security, climate change, environment and other developmental policies of many Asian countries. The development of new and renewable energy resources is dependent on the availability of these resources in each country. Not all East Asian countries are richly endowed with renewable energy resources. Policies to promote grid-based renewables in East Asia include removal of entry barriers to renewable energy development and electricity generation through legislation and renewable energy producers programs, development of national frameworks to facilitate investments, establishment of renewable energy funds, financial incentives and subsidies to improve renewable energy competitiveness, renewable energy targets, portfolio standards, green pricing and tradable green certificates. These policies are summarized in Table 6.9.

Table 6.8
Technology Comparative Costs

Technology	Generating Costs (US cents/kWh)		Investment Costs (US$/W)	
	Mean	Range	Mean	Range
Gas combined cycle	3.5	3.0-4.0	0.6	0.5-0.7
Coal	4.8	4.0-5.5	1.2	1.0-1.3
Nuclear	6.0	3.3-8.0	1.6	1.2-2.0
Wind	5.5	3.0-8.0	1.4	0.8-2.0
Biomass – 25 MWe combustion	6.5	4.0-9.0	2.0	1.5-2.5
Small hydro	7.5	5.0-10.0	1.0	0.8-1.2
Solar thermal power	15.0	12.0-18.0	5.0	4.0-6.0
Solar PV	55.0	30.0-80.0	7.0	6.0.8.0

Source: *Langcake,* 2003.

[254]

Table 6.9
Renewable Energy Policies in Selected East Asian Countries

Country	Grid-Based Renewable Energy (RE) Policy
Southeast Asia	
Indonesia	i) Small Power Generation from renewable energy (PSK) legislation issued in 1998 allowed small RE generators to be interconnected to the grid. ii) New legislation issued in June 2002 allowed RE power plants up to 1 MW to be connected to the grid. Purchase rate is calculated at 80% and 60% of the announced electricity base price at medium and low voltage.
Malaysia	i) Small Renewable Energy Power program (SREP) launched in May 2001 facilitates grid connection of small renewable energy projects through the framework of the Renewable Energy Power Purchase Agreement (REPPA). ii) Malaysia Electricity Supply Industry Trust Account (MESITA) fund provides financial assistance to renewable energy projects. The fund receives contribution from power generators equivalent to 1% of their audited revenue.
Philippines	i) Presidential Decree 1442 (Act to Promote the Exploration and Development of Geothermal Resources) provides private sector incentives to develop the geothermal resources. ii) Republic Act (RA) 7156 (Mini-Hydroelectric Power Incentives Act) defines various tax incentives to private sector developers on the development of the country's mini-hydro resources. iii) Executive Order 462 enables the private sector to participate in the exploration, development, utilization and commercialization of ocean, solar and wind (OSW) energy resources for power development. iv) RA 9136 (Electric Power Industry Act) is also seen to have positive implications on large-scale renewable energy power project development. v) House Bill 4839 (Act to further promote the development, utilization and commercialization on new and renewable sources of energy and for other purposes) is pending with the Philippine Congress.
Thailand	i) The Small Power Producers (SPP) Program introduced in 1992 is the main program to encourage private sector investments on grid-based renewable energy projects. ii) To further boost investments on grid-based renewable energy, the government launched the Subsidy Program for Renewable SPPs in 2001. iii) The government introduced the Very Small Renewable Energy Power Producers (VSREPP) Program in 2002, which supports the use of renewable energy for electricity generation by small-scale generators (less than 1 MW).

Vietnam	i) Renewable Energy Action Plan (REAP) is a coordination framework for renewable energy development and resource mobilization activities. Calls for the establishment of Remote Area Renewable Energy (RARE) Fund. REAP targets: 25-51 MW renewable energy capacity under phase 1 and 175-251 MW under phase 2.
Northeast Asia	
China	i) White Paper on New and Renewable Energy in China issued in April 2000 provides 5-year and 10-year planning perspective on renewable energy.
Japan	i) Renewable portfolio standard (RPS) effective in April 2003, target of 1.35% renewable energy share in power generation by 2010. ii) Green pricing program in Hokkaido launched in 1999 iii) Tradable green certificate implemented in 2001.
Republic of Korea	i) Target of 5% renewable energy share of the primary energy demand in 2011. ii) Price support for the price-cost differentials (base price or production cost less average market price of electricity in the previous year) for a 5-year period from the start-up of commercial power plant operation. This is applied to photovoltaic, wind, small hydro, landfill gas, and waste incineration.
Chinese Taipei	i) Target of 3% renewable energy share of the primary consumption in 2020. Subsidy of up to 50% of investment costs is provided for photovoltaic and wind turbine users. ii) A renewable energy bill, which provides further incentives for investment in renewable energy technologies, is being studied by the parliament.

Sources: Indonesia and Malaysia – T. Tjaroko, M. Cabrera and T. Lefevre (2003); Philippines and Thailand– R. Pacudan-a (2003); Vietnam – R. Pacudan-b (2003); China, Republic of Korea and Chinese Taipei – APERC 2002; Japan – http://www.isep.or.jp/img/chalmers. pdf.

Electricity Trade

Power Grid Interconnection

Except for few countries in Southeast Asia, most national electricity grids are isolated. The geographic distribution of energy resources does not match the electricity market location centers. Therefore, options to interconnect the electricity grids regionally are also being considered. The benefits of power interconnection include the following aspects.

1. Supply security improvement
   - promotes power system supply security
   - provides new energy supply options
2. Economics and efficiency
   - exploits economies of scale
   - shaves peak load
   - facilitates market restructuring and competition
   - extends economic benefits of the regions with energy resources
3. Environmental benefits

There are two power interconnection projects being considered in East Asia: the Northeast and Southeast Asian interconnections. Japan, South Korea and China are the market centers of the proposed Northeast Asian Power Interconnection, while Malaysia, Philippines, Thailand and Singapore are the market centers for the Southeast Asian Power Interconnection.

China has experienced rapid electricity demand in the past decades and is forecasted to maintain its rapid electricity demand. Also, north and northeast China have experienced serious environmental problems due to coal power generation. Imported electricity is considered as the potential solution to meet the fast growing market demand in an environmentally friendly way. Despite the moderate demand growth forecast, Japan has serious problems in meeting its commitment to reduce GHG emissions under the Kyoto Protocol. Nuclear power is considered as an alternative for Japan but safety concerns have become a public issue in the recent past. The Republic of Korea has similarly experienced fast growing electricity demand over the past decades and is forecasted to sustain this rapid growth in the following decades. Nuclear development has been an option for the Republic of Korea but this requires huge capacity investments. Electricity imports would be a possible alternative through routes across China and North Korea. Figure 6.2 and Table 6.10 show the potential scope of the Northeast Asian Power Grid Ring.

Figure 6.2
Northeast Asian Proposed Power Grid Interconnection

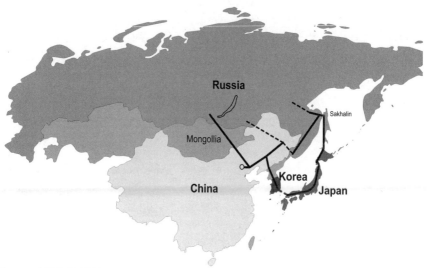

Source: APERC, 2000.

Table 6.10
Northeast Asian Proposed Power Grid Ring

1. East Siberia to China through Mongolia	Preliminary studies show that the Irkutsk power system (one of the ten components of the Siberian UES grid) is the most suitable source of electricity for China.
	A transmission corridor could be developed from one of the hydropower stations of the Irkutsk system and Beijing through Mongolia with the total length of around 2,500 km. A 2-3 GW transmission capacity using 600 kV HVDC lines could transport an annual volume of 10-15 TWh of electricity.
	Two export project studies being undertaken are:
	i) Russia-China Power Export Project: A pre-feasibility study was developed jointly by the Russian regional power company Irkutskenegro and State Power Grid Development Corporation of China in 1997. The project aims to export a power surplus of 18 TWh per year and a power transfer capacity of 3 GW. The cost of construction was estimated to be US$1.5 billion.
	ii) Amur region (Far East Russia) and Kharbin (Northeast region of China) Interconnection: The unfinished 2.3 GW Bureyskaya hydropower plant in Russia could export 3 TWh of electricity annually to Kharbin. The transferred capacity could be 1 GW. The investment requirement is estimated to be US$ 2 billion.

2. China to the Democratic People's Republic of Korea (DPRK), and to the Republic of Korea (ROK)	The ROK may be interested in developing power connection with DPRK as means of providing aid and reducing political tensions. On the other hand, DPRK may also be interested in avoiding supply shortfall in the future. A power interconnection between two countries would optimize the systems of both economies. In the longer term, this interconnection would be extended to China and perhaps to Russia.
3. Far East of Russia to Japan with potential connection to South Korea	Electricity from Siberia and Russian Far East could be transported to Japan through Sakhalin and Hokkaido. A concept developed in 1997 by the United Energy System (UES) of Russia and the Russian Academy of Sciences was to export electricity to Japan. Two thermal plants would be constructed in Sakhalin island: 4 GW shelf gas-power Sakhalinskaya plant and 2 GW coal-fired Solntsevskaya power plant. Power could be transported through a 500 kV HVDC transmission line traversing Sakhalin island (420 km) and a submarine cable (50 km) with a capacity of 6 GW through the Laperuza channel. Total investments are estimated at US$ 11.9 billion.

Sources: Energy Argus, 2001; Energy Argus-a, 2003; APERC-a, 2002; APERC, 2001.

The regional power grid interconnection in Southeast Asia can be divided into the Greater Mekong Sub-region (GMS) and Southeast Asia power interconnections. GMS interconnection consists of countries comprising the Mekong river basin, Cambodia, Lao PDR, China (Yunnan Province), Myanmar, Vietnam and Thailand. The GMS through Thailand is to be connected to the rest of Southeast Asia: Thailand to Peninsular Malaysia to Singapore. Java and Sumatra islands of Indonesia will be interconnected and Sumatra will be connected to Peninsular Malaysia. Peninsular Malaysia will be connected to Sarawak, Brunei, Sabah and to the Philippines. This regional power grid interconnection is part of the ASEAN's long-term energy development and cooperation under ASEAN Vision 2020. Figure 6.3 shows the existing and the potential border crossing of electricity in Southeast Asia. Similar to natural gas, cross-border power interconnection already exists in some countries in Southeast Asia. The status of the interconnection projects is summarized in Table 6.11.

Figure 6.3
Power Grid Interconnection in Southeast Asia

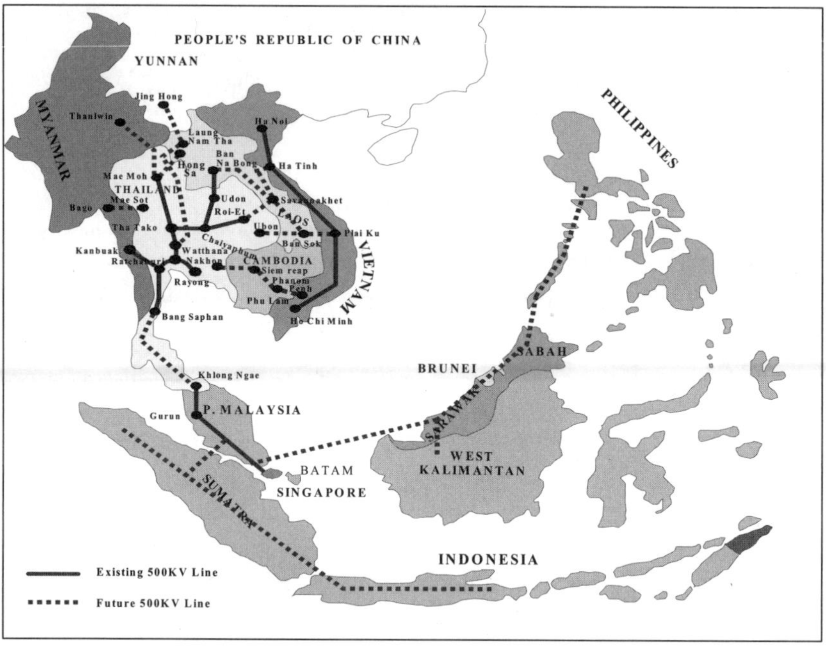

Source: Chonglertvanichkul, 2000.

Table 6.11
Southeast Asia Power Interconnection Projects

No	Project Description	Coordinating Utility	Status
1	Peninsular Malaysia-Singapore (in operation)	TNB	Availability of the interconnection is more than 96.77%
2	Thailand-Peninsular Malaysia • Sadao – Bukit Keteri (in operation) • HVDC Links between Khlong Ngae – Gurun (Medium term)	EGAT	The interconnection project is in progress.
3	Sarawak-Peninsular Malaysia (Long term)	SESCo	The interconnection project has been deferred indefinitely.
4	Peninsular Malaysia-Sumatra (Long term)	TNB	Terms of reference (TOR) for the pre-feasibility study will be done once a task force is set up.
5	Batam-Bintan-Singapore-Johor (Long term)	PLN	Seeking sponsors for studies or cost sharing between related utilities.

[260]

6	Sarawak-West Kalimantan (Long term)	SESCO	No progress
7	Philippines-Sabah (Long term)	NPC	This interconnection project may be needed only after 2010.
8	Sarawak-Sabah-Brunei (Long term)	SESCO	No progress
9	Thailand-Lao PDR • Udon Thani-Nabong (Medium term)	EGAT	No progress. Feasibility study and a survey for suitable interconnection locations have been carried out
	• Mae Moh No. 3 – Hong Sa (Medium term)		-ditto
	• Roi Et-Savannakhet (Medium term)		-ditto
	• Ubol Ratchathani-Ban Sok (Long term)		-ditto
10	Lao PDR-Viet Nam • Ban Sok-Pleiku (Medium term) • Nam Theun No.2-Ha Tinh (Long term)	EdL	MOU has been signed by Viet nam and Lao PDR to carry out these projects. Further study on the master plan will be carried out
11	Thailand-Myanmar • Mae Sot-Bago (Medium term)	EGAT	A feasibility study of system interconnection is being carried out by EGAT
	• Mae Moh No.3-Ta Sang (Long term)		Feasibility study is being carried out
12	Vietnam-Cambodia (Short term)	EVN	No report
13	Lao PDR-Cambodia (Long term)	EdL	No report
14	Thailand-Cambodia (Medium term)	EGAT	Agreement on power cooperation has been signed. The study for the system connection to export power from Thailand to the provinces in the Western part of Cambodia is being carried out by EGAT

Source: Report of the 16th Meeting of the Heads of ASEAN Power Utilities/Authorites HAPUA, April 25-28, 2000.

Electricity Trade and World Energy Prices

The coal and hydro resource potential in the Russian Far East and the huge market of electricity in Japan and South Korea drive the development of the power grid interconnection in Northeast Asia. Similarly, the interconnection projects in the GMS are also driven by the huge hydro resources in China (Yunnan Province), Laos, Myanmar and Vietnam and the high electricity demand in Thailand. Interconnection between other Southeast Asian countries were initially conceived for emergency purposes and for network system stability. However, several proposals have come out to upgrade the interconnection for the purpose of electricity trade.

The current upward trend of world energy prices would make the economics of long distance high voltage transmission favorable and the exploitation of hydro resources in the remote areas in Asia would become cost-effective. Thus, the overall implication of rising world energy prices would be the overall increase in electricity trade and the development of the regional power grids in Asia. Moreover, once this regional grid has been put in place, it would probably improve the economics of the exploitation of small reserves of other conventional resources such as coal and natural gas in remote areas for electricity generation.

Electricity Supply Industry Reforms

The rapid economic growth in Asia in the past decades brought significant transformation of the electricity supply industry. To meet the ever-growing demand for electricity to satisfy the needs of economic and socioeconomic activities, many governments have initiated institutional and structural reforms in the industry. These reforms in general were intended to alleviate the financial burden facing the government-owned utilities and to improve the overall efficiency of the electricity supply industry.

Most of the power industries in Asia are public sector-owned and vertically integrated in generation, transmission and distribution. With recent developments in the industry, the electricity business is now composed of 4 key functions, namely generation, transmission, distribution and supply. It is also well recognized that the generation and retail businesses are competitive in nature while the transmission and distribution segments are natural monopolies.

Among the key changes in the power industry reforms are the unbundling of the key components, separating the competitive and natural monopoly functions, and the privatization of the government-owned

[262]

utilities. With privatization, the role of the government is also changed from provider of electricity services to promoter of competition in competitive segments and regulator in the monopolistic sectors of the industry.

Unbundling

Based on developed country experiences, the restructuring programs of the electricity supply industry are following four main stages: vertically integrated, single buyer, wholesale competition and retail competition. This is shown in Figure 6.4.

The initial stage is a *vertically integrated industry* where all of the 4 main industry functions are undertaken by a single utility, and in most cases government owned-utilities. The said utility generates, transmits and distributes electricity in its specific franchise area. In the *single buyer model*, the government allows competition in generation, opening the generation business to independent power producers (IPPs), mainly private investors but in some cases government corporations. Each IPP secures a long-term contract, the power purchase agreement from the electric utility, which transmits and distributes electricity.

Figure 6.4
Electricity Supply Industry Structural Models

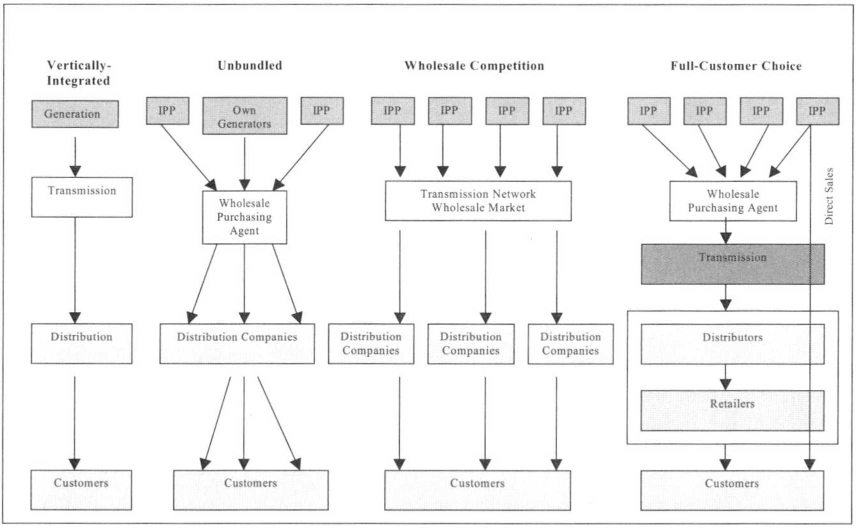

Source: Hunt and Shuttleworth, 1996.

In the *wholesale competition model*, the government unbundles the generation, transmission and distribution segments, and establishes the wholesale electricity market. The wholesale market consists of independent market operator, system operator and settlement administrator. The generators sell electricity to bulk electricity consumers through the power pool or bilateral trade. Access to transmission is universal and the transmission business becomes a wire business. End-use consumers, however, have no free choice and buy electricity directly from the distributors. Both the transmission and distribution companies are under the oversight of an independent regulator.

The competition is brought down into the end-use levels under the *retail competition*. The distribution and supply functions are differentiated and the end-use consumers have the choice of buying electricity from different suppliers, who in turn are purchasing electricity from the wholesale market. Distribution becomes purely wire business and suppliers have access to distribution networks. With this structure, firms are free to enter into the competitive functions of generation and retail. The high and low voltage networks, which are natural monopolies, are regulated.

Change of Ownership

In many cases, the privatization of public utilities also transpires in the course of restructuring. The privatization process is also divided into 4 phases: government agency, commercialization, corporatization and privatization.

A public utility is considered *government agency* when the central government directly controls the day-to-day management and operation of the utility. *Commercialization* occurs when commercial incentives are introduced to the state-owned utility. In *corporatization*, the state-owned utility is turned into a state-owned enterprise by subjecting the enterprise to normal business laws and competes on a level playing field with private firms. *Privatization* is the selling of state-owned enterprise assets and transfer of ownership to the private sector.

Regulation

Restructuring as discussed earlier involves separation of the competitive and monopolistic functions of the electricity supply industry. However, both the competitive and monopolistic components of the industry require effective regulation. The introduction of competition implies that the competition law must be enforced. Regulatory authorities must ensure that a level playing field is sustained for competition, that anti-competitive practices are being controlled through merger policies, and that subsidy policies do not provide unfair competitive advantage to some industry players. On the other hand, transmission and distribution networks remain natural monopolies and therefore electricity regulation must address the grid allocation issue including congestion management in the short term, and the provision of adequate incentives for investment and cost efficiency in the long-term, through efficient pricing of network services.

Current Status

Among the Asian countries, Singapore has implemented the most advanced electricity supply industry structure. This is shown in Figure 6.5. Wholesale competition has been introduced and transformed into limited retail competition. End-use consumers with an annual consumption exceeding 240 MWh will be allowed from June 2003 to freely select their electricity suppliers. This consumer group will join the current contestable users with an annual demand of 2 MW and above. Future liberalization will extend to consumers of at least 120 MWh/yr, followed by full liberalization expected in 2004. In terms of the change of ownership, the government has created several state corporations to take over the electricity industry functions from the Public Utilities Board. These state corporations will be privatized in the future through public offerings.

As shown also in Figure 6.5, most of the Asian countries have a monopsony structure of electricity supply industry, at different stages of ownership level. Independent power producers are permitted to enter into the generation business. However, there is a wide range of ownership arrangement for the single buyer of electricity. Japan on the other hand has 10 privately-owned vertically integrated electric utilities. IPPs have secured power purchase agreements from these companies. Japan's partial liberalization plan allows contestable consumers to freely select their electricity suppliers and these suppliers must be given access to the electricity network. The contestable market consists of consumers with more than 2 MW of electricity demand.

Another variant of the utility's ownership structure is represented by Malaysia's Tenaga Nasional Berhad (TNB). TNB took over the assets of the National Electricity Board (NEB) and was corporatized, then privatized through flotation in the stock market. The government however maintained a majority share. Initially, the government of Malaysia is planning to introduce a power pool. The government however recently decided not to adopt this model and instead maintain the current ownership arrangement. New private power contracts will be tendered in a competitive manner.

Most of the electric utilities in East Asia are state-owned corporations. The plans to reform the industry vary from country to country. Table 6.12 shows the status of reforms in selected East Asian Countries. However, a certain pattern has clearly emerged.

The Taiwanese government is planning to privatize the power utility through the divestiture of assets. The Philippines is currently introducing wholesale competition and at the same time carrying out privatization through assets divestiture. Indonesia, Thailand and South Korea plan to simultaneously introduce wholesale competition and privatization with the privatization process being implemented through public offerings at the stock market. Finally, China plans to introduce wholesale competition while maintaining the current ownership status.

Figure 6.5
Electricity Industry Structure and Ownership in Asia

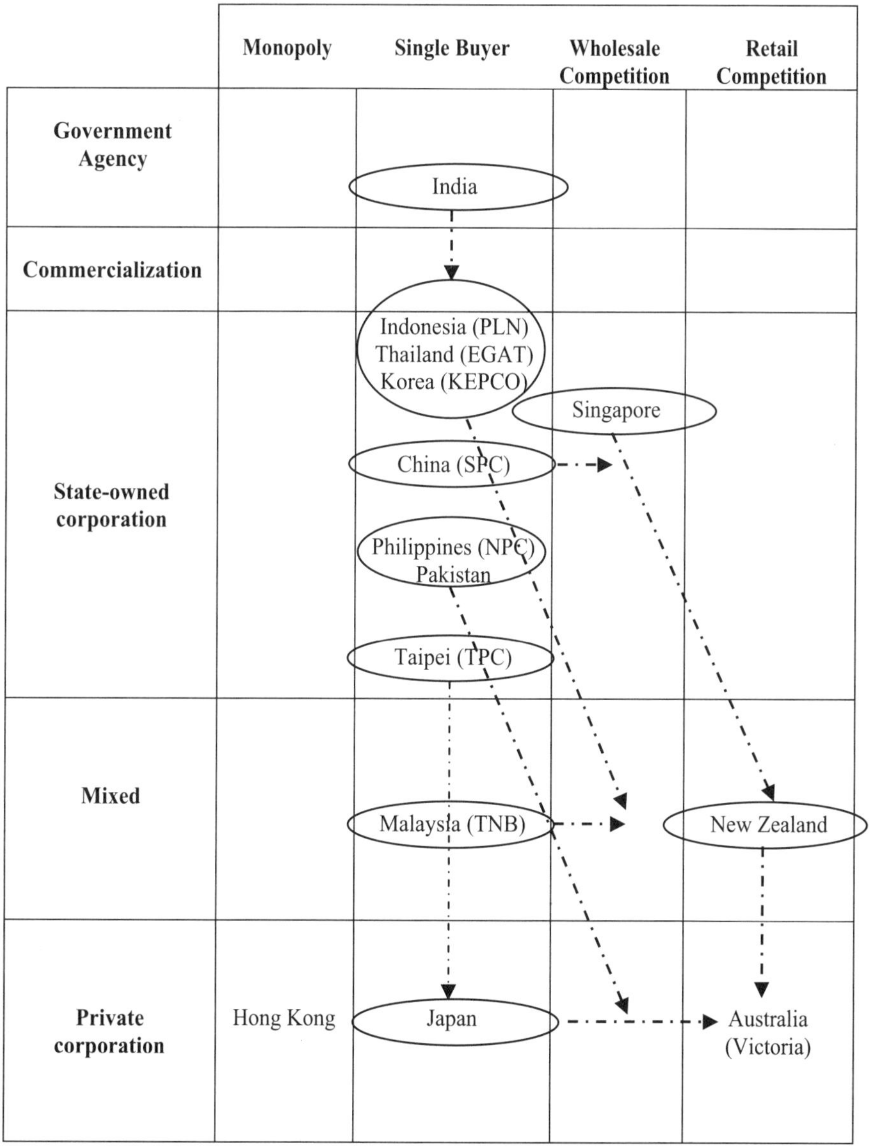

Source: Author's elaboration

Table 6.12
Status of Reforms in Selected East Asian Countries

Country	Status of Reforms
China	IPPs have long-term contracts with the State Power Corporation (SPC). Unbundling of the SPC into separate generation, transmission, and distribution companies is planned. Early and extensive adoption of competitive wholesale market is considered to be unlikely.
Japan	The amendment of the Electricity Utilities Industry Law in 1995 permitted entry of IPPs. The most recent amendment in 1999 allowed partial liberalization of the retail segment. High voltage consumers (20 kV) or users with demand over 2 MW are classified as contestable consumers.
Korea	The Korea Electric Power Corporation (KEPCO) was divided into 6 companies. The Korea Power Exchange and Korea Power Commission were established in April 2001. Generating companies will be privatized step by step.
Malaysia	Power Supply Act of 1990 allowed partial privatization of the National Electricity Board, now the Tenaga Nasional Berhad (TNB). Full privatization is not being considered. The energy regulator was recently established with the passage of the Energy Commission Act in 2000. Malaysia will implement an open bidding system for power plant construction projects after 2005.
Philippines	The Electric Industry Reform Act was enacted in June 2001 which mandates the restructuring of the power industry and the privatization of the National Power Corporation. The Implementing Rules and Regulations for the Reform Act became effective in March 2002 while the rules for the Wholesale Electricity Spot Market became effective in July 2002.
Singapore	Restructuring and the introduction of competition in electricity generation were implemented in 1995. The Singapore Electricity Pool started operation in April 1998. The Energy Market Authority of Singapore was established in April 2002. Consumers with power demand of more than 2 MW became contestable consumers in July 2001. Customers with consumption of more than 240 MWh/year became contestable in June 2003.
Chinese Taipei	Electricity generation was opened up to private investments. The government is planning to restructure and introduce competition in the electricity supply industry and privatize Taipower.
Thailand	The government plans to privatize state-owned electric utilities, the Electricity Generating Authority of Thailand (EGAT), Provincial Electricity Authority (PEA) and Metropolitan Electricity Authority (MEA). A regulatory authority will be established.

Sources: *Asia Gas and Power*, May 2003 and December 2001; APERC, 2002.

Industry Reforms and World Energy Prices

As revealed earlier, the electricity supply industry in most Asian countries falls into the single buyer model with dominant ownership from the government. In a single buyer model, the independent power producers (IPPs) secure long-term contracts known as the power purchase agreements (PPAs) with the government utility. The fundamental weaknesses of this present arrangement were exposed during the Asian financial crisis. The financial crisis that occurred in 1997 was characterized by falling electricity demand, and depreciation of local currencies. It must also be recalled that during this period, world energy prices were on the downward trend. The structural flaws of the IPP-based structure were related to allocation of market risks and electricity pricing.

A competitive electricity market reacts to macroeconomic crisis. When electricity demand falls during a crisis, there will be a downward trend of electricity spot prices as excess capacity develops. Contracts (both the fuel supply contract to generators and long-term electricity supply contracts to consumers), which depend partly on spot prices lose their value. The losers are the equity providers, speculators who have taken the price risk, and debt providers. Taxpayers are not asked to pay the bill. The falling electricity prices however stimulate demand for electricity.

The long term PPA insulates the IPPs from market risk (e.g. shift of prices and quantity of electricity consumed) and other guarantees protect IPPs from other risks (fuel supply, currency, political, etc). Investors are protected from risks and these risks are passed on to the off-takers and will eventually be borne by the consumers or taxpayers. These risks however can be shared with investors when there is a competitive market.

The existing tariff-setting mechanisms practiced in many Asian countries result in higher prices when electricity demand falls, and excess capacity increases. This is necessary in order to maintain the financial performance of the government-owned utilities and to meet their financial agreement requirements with multilateral lending institutions. However, difficulty arises because, with the political implications of price increases, the electricity tariff cannot be sufficiently raised by the governments to reflect total costs. Therefore, there is a high possibility that the utility will not be able to meet its obligations with the IPPs. In case of defaults, the government normally assumes the obligations of the utility or bails out lending institutions that lose due to the failure of the utility to meet its obligations. While the IPPs can fully recover their costs, the taxpayers are asked to pay for the bill.

After the crisis, several Asian governments have realized the need to accelerate the reform process in order to get away from structural flaws. An upward trend in world energy prices could again expose the Asian governments to the same problems encountered during the crisis. Fuel supply risks will be passed on to the governments and finally to the consumers. Moreover, difficulties will be encountered in raising electricity prices due to the highly political price-setting process under the single buyer model. The current upward trend in world energy prices reinforces the incentive for the government to free up the electricity supply industry.

Conclusion

The electricity supply industry is one of the most dynamic sectors in the economies of Asian countries. Over the past decades, several segments of the industry have undergone changes influenced by several factors at the national, regional and global levels.

During the past decades, energy security policies have shaped the fuel generation mix, resulting in the decrease of shares of oil in power generation. Electricity generation fuels that are either available as indigenous resources or traded commodities in the regional market have dominated the generation mix of the Asian economies. The current development of world oil prices strengthens these energy security policies in Asia. With these, nuclear and coal would remain the mainstay fuels in Northeast Asia while natural gas and coal would continue to shape the fuel mix in Southeast Asia. Natural gas infrastructure development, LNG terminals and pipelines envisioned by Asian governments could receive strong support from private sectors due to improved project economics. Moreover, with the improved economics of renewable energy technologies, there will be an increase in the use of renewable energies for power generation.

Aside from the development of input fuels for power generation, the upward surge in world oil prices could reinforce the existing electricity trade in the region. The economics of long distance high voltage power transmission would be improved and would render the development of huge hydro resources, and to some extent coal and natural gas, in remote areas in Asia, attractive to private developers.

Lastly, with the electricity supply industry reforms currently being undertaken or planned in most Asian countries, rising world energy prices could provide strong incentives for the governments to accelerate reforms. Structural flaws have been identified with the current structure during the Asian financial crisis. The same issues of allocation of risks and electricity pricing would arise with high fuel input prices. Moreover, these issues can only be rectified with structural changes in the industry.

FOCUS ON CHINA AND INDIA

7

The Present Status and Future Prospects of Energy in China

Kenneth B. Medlock III, Ronald Soligo and Amy Myers Jaffe

China has achieved remarkable economic progress over the past two decades. Real GDP (1995 PPP$) has grown at an average annual rate of over 9 percent, which is substantially higher than the average growth rate for developed countries. In addition, population growth rates in China have topped 1.2 percent per year. Energy is vital to economic development and sustaining populations, and China is no exception. Chinese total primary energy supply (TPES) increased from 493 million tons of oil equivalent (mtoe) in 1980 to 905 mtoe in 1999, an average increase of over 3.2 percent per year (Interestingly, TPES fell in 1998 and 1999 by an average of 1.03 percent per year despite positive GDP and population growth rates and this point will be discussed later). As a benchmark for comparison, US growth rates for real GDP, population, and TPES were 3.14 percent, 0.96 percent and 1.19 percent respectively.

China's rapid economic development and consequent rapid growth in energy requirements has pushed it into the forefront of international energy policy discussions. China accounts for roughly 10 percent of total world energy consumption, but was self-sufficient until 1993. Since 1979 the rate of growth in oil demand has exceeded the rate of growth in oil production, and China is now a net importer of crude oil. In fact, economic growth has led to an increase in oil consumption from 2.1 million barrels per day in 1990 to an estimated 4.4 million barrels per day in 1999, an average annual increase of 4.0 percent. Economic expansion has also led to an increase in coal use, from 659 million short tons in 1980 to 1341 million short tons in 1999, and natural gas consumption, from 392 billion cubic feet in 1980 to 854 billion cubic feet in 1999, average annual increases of 3.8 percent and 4.1 percent respectively.[1] However, due to enormous domestic coal reserves, China remains a net exporter of coal. Furthermore, while China is still self-sufficient in natural gas, active promotion of natural gas utilization could push China to consider imported gas in the near future.

Total crude oil imports are expected to grow substantially in the coming years as China's domestic oil requirements increase and its domestic oil production fails to keep pace. Depending on its pace of economic growth, China's oil use is projected to increase by up to 3.8 million barrels per day by 2010, and up to 11.1 million barrels per day by 2020 (as shown in Table 7.3). If China's oil production levels remain relatively stagnant, as has been the case for several years, oil imports will grow by equivalent amounts as China will be forced to become increasingly import dependent.

Growing Chinese dependence on imported oil has important implications for world oil markets. Equally significant are the implications of economic growth for natural gas demand. As demand for gas increases with the development of international pipelines and/or LNG facilities, China portends to become a major factor in the international natural gas trade as well. Increasingly, China will have to participate in international energy trade on a sustained basis, form energy alliances, and make security and environment choices about fulfilling its future energy needs. These energy trade alliances and policy options will be constrained by the unwieldy organization of China's oil and gas industry and the aged and inefficient infrastructure that exists in China today.

Economic Development and Energy Demand

Economic growth and energy requirements are closely related. Medlock and Soligo[2] show this relationship to be non-monotonic, characterized by a declining energy intensity of GDP (energy use per unit output), largely motivated by shifting structures of production and consumption. As the composition of GDP (the output shares of the agriculture, industry and service sectors) and the composition of consumption changes (the budget shares of food, clothing, transport etc.), the sources of growth in aggregate energy demand also change. This has direct implications for the rate of growth in energy demand relative to the rate of economic growth.

The relationship between economic development and the structure of production is well documented.[3] In the initial stages of development, the share of agriculture in total output falls while the share of industry rises. As development continues, the domestic demand for financial services, communications and transportation rises, and the share of services in total output increases relative to industry and agriculture.

Figure 7.1

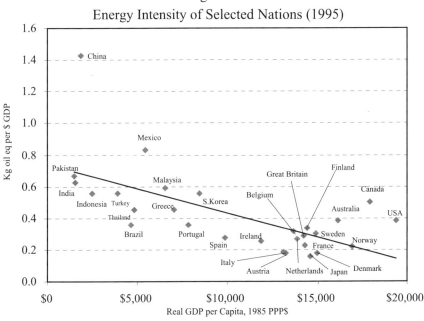

Energy Intensity of Selected Nations (1995)

Source: Compiled from the *World Bank Development Indicators, 1997.*

[277]

Shifts in the structures of production and consumption, coupled with innovations that increase energy efficiency, result in a long run reduction in energy intensity. In Figure 7.1, a cross-section of the energy intensity of selected nations from differing levels of per capita GDP illustrates this point. There is a distinct trend of declining energy intensities as per capita incomes rise.

At the outset of economic development, the shift to industrialization results in rapid increases in energy consumption. Increases in energy demand generally begin to slow down, however, as economies enter the "post-industrial" phase of development. The result is a declining energy intensity of output. This is largely driven by growth in less energy intensive production, such as light finished goods and financial and leisure services, relative to heavy industry, which is infrastructure intensive. Thus, energy requirements per unit of output decline. Note that this does not imply declining energy use, nor does it infer that heavy industry ceases to grow. Rather, it only implies that energy demand growth rates decline relative to growth in output.

Economic development is also characterized by a shifting structure of consumption. As per capita incomes rise, consumers are more able to afford particular items such as air-conditioners, furnaces, refrigerators and automobiles. The direct implication of growth in household vehicle and durable goods stocks is growth in energy demand for transportation (crude oil) and for residential and commercial uses (natural gas and electricity) since energy is required for the utilization of durable goods such as household appliances and motor vehicles. Table 7.1 illustrates the manner in which the consumer bundle changes with per capita income. The share of consumer expenditures devoted to transportation and durable goods approximately doubles at levels of per capita income between 4,000 and 10,000 US$.

Table 7.1
Structure of Consumption

GDP/cap	Share of Total Consumer Expenditure					
1995 PPP $	Food and Clothing	Rent	Health Care	Education	Transport and Communication	Durables and Other
$0 - $1,000	39	23	6	13	5	15
$1,001 - $4,000	35	18	8	14	6	19
$4,001 - $10,000	25	23	11	13	6	23
$10,001 - $20,000	20	16	11	9	11	33
$20,001 -	16	18	14	9	11	31

Source: *World Bank Development Indicators, 1997.*

The growing importance of energy for transportation has led to an increased focus on the growth of motor vehicle stocks in the economic literature.[4] The implication being that as motor vehicle stocks increase so will the demand for motor fuel and hence the demand for crude oil. Figure 7.2 illustrates a time-series/cross-section of motor vehicle registrations for 28 countries from different levels of development. Apparent in the data is the existence of a *saturation* level of motor vehicle stocks. Specifically, as demonstrated by Medlock and Soligo[5] the income elasticity of motor vehicle stocks declines as income rises, which is a result of declining marginal benefit to the consumer of additional motor vehicles. This eventually leads to no growth in per capita motor vehicle stocks, or a point of saturation.[6] For developing nations such as China, however, there portends to be significant increases in motor vehicle stocks. Utilization of the growing vehicle stock requires a commensurate increase in motor fuel demand. This means that for developing countries not rich in domestic oil resources, dependence on imported oil must also rise.

[279]

Figure 7.2

Vehicle Registrations for Selected Nations (1979-1995)

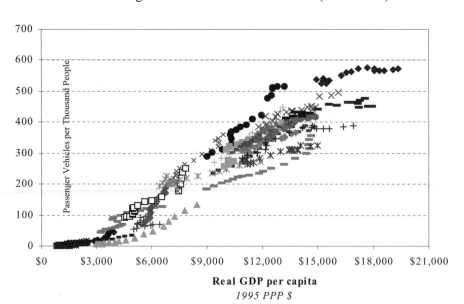

◆ Turkey	■ India	▲ Pakistan	✕ China	✳ Sri Lanka
● Indonesia	+ Mexico	▬ Thailand	▬ Malaysia	◆ Greece
□ Portugal	▲ South Korea	✕ Spain	✳ Ireland	● Italy
+ Austria	▬ Finland	▬ Japan	◆ Netherlands	■ Great Britain
▲ France	✕ Australia	✳ Denmark	● Sweden	+ Norway
▬ Belgium	▬ Canada	◆ United States		

Source: *World Motor Vehicle Data Book, 1997*, and Penn World Tables 5.6

Using panel data for 28 countries over the time period 1978-1995, Medlock and Soligo estimated the effect of increasing income on the growth of total final energy consumption (TFC) by sector.[7] The estimated relationship is:

$$\ln(ec_{s,t}) = \alpha_{s,i} + \beta_1 \ln(gdp_t) + \beta_2 (\ln(gdp_t))^2 + \beta_3 \ln(p_{s,t}) + \beta_4 \ln(ec_{s,t-1})$$

where, $\ln(ec_{s,t})$ is the natural logarithm of per capita energy use in sector s at time t, $\ln(gdp_t)$ is the natural logarithm of gross domestic product in real purchasing power parity (PPP) dollars at time t, and $\ln(p_{s,t})$ is the natural logarithm of the price of energy in sector s at time t. The term $\alpha_{s,i}$

is a country-specific intercept term for country i and sector s. Notice the equation is quadratic in the term $\ln(gdp_t)$. Thus, if β_1 is positive and β_2 is negative, the income elasticity of energy demand declines as income rises. Likewise, the energy intensity declines as income rises.[8]

A principal advantage to this technique is that it captures the effects of changing economic structure through the course of economic development. Figure 7.3 illustrates the energy-income relationship for the "average" country as estimated by Medlock and Soligo.[9] The country-specific intercept term $\alpha_{s,i}$ differentiates the estimated "paths" of energy demand by end-use sector across countries. These terms basically act to shift any given country above or below the paths illustrated in Figure 7.3. These country effects can be used to generate similar curves for each country in the sample, and hence, forecast energy demand.

As indicated in Figure 7.3, the industrial and other sector grows the most rapidly at the beginning of economic development. This is motivated by the industrialization process, which is typically characterized by the development of heavy industry and the growth of infrastructure and urbanization. Energy use in the residential and commercial sectors grows and follows suit, growing rapidly through the range of incomes in which durable goods purchases rise significantly (see Table 7.1). Eventually energy used in the transportation sector surpasses the energy consumed in all other sectors.

It should be noted that the estimated relationship in Figure 7.3 also reflects the effects of technology acquisition during the course of development. Specifically, as less developed countries become wealthier they will be able to afford the more energy efficient technologies already in use by more developed nations. The development path in Figure 7.3, therefore, implicitly incorporates the effects of both changes in economic structure and technological improvements though the course of development. It does not, however, incorporate the impacts of new innovations by frontier countries, which would serve to reduce demand at any given level of per capita income.

[281]

Figure 7.3
Energy Demand by End-Use Sector for a Hypothetical Country

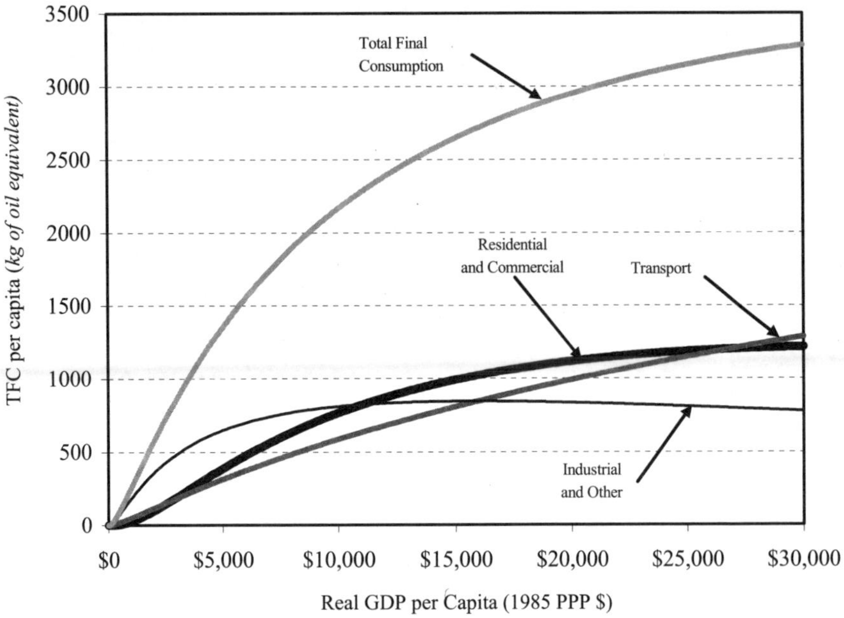

Source: Graph reproduced from Medlock and Soligo (2001).

Chinese Energy Demand

Figure 7.4 shows total energy use by China for the period 1978-1999 as well as energy consumption by end-use sectors: defined as residential and commercial, transportation, and industrial and other.[10] During this period total final energy demand increased by approximately 150 percent, with most of the increase coming in the industrial and transportation sectors.

As indicated in Figure 7.5, growth in energy use has been most rapid in the transportation sector, capturing share of total energy from other sectors. From 1980 to 1999, motor vehicle stocks in China grew from 0.3 to 3.2 passenger vehicles per thousand people, an increase of almost 1,000 percent. The subsequent utilization of these motor vehicles has contributed to an increase in transportation energy use of 1,823 percent (a 5.6 percent average annual rate) over the same period. Since crude oil is the primary fuel in transportation, satisfying approximately 89.5 percent

[282]

of all transportation energy needs, this has also contributed to a rapid increase in crude oil consumption.[11]

Figure 7.4

Chinese Total Final Energy Consumption (1978-1999)

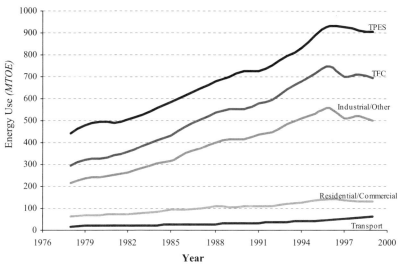

Source: Energy Statistics of Non-OECD Countries (IEA) and *China Energy Statistics Yearbook*, 2000.

Figure 7.5

Chinese TFC by Sector (1980 and 1999)

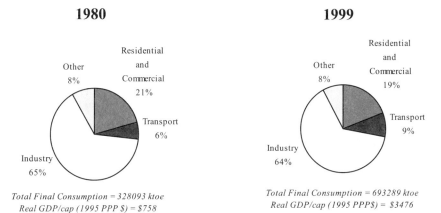

Source: Energy Statistics of Non-OECD Countries (IEA) and *China Energy Statistics Yearbook*, 2000.

There are distinct traits within the Chinese experience that distinguish it from other countries in our sample. Energy demand in transport has historically been lower than what is typical in other countries at similar levels of per capita income, and energy demand in the industrial and other sector has been higher. This is typical of command economies, which have emphasized investment in heavy industry to the detriment of investment in light (consumer goods) industry. China severely restricted the production of automobiles and transport infrastructure, emphasizing the utilization of bicycles as the chief mode of personal transportation. In addition, the use of somewhat arbitrary fixed prices masked the true costs of energy inputs, and the de-emphasizing of profits as a determinant of managerial performance, resulted in very inefficient energy use in industrial practices. This can be seen in Figure 7.1, which shows an unusually high energy intensity for China relative to other countries. However, economic liberalization will most likely result in a 'correction' toward the average global trend, and the manner in which this happens will have a significant impact on future Chinese energy demand. In fact, the effects of liberalization are already apparent. As noted earlier, China's TPES declined in 1998 and 1999 despite positive GDP growth. Figure 7.6 notes a decline in energy intensity from 0.663 toe/thousand 1995 PPP$ in 1980 to 0.208 toe/thousand 1995 PPP$ in 1999, and Figure 7.5 shows a declining share of industrial energy use. Each of these facts supports increased efficiency in production, albeit this increase need not be technology induced.[12]

Figure 7.6 illustrates the sum and composition of China's TPES in 1980 and 1999. Apparent from Figure 7.6 are both the rapid growth in TPES and the increasing share of crude oil in total requirements. Also worthy of note is the rising share of coal in TPES. This is reflective of the enormous coal reserves indigenous to China. From an energy policy perspective, exploiting domestic energy reserves has shielded China from world energy market volatility. However, mounting environmental

[284]

domestic and international pressure will make it difficult to continue to exploit coal, the most polluting of the fossil fuels, as a primary source of energy. This could push China to develop natural gas infrastructure capable of transporting and delivering imported natural gas, the cleanest of the fossil fuels, in effort to displace coal, particularly for residential use and electricity generation. However, the infrastructure investment that must be undertaken is substantial, and the exposure to international energy markets is undesirable. Thus, the environmental savings and efficiency gains must be viewed as delivering a net benefit before this takes place. Additional pressure to turn outward for energy resources is mounting from the growth of transportation energy demand, which will push China to turn to international crude markets.

Figure 7.6
Chinese TPES and Composition by Source (1980 and 1999)

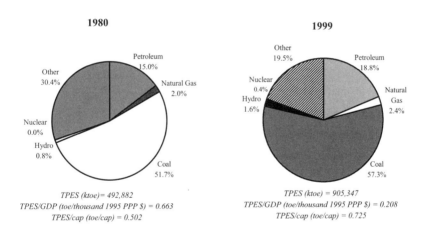

Source: Energy Statistics of Non-OECD Countries (IEA) and *China Energy Statistics Yearbook*, 2000.

Energy Demand in China to 2020

Using the methodology outlined in Medlock and Soligo we have forecasted Chinese energy demand growth under various growth

[285]

scenarios. These projections are indicated in Table 7.2 and Figure 7.7.[13] (Figure 7.7 is an illustration of our reference case forecast from Table 7.2.) Alternative assumptions about the rate of economic growth are made holding the real price of energy constant at 1999 levels. We take as our reference case the scenario in which real GDP growth averages 6.0% per annum. Other illustrated cases include a much more conservative growth scenario of 3.7 percent GDP expansion and 8.3 percent GDP expansion, of which the latter is the historical rate of growth over the past 10 years.

The projections are for energy demand by end-use sector, the sum of which is total final consumption (TFC). To arrive at projections for Chinese TPES, which is the amount of energy necessary to facilitate a given level of final demand, it is necessary to make some assumptions about the transformation and conversion loss that will be incurred in the future. Transformation and conversion loss is the energy that is used up in the production of delivered energy goods such as electricity and domestically produced petroleum products. This loss can vary between countries. Factors that can affect this value are the composition of the primary fuel requirement and the technologies used in the production of final energy products (electricity and petroleum products, for example). Therefore, transformation losses may change over time if there is a change in either of these factors. For the purposes of forecasting, the loss is assumed to hold to its average value for 1994-1999, about 22 percent of primary requirement.

The results in Table 7.2 indicate, for the reference case, a rate of growth in energy use of about 4.3% per year to 2020. This compares with a projected rate of growth of 4.7% per year in the US Department of Energy's (DOE) *International Energy Outlook, 2002* Reference Case. Note, however, that our reference case assumes a 6% rate of economic growth while the DOE's is 7%. Our projections also indicate a slightly higher rate of growth in the transportation sector of 6.8% per year, than the DOE's rate of 6.2% per year.

[286]

Table 7.2
Energy Demand Forecasts for China to the Year 2020

	Historical		Projected 2010			Projected 2015			Projected 2020		
General Data	**1995**	**1999**	**Low**	**Reference**	**High**	**Low**	**Reference**	**High**	**Low**	**Reference**	**High**
Average Annual GDP Growth			3.7%	6.0%	8.3%	3.7%	6.0%	8.3%	3.7%	6.0%	8.3%
GDP (billion 1995 PPP$)	$ 3,166	$ 4,358	$ 6,499	$ 8,272	$ 10,476	$ 7,793	$ 11,070	$ 15,607	$ 9,346	$ 14,815	$ 23,252
Population (millions) (a)	1200	1248		1329			1367			1406	
GDP/cap (1995 PPP$)	$ 2,639	$ 3,491	$ 4,801	$ 6,112	$ 7,739	$ 5,560	$ 7,898	$ 11,135	$ 6,439	$ 10,207	$ 16,021
Energy (Units: mtoe)											
Residential/ Commercial	136.5	131.7	264.6	299.6	336.4	319.3	389.9	467.2	376.8	493.9	626.2
Transportation	44.4	60.5	114.6	143.5	178.2	139.5	195.9	270.8	169.5	265.7	406.3
Industrial/Other	532.5	501.0	600.6	683.0	765.8	680.3	814.1	945.5	766.2	953.3	1126.8
TFC	713.4	693.3	979.8	1126.2	1280.5	1139.2	1399.9	1683.5	1312.4	1712.9	2159.3
TPES (b)	889.5	905.1	1254.6	1441.9	1639.5	1458.6	1792.4	2155.5	1680.5	2193.3	2764.8

Notes: (a) Population is assumed to grow at 0.6% per year (World Bank Development Indicators, 1999).
(b) To obtain projected TPES we assume the 1994-1999 average transformation and conversion loss.

Source: Projections: Authors' own estimates; Historical: Energy Statistics of Non-OECD Countries (IEA) and *China Energy Statistics Yearbook*, 2000.

We can expect the bulk of China's total energy demand to continue to come from industrial activities for the foreseeable future since a high proportion of Chinese GDP originates in the industrial sector (around 50% in 1995). However, residential and commercial energy use and transportation energy use will begin to account for an increasing share of total energy consumption as more and more consumers achieve higher levels of income. Medlock and Soligo predict that motor vehicle stocks in China could grow to 30 vehicles per thousand individuals by 2015 at a per capita GDP growth rate of 5.0% per annum.[14] With a projected population of about 1.4 billion, this amounts to a total stock of automobiles of about 42 million, an increase of about 37.5 million from 1995 levels. Given the nature of the transportation sector, increased utilization translates into a huge increase in the demand for oil and petroleum products.

Figure 7.7

Reference Case Energy Demand Forecast for China to the Year 2020

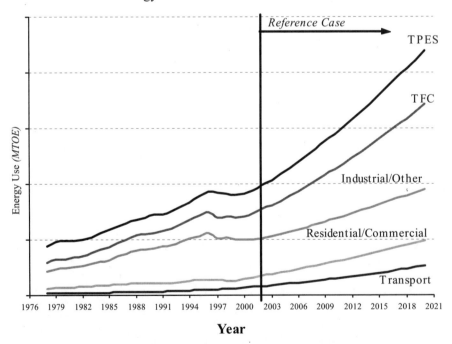

Source: Authors' own estimates, Energy Statistics of Non-OECD Countries (IEA) and *China Energy Statistics Yearbook*, 2000.

The estimates in Table 7.2 assume that while China's economy will follow the general trends exhibited by other countries, its energy efficiency will not quickly converge to levels for non-command economies at comparable per capita income. In the transportation sector China's energy use is considerably below that of non-command economies with similar per capita income. Given the existing infrastructure and environmental obstacles, it seems unlikely that such a correction will be rapidly forthcoming. Rather, the process must involve massive infrastructure investment as well as the replacement of outdated transport equipment, both of which could take considerable time.

In the industrial sector, China's energy use is much higher than that of non-command economies with similar per capita income. However, as the Chinese economy liberalizes, managers will place greater emphasis on profits. Inevitably, this will result in the extinction of inefficient processes, which will lead to a reduction in the energy intensity of production and to a downward 'correction' to the global development trend. In addition, the effect of moving from very energy intensive heavy industry, the child of the command economy era, to less energy intensive consumer-oriented production can itself create a downward correction. Nonetheless, China has had difficulty in increasing efficiency in the state owned firms and closing those that are beyond improvement. These firms will continue to act as a drag on energy efficiency for some time to come.[15]

Figure 7.8 and Table 7.3 illustrate the effect of such a 'correction' toward average global tendencies in the Reference Case growth scenario. Specifically, it is assumed in generating these forecasts that the country-specific effects for China (the $\alpha_{s,i}$'s) converge to the average country-specific effect within each sector at an arbitrary rate of 5% per year. (We are effectively forcing China to converge toward the sector curves illustrated in Figure 7.3 as economic development continues.) Notice the industrial sector energy use growth is lower, the transportation sector energy use growth is higher, and the residential and commercial sector energy use is virtually unchanged. The adjustment as illustrated is meant to give some indication of the effects of the liberalization of the Chinese economy, albeit the adjustment need not occur with the timing or at the rate conjectured.

[289]

Table 7.3

Reference Case Energy Demand Forecasts for China
to the Year 2020 with Adjustment to Global Tendencies

	Historical		Projected		
	1995	1999	2010	2015	2020
General Data					
Average Annual GDP Growth			6.0%	6.0%	6.0%
GDP (billion 1995 PPP$)	$3,166	$4,358	$8,272	$11,070˙	$14,815
Population (millions) *(a)*	1200	1248	1329	1367	1406
GDP/cap (1995 PPP$)	$2,639	$3,491	$6,226	$8,098	$10,533
Gross Energy Demand by Sector (MTOE)					
Residential/Commercial	136.5	131.7	294.0	378.7	475.8
Transportation	44.4	60.5	197.0	302.4	449.2
Industrial/Other	532.5	501.0	585.5	659.6	739.4
TFC	713.4	693.3	1076.5	1340.8	1664.4
TPES *(b)*	889.5	905.1	1378.4	1716.8	2131.1

Source: Projections: Authors' own estimates; Historical: Energy Statistics of Non-OECD
Countries (IEA) and *China Energy Statistics Yearbook*, 2000.

Figure 7.8

Reference Case Energy Demand Forecast for China
to the Year 2020 with Adjustment to Global Average Tendencies

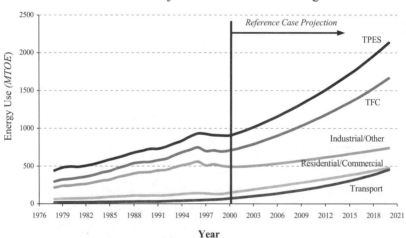

Source: Authors' own estimates, Energy Statistics of Non-OECD Countries (IEA) and
China Energy Statistics Yearbook.

Since the country-specific biases (that is, deviation from the mean of the estimated intercept term) in China for the industrial and transportation sectors work in opposite directions, they tend to cancel one another, thereby diminishing the importance of our assumption about the degree to which China will converge to international "standards" of energy intensity. However, the sector-by-sector breakdown of TFC indicated in Table 7.3 and Figure 7.8 will result in a different composition of energy requirements. In particular, higher relative growth in transportation and lower relative growth in industrial energy use will most likely result in greater oil dependence and lower natural gas dependence. Hence, projected views of economic policy play a major role in forecasting the Chinese energy situation. For the remainder of this chapter, we will focus only on the primary set of results given in Table 7.2 and Figure 7.3, but the reader should be conscious of the sensitivities herein.

Crude Oil and Natural Gas Demand in China to 2020

What do the forecasts of China's energy demand presented in Table 7.2 imply for future Chinese crude oil and natural gas requirements? In Tables 7.4 and 7.5, we have illustrated some forecasts for Chinese crude oil and natural gas demand to the year 2010 and 2020. These forecasts have been generated under certain assumptions about the fuel mix within each end-use sector.

As indicated in Table 7.4, in 2010 oil demand is estimated to be between 6.59 and 8.15 million bpd, corresponding to GDP growth rates of 3.7 percent and 8.3 percent. In 2020, demand is estimated to be between 9.12 and 15.4 million bpd, again for growth rates of 3.7 percent and 8.3 percent. The reference case projections are for 7.3 million bpd in 2010 and 11.8 million bpd in 2020, which compares with DOE's *International Energy Outlook, 2002* reference case projections of 6.8 million bpd in 2010 and 10.5 million bpd in 2020 (The DOE Reference Case assumes GDP growth of 7 percent). A major reason for the difference between our projection for oil demand and that of the DOE is the growth of the transportation sector. For example, in our high growth scenario, oil use in the transport sector surpasses oil use in the industrial sector by 2020, and accounts for almost half of all oil consumption in China. In fact, the transportation sector accounts for the largest increases in oil use in all growth scenarios.

The oil demand numbers are generated under the assumption that the fuel mix within each sector remains constant at 1999 levels. In particular, these forecasts do not allow for the possibility of environmentally motivated substitutions away from coal, nor do they account for the fact that increases in energy demand in transportation will be largely dominated by the growth of private transportation, which is typically oil dominated. These would both have the effect of increasing the share of oil in total energy demand. In fact, making some arbitrary yet very modest assumptions about the oil share of end-use sector consumption causes the oil and gas demand figures in Tables 7.4 and 7.5 to change significantly. For example, assume that the oil component in the energy mix in transportation rises to 95 percent by 2020. Assume further that oil, which now accounts for only 17 percent in the residential/commercial sector, rises to 23 percent and, finally, that the oil share in the energy mix of the industrial sector increases from 19 percent to 26 percent. In this case, oil demand in 2020 will be between 11.0 million bpd and 19.0 million bpd in 2020, dependent on the assumed GDP growth rate.

It is important to note that the growth in energy demand for transportation is conditioned on the future development of complementary infrastructure and the extent to which environmental concerns are addressed. In developed countries, the existence of infrastructure serving gasoline and diesel vehicles is often cited as a barrier to the adoption and spread of vehicles powered by fuel cells. The relative absence of such infrastructure in China could allow such new technologies to take hold much more readily.[16] If such technologies were adopted rapidly, our estimates would greatly overstate the growth in demand for crude oil.

Table 7.4
Projected Chinese Crude Oil Requirements by Sector

Year	Case	Primary Oil Requirement	
		(mtoe)	*(million bpd)*
1995		175.48	3.36
1999		219.40	4.41
2010	Low	305.04	5.99
	Reference	359.65	7.06
	High	420.41	8.25
2015	Low	359.24	7.05
	Reference	460.02	9.03
	High	579.87	11.38
2020	Low	420.32	8.25
	Reference	582.25	11.43
	High	787.95	15.47
Average annual percentage change	Low	3.14%	
	Reference	4.76%	
	High	6.28%	

Source: Authors' own estimates.

[293]

Table 7.5

Projected Chinese Natural Gas Requirements by Sector

Year	Case	Primary Gas Requirement	
		(mtoe)	*(bcf)*
1995		15.69	622.76
1999		21.22	842.21
2010	Low	52.82	2095.70
	Reference	60.14	2386.33
	High	67.61	2682.69
2015	Low	92.79	3681.82
	Reference	111.90	4440.09
	High	131.42	5214.65
2020	Low	146.62	5817.83
	Reference	185.76	7371.04
	High	225.18	8935.25
Average annual percentage change	Low	9.64%	
	Reference	10.88%	
	High	11.90%	

Source: Authors' own estimates.

Table 7.5 indicates the forecasts for natural gas use in China. In 2010, natural gas demand is estimated to be between 2,095 billion cubic feet (bcf) and 2,682 bcf, corresponding to GDP growth rates of 3.7 percent and 8.3 percent. In 2020, demand is estimated to be 5,187 bcf and 8,935 bcf, again for growth rates of 3.7 percent and 8.3 percent. These estimates compare with DOE reference case projections of 7,596 bcf in 2020. (Again, the DOE Reference Case assumes GDP growth of 7 percent.)

Given the recent initiatives to increase natural gas utilization, projections holding natural gas share in each end-use sector constant are most likely not very indicative of the direction of Chinese energy policy. Accordingly, the projections in Table 7.5 indicate that the share of natural gas in total energy increases to about 8.7 percent of total energy requirements by 2020.[17] (The DOE projects Chinese natural gas demand will account for 9% of total energy requirements by 2020, up from about

2.4% in 1999). The increase in natural gas share is driven primarily by increases in natural gas use in the industrial and other sector, rising from about 3.4 percent of total industrial energy demand to 12 percent of total industrial energy demand.

Crude Oil and Natural Gas Production in China

Total crude oil production in China is estimated to be 3.3 million barrels a day in 2001, most of which is concentrated in a small number of highly productive fields.[18] As indicated in Table 7.6, most of China's oil production in 1996 originated in a few fields. At present, about one-third of China's oil output comes from just one mature field, Daqing, which is located in Northeast China. Two smaller fields, Shengli, which is located in the Northern Shangdong province and Liaohe, which is located in the Liaoning province, account for an additional 24 percent of production.

China's largest oil field, Daqing, produces about 1.4 million barrels a day. A small portion of this crude (about 50,000 bpd as of early 2002) is exported to Japan, but most is transported by pipeline or railcar to refineries in North and Northeast China. Some Daqing oil is shipped to the Lower Yangtze region and the southern provinces by small coastal vessels where it is refined. Shengli production averages about 519,000 bpd, of which about 220,000 bpd remains in the Shangdong province for refining. The remainder is shipped by pipeline to the coast or to refineries along the Yangtze river. Production from Liaohe averages around 268,000 bpd, and is shipped mainly by pipeline to refineries in the Lower Yangtze region. Both the Daqing and Shengli fields are considered over-drilled and are poor candidates for additional tertiary recovery schemes. While production from these fields has remained flat for the past six years, some decline in production rates is expected from both fields over the next five to ten years.

The next tier of smaller fields includes Xinjiang. The Xinjiang Uigur autonomous region in Western China has three giant crude oil basins: Tarim, Junggar and Tu-Ha. Although current output from the region is small, China believes this region could see a large boost in output from exploration and development activities, possibly as high as one million bpd by 2008. However, such development would require massive investment, including construction of a major 4,000-kilometer pipeline to more populous East and Southeast regions.

Table 7.6

China's Oil Production by Field

Field	Province	Region	1998 Output thousand bpd	1999 Output thousand bpd	2000 Output thousand bpd
Daqing	Heilongjiang	Northeast	1493.2	1462.2	1424.1
Shengli	Shandong	North	531.0	509.0	519.0
Liaohe	Liaoning	Northeast	278.5	274.3	268.7
Xinjiang	Xinjiang	West	178.5	184.1	188.5
Changqing	Gansu	Northwest	81.4	87.6	94.5
Nanhai East	N/A	Offshore	105.5	88.0	90.0
Tarim	Xinjiang	West	78.8	85.7	89.0
Dagang	Hebei	North	86.5	82.5	80.5
Jilin	Jilin	Northeast	80.8	77.4	76.4
Zhongyuan	Henan	North	78.0	72.0	73.0
Bohai	N/A	Offshore	45.1	45.2	63.7
Tu-Ha	Xinjiang	West	63.6	63.6	61.5
Nanhai West	N/A	Offshore	20.3	35.1	46.4
Tahe	Xinjiang	West	0.0	29.2	42.7
Yanchang	Shaanxi	Northwest	32.5	42.3	41.3
Qinghai	Qinghai	West	35.2	38.0	40.0
Henan	Henan	North	37.1	37.1	36.9
Jiangsu	Jiangsu	Lower Yangtze	25.1	25.1	30.9
Jianghan	Hubei	Middle Yangtze	15.1	15.1	19.2
Jidong	Hebei	North	12.7	12.6	12.9
Yumen	Gansu	Northwest	8.0	8.0	8.2
Sichuan	Sichuan	Southwest	4.3	4.0	4.0
Anhui	Anhui	Lower Yangtze	1.6	1.6	1.6
Dian-Qian-Gui	Yunnan	Southwest	1.0	1.0	0.6

Sources: Data are reproduced from Lewis (2000). Data obtained from CNPC, Zhongguo shiyou tianranqi jituan gongsi nianjian, 1999 (China National Oil and Gas Enterprise Group Corporate Yearbook 1999) Beijing: Shiyou gongye chubanshe, 2000, 74; Sinopec, Zhongguo shiyou huagong zonggongsi nianjian 1999 (Yearbook of the China National Petrochemical Corporation, 1999) Beijing: Zhongguo shihua chubanshe, 1999, 274, 279, 283, 287, 291, 293, 296; Annual reports and SEC forms submitted by PetroChina, Sinopec and CNOOC in 2000; numerous energy sector news sources.

Construction of a pipeline from the Tarim area to Shanshan was completed in 1997, and plans exist to extend the line to Lanzhou and points east, with a spur to energy-short Sichuan province. Eventually the system could be extended to Shanghai and its environs.[19]

Certain onshore exploration blocks have also been targeted for foreign investment. China began to open up its industry in the 1970s, originally permitting joint ventures in the southern provinces, and later expanding to other parts of the country. The China National Oil Development Corporation has handled ventures with foreign companies. Western oil company activities onshore have been limited mainly to smaller oilfields and to wildcat exploration. Among the companies with upstream investment in China are Exxon, Texaco, Agip, BP, Amoco, Shell, and a number of Indonesian and Japanese companies. China has placed some hopes on developing the western oilfields of the Tarim Basin, but the absence of pipeline infrastructure and the economics to support its construction as well as an uncertain environment for foreign investors has slowed the development of the region.

Offshore oil production represents about 6 percent of total oil production at around 200,000 bpd. About a third of the offshore production is sold abroad, mainly to refiners in Singapore, with the rest sent to China's southern provinces. Recently, there has been some successful exploration activity by foreign oil companies in China's offshore at the Pearl River Mouth area and Bohai Sea, of which the latter is thought to hold more than 1.5 billion barrels of reserves. Phillips Petroleum has announced plans to produce more than 200,000 bpd by 2004 from its discovery in Peng Lai, and Shell has an agreement with Chinese National Offshore Oil Company (CNOOC) to begin drilling in the Bonan area in 2003. In addition, a consortium comprised of Italy's Eni, Chevron and Texaco and CNOOC has been producing in the Pearl River Mouth area since early 1999 and has announced a new oil find in the South China Sea.[20] Canadian Huskey Oil and CNOOC, which are already producing 50,000 bpd in the Pearl River Mouth near Wenchang, have also recently signed an agreement to carry out further exploration in the area.

Natural gas production in China in 2000 was slightly less than one trillion cubic feet (Tcf), reflecting small domestic demand, which was only about 2 percent of TPES. However, given the environmental benefits of natural gas versus coal, the importance of natural gas to China's energy mix should increase. The EIA estimates Chinese natural gas reserves to be approximately 48 Tcf. The majority of these gas reserves are located in the western and northern provinces while the major population centers are located in the southern and eastern provinces, which makes the development of infrastructure crucial to the viability of natural gas as a fuel source. A major hurdle to attracting capital for the development of pipeline infrastructures exists in the lack of a unified regulatory framework. Pipelines that would span multiple provinces within China would be subject to different regulatory guidelines in each province thereby limiting the opportunity for commercial success of the project. In effect, each province could extract maximum rents through tariff structures that vary from region to region, leaving little-to-nothing for equity stakeholders. Concerns about the commercial success of trans-China projects will be alleviated to some extent as the Chinese government moves toward a unified regulatory framework.

One major project currently being considered is the West-to-East Pipeline, which would connect natural gas reserves in the Xinjiang province (Tarim Basin) to demand in Shanghai. The project is meeting resistance, however, from its potential financiers (Shell, ExxonMobil, and Gazprom are majority stakeholders) due to concerns about its long-run profitability. The reserves are not considered significant enough to supply gas beyond a 20-year time horizon, making the required rate-of-return on capital considerably higher than is viewed possible. One potential long-term solution is to use the pipeline as a trunk for connecting Central Asian gas supplies to Eastern Chinese markets, but the political and economic considerations have yet to be negotiated and could take some time.

Another potential source of gas supply to China is the Russian gas fields in Eastern Siberia, near Irkutsk. However, this option is problematic in that its commercial success hinges on the ability to link to the Korean peninsula. The political turmoil and the necessity of multi-government cooperation in the region render this option infeasible at the moment.

Given the substantial costs of developing pipeline infrastructure, LNG imports have been cited as a prospect for overcoming infrastructure deficiencies in southeastern China. British Petroleum (BP) has taken a lead role in the construction of an LNG terminal in the Guangdong province. The project would be used to provide fuel primarily to power plants that are being constructed in the region, with potential supplies projected to come from the Middle East (Qatar), Indonesia, and/or Australia's Northwest Shelf.

The Outlook for Future Chinese Oil and Gas Production and Imports

In November 2001, Zhang Zhigang, Vice Minister of the SETC, explicitly identified several factors essential to China's energy security. In particular, he claimed that China must increase efficiency in energy consumption, expand domestic exploration and production of crude oil and natural gas, promote the diversification of state oil and gas companies to endeavors beyond China's borders, move to market-oriented pricing of oil and gas, encourage the development of domestic natural gas infrastructure, and promote alternative energy technologies.[21] An over-riding theme in these comments is a decreased reliance on imported energy through the development of domestic resources as well as increased energy efficiency. However, we do not expect such a scenario to emerge in its entirety in the near future.

Despite an opening to foreign investment, China's domestic oil and gas production is not expected to increase substantially in the near term. Among the many factors that account for this are: capital constraints within China's major industries, general ineffectiveness of oil sector corporate reforms, concern about the patchwork of regulatory environments that multi-province pipelines face, cautious interest among foreign investors in acreage offered for exploration, and the prospects that oil prices could remain low over the longer term.

For these and other reasons, we expect that domestic oil output will stagnate for the next 10 years and remain close to 3.3 million bpd through

[299]

2010. Other forecasts range from 3.0 million bpd to 3.7 million bpd. The DOE reference case forecasts production at 3.6 million bpd.

The outlook for 2020 is not much better. The DOE forecasts 2020 oil production at 3.5 million bpd. This is a reasonable projection given the possibility that technological improvements and efficiency gains will be made in China's energy sector over the next twenty years, which could eventually arrest decline in production rates. Furthermore, there is the prospect that needed pipeline infrastructure will be built.

Should domestic oil output increase only modestly over the next two decades, Chinese imports of crude oil and petroleum products will increase steadily. Depending on which of the growth scenarios we choose from Table 7.2, oil imports will range from 2.7 to 4.9 million bpd in 2010 and 4.9 to 12.2 million bpd in 2020. Using our reference case scenario of 6 percent GDP growth, imports would be 3.6 million bpd in 2010 and 7.9 million bpd in 2020.

Natural gas imports are also likely to increase. Current production of natural gas in China is about one trillion cubic feet (tcf). China has ample gas resources in the Ordos, Sichuan, Tarim Basin, Juggar, and Qaidam areas as well as in the western South China Sea. If concerns regarding the commercial viability of developing domestic reserves ease and China looks to diversify its domestic resource base, natural gas production should increase. Nevertheless, it is unlikely that China can meet its projected natural gas needs without turning to imports. Using our reference case scenario of 6% GDP growth, demand will approach 7.4 tcf, which will most likely result in China becoming a net importer of natural gas.

Energy Supply Options

Becoming increasingly energy import dependent leaves Chinese policy-makers with some difficult choices. The government has launched a program to diversify its portfolio of energy supplies by expanding natural gas resources inside the country, targeting increases for natural gas utilization from 2 percent in 2000 to 8-10 percent by 2015. In order to meet this goal, however, China must look to import LNG and/or develop its domestic reserves. The latter option would inevitably require the development of oil and gas resources in Western China, but this requires the construction of a costly pipeline to east and/or southeast markets within China.

Another option to diversification is to increase energy trade with Russia. In July 2001, Chinese leader Jiang Zemin visited Russia and signed several important agreements to pursue energy trade between the two countries. One agreement calls for the feasibility study of a 400,000 bpd oil pipeline (projected to cost $1.7 billion) from East Siberia to Beijing. This project would link the Chinese market to the 11 billion barrel reserves of the Yurubcheno-Takhomskaya zone currently controlled by Yukos and Slavneft. Also being discussed is the option to import oil from Kazakhstan via an all land route that could connect with fields in the Tarim basin on its way to the major markets. China and Russia are also discussing a major natural gas pipeline between Irkutsk and Yakutia and Chinese markets. Three groups are competing to build a 4,000-kilometer pipe capable of transporting up to 1.93 billion cubic feet per day from Western China to Shanghai. A BP-led group is trying to develop the 1.5 trillion cubic meter Kovykta East Siberian gas field for export to China.[22]

The main alternative to oil pipeline proposals is to import crude by tanker. The two oil pipeline options (one from East Siberia and the other from Kazakhstan) develop routes that avoid the potential security risks associated with transporting oil by tanker through relatively narrow and congested sea-lanes of the South China Sea. However, since tankers offer lower transport costs than pipelines for oil transported over large distances, the issue becomes one of how much China is willing to pay for diversification of supply and the perceived risk associated with each of these options.

Table 7.7 shows the transport costs for oil for various routes including Tarim to Guangdong. Under conservative assumptions, the cost of transporting Tarim Basin (Korla) oil to Guangdong will be around $2.84 per barrel, excluding right of way costs. This estimate assumes that there would be sufficient production at Tarim to support a large capacity pipeline of 1 million bpd. Economies of scale dictate that a smaller pipeline would produce higher per barrel costs. For example a 30-inch pipeline capable of transporting 500,000 bpd would increase transport costs to $4.48 per barrel. If a 40-inch pipeline were built in anticipation of large volumes, but only initially transported 500,000 bpd, the cost per barrel for 500,000 bpd would be $5.67.

A comparison of the cost of Tarim Basin oil with imports from the Middle East delivered to southern China shows that the Tarim Basin oil is competitive only when FOB oil prices for sour crudes from Iran, Iraq and Saudi Arabia hold above $11-$13 per barrel. Production costs at the Tarim Basin are roughly $10 per barrel at the field. Adding transport costs of $2.84 per barrel (the most optimistic of our estimates) puts the total cost of Tarim oil in the Southern Chinese market at around $13 per barrel. Right-of-way costs of up to $2 per barrel could push that to $15 per barrel. Accounting for tanker costs from the Middle East of approximately $1 per barrel and a quality premium of about a $1 per barrel yields the $11-$13 per barrel figure noted above.

Table 7.7
Cost Estimates of Alternative Routes

Route	Length (Km)	Diameter (inches)	Capacity (Mbpd)	Total Cost (billion US$)	Cost per barrel (US$)
Uzen/Arkbinsk-Xinjiang	3,000	40	1,000	$3.35	$2.03
Korla-Guangdong	4,200	40	1,000	$4.69	$2.84
Korla-Guangdong	4,200	40	500	$4.69	$5.67
Korla-Guangdong	4,200	30	500	$3.70	$4.48
Kazakh border-Guangdong	5,000	40	1,000	$5.58	$3.38
Azeri/Turkmen/Kharg	2,150	40	1,500	$3.00	$1.21
CNPC to China	3,000	40	1,000	$3.50	$2.12
Summary: Per Barrel Costs to Southern China					
CNPC to China to Shanghai/Canton ($2.12 + $3.38)					$4.90
Kharg Island to China via tanker					$1.00
Azeri/Kazakh via pipeline through Iran					$2.21
Tarim Basin to Guangdong					$2.84
Assumptions:					
Cost of capital					20%
Length of life (years)					30
Operating costs (% of capital cost)					2%

While world oil prices have recently posted a substantial increase, past history shows that they can be highly volatile. It would not make economic sense to develop the Tarim Basin fields and build the pipeline infrastructure until there is some reasonable expectation that prices will remain high enough for a period of time for investors to recover their costs. The same prerequisite holds for natural gas, only it must remain competitive with LNG, which requires the development of LNG import facilities.

Even if Tarim were developed, it is unlikely that production could be increased sufficiently over the next two decades, which dispels the notion that these reserves would obviate the need for growing imports. An alternative to Tarim oil is to import oil from Kazakhstan via a 7,200-kilometer pipeline crossing both Kazakhstan and China. This pipeline, assuming a 40-inch/1 million bpd capacity and excluding right-of-way costs, carries with it a per barrel transport cost of $4.90.

Following the logic above, the FOB price of Kazakh oil via this long pipeline would have to be $3.90 per barrel (=$4.90-$1.00) less than the FOB price of Middle East oil in order to be competitive. Since there are alternative markets for Kazakh oil in the Mediterranean where transport costs are much less than to Southern China, it is unlikely that Kazakh producers would agree to sell in Asian markets at a discount. Hence, the overland route to China would require a substantial subsidy.

The least cost route to transport Kazakh oil to Southern China is by pipeline through Iran to Gulf ports (e.g. Kharg Island) and then by tanker to China at an estimated cost of $2.21 per barrel. Hence, the overland route would require a subsidy on the order of $2.70 per barrel, plus the overland right-of-way costs and any transit fees that might be charged by the many jurisdictions through which the pipeline would pass, to make it competitive. However, during the 1990s Gulf FOB prices for Asian delivery have been higher than for European delivery by an average of $0.83 per barrel.[23] This price differential, if it persists, reduces the cost disadvantage for sales of Kazakh oil to Asia as compared to Europe.

China's policy-makers may view these transport cost differentials and the required subsidies as the cost of diversifying transport routes in order

[303]

to achieve a greater degree of oil security. The issue for policy makers in China is whether the security benefits of this diversification are worth the cost in terms of higher total import dependency.

Additional complexity is added as a result of the ongoing policy of liberalization of the domestic energy industry. In particular, production of existing fields in China may be reduced when the Chinese market is open to relatively unfettered competition from imports. The costs of transporting domestic Chinese production to markets within China are especially high, given that the rudimentary nature of the domestic pipeline network requires the use of rail car to transport oil in many cases. While a decreasing share of oil is being shipped in this way, these shipments accounted for 10 percent of total oil use in recent years. Jaffe and Soligo[24] have shown that at FOB prices of $10 in the Gulf, production at Xinjiang and Tarim will have to be curtailed unless China invests in additional pipeline infrastructure. At import prices of $9 per barrel, Daqing will still be competitive with imports when transported by small vessel to markets in the Lower Yangtze and Southern provinces. Shengli and Liache will also continue to be competitive as long as import prices remain above $8 per barrel. Oil produced in the northwest, however, would be uneconomic under some price scenarios even when transported by pipeline. As discussed above, at Gulf prices below $11 per barrel, Tarim oil would not be competitive with imports in the southern provinces. However, Tarim oil could still be competitive in the North and Northwest. Similarly, oil from Xinjiang would be competitive in north and northwestern provinces.

The implications of this analysis are that if oil prices fall again to relatively low levels and China frees its internal prices to move directly with international market levels, Chinese oil companies may decide it makes more sense to shut-in high cost fields in Western China in favor of higher imports of foreign crude oil in certain markets. This will be particularly true for shipments carried by rail car. Thus, unless oil prices are sustained at current levels, China's Western oil production levels may not increase significantly as privatization takes place.

[304]

China's Refining Sector: Challenge of Meeting Regional Imbalances

The refining industry in China includes over 100 refineries and petrochemical plants with a total capacity of around 4.75 million bpd (not including a large, uncounted number of very small, locally operated refineries) making China one of the largest refiners in the Asia Pacific region. Worldwide, only the United States, Russia and Japan have larger refining capacity than China. Sinopec still controls about 3.36 million bpd of the country's total refining capacity. CNPC holds another 505,000 bpd with the rest controlled by local independents.

Table 7.8 gives projected refinery capacities by type of crude that can be refined to the year 2005 as compiled by Asia Pacific Energy Consulting (APEC). Assessing projects already announced and planned, APEC anticipates that China's refining capacity will rise to about 5.8 million bpd by 2005.

Table 7.8

China Refinery Capacity by Crude Types

(thousand bpd)

Crude Type	1998	2000	2002	2005
Sweet (< 0.9% sulfur)	4,350	4,050	4,050	3,700
Medium Sweet (0.9-1.15% sulfur)	160	300	550	750
Sour (2+% sulfur)	240	600	700	1,350
Total	**4,750**	**4,950**	**5,300**	**5,800**

Note: The Chinese central government announced in early 1999 that up to 500 thousand bpd of 'illegal' refining, basically simple distillation would be closed down by 2000. We have included in our 1998 numbers approximately 300 thousand bpd in base refining capacity that is run mainly by provincial and municipal state oil companies and have deleted that from our base capacity for the year 2000. All of this capacity ran on domestically produced waxy sweet crudes.

Source: APEC.

Depending on China's economic growth rates and future refinery construction plans, the country may increasingly have to import petroleum products if high demand growth scenarios ensue and large refinery investments are not made between 2005 and 2010. Much of China's existing refining capacity is aged and designed to refine the waxy high

[305]

quality oil that is produced domestically. This physical limitation restricts China's import choices.

China does not have the right kind of capacity to refine large amounts of the lower quality supplies that are produced in Gulf countries such as Iraq, Iran, Saudi Arabia and Kuwait. As shown in Table 7.8, China is projected to have only a little more than 1.35 million bpd of capacity to process this lower-quality Gulf oil by 2005. China will have to import low sulfur supplies, some of which will come from Abu Dhabi, Oman and Yemen. China's first refineries were built in the Northeast, so as to be close to the Daqing oil field and northern and eastern coastal regions with high refined product demand. A series of refineries were also built in the Middle and Lower Yangtze regions and on the coast along the Bohai, Yellow and East China Seas. More recently, however, refineries have sprung up in the South, partially in response to rapid economic growth in that section of China and in anticipation of an increasing reliance on imported Middle Eastern oil.

China's oil demand and petroleum product manufacturing capability are not efficiently matched, creating additional challenges for its oil industry. North, Northeast and Southern coastal China are the areas that currently have the largest demand for oil. Northeast China has traditionally been the country's most important industrial area, and that region houses not only the large Daqing oilfield but also some 1.2 million bpd in refining capacity. The region is a major exporter of crude and petroleum products to both other parts of China and to Japan and is expected to maintain this surplus status well into the 21st century. North China, which includes the Shangdong, Shanxi and Hebei provinces as well as the cities of Beijing and Tianjin, is home to the Shengli and other smaller oilfields and has close to 1 million bpd of refining capacity. However, oil demand in the region is growing rapidly, and is expected to maintain a small refined product deficit into the coming decade. The other areas of the country have smaller demands, and have either small deficits or surpluses.

The Lower Yangtze region, which includes the eastern seaboard around Shanghai, and Southern provinces (Fujian, Guangdong and Hainan) are two of the fastest growing regions in China in terms of economic development and energy demand and has only a small refined products deficit at present. The Lower Yangtze region has around 750,000 bpd of refining capacity while the south, with two refineries in Guangdong at Maoming and Guangzhou and one at Fujian, has a capacity of over 425,000 bpd. The oil deficit in both the south of China and the Lower Yangtze region is expected to grow rapidly over the next five years.

Saudi Aramco, the Saudi state oil company, and Exxon have signed a Memorandum of Understanding to invest in upgrading a refinery at Fujian. Foreign entry into the downstream industry has proved very difficult, however, and few ventures have proceeded smoothly. Total SA of France hold a 20 percent stake in West Pacific Petrochemical Company (WEPEC) for an investment in the refinery Dalian. Exxon, ARCO and Caltex have also pursued downstream ventures in China. BP currently owns over 20 percent in the Zhenair refinery. The overall difficulty of China's investment climate in the refining sector will likely inhibit wide-scale construction of new facilities to meet rising internal demand for petroleum products, barring major reforms in the oil sector.

Concluding Observations:
The Geopolitics of Chinese Oil Supply

China's central government has encouraged its state oil companies to become more outward looking in their orientation in an effort to diversify and identify secure supplies of oil and gas. In 1986, China's State Planning Commission, acknowledging that its domestic oil industry could not maintain oil self-sufficiency in light of the country's growing energy demand, officially gave the go-ahead to allow foreign crude imports.[25]

In 1996, facing this trend of rising demand for oil and flagging domestic oil production, China unveiled a plan to attain around a third of its energy needs through international exploration and acquisition activities.[26] In 1997, state CNPC outbid the international majors for oil fields and exploration acreage in Venezuela, Sudan, southern Iraq (on hold until United Nations sanctions are lifted), Iran and Kazakhstan, where it has acquired a 60% stake in Aktybinskmunai production association, and the Uzen oil field.[27]

China has also looked at Iraqi and Iranian oil fields that might open to foreign investment—the former should political circumstances for foreign investment change. CNPC has on the books a $1.2 billion commitment to develop the Al-Ahdab oil field in southern Iraq, and has also signed a Memorandum of Understanding with Iran's National Iranian Oil Company to explore for offshore reserves in Iran, China and elsewhere. So far, however, United Nations sanctions and lack of hard currency have prevented CNPC from doing either.

Gaye Christofferson argues that China's move into Central Asia and elsewhere is aimed not only to provide stable oil imports but also to develop economic zones around China:

> China's strategy for Central Asia and the Asia Pacific has not been formulated unilaterally but rather in consultation with countries in each of these regions. This strategy involves the formation of natural economic territories that transcend borders, extending from China's domestic economy into surrounding countries. Called the Northwest Economic Circle and the Northeast Economic Circle, they open up inner border areas to international trade, with the hope that the interior will gain the same benefits as the coastal region. Oil and gas pipelines are the sinews that integrate and link these natural economic territories.[28]

China's activities to deepen its oil trading relationships with Iraq and Iran have fueled concerns that Beijing will form oil-for-arms, military-client relationships with these nations. Ironically, however, China's oil sector may not be able to benefit directly from access to large volumes of oil from Iraq and Iran. Aged and unsophisticated oil refining equipment throughout most of China means that China is limited in the quality of oil it can process. China cannot refine large amounts of most of the lower quality supplies that are produced in Gulf countries such as Iraq, Iran, Saudi Arabia and Kuwait. By 2005, China is only likely to be able to process little more than 1 million bpd of this lower quality Gulf oil, though it will be able to import supplies from places like Abu Dhabi, Yemen or Oman.

China's expanding ties with Russia and with Middle East oil producers will complicate its relations with the United States. On the one hand, increased dependence on foreign oil imports will make China more dependent on the US Navy that patrols the sea-lanes, ensuring the free flow of oil to Asia. On the other hand, China is not comfortable with the rise in US power internationally and its plans to pursue new missile defense strategies. While not decisive, China's strategic energy situation will limit its foreign policy choices.

8

The Present Status and Future Prospects of Energy in India

Leena Srivastava and Megha Shukla

A s a country grows, demographically and economically, the need for energy and energy services also increases. Following the current trends, global energy use is expected to increase substantially in the future. In fact, energy use is growing fastest in developing countries like India, at a rate up to 2.5 times more than that prevailing in developed countries. Hence, there is an urgent need to devise an energy strategy for India that follows a path that is 'sustainable' in energy use, by promoting the efficient utilization of available energy resources.

Total primary energy consumption in India has increased nearly five-fold in the past three decades during the period from 1970 to 2001. This consumption stood at 314 MTOE in 2001, which made India the sixth largest energy consumer in the world.

Moreover, it must be noted that the share of commercial energy in the total primary energy consumed has risen to more than 70 percent in 2001, up from 28 percent in 1950 and this level is expected to rise even further in the future with the development of the economy.

[311]

Figure 8.1
Comparative Trend in GDP and Total Primary Energy Consumption

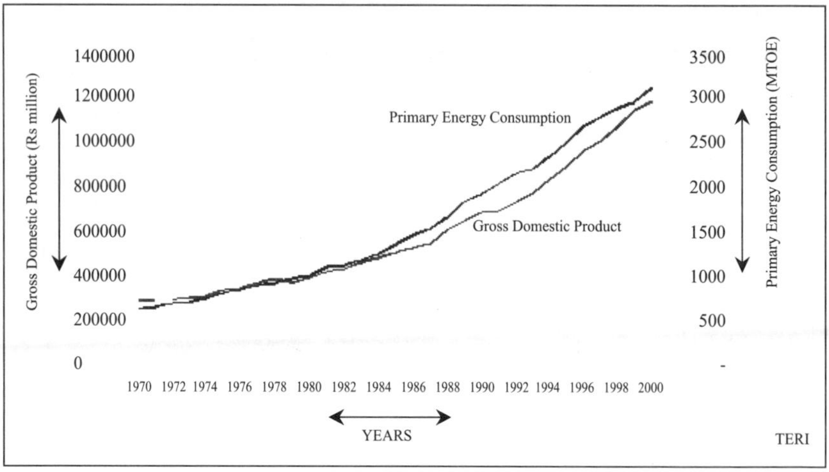

Source: GDP figures are from Economic Survey 2001-2002; Primary energy consumption figures are from *BP Statistical Review of World Energy*, 2002.

Figure 8.1 shows the trend in GDP and primary energy consumption for India since 1970 and indicates a strong linkage between energy and the economy. It may be noticed that since 1985, there is a gradual distancing between the two curves indicating the growing share of the services sector, which is less energy intensive as compared to the industrial sector. In fact, many industries in India such as steel and cement have very high energy intensities compared to similar industries operating in other parts of the world (see Table 8.1).

Table 8.1
Major Challenge–High Energy Intensities

Specific energy use (Million kcal/ton)	India	Other countries
Steel	9.5	4.18 (Japan)
Cement	2.0	0.95 (US)
Refrigerators (kWh/day)	1.25	0.90 (World average)

Source: *Hand Book on Energy Management and Audit*, published by TERI, 2000.

[312]

Also, the energy elasticity for commercial energy is less than that estimated for non-commercial energy which shows that the importance of commercial energy is more in the context of Indian energy mix. Elasticity for almost all the fuels, except solid fuels, is greater than unity, implying that the investments in the energy sector have to grow by more than the anticipated investments in the other sectors of the economy in order to avoid derailing the economic expansion process.

However, the elasticity of solid fuels with respect to various parameters in different sectors is negative, which is indicative of the lower efficiency of the solid fuels, which means a gradual shift away from solid fuels as the economy develops and discovers more effective processes demanding more efficient fuels. Moreover, the elasticity of solid fuels has become more negative in the later period indicating clearly that there are higher rates of substitution.

The elasticity is lowest for the household sector, which probably explains the phenomenal growth of LPG as the preferred household fuel due to rapid urbanization of the economy. The high growth of urbanization also explains the high elasticity of power for the household sector.

It may also be noted that the elasticity of oil and gas and power has increased in the period 1980-87 as compared to the earlier decade, while that of solid fuels and non-commercial energy has declined, which is in line with the growing urban centres in the country. Both oil and power show high elasticity in the agriculture sector. However, with the increased usage of electrified pump sets, the dependence of agriculture on the power sector is bound to grow. Moreover, the diminishing returns in agriculture means that more inputs are required to produce more from the same cultivable land. This also translates into high energy intensity for the agriculture sector.

Coal shows a negative elasticity in the transport sector, which is primarily due to the shift of railways towards electrified/diesel engines for higher speed and performance. Across the sectors, solid fuels, primarily coal, show a negative elasticity, while power, followed by oil and gas, shows the highest positive elasticity. This is due to the versatility of uses for which energy in the form of power and oil and gas can be utilized. This high elasticity of energy derived from electricity points towards the importance of reforms in the power sector for the rapid development of the economy, an issue that is discussed in detail later.

Even though India's total energy consumption level is growing, the per capita energy consumption is still 318 Kgoe, indicating very low levels compared to the world figures (see Figure 8.2). It represents only about 20 percent of the global average. Also, the per capita electricity generation and per capita oil consumption levels in India are among the lowest in the world, even lower than the neighboring countries, as shown in Figures 8.3 and 8.4. Therefore, with India targeting ambitious GDP (Gross Domestic Product) growth rates of about 8 percent over the next two decades, it is quite likely that per capita energy consumption levels will also rise in the future.

Figure 8.2
Low Levels of Per Capita Consumption in India

Per capita commercial energy consumption in 1998

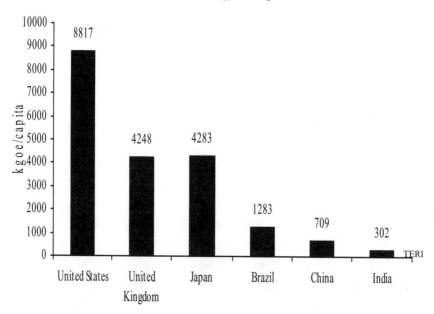

Source: World Development Report 2000.

[314]

Figure 8.3
Comparison among Countries with Respect
to Per Capita Electricity Generation

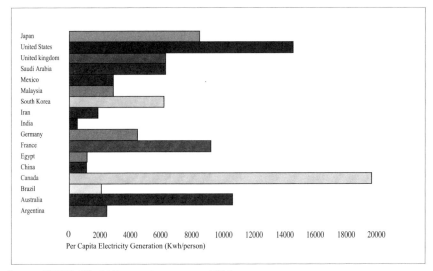

Source: UNDP, World Energy Assessment, 2000.

Figure 8.4
Comparison among Countries with Respect to Per Capita Oil Consumption

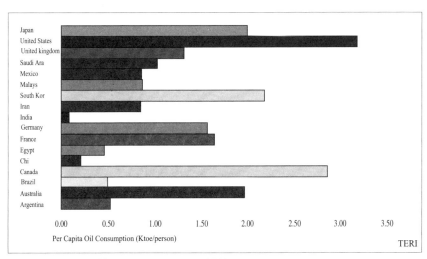

Source: UNDP, World Energy Assessment, 2000.

On the whole, India has remained a net importer of energy. The share of oil imports in the total energy imports is increasing. In fact, about 74 percent of the total refinery throughput was imported during the year 2001 (see Figure 8.5).

Figure 8.5
Increasing Reliance on Oil Imports

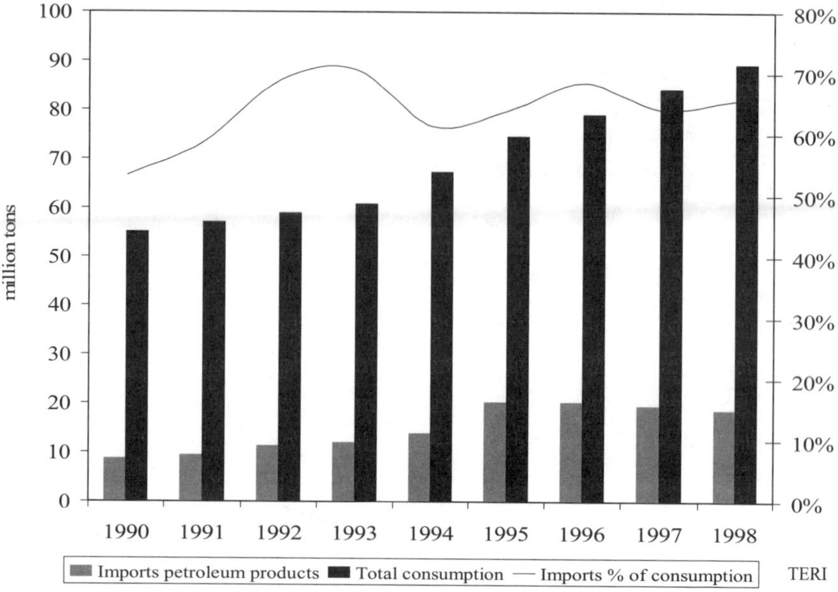

Imports petroleum products ■ Total consumption — Imports % of consumption   TERI

Source: TEDDY 2000/2001.

From the past experience, crude oil supply disruptions have a significant impact on a country's economy. A recent United Nations study has determined that with the upward oil price rally in 2000, oil imports of developing economies were higher by US$60 billion in 2000 as compared to 1999, and that the increase was equivalent to 1.3 percent of the GDP of developing economies, which is quite substantial.

Therefore, it becomes very important that India should adopt measures that improve the efficient utilization of energy resources, thereby reducing the need to produce more energy. These measures will not only enhance the security of energy supplies, which is an area of concern for the country today, by spreading available energy resources over a long period of time

[316]

but also mitigate environmental impacts and reduce their cost of delivery. Thus, this chapter highlights several initiatives that can be taken by the government in various energy sub-sectors viz., power, coal, oil and gas and renewables. It further identifies the initiatives that the government should undertake immediately.

Figure 8.6

Current and Projected Energy Mix for 2001 and 2025

(in percentages)

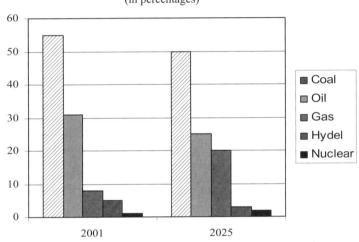

Source: Current figures are from *BP Amoco Statistical Review of World Energy* 2002 and projected figures are from the Government of India's Hydrocarbons Vision–2025 Report.

Characteristics of Past Energy Policy

India's energy mix has not undergone much change in the past thirty years. Coal still remains the dominant fuel with 55 percent of total primary energy accounted for by coal, down from 58 percent in 1970, though the consumption of coal has grown by 5.21 percent annually. The share of crude oil has increased marginally from 30 percent in 1970 to 31 percent in 2001, while growing at 5.50 percent annually since 1970. Natural gas has witnessed major gains to notch up a share of 8 percent, up from virtually nothing in 1970, and growing at 13.73 percent annually, though it is since the 1980s that the gas sector has really seen

[317]

major improvements with domestic discoveries. The share of hydropower has declined, although it displayed an annual growth rate of 2.38 percent over the past thirty years. This is primarily due to high growth rates achieved by the oil and gas sectors. As for nuclear energy, India has fourteen nuclear reactor units in operation in addition to four 220-MWe reactor units that were commissioned in 1999-2000. The plan envisages boosting capacity to 7300 MWe by 2007 and further to 20000 MWe by 2020, representing 7 to 10 percent share in the total electricity generation. The current and projected energy mix of these sources is shown in Figure 8.6.

With regard to the policies pertaining to energy sector in India, these are formulated by the various ministries of the government. The important ministries for energy are the Ministry of Petroleum and Natural Gas (MOP&NG), the Ministry of Coal (MoC), the Ministry of Non-Conventional Energy Sources (MNES), the Ministry of Environment and Forests (MoEF), the Department of Atomic Energy and the Ministry of Power (MoP).

Within the Ministry of Power, the Central Electricity Regulatory Commission (CERC), constituted in response to power sector reforms, works closely with the State Electricity Boards (SEBs) and utilities in the power generation, transmission, and distribution of electricity. Under the MOP&NG is the Directorate General of Hydrocarbons (DGH). The DGH oversees petroleum exploration programs, develops plans for the state-owned oil enterprises and private companies, and oversees the efficient utilization of gas fields. The Gas Authority of India Limited (GAIL) is responsible for transportation and marketing of natural gas. Other state-owned oil companies like the Oil and Natural Gas Corporation (ONGC), Oil India Limited (OIL), Indian Oil Corporation (IOC), Bharat Petroleum Corporation Limited (BPCL), Hindustan Petroleum Corporation Limited (HPCL) among others, help in shaping the direction of energy policies. Similarly, other ministries have their respective charters. The ministries that oversee transportation of fuels are also very important. For instance, the Ministry of Shipping Transport (MoST) is responsible for the importation of energy aboard ships of the state-owned Shipping Corporation of India (SCI).

However, in recent years it has been felt that energy policies in India lack overall coordination. This has, to a great extent, acted as a barrier against private investments in energy projects. Therefore, it becomes critical to develop a strategy and implement it in a coordinated manner, in order to respond effectively to any kind of supply disruption. For instance, in the power sector, the lack of a coordinated energy policy has led to the scrapping of many private projects based on liquid fuels such as naphtha and fuel oil. In 1996-1997 the government had allowed private companies to set up small to medium-sized power plants based on liquid fuels. However, with the hike in fuel prices, many such projects have been rendered economically unviable. The promoters of these projects are still struggling to tie up finances and negotiate escrow covers. The MoP withdrew the clearances of many projects, as the promoters have not been able to firm up the natural gas or LNG linkages, to take care of their future fuel requirements. This has impacted on the power capacity installation that was planned during the Ninth Five-Year Plan.

India is the third leading coal producer in the world after China and the United States. As such, most of India's coal demand is met through domestic production, with the exception of coking coal, which is imported to make up for the shortage. Presently more than half of the power needs are met by coal. Although the government is also forecasting a huge increase in coal-based power capacity, a massive increase in coal supply is required to achieve this increase. Analyzing past policies in the power and coal sectors, it is clear that the two sectors need to be viewed in a more coordinated manner rather than in a mismatched fashion, so that policies lead to overall development of the energy sector. In this regard, it might be worthwhile to assess the potential of coal imports, for blending purposes, especially in locations far away from the coal fields and along the Indian coastal belts (such as Gujarat and Maharashtra states).

In the hydrocarbon sector, although India has the advantage of being situated near the Caspian region, which has about 2-3 percent of proven world energy reserves, several proposals made to transport oil and gas from Kazakhstan and Turkmenistan to Asian countries, particularly India, have not materialized so far. This has been due to many factors. First of all, the natural gas markets have not been able to develop. Also, unlike other fuels, natural gas trade requires long-term contracts between buyers and sellers, which necessitate significant financial and political commitments. Owing to the lack of such commitments from the parties involved, no imports have materialized till date. Further, the gas discovery by Reliance Industries Limited (RIL) in the Krishna-Godavari Basin in the state of Andhra Pradesh, has also led to a renewed look at various gas import options from neighboring countries like Burma and Bangladesh.

The transport sector also contributes significantly to the economic development of a country. The past figures in this sector clearly indicate that the Indian economy is locked into a system based on inefficient use of energy. There is a major change in the transport mix with regard to the respective shares of the railways and roadways in the movement of freight and passenger traffic. The shift has been experienced more from rail to road movement for various reasons such as the absence of a good public transport system, which has led to an increase in the share of personal motor vehicles. This in turn, has increased the levels of congestion and lowered speed, leading to poor fuel efficiencies in most cases (see Table 8.2). Figure 8.7 depicts the inter-modal share of freight traffic.

Table 8.2

Increasing Share of Roads in Freight and Passenger Movement

	Railways	Roads
Freight	40%	60%
Passenger	20%	80%

Source: CMIE Basic Statistics (Various issues); MoR Status Paper on Indian Railways 1996/97; MoF Economic Survey 1999.

Figure 8.7
Inter-Modal Share of Freight Traffic

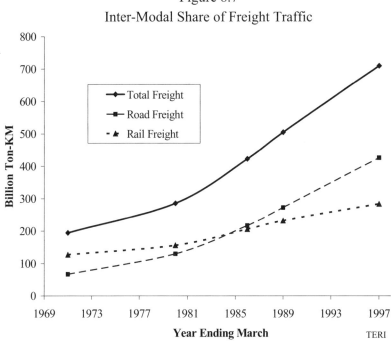

Source: Economic Intelligence Service, 2001, CMIE Publication.

As far as renewable energy options are concerned, the last couple of years have seen considerable progress in the generation of power from sources such as wind, small hydro, biomass and solar energy. Although the total installed capacity of power generation from various renewable energy sources has reached about 1700 MW, this represents merely 1.76 percent of the total installed capacity in 2001, which is quite insignificant. Hence, along with this there is a need to make use of renewable energy options substantially with the use of energy efficient technologies and promotion of rural energy programs that will help in the overall development of the rural areas in the long run.

Hence, review of the past policies in energy sub-sectors (coal, oil & gas, power, renewables and transport) clearly show that inadequate attention has been given to various decentralized energy options. In fact, government policies should be framed such that proper attention is given to all energy forms, leading to a more balanced mix in the total energy supply.

[321]

India's Significant Untapped Potential

Coal is the most abundant fossil fuel resource in India. The principal deposits of hard coal are located in the eastern parts of the country (as in the states of Andhra Pradesh, Bihar, Orissa, Madhya Pradesh and West Bengal) which accounts for about 85 percent of the total reserves. The reserve to production ratio of 212 for coal indicates that coal has huge potential in meeting India's energy needs in the future. Hence, the government plans/policies should be framed in a way that encourages coal exploration in the country.

As far as oil and gas exploration is concerned, India remains one of the least explored regions in the world. The country has a well density of 20 per 10000 sq. km against a world average of 20. Of the 26 sedimentary basins, only 6 have been explored so far. The Oil and Natural Gas Corporation (ONGC) and the Oil India Limited (OIL), two upstream public sector oil companies, have been undertaking oil and gas exploration work and hence there is an increase in the meterage and the number of wells drilled. Still, the current reserve accretion continues to be very low. The government's initiative, the New Exploration Licensing Policy (NELP), introduced with the objective of exploring more hydrocarbon reserves in India, has started bearing fruit, as shown by the NELP I fields in the Krishna Godavari (KG) basin. Such initiatives are likely to evoke interest in the private sector also in the future.

Additionally, India has vast untapped hydroelectric potential. Estimates place the hydroelectric potential at 64000 MW, of which only about 37 percent (or 24,000 MW) has been utilized. Only about one-fifth of India's total electricity generation comes from hydroelectric power plants. Other alternative energy sources such as wind, solar photovoltaic (PV) technologies and biomass have a future in India. Since India wants to see 10% of all additional electric capacity coming from renewable energy sources by 2012, the Indian Renewable Energy Development Agency (IREDA), a part of the Ministry of Non-Conventional Energy Sources (MNES), which oversees the development of these energy sources from the government's side, has the immense task of tapping these resources.

[322]

Considering the untapped potential of wind energy alone, which has been revised in the recent studies to 45000 MW (at 50 meters hub height) compared to the initial estimates of 20000 MW (at the micro level), the potential locations identified are in the flat coastal terrain of southern Tamil Nadu, Kerala, Gujarat, Lakshadweep, Andaman & Nicobar Islands, Orissa and Maharashtra. Other favorable sites have also been identified in some inland areas of Karnataka, Andhra Pradesh, Madhya Pradesh, West Bengal, Uttar Pradesh and Rajasthan. Although in terms of currently installed wind turbine capacity of 1175 MW (57 MW demonstration projects and 1118 MW commercial projects as of mid-2000), India ranks fifth in the world behind Germany, USA, Denmark and Spain, there is still much scope for the development of wind energy in India.

In the field of solar water heaters and solar cookers, India has developed substantial manufacturing capability and has become a leading producer in the developing world and the MNES has been promoting various programs related to the sales of box solar cookers, solar steam cooking systems, solar buildings etc., by creating an awareness of the potential for solar-efficient technologies. This potential needs to be tapped further if the country wants to see a rise in the share of renewables in the total energy mix of the country.

The potential sites for tidal power generation are the Gulf of Kutch and the Gulf of Khambat (Cambay) both in the western state of Gujarat, and the Gangetic delta in the Sunderbans area of West Bengal in eastern India. The tidal ranges of the Gulf of Kutch and the Gulf of Khambat are 5 and 7 metres respectively, with theoretical capacities estimated at 900 MW and 7000 MW and the estimated annual output at approximately 1.6 TWh and 15 TWh respectively. This potential remains untapped.

The contribution of biomass fuel in the total primary energy supplies is presently about 41 percent. In India's rural areas, the percentage of biomass (wood, animal dung and agricultural residues) supplied has risen to about 95 percent. Although the use of dried dung and waste as fuels is widespread in agriculturally prosperous regions, wood is still the principal domestic fuel in poorer and less well-endowed regions. Overall, fuel wood alone is estimated to provide almost 60 percent of energy in rural areas and around 35 percent in urban areas. Apart from its use in domestic cooking and heating, it is also used in bakeries, hotels, brick manufacture, tile manufacture and numerous small cottage industries. Hence biomass holds great potential for use as energy source in India. Table 8.3 shows proposed renewable energy (RE) capacity addition upto 2012.

Table 8.3
Proposed Renewable Energy (RE) Capacity Addition, 2012

S No.	RE	Capacity (MW)
1	Wind	6000
2	Small hydro	2000
3	Biomass	1500
4	Others	500
	Total	**10000**

Source: Presentation made on "Renewable Energy in India—A Viable Mitigation Option" by Mr A. K. Mangotra, Joint Secretary, Ministry of Non-Conventional Energy Sources in the "Workshop on Climate Change: Policy Options For India" on 5-6 September 2002, New Delhi.

Given the huge coal reserves in India, there also exist large quantities of coal bed methane (CBM). Considering the fact that CBM is less polluting and is environmentally benign, it will attract a lot of interest by the various players for its exploitation and use. However, since CBM exploration is quite time-consuming and capital-intensive, unless fiscal and other incentives are put in place, the possibility of investors getting interested in this activity in India is remote. There is a need to undertake activities to develop CBM, which will definitely supplement the available fuels for power generation and other uses.

India also holds huge potential (of about 15000 MW) to generate power from co-generation in selected industries like sugar, fertilizer, steel, cement, paper, man-made fiber, and chemical/petrochemical industries. The power fed into the grid by industrial co-generation is beneficial to both the country as well as the individual units. The case studies carried out for a few sugar mills clearly indicate that, assuming several options that reflect alternative combinations of output, investment costs and power purchase prices along with a pre-tax return on investment (internal rate of return) of 25 percent, the cost of power generation will range from Rs 1.26 per kWh to Rs 1.64 per kWh (by conservative estimates) that is, below Rs 2.00 per kWh.

In a nutshell, India holds huge potential for various energy sources, which has not yet been explored adequately. Given a thrust by the government, these options could be explored properly and provide a cushion to the energy supply in order to meet the growing demand in the long-term.

The Emerging Energy Scenario

The emerging energy scenario in India is discussed in greater detail in the subsequent sections. The focus is on the issues in the various sub-sectors such as power, coal, oil and gas as well as renewables.

Power Sector

The total installed generating capacity as on March 31, 2001 has increased to 101154 MW in utilities. The share of thermal power in total generation has increased from 71 percent in 1991-1992 to 81 percent in 2001-2002. Though plans have been made to increase the share of hydro in the total hydro-thermal mix for generation, unfortunately hydro has not been able to attain that share. A review by Ministry of Power (MoP)/Central Electricity Authority (CEA) carried out in 2001 assessed the likely capacity additions during the Ninth Five Year Plan period. It revealed that additions would be to the tune of 19213 MW during this period, much below the targeted additions. The likely additions comprise 4590 MW (24 percent) from hydro, 13743 MW (71 percent) from thermal and 880 MW (5 percent) from nuclear projects.

The 'Working Group Report on Power for the Tenth Plan' revealed that the state governments are expected to achieve 85 percent of the original capacity addition as against the targeted addition of 10,748 MW. While, the central government is expected to achieve capacity addition of 4774 MW as against the targeted 11909 MW, while the private sector is expected to add a mere 5322 MW as against the targeted 17588 MW. The report also anticipated the peak shortages in the sector (which is the maximum power shortage during a specified period of time) of 16.5 percent and energy shortages (which are overall shortages of energy during the entire period) of 10.2 percent respectively by the end of Ninth Plan period. In addition, CEA also has made projections for the Tenth Plan. As per their projections, the capacity addition of 10000 MW per year is likely to materialize till the year 2011-2012. It is also expected that about 25 percent of this generation will come from the Independent Power Producers (IPPs) in the private sector, while the rest will come from the public sector and mostly from the central units.

A review of the power supply industry over the years shows that the sector has undoubtedly made significant progress. The installed capacity and power generation has increased several times between 1951 and 2001. Figure 8.8 indicates the actual and projected electricity capacity additions during the Fifth Plan (1974-1979) and Eleventh Five-Year Plan (2007-2012). The size and expansion of the transmission and distribution network has also increased substantially. Besides all urban centres, over 85% of the total villages of the country have access to power.

Figure 8.8
Electricity Capacity Additions in Plan Periods

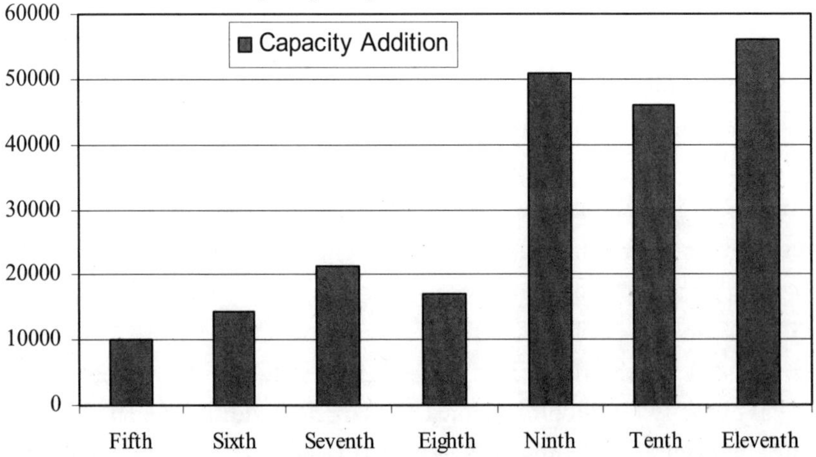

Source: Central Electricity Authority. Report of the Working Group on Power for the Tenth Plan. 2002.

There has also been progressive interconnection of power systems at the state level to start with and subsequently at the regional level. The entry of Central Public Sector Undertakings (CPSU) into power generation and transmission has helped to consolidate the power system in the country. A National Power Grid, which has been approved in principle by the government, is already on the horizon. However, energy and peak shortages still continue to plague the economy.

Although the growth achieved through investments in the public sector has been impressive in the past, there are certain areas of concern. One is that the high growth achieved in the past may not be sustainable through public funding alone. Looking at the capacity additions in the earlier Plan period, it may be noticed that during the Fifth Plan (1974-1979), the capacity addition was 10202 MW, during the Sixth Plan (1980-1985) it was 14226 MW and for the Seventh Plan (1985-1990) it was 21401 MW. However, in the Eighth Plan (1992-1997) it was only 16423 MW. Though the share in the Ninth Plan has increased substantially compared to the previous Plan, there have been many slippages (of 52 percent against targeted) in the materialization of many projects.

The emerging scenario in the power sector now clearly shows low prospects of capacity additions by the public sector because of their growing financial constraints. The deteriorating financial health of the State Electricity Boards (SEBs) has adversely affected the ability of the utilities to make adequate investments in future capacity additions and the system improvement programs. In fact, the public sector thermal generation projects also require budgetary assistance. The requirements of coal and its transportation for these projects are expected to rise. To meet these requirements, large investments in the coal sector as well as in the railways and the ports for coal transportation need to be made. In fact, for the Ninth Plan, the investment requirement in the coal sector is estimated as Rs 20000 crores against the anticipated investment of Rs 2000 crores.

Alternatively, it becomes crucial that the role of the 'private' sector is spelled out clearly by the government. There is an urgent need to encourage investments by the private players and introduce more competition in order to achieve improvements in the functioning of the system. Estimates indicate that an investment of US$ 80 billion (Rs 384000 crores) is required for meeting capacity additions in each Five Year Plan period. This translates into an annual investment of about Rs 76800 crores (at the rate of Rs 48 per US$). This is much less compared to the Ninth Plan's approved outlay for the central sector of about Rs 53000 crores (1 crore = 10 million). Further, as indicated by the Working Group Report, the magnitude of the task for the Tenth Plan is huge when compared with the Seventh, Eighth and Ninth Plans. (See Table 8.4).

Table 8.4

Capacity Additions per Annum in Plan Periods

Capacity additions per annum	VII Plan (1985-1990)	VIII Plan (1992-1997)	IX Plan (1997-2002)	X Plan* (2002-2007)
(MW)	4210	3285	5000	10000

Source: Central Electricity Authority. Report of the Working Group on Power for the Tenth Plan, 2002.

Critical Issues in the Power Sector

The privatization of the power sector started more than a decade ago in 1991, with the objectives of bringing improvement in the efficiency of the system, providing quality power, lowering power costs and offering better service to the consumers. Many new power policies were introduced to attract private investments. However, the experience in this regard in the 1990s has been totally dismal, with capacity addition targets slipping more than 50 percent and power costs increasing almost thrice during 1991 to 2002. The increase in costs has been more pronounced in the case of SEBs, which are over reliant on power purchase from the central stations.

All this has led to greater thrust on distribution reforms in recent times. It is believed that the improvements in the power distribution sector will induce private investments in generation as well. Certain states like Orissa have already identified and handed over specific areas to the private sector. Rajasthan has proposed priority to attract private investments into distribution below 32 KV lines. The MoP has also put in place a set of conditions to which disbursement of funds under the Accelerated Power Development and Reform Program (APDRP) is to be done for transitional financing of reform steps undertaken by the state governments. Four states have already secured 43 percent of power reform funds against the approved funds for upgrading of the power transmission and distribution system, which indicates clearly that this alone will not provide the solution. On the contrary, the reforms in the distribution sector will generate better results if the existing decentralized institutional mechanisms like cooperatives, local service providers etc. are utilized more effectively and efficiently in the states.

However, the regulating commissions, Central Electricity Regulatory Commission (CERC) and State Electricity Regulatory Commissions (SERCs), which are agencies at the central and state level formed for fixing tariffs and ensuring level playing fields lack independence. There should be transparency in the procedure of selection of their expertise. The government should make these Commissions autonomous bodies that can undertake and execute decisions, thereby providing them with stability. Hence, there is an urgent need to strengthen these commissions in the power sector if any major reform has to be implemented.

The high transmission and distribution (T&D) losses[1] in the power sector are another problem. The government needs to focus on the reforms in the T&D sector that were neglected and has thereby created bottlenecks. However, it is now conceded by policy makers that T&D should be given due attention. To tackle this issue, the government has announced an action plan to improve the sub-T&D systems in the country. The Committee constituted for this purpose has recommended the T&D schemes that primarily focus on reducing "commercial losses" in a shorter time-span and reducing "technical losses" over a longer period of time. This in turn will bring improvements in the efficiency of the system.

Figure 8.9
T & D Losses in Uttar Pradesh (TERI study)

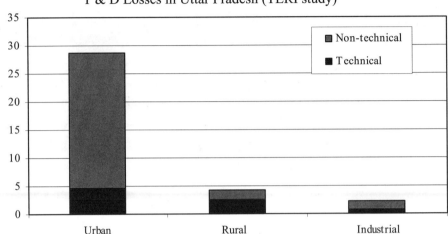

Source: TERI 1998.

A study undertaken by the Tata Energy Research Institute (TERI) on T&D losses in one of the Indian states, Uttar Pradesh, has shown that power thefts (usually referred to as "non-technical losses") in urban areas is more widespread compared to the rural areas or the industrial sector (See Figure 8.9). The improvements in efficiencies will also bring about improvement in the quality of power supply and the services that are offered to the consumers. This in turn will help in the better utilization of existing energy resources to meet the existing power shortages in the country.

The issue of subsidies also requires attention. The government is providing subsidies to the poorer sections of society. In the power sector, industrial consumers are cross subsidizing tariffs for agriculture consumers. Such subsidies have sunk the finances of the state government completely. As a result of this, utilities have been forced to sell power below its cost, which is contributing to their bleak financial picture. In the light of regulatory reforms happening in India, it is very important that proper estimation of subsidies is carried out. If the government has to provide the subsidy, it can be provided on the basis of the metered power for the agriculture sector.

Taking a holistic view of developments in the sector, in addition to the remedies mentioned above, a complementary package including other measures such as energy conservation and demand side management also needs to be taken up gradually. Such measures, combined with the additional energy availability through renovation and modernization, would enable India to overcome the situation of power cuts and power shortages in the years to come.

Coal Sector

India is the third largest producer of coal in the world. It is one of the primary sources of energy, accounting for about 67 percent of the total energy consumption in the country. India also has some of the largest reserves of coal in the world (nearly 197 billion tons). Coal deposits in India occur mostly in thick seams and at shallow depths. Non-coking coal reserves aggregate 172.1 billion tons (85 percent) while coking coal reserves are 29.8 billion tons (the remaining 15 percent). Indian coal has a high ash content (15 to 45 percent) and low calorific value. It is also relatively low in sulfur (0.5 percent) and chlorine content. Lignite, sub-bituminous and bituminous coal are predominant in India, and only small amounts of anthracite are available. Due to the high ash content of coal, environmental measures are being taken by many Indian states in using this resource. Coal India Limited (CIL), the major player in the industry, accounts for 90 percent of the country's coal output. CIL oversees the operations of its regional subsidiaries as well.

With the present rate of around 0.8 million tons of average daily coal extraction in the country, the reserves are likely to last over a hundred years. As a matter of fact, the energy derived from coal in India is about twice that of energy derived from oil, as against the world, where energy derived from coal is about 30 percent lower than energy derived from oil. Also, the use of beneficiated coal[2] has gained acceptance in steel plants and power plants located at a distance from the pithead.

At the same time, India is the eighth largest coal importer. Imports of low ash-content coal are principally meant for use by the steel plants, for which it is blended with Indian coal. Against an annual coal production of

310 million tons within the country, India also imports almost 25 million tons. The government forecasts huge increases in electricity capacity based on coal. Coal demand is also expected to increase manifold in the next few years due to an increase in demand from metallurgical and other industries. As a matter of fact, the demand for coal has been rising at an annual rate of 6 percent since 1992-1993 and CIL and its subsidiaries will be unable to meet the projected demand alone. The investment needed to bridge the gap of about 400 million tons, between the level of production in the public sector (290 million tons in 1995-1996) and the projected demand of 690 million tons (2009-2010) is estimated to be US$ 18 billion. The public sector corporations are expected to increase their production by about 250 million tons by 2009-2010, subject to their making an additional investment of US$ 8-10 billion. The balance requirement of 150 million tons will have to be met by imports in the short run and by new investments in the long run. Hence, in the long term, the principal objective of coal policy for India should be to improve the financial performance of the industry by creating a freely competitive situation. A financially viable electricity industry will necessarily support reforms in the coal industry as well.

With the advent of recent economic reforms, the government controls on pricing and distribution of coal have been relaxed and it is fully deregulated now. With effect from January 1, 2000, pricing and distribution of all grades of coal are fully deregulated after notification of a new Colliery Control Order, 2000 which supersedes the Colliery Control Order, 1945. Under the Colliery Control Order, 2000, the Central Government has no power to regulate coal prices.

Presently, coal imports are allowed under the Open General License (OGL) system. Also, a new coal policy has been announced that permits private sector participation in commercial coal mining. In order to attract private investments, the government should offer financially attractive reserves and put them on a similar platform as the public sector companies. The government should also introduce competitive bidding for coal mining blocks. All public and private companies must bid for the blocks freely without CIL being given a preference. There is a considerable need for such initiatives to be undertaken by the government to improve the efficiency and competitiveness of the Indian coal sector.

Oil and Gas Sector

The share of oil in the country's fuel mix has steadily risen from 25 percent in 1960s to about 33 percent in the 1990s. Though energy elasticity is projected to decline to 0.55 in 2025 from the present 0.70, the share of oil in overall energy availability is projected to increase to 40 percent over the same period. Since Indian domestic production has failed to keep pace with this rapid rate of growth, import dependence for oil has risen from 44 percent in 1991 to over 70 percent in 2001. As per the *Hydro Carbon Vision 2025* document, crude oil demand in 2025 is placed at around 276 million metric tons (MMT) and most of which is likely to be met only by imports. Also, the Tenth Plan document forecasts the import dependency of 85 percent by 2006-2007 out of which sour crude will be 78 percent, which is likely to be sourced mainly from the Middle Eastern countries. However, with the new discoveries proving fruitful in NELP 1, there are chances that India is also likely to meet some of the growing demands by its indigenous production.

Compared to crude oil, natural gas is expected to play an important role in the energy future due to growing environmental concerns. According to the *Hydro Carbon Vision 2025* document, the share of natural gas in total energy consumption is projected to be 16 percent by 2025, up from 8 percent at present (with the demand expected to range from 216 to 313 MMSCMD in the year 2011-12). However, in the light of restricted gas production from indigenous sources, the government has been encouraging the gas import projects in the form of either liquefied natural gas (LNG) or piped imports (such as the Indo-Iran pipeline, Indo-Oman pipeline and Indo-Bangladesh gas pipeline projects). It must be noted though, that most of these projects are stalled and nothing much is being achieved due to various reasons.

Reforms in the hydrocarbon sector started in 1997. The government laid down a timetable for abolishing the Administered Pricing Mechanism

(APM) by 2002. Though the APM has been abolished since April 2002, the sector has not yet been completely opened to market forces. The pricing of sensitive fuels such as petrol (MS), diesel (HSD), domestic gas (LPG) and kerosene, though free, is still set after consultation with the government.

The domestic exploration and production companies are still negotiating with the refineries for an internationally competitive price regarding crude oil. In case of gas prices also, it has not been linked completely to the international parity levels. According to the plans proposed by the MOP&NG a gradual increase in gas prices was to begin in January 2003 with complete deregulation by October 2003. According to it, the ceiling on gas prices was to be raised from the current level of Rs 2850 (US$59.38) per MCM to Rs 4300 (US $89.58) per MCM from January 1, 2003. Further, gas prices were to be linked to 100 percent fuel oil parity from April 1, 2003 and the price ceiling raised to Rs 5800 (US$120.83) per MCM. The Ministry proposed deregulation of gas prices from October 1, 2003, so that market forces could determine the real price. It also proposed that the consumer price would include royalty in a manner that the final price would not exceed the international fuel oil price after the deregulation. Unfortunately, such policies still need to be implemented before the sector is "fully deregulated" in the real sense.

The Petroleum Regulatory Board Bill, which has already been introduced in Parliament, has not yet led to the formation of a Regulatory Board, which will regulate the sector. These are many issues that still have to be clarified with regard to the role of that Board as outlined in this Bill. The crude pipelines put up by domestic oil companies under the APM regime should be given the status of "common carrier" and open access should be provided to all players subject, of course, to regulation by the Board.

With regard to the new product pipelines, the government has introduced a new petroleum product pipeline policy. According to this, all pipelines to be laid in future will be based on the "common carrier" principle. In fact, this means that the oil companies interested in laying a product pipeline from a refinery over a length of over 300 km length or any pipeline from a port would be required to publish the proposal inviting other interested companies to take capacity in the pipeline on mutually agreed commercial terms. At least 25 percent extra capacity would necessarily have to be provided for other users. The tariff to be charged for pipeline use will be subject to the government regulations. These proposed guidelines are not supposed to be applied to the crude oil pipelines. Companies will also be free to construct pipelines originating from refineries for their captive use.

Concerning retail marketing, there is no policy announcement by the government clarifying the policies encouraging entry of private players. To encourage private sector investments, many issues need to be clearly defined. As is evident in case of LNG imports, the importers are demanding the grant of infrastructure status for LNG projects. The idea here is that if infrastructure status is given to LNG projects, only 4 percent Central Sales Tax (CST) will have to be paid as against the state sales tax rates which vary widely from one state to another, and which would make LNG costlier than coal and jeopardize the investments being made by the companies in building LNG terminals.

Another limitation that India faces relates to the available port capacity to import fuels from various parts of the world. Port capacity for oil imports in 1994-1995 was 78 MMT as against 8 MMT for coal. Till the pipelines and port ancillaries are given infrastructure status, developments will happen at a very slow pace. Moreover, India also needs to devise a strategy to have supply of energy from diversified sources especially for hydrocarbons as against depending upon one source, the Middle East. To further boost energy security, the government should frame suitable policies that help in the development of non-conventional gas resources such as coal bed methane (CBM) and gas hydrates, and attract private investors to these sectors.

Renewable Energy Sector

In India, renewable sources of energy have been promoted since the 1980s. The strategy used was state subsidy in the initial period, followed by fiscal incentives. The draft renewable energy policy sets a goal of installing 10000 MW of renewable power generation capacity. The strategy involves mainly fiscal incentives like tax benefits and financial incentives such as low interest loans. In fact, the strategy followed in India differs from that followed in other developed countries like Europe, where the legislation makes it mandatory to generate a certain portion of power using renewables.

Also, in the ongoing reform process in the power sector, renewables require repositioning. Due to the overall financial weakness of utilities and the fact that the tariff issues are politically sensitive, the higher cost of renewables calls for government support at the present time. There is an urgent need to promote competitive bidding for the procurement of renewable based electricity by utilities as well.

The comparison of potential with achievement made in this sector paints a sorry picture (see Table 8.5). Though India ranks first in the world in utilization levels of solar cookers and biomass gasifiers and can claim decent utilization levels in biogas plants, cooking stoves, solar photovoltaics and wind power, the levels achieved are not true indicators of the country's potential, most of which remains unfulfilled.

Table 8.5
Potential and Achievement in Renewable Energy

Source/System	Approximate Potential	Achievement (as on 31-10-2002)
Power from renewables:		
Solar photovoltaic power	—	2.30 MW
Wind power	45,000 MW	1702.3 MW
Small hydro power (up to 25 MW)	15,000 MW	1461.43 MW
Biomass cogeneration power	19,500 MW*	456.93 MW
Biomass gasifier	—	51.6 MW
Energy recovery from wastes	1,700 MW	21.98 MW
Power from renewables (Total)	**81,200 MW**	**3695.54 MW**

Source: http://www.renewingindia.org/newsletters/repsovision/current/news_rep_oct0202.htm.

One of the main reasons for these relatively low levels of utilization is the high cost of using these technologies. However, as Table 8.6 shows, these costs are slated to decline in the coming years and these technologies will become economically competitive.

Table 8.6
Current and Estimated Future Costs of Renewable Energy Technologies

Technology	Current Energy Costs (cents/kWh)	Potential Future Energy Costs (cents/kWh)
Biomass electricity	5-15	4-10
Wind electricity	5-13	3-10
Solar photovoltaic	25-125	6-25
Solar thermal electricity	12-18	4-10
Small hydro	4-10	3-10

Source: World Bank website.

The last decade and a half of the promotion of wind, biomass, solar energy and other renewable energy technologies (RETs) in the Indian energy economy has provided a great deal of empirical knowledge about strategies for their successful commercialization. One of the crucial requirements in the development of renewable energy is the government's involvement in order to ensure a conducive policy environment (through the provision of remunerative prices for RET generated electricity or of fiscal incentives) and to provide backup financial support (through direct and indirect subsidies) in order for RETs (that have yet to mature technologically) to move towards sustainable financial viability. Low cost working capital credit should be provided to encourage its use and decentralize the renewable energy technologies. Additionally, providing both technology-push and consumer-pull might help in the creation of a sustainable market for these. Consequently, it is important to continuously monitor and fine tune the incentive structure so as to keep pace with market developments.

The 73rd and 74th constitutional amendments also assure more power for village *panchayats* (local bodies) in the field of energy as it enables the *panchayats* to promote and propagate non-conventional renewable energy. There is also a need to create local institutional capacity for the energization of villages using renewable technologies.

Enhancing Energy Efficiency in India: Long Term Solutions

The rate of growth of energy intensity of the economy has been slower than that of total energy consumption and in the 1990s the energy intensity has in fact declined. This decline is made possible due to the high growth observed in the services sector of the economy and/or improvements in the energy efficiency of the economy.

Sectoral trends in energy intensity also offer important insights into the country's energy efficiency. The energy intensity of industry has declined since the 1980s primarily due to the decline in the oil intensity of the industry, although the intensity of gas usage has increased. This is expected to continue for years to come, as gas supplies have increased and the gas demand in the country is constrained by supply, given that gas is more efficient than oil in industrial applications. The energy intensity of the agriculture sector has risen, primarily due to the huge rise in electrical energy intensity of the sector. This trend is also expected to continue as Indian agriculture tries to rely more on man-made irrigation options than on the monsoons. Also, new age farming processes require measured irrigation at the right time to yield desirable results. This will further necessitate the use of pump sets in irrigation. According to UNDP estimates, there is still room for improvement in the energy efficiency of various sectors of the economy.

The energy intensity of transport (excluding railways) rose till 1989-1990, when it reached its peak and declined thereafter. This is probably due to introduction of more fuel-efficient vehicles since the liberalization of the economy in 1990-1991.

Table 8.7
Potential for Improvement in Energy Efficiency

Sector	Percentage
Industry	
Iron and steel	15
Cement	17
Pulp and Paper	20-25
Textile	23
Aluminium	15-20
Household	
Lighting	10-70
Refrigeration	25
Air-Conditioning	10
Agriculture	
Pump sets	25-55
Transportation	
Cars	7.5-10.0
Trains (diesel)	5-10
Trains (electric)	5-10

Source: Compiled from various TERI reports.

Improving the efficiency in the sector would entail introducing market-based reforms (see Table 8.7 above). Some progress has been made along these lines, as the Energy Conservation Act has been passed and the Bureau of Energy Efficiency has been established. The Energy Conservation Act, 2001 seeks to set up a Bureau of Energy Efficiency whose Governing Council will be headed by the Union Minister of Power. It will work out stringent norms for the conservation of energy in all forms, wherein there will be no room whatsoever, for sub-standard equipment. The Bureau will also exercise the powers of the central government for enforcement of efficient use of energy and its conservation. The states will emulate the center at the regional level. Besides, the existing Energy Management Center will merge its assets, liabilities and employees with the Bureau. Also, this is a unique law with India being the second country in the world to have such a legislation.

[339]

Some of the other measures that India should adopt to enhance energy efficiency include following innovative market incentives (such as differential excise duties) to promote end-use efficiency. Support should be given to develop and disseminate energy efficient technologies in small scale industries as well. Further, there is a need to accredit energy audit organizations and facilitate energy audits for hotels, large commercial complexes and industries. Adoption of these measures will not only provide efficient utilization of energy resources in India but will also help in building the security of supplies for the country in the future.

Conclusion

Ensuring affordable supplies of energy in various forms is central to the socio-economic development of a country. As shown above, the link between energy and economy in India is still strong and any disruption in energy supplies is bound to have a negative impact on the economy. Hence, it becomes important to protect India's economy from any kind of external supply shock and maintain a cushion against such shocks.

In this regard, several initiatives still need to be undertaken by the Indian government in the energy sector apart from just allowing the entry of the private sector to bring about reforms in the power, coal and hydrocarbon sectors. It also becomes important that market forces are allowed to play a role and induce further competition, which will ultimately provide better services to the end-users at a competitive price. The market forces will also ensure that during times of crisis, demand and supply are balanced, as in such a situation the prices will indicate relative shortage and surplus in the sector. All these initiatives in various energy sub-sectors will boost the country's energy security in the long run.

Concluding Observations

John V. Mitchell

Internationalizing Asian Energy

The trends described in this book point to a continuing internationalization of the Asian energy scene. This has three dimensions: trade, investment and security. The drama is developing within a larger saga. There is a momentum created by economic globalization and the attempts to "manage" it to produce politically and socially acceptable outcomes. The perception is growing that energy security (both economic and strategic) may be more easily achieved by international cooperation than by doomed attempts at the "independence" of self-sufficiency. Finally, the geopolitical script is changing, both globally and in Asia.

Policy or Markets

Manning in his paper suggests a contrast between a "pessimistic view of strategic competition" and a "market-led" scenario. In the first scenario, the growing energy interdependence between Southwest and Northeast Asia leads to a political and bureaucratic "nexus" of Asia-centric relationships. In the second scenario, the growing interdependence engages Asia more not only with itself but also in the wider international system of trade and investment in energy. Manning suggests some ways in which the growing relationships between the two wings of Asia can contribute to the economic solution: some of these are based on the capacity of China, through its national oil companies, to contribute management as well as finance to investments in Southwest Asian oil. Chinese state companies have also signed both oil and gas Memoranda of Understanding for projects in Kazakhstan and Turkmenistan. The Malaysian state company Petronas, though not an importer, has engaged in projects in Iraq and Iran. Japanese companies have long invested in oil in the Neutral Zone,[1] and also in gas and oil in the UAE, Oman, and Yemen, and most recently in oil projects in Iran. In the reverse direction, Saudi Aramco has significant shareholdings in a Korean and a Philippine refinery and is pursuing various interests in China. These developments are quite consistent with normal commercial relations within the open framework of the international oil market, but they could also be the first steps towards an "Asian system." Manning sketches a scenario along these lines, with China as the key to the importing side of the relationship.

Limits to Policy

Manning's question about forming an "Asian nexus" between importers and exporters is important and interesting. The most serious obstacle to an "Asian nexus" between energy exporters and importers is the determination of the governments of Saudi Arabia, Iran and other Southwest Asian countries to retain either total ownership and control or majority ownership and effective control of their upstream oil industry. The failure of the (Japanese) Arabian Oil Company to reach agreement to extend their concession in the Saudi portion of the Neutral Zone illustrates this point. Iranian terms for foreign investment, though apparently acceptable to the Japanese in the case of the Azadegan field yield neither ownership nor control to the foreign investors. Kuwait, after a decade of discussion, has yet to finalize investment contracts for foreign companies. In any case, the companies selected in Kuwait are essentially the companies associated with the US and European countries with military capability, as are the concessionaries chosen for the Saudi Arabian gas contracts.

Among the importing countries, the refining industry in Japan and Korea is not economically attractive to foreign investors. In the Japanese case, attempts by Saudi Aramco to buy significant interests in the 1990s were rejected, apparently on policy grounds. China has similarly limited all foreign investment in its refining and downstream industries with no hint of special relationships.

Even in the oil trade, the restrictions placed by major Southwest Asian exporters on the resale of their crude oil have limited competition in the market and have frustrated the development of a large liquid spot market.[2] The result has been a tendency for exporters to extract a higher netback price from Asian markets than from the US or Europe (the so-called "Asian premium.")

What is distinctive is that in Asia the international oil companies have a limited role. They are involved in some major exporting countries, but not in some of the most important of these. They have dominant roles downstream in some oil importing markets: Australia, New Zealand, Singapore, Thailand and the Philippines. In Japan and Korea they have important positions alongside the national private sector companies. In China, India, Indonesia, the great markets of the future, the international oil companies have no material downstream positions. If there are openings and privatization takes place, these international companies will have to make their way against the incumbent state or privatized companies. The technical, financial and managerial strengths of the international companies may be instruments of change in the Asian oil markets, but the advance of these companies is not a driving force. Change will enlarge their role, but will not make them dominant.

The Gas Sector

The gas sector is a slightly different story. Japanese commercial interests (and recently Korean) have for decades been involved in investment in LNG facilties and shipping from the UAE, Qatar, Yemen and Oman, just as in Indonesia and Australia. The problem for the future is not so much the strategic acceptability of such investments as the degree to which they can be financed now that the Japanese (and Korean) gas markets are being liberalized. In domestic liberalization, as in the European gas market, the tendency is to isolate the transportation system from the upstream and downstream interests and provide open access. In an existing infrastructure this is not an especially challenging policy. For international pipeline or transportation systems the situation is different. International agreements have generally been used not to isolate the new transportation system, but to support its financial credibility by locking in long term supply and off-take commitments in the exporting and importing countries. How such a new international infrastructure is to be financed in future, with liberalized import markets, is a difficult question everywhere. It may delay the development of gas infrastructure between the East Asian importers and long distance suppliers such as Iran, Qatar and central Asia.

The role of international companies in the gas sector may be more important than in oil. They are already key players in international gas trade in Asia, such as it is. In contrast to oil, the companies' role in gas is mainly upstream, while the downstream is either in the hands of local utilities or has yet to be created for new markets. Gas on the scale envisaged is a new game for everyone, but the game cannot be played without the companies, and their participation will be on the side of an "international market" scenario rather than an "Asian nexus."

In short, increased openness, to both trade and investment is more likely to deepen and reinforce the links between East Asian importers and Southwest Asian exporters than any development of bilateral and exclusive connections. There may be important exceptions to this, particularly in the development of oil and gas pipelines from Russia or central Asia to China, which absolutely need a solid foundation in bilateral agreements. Such agreements, however, are unlikely to supply all or even most of China's projected needs for oil or gas imports: the larger and more open system will still be necessary.

Manning and some of the other authors also draw attention to the connection between energy trade and investment relations and the broader issue of international security. The headline here is the dependence of Asian importers on US-led protection of the South West Asian sources of energy exports. Some importing countries like Japan contributed to the

[344]

cost of the Gulf War and took important symbolic steps to support the UN action, but the future is less well defined. Manning points out that China is or has been a supplier of arms to several South West Asian countries. By comparison with the US, these efforts carry little weight. For both exporting and importing countries in Asia, the best military security for growing energy interdependence is that available from outside Asia— though of course Asian countries would prefer to be at their call rather than that of US domestic political interests.

Conclusions

The energy trends in Asia that are described in this book are intriguing. Numbers may be uncertain but some directions are clear: greater liberalization of domestic markets, more imports of oil and gas, increasing use of gas, widening engagement in the evolving practices and institutions of international trade and investment, continuing dependence on out-of-Asia military and political support for the security of international oil supplies. For natural gas, there is important regional work to be done to provide institutional and commercial frameworks for the infrastructure investments needed to satisfy the ambitions of most energy importing governments with regard to the diversification of gas supplies and clean fuel for their cities. The participation of international companies will tend to internationalize the growing gas trade, but inter-government agreements may be needed to provide the conditions for major cross-border infrastructure investment. As the volumes of oil and gas trade grow in international importance, there may be some shifts in market structure. The policy choices of the exporting governments, and the governments and companies of the main importing countries, will determine those shifts. Present policies in important oil exporting and importing countries are likely to limit internationalization of investments in oil either globally or within Asia.

CONTRIBUTORS

PHILIP ANDREWS-SPEED is Director of the Centre for Energy, Petroleum and Mineral Law and Policy at the University of Dundee in Scotland. He spent fourteen years as a geologist in the international mining and petroleum industries before coming to the Centre in 1994, gaining an LLM in Energy Law and Policy, and joining the academic staff. Dr. Andrews-Speed leads the Centre's China Program, which covers research, consultancy and professional training in the petroleum, electricity, mining and water sectors. The focus of the research is on policy, regulation and reform especially in gas, electricity and coal. In 2001-2002 he carried out a project supported by the British Academy and by the International Institute for Strategic Studies examining the interaction between China's foreign policy and its energy policy, and the wider strategic implications of China's energy needs. He has recently completed a book entitled *Energy Policy and Regulation in the People's Republic of China*, which is due to be published by Kluwer Law International.

JAMES P. DORIAN is a Washington-based International Energy Economist specializing in Eurasian oil and gas issues and renewable energy. With twenty years experience in analyzing energy markets and policies, Dr. Dorian is an expert on energy and economic development strategies of the former Soviet Union, China and Asia, oil and gas development and investment trends, renewable energy technologies and policies, and the geopolitical forces affecting the global energy industry. Prior to his relocation to Washington, Dr. Dorian was an Energy and Resources Economist with the State of Hawaii Government in Honolulu, where he managed several collaborative projects on energy efficiency and renewable energy involving Hawaii and the Chinese and Philippine governments. Formerly, Dr. Dorian was a Research Fellow at the East-West Center in Honolulu, where he served as Coordinator of the Center's *Central Asia and Caucasia Energy and Minerals Project* and the *China Energy Project*. In 1997 Dr. Dorian was based in Uzbekistan and served as the Chief Energy Sector Specialist of an Asian Development Bank study on economic cooperation prospects in Central Asia and Xinjiang, China. Since the mid-1980s he has provided consultancy services to several businesses and international lending agencies.

Dr. Dorian has to his credit more than 90 scholarly and business-oriented publications, including the May 2001 management report, *Oil and Gas in Central Asia and Northwest China*, published by The CWC Group of London. In 1997, *The Financial Times* of London published Dorian's business executive report, *Oil and Gas in Russia and the Former Soviet Union*. In 1994, Oxford University Press published a sole-authored book of Dr. Dorian entitled *Minerals, Energy and Economic Development in China*, which is now in its second printing. Dr. Dorian is a member of the International Association of Energy Economists, and serves on the international editorial board of the UK-based *Journal of Energy Policy*. He is also a member of the Harvard-based Central Eurasian Studies Society. Dr. Dorian has a doctorate degree in Resource Economics from the University of Hawaii, where he served as an Affiliate Graduate Faculty member between 1989 and 2002.

AMY MYERS JAFFE, a Princeton University graduate in Arabic Studies, is the Associate Director of the Rice University energy program and the Wallace Wilson Fellow for Energy Studies at the James A. Baker III Institute for Public Policy, Rice University. Her research focuses on the subject of oil geopolitics, strategic energy policy including energy science policy, and energy economics. Her work has been published widely in academic journals and several book volumes including a co-authored article in *Foreign Affairs* "The Shocks of a World of Cheap Oil," published in January 2000 and the chapter on "Oil Geopolitics" in the Encyclopedia of Energy. She served as co-editor of *Energy in the Caspian Region: Present and Future* (Palgrave, 2002). Her other works include economics surveys on the role of Saudi Arabia's price discrimination in the oil market and the public goods aspect of petroleum inventories in energy policy formation as well as several articles and book chapters on oil in the Middle East, Russia, China and the Caspian Basin.

Amy Myers Jaffe received the 1994 Award for Excellence given by the International Association for Energy Economics and is a member of the Council on Foreign Relations (CFR). She is a principal author of the Baker Institute's first nine energy studies that covered energy policy and trends in the Middle East, Caspian Basin, China and Japan as well as emerging technologies in the nuclear, nanotechnology and natural gas sectors. She is currently organizing a major study on energy in Russia for the Baker Institute and was a major contributor to the joint Baker Institute/CFR task force on "Guiding Principles for US Post-Conflict Policy in Iraq." She serves as Project Director for the joint Baker Institute/CFR task force on "Strategic Energy Policy: Challenges in the 21st Century." Prior to joining the Baker Institute, Amy Myers Jaffe was the Senior Editor and Middle East analyst for *Petroleum Intelligence Weekly*, a respected oil journal. She has written for several publications including the *New York Times*, *Dow Jones International*, *The Asian Wall Street Journal* and the *Mideast Report* and is a widely-quoted commentator on oil and energy policy in the US and international media.

ROBERT A. MANNING is currently Senior Counselor, Energy, Technology and Science Policy at the US State Department. This article was written while Mr. Manning held the position of C.V. Starr Senior Fellow and Director of Asian Studies at the Council on Foreign Relations and it represents his personal view, not that of the US Department of State or any US government agency. He is author of *The Asian Energy Factor: Myths and Dilemmas on Energy, Security and the Pacific Future* (St. Martin's Press, September 2000) and co-author of *China, Nuclear Weapons and Arms Control: A Preliminary Assessment* (Council on Foreign Relations Press, 2000). He is also on the Executive Board of the Council for Security Cooperation in the Asia-Pacific (CSCAP). Earlier, Robert Manning was a Senior Fellow at the Progressive Policy Institute (PPI); Chair of PPI's Defense Working Group; co-author of the monograph *Defense in the Information Age: A New Blueprint* (December 1995); editor of *Missile Defense and American Security* (May 1996) and the author of a study on post-Cold War nuclear strategy and proliferation

Back to the Future: Towards a Post-Nuclear Ethic (Progressive Foundation, 1994). He has also written numerous monographs on Korea, Japan and Asian security. From 1989 until March 1993, he was Advisor for Policy to the Assistant Secretary for East Asian and Pacific Affairs, Department of State. He was involved in policy planning, political/military and a wide range of policies, particularly those towards Korea, Japan, China, political-military affairs and Asian security, Asia-Pacific economic cooperation, Vietnam and Cambodia. He has also been an Advisor to the Office of the Secretary of Defense (1988-89).

Robert Manning has written, edited or contributed to more than a dozen books and written more than 40 academic papers and published studies related to the US-Japan security alliance; China, Japan, Korea; APEC and Asia-Pacific trade issues, including the monograph *Starting Over: From MFN to a China Policy for the Future*. He has written extensively and testified before Congress on Korea and US policy. He has written widely on international affairs, in professional and policy journals such as *Asian Survey, Survival, Foreign Affairs, Foreign Policy, Washington Quarterly, World Policy Journal, The New York Times, Wall Street Journal, Washington Post, Los Angeles Times, The New Republic, International Herald Tribune, Politique Internationale, Le Monde Diplomatique, Asahi Shimbun, Nikkei, Chuo Koron, Shokun, Chosun Ilbo* (Korea) and other publications.

KENNETH B. MEDLOCK III is currently a Visiting Professor of Economics at Rice University and Energy Consultant to the James A. Baker III Institute for Public Policy. He previously held the position of Corporate Consultant at El Paso Energy Corporation. While at El Paso, he was responsible for fundamental analysis of North American natural gas, petroleum and power markets. He also served as the Lead Modeler on the Modeling Sub-group for the National Petroleum Council study of long term natural gas markets in North America, released in 2003. From May 2000 to May 2001, Kenneth Medlock held the M.D. Anderson Fellowship at the James A. Baker III Institute for Public Policy. There, he successfully organized the conference "Global Warming: Science and Policy" (September 2000) and edited the conference volume.

Kenneth Medlock has peer-reviewed publications in *The Energy Journal*, *The Journal of Transport Economics and Policy*, has featured in the *IAEE Newsletter*, and has several articles both under review and pending publication. He also has several working papers drafted in conjunction with studies conducted with the Baker Institute. Kenneth Medlock has spoken at a number of conferences with regard to energy and the environment. In addition, he has fielded numerous media (print, television and radio) inquiries with regard to energy and energy policy. He has appeared in *Time Magazine*, *Business Week*, the *Boston Globe*, *Dallas Morning News*, *Times-Picayune*, *Detroit Free Press*, and the *Houston Chronicle*. Kenneth B. Medlock III received a Ph.D in Economics from Rice University in May 2000. His areas of specialization are in the fields of Energy and Environmental Economics and Policy and Macroeconomic Theory, with an interest in Applied Econometrics and Applied Microeconomics.

JOHN V. MITCHELL is an Associate Research Fellow of the Royal Institute of International Affairs (Chatham House). From 1994 to 2001 he was Chairman of the Energy and Environment Programme there (now called the Sustainable Development Programme). He is Research Advisor at the Oxford Institute of Energy Studies. His publications include: *Iraq's Oil Tomorrow* (with Valerie Marcel), RIIA 2003; *The Changing Geopolitics of Energy,* RIIA 2003; *Renewing Energy Security*, RIIA 2002; *The New Economy of Oil*, (with Koji Morita, Norman Selley and Jonathan Stern) RIIA/Earthscan, London, 2001; *Companies in a World of Conflict* (editor) RIIA, London, 1998; *The New Geopolitics of Energy* (with Peter Beck and Michael Grubb), RIIA, London, 1996.

John Mitchell retired in 1993 from British Petroleum where his posts included Special Advisor to the Managing Directors, Regional Coordinator for BP's subsidiaries in the Western Hemisphere, Non-Executive Director of various BP subsidiaries, and head of BP's Policy Review Unit. Before joining BP in 1966 he worked in the Ministry of Trade and Industry, first of the Federation of Rhodesia and Nyasaland, and then of Southern Rhodesia. He was born and educated in South Africa and left the country in 1956, after graduating from the University of Natal.

ROMEO PACUDAN is a Senior Energy Economist at the Systems Analysis Department, UNEP Risoe Centre (URC) of the Risoe National Laboratory in Roskilde, Denmark. At URC, he is involved with projects related to energy sector reforms, energy industry regulation, renewable energy and energy efficiency policies and regulation, and capacity development for the Clean Development Mechanism in developing countries.

Prior to joining URC, Dr. Romeo Pacudan was a Senior Energy Policy Expert at the International Institute for Energy Conservation (IIEC), an international non-profit organization affiliated with the Civil Engineering Research Foundation (CERF), based in Bangkok, Thailand during the period 2001-2002. He was also an Assistant Professor of the Energy Program of the Asian Institute of Technology in Bangkok, Thailand during the period 1996-2000. Dr. Pacudan obtained his doctorate degree in Applied Economics at the Université de Grenoble, in Grenoble, France while doing his research work at the Institut d'Économie et de Politique de l'Énergie (IEPE), also in Grenoble, France. He has a Master's degree in Engineering specializing in Energy Economics and Policy from the Asian Institute of Technology in Bangkok, Thailand.

MEGHA SHUKLA is currently a Research Associate working at The Energy and Resources Institute (TERI), Bangalore, India. TERI's Southern Regional Centre was set up at Bangalore with initial support from the Government of India and the European Commission. She became the Area Convenor of the Oil and Gas Area of the Policy Analysis Division from April to August 2001 and later from April to December 2002. She then moved to the Regulatory Policy and Governance Division during her work tenure at TERI, New Delhi. As the Area Convenor she provided research direction and guidance in developing research projects and programs in this sector.

[352]

Megha Shukla's present scope of activities involves project management in order to undertake research and consultancy work in the infrastructure sector projects, with particular focus on oil and gas, power and other energy sectors. She has been awarded a Master's degree in Business Economics from the University of Delhi in India and has published some studies in various international journals dealing with energy issues.

RONALD SOLIGO is Professor of Economics at Rice University and holds a Ph.D. degree from Yale University. Dr. Soligo's fields include economic growth and development and energy economics. Some of his published articles are: "The Role of Inventories in Oil Market Stability" (with Amy Myers Jaffe), *Quarterly Review of Economics and Finance* (vol. 42, 2002); "Automobile Ownership and Economic Development: Forecasting Passenger Vehicle Demand to the Year 2015" (with Kenneth B. Medlock III), *Journal of Transport Economics and Policy* (May, 2002); "The Economics of Pipeline Routes: The Conundrum of Oil Exports from the Caspian Basin" (with Amy Myers Jaffe), in *Energy in the Caspian Region: Present and Future* (Palgrave Press, January 2002); "Economic Development and End-Use Energy Demand" (with Kenneth B. Medlock III), *Energy Journal* (April 2001); "Potential Growth for US Energy in Cuba" (with Amy Myers Jaffe), ASCE Volume 12 Proceedings, *Cuba in Transition* (web site); "The Saudi Arabian Economy," James A. Baker III Institute for Public Policy, Rice University (July 2002); "Impact of the Reopening of Persian Gulf Upstream Sectors to International Investment in International Oil Markets" (with Amy Myers Jaffe) in *Middle East Economic Survey,* August (2000); "Japanese Energy Demand to 2015" (with Kenneth B. Medlock III), James A. Baker III Institute for Public Policy, Rice University (May 2000); "A Note on Saudi Arabian Price Discrimination" (with Amy Myers Jaffe), *The Energy Journal*, August (1999); "The Composition and Growth of Energy Demand in China" (with Kenneth B. Medlock III), James A. Baker III Institute for Public Policy, Rice University (May 1999); "China's Growing Energy Dependence: The Costs and Policy Implications of Supply Alternatives" (with Amy Myers Jaffe), James A. Baker III Institute for Public Policy, Rice University (May 1999).

LEENA SRIVASTAVA is currently Executive Director, The Energy and Resources Institute (TERI), New Delhi, an independent, non-profit research institution working in the areas of energy, environment and sustainable development. She was Director of the Regulatory Studies and Governance Division, TERI from April 1999 to March 2003. During this time she became Project Director for the South Asia Forum for Infrastructure Regulation (SAFIR), which is a network of regulatory commissions, regulated entities, academic/research organizations and civil society working towards experience sharing and capacity building in the region and beyond.

Since June 2000, Dr. Leena Srivastava has been holding additional charge as Dean, Faculty of Policy and Planning, TERI School of Advanced Studies, where she is teaching doctoral courses on Energy Policy and Planning and Infrastructure Economics. She has a Ph.D. in Energy Economics from the Indian Institute of Science in Bangalore, India. She has a number of publications to her credit and serves on the editorial boards of various international journals dealing with energy and environment issues.

DAVID VON HIPPEL is an independent consultant and Nautilus Institute Senior Associate whose training and experience cover a broad range of topics and applications in the fields of energy and resource planning and environmental management. Much of his recent work has centered on energy and environmental issues in Asia, particularly Northeast Asia. He has prepared models of future energy demand and supply, and of related environmental impacts, covering several of the countries of Northeast Asia, including preparation of "business as usual," "clean coal" and "alternative" energy scenarios for China, and scenarios of energy use for Japan, the ROK and other nations. Dr. Von Hippel has also undertaken extensive analyses of the patterns of fuels use and prospects for energy efficiency in North Korea, as well as options for assisting with energy-sector redevelopment in that country, prepared reviews of rural electrification options and the impact of climate change/sea-level rise in Asia and the Pacific, and also evaluated nuclear fuel and nuclear waste scenarios for the countries of Northeast Asia. He is currently involved in a collaborative project with teams from Northeast Asian countries to develop "business-as-usual" and "alternative" scenarios for each country, as well as scenarios related to regional integration of energy systems (including power grid interconnections). In the context of this "East Asia Energy Futures" project and other projects over the last decade, Dr. Von Hippel has trained professionals from various countries in the use of energy/environmental planning and demand-side management planning tools and methods.

Dr. Von Hippel has also focused on electric utility planning in the Arab states. He has worked extensively on integrated resource planning (IRP) and demand-side management (DSM) issues in Syria, Saudi Arabia, and Egypt, and been a resource person at a region-wide workshop on the topics of IRP and DSM. In recent years, Dr. Von Hippel has worked on several DSM resource assessments for regions and states in the western United States. In the context of these projects he has worked with a number of private and public agencies, including Nautilus Institute, the World Bank, the United Nations, a US gas utility, and Tellus Institute (Boston, Massachusetts). Dr. Von Hippel holds M.S. and Ph.D. degrees in Energy and Resources from the University of California at Berkeley, and M.A. (Biology) and B.S. degrees from the University of Oregon.

NOTES

Introduction

1. In this chapter, the Asian region does not include the Central Asian republics formerly part of the Soviet Union, Turkey, or Asian Russia.

2. *International Energy Outlook* 2002, US Department of Energy, Washington DC, 2002.

3. This number, and other oil and gas numbers in this paragraph, are taken from the *BP Statistical Review of World Energy*, BP, London, 2002.

4. *International Energy Outlook*, 2002.

5. See John V. Mitchell et al., *The New Geopolitics of Energy* (London: Royal Institute of International Affairs, 1996).

Chapter 1

1. For purposes of analysis, the Asia-Pacific is comprised of Greater China (People's Republic of China, Hong Kong, Taiwan), Japan, North and South Koreas, the ASEAN states and India.

2. *BP Statistical Review of World Energy*, June 2003.

3. Ibid.

4. Dr. Fadhil Chalabi, "Asia's Dependence on Middle Eastern Oil," unpublished presentation at Asia Society Conference on "Energy and the Economic Recovery of Asia," Houston, Texas, April 28, 2000.

5. See Robert A. Manning, *The Asian Energy Factor* especially chapters two and three (New York and London: Palgrave/St Martin's Press, 2000)

6. See Kent E. Calder, "Asia's Empty Tank," *Foreign Affairs* (March/April 1996) 56.

7. See Unclassified CIA report to Congress on "Acquisition of Technology Relating to Weapons of Mass Destruction and Advanced Conventional Munitions," January 30, 2002).

8. See Daniel Yergin, "Asian Energy Needs and Security Implications," paper for the International Institute for Strategic Studies, September 1997; Also Yergin et al., "Fueling Asia's Recovery," *Foreign Affairs*, (March/April 1998): 34-50.

9. See *BP Amoco Statistical Review of World Energy* (1999): 10.

10. See Keun-Wook Paik, *Gas and Oil in Northeast Asia* (London: Royal Institute of International Affairs, 1995) 3-5.

11. *BP Amoco Statistical Review of World Energy*, 1999.

12. See Kent E. Calder; *Asia's Deadly Triangle: How Arms, Energy, and Growth Threaten to Destabilize Asia-Pacific;* Nicolas Brealey Publishing, London, 1996 (published in the US as *Pacific Defense*, New York, NY: William Morrow). This is most cogent articulation – and most frequently cited rendition – of the resource scarcity-territorial dispute-conflict energy security logic. See also Calder, "Asia's Empty Tank, *Foreign Affairs*, March/April 1996, or for example, Mamdouh G. Salameh, "China Oil and the Risks of Regional Conflict," *Survival* (Winter 1995-1996).

13. For an analysis of the financial crisis see Robert A. Manning, "The Asian Financial Crisis: Security Risks and Opportunities," 1998 Pacific Symposium, National Defense University, Institute of National Strategic Studies, Washington, DC.

14. See, for example, David E. Sanger and Mark Landler, "Asian Rebound Derails Reform as Many Suffer," *The New York Times*, July 12, 1999, 1; and Peter Montagnon, "False Dawn in Asia," *Financial Times*, April 19, 1999, 17. See also *Business Week*, "Asia: How Real is the Recovery? May 3, 1999; and Paul Krugman, in *Time* magazine, "Has Asia Recovered?"

15. *Petroleum Intelligence Weekly*, October 24, 1999, 14.

16. See "World Energy Outlook and the Impact of Economic Turmoil in Asia on Oil Prospects," June 1999, International Energy Agency. Also, IMF *World Economic Outlook*, Washington, DC 1999.

17. US DOE, Energy Information Administration, *International Energy Outlook*, 1999, 141.

18. See *Northeast Asian Energy in a Global Context*, The Royal Institute of International Affairs, 1996, 11.

19. My calculations from IEA *World Energy Outlook* and EIA *International Energy Outlook*. 1999.

20. Own calculations derived from *BP Statistical Review of World Energy*, 1999, and Ichizo Aoyama and Richard Berard, "The Asian Oil Imbalance 1996-2010," Research paper for Gulf energy study of the Baker Institute for Public Policy, Rice University, 1997.

21. Own extrapolations based on calculations in Paul Horsnell, *Oil in Asia* (London: Oxford University Press, 1997) 22.

22. *Northeast Asian Energy in a Global Context*, op. cit., 3.

23. Own calculations from BP Amoco, *Statistical Review of World Energy, 2001, 2002*.

24. Paik, op. cit., and own calculations from BP Amoco *Statistical Review of World Energy*.

25. World Automobile Association statistics.

26. Jonathan Simon (ed.), *China Energy Databook*, Lawrence National Laboratory, 1996; China State Statistical Bureau; and own calculations.

27. Own calculations based on IEA and Asian Development Bank energy statistics.

28. See "China and Long Range Asian Energy Security," study of the James A. Baker III Institute for Public Policy, Rice University, April 1999, 6-7.

29. Own calculations from BP Amoco *Statistical Review of World Energy*.

30. Own calculations from BP Amoco *Statistical Review of World Energy*; APEC Energy Advisory Committee, June 1995, cited in Kent Calder, "Energy and Security in Northeast Asia: Fueling Security," IGCC Policy Paper, University of California, February 1998.

31. *BP Statistical Review of World Energy*, June 2001.

32. Own calculations based on IEA forecast, EIA, and Fereidun Fesharaki of East-West Center (1998).

33. Chinese nuclear officials in interviews with the author, Beijing and Guangzhou, March 1999.

34. Own calculations based on Fesharaki, presentation to Council on Foreign Relations Energy Security Study; also background interview with US Department of Energy official, June, 1999.

35. This assertion is based on numerous interviews with Chinese energy officials and Western oil and gas multinationals.

36. See the APEC website, APEC Energy Working Group for notional ideas of an ASEAN energy grid. See Paik (1995) op. cit., for a plethora of ideas for a Northeast Asia gas grid. Both ideas are still at an embryonic stage of development.

37. See EIA *International Energy Outlook*, 1999.

38. BP Amoco *Statistical Review of World Energy*, 1998.

39. Ibid.

40. It is possible that Tarim will prove to contain 20 billion barrels of commercially extractable oil, and that the South China Sea holds 100 trillion cubic feet of natural gas. However, so far, no major oil companies believe either to be the case.

41. See Paul Horsnell, *Oil in Asia* (London: Oxford University Press, 1997), Chapter 10, 251-277.

42. See Horsnell, op. cit., Chapter 10, "Asian Producers." Also author's background interviews with oil executives from three major firms active in Asia, September 1999.

43. See Horsnell, op. cit., Chapter 11, "Middle East Exporters and Asia" for a detailed discussion of oil supply relationships, particularly pricing in the Dubai forward market and the Saudi "Asian premium."

44. See Fadhil Chalabi in "Gulf-Asia Energy Interdependence," Middle East Institute, 1998.

45. EIA, *International Energy Outlook* 1999, and Fesharaki, et al. *Pacific Energy Outlook* (Honolulu, HI: East-West Center, 1995).

46. Ahmed Zaki Yamani, speech to the Centre for Global Energy Studies, Eighth Annual Conference, April 27, 1998, London.

47. Rilwanu Lukman's speech in John Calabrese (ed.) *Gulf-Asia Energy Security*, Middle East Institute, Washington, 1998.

48. See *South China Morning Post* (online edition) November 4, 1999, also *China Daily* November 4, 1999.

49. See Xiaoje Xu, "China and the Middle East: Cross-Investment in the Energy Sector," Middle East Policy Council, *Middle East Policy* journal vol. VII, no. 3, June 2000.

50. See *Japan Times* (online edition) September 11, 2001.

51. See Guy Dinmore, "Japan Deal Over Work on Iran Field," *Financial Times*, July 9, 2001.

52. See *Middle East Digest*, June 9, 1995.

53. See Kent E. Calder, "Japan's Energy Angst and the Great Caspian Game," National Bureau of Asian Research, Seattle, Washington, March 2001; see also Michael J. Green, *Japan's Reluctant Realism* (New York, NY: Palgrave, 2001).

54. Cited in Aoyama and Berard, "The Asian Oil Imbalance 1996-2010," Working Paper for Middle and the Gulf study, James A. Baker IIII Institute for Public Policy, Rice University, 1997.

55. See Calder, "Asia's Deadly Triangle," op. cit.

56. See Ronald Soligo and Amy M. Jaffe, "China's Growing Energy Dependence," Working Paper for "China and Long-Range Energy Security," study of the James A. Baker II Institute of Rice University, April 1999.

57. Figures cited in Michael C. Lynch, "The Nature of Energy Security," in the M.I.T. Japan Program Report, September/October 1997.

58. *Financial Times*, November 6, 1999, 1.

59. *Washington Post*, July 15, 1997.

60. See Jonathan Rynhold, "China's Cautious New Pragmatism in the Middle East," *Survival*, vol. 38, no. 3 (Autumn 1996): 102-16, for a discussion on how China balances strategic considerations with the demands of modernization.

61. Author's background interviews with Chinese officials in July 1997, and with US officials in September 1997 and February 1998.

62. See Bates Gill, "Chinese Arms Exports to Iran," *Middle East Review of International Affairs* (MERIA) online edition, Tel Aviv, vol. 2, no. 2, May 1998. See also Gill, "Two Steps Forward, One Step Back: The Dynamics of Chinese Non-Proliferation and Arms Control Policy-Making in an Era of Reform," in David M. Lampton (ed.), *Chinese Foreign and Security Policy Decision-Making in an Era of Reform, 1985-2000* (Stanford, CA: Stanford University Press, 2001).

63. See Ji Guoxing, "SLOC Security in the Asia-Pacific," Asia-Pacific Center for Security Studies, Honolulu, Hawaii, 2000.

64. See John H. Noer, *Chokepoints: Maritime Concerns in Southeast Asia* (Washington, DC: NDU Press/Center for Naval Analysis, 1996).

65. John H. Noer, "Chokepoints," op. cit.

66. Noer, op. cit., 52.

67. See Geoffrey Kemp, *Energy Superbowl* (Washington, DC: The Nixon Center, 1997) for a thoughtful discussion of the Gulf, Caspian and energy security.

Chapter 2

1. Though as a region Asia will enjoy strong economic growth to 2020 and a growing thirst for energy, it must also be recognized that there are some significant problems in the region, including the realization that most of the world's 800-900 million poor live in Asia. In addition, Japan, the region's powerhouse, continues to have economic problems that are damaging prospects for regional economic activity. Japan's economic problems are structural in nature and deep-rooted (for example in the banking sector), and macroeconomic policies alone cannot prompt a turnaround. Nonetheless, Asia's economic prosperity is expected to help eliminate some poverty in the region. In this context, the Asian Development Bank has set a goal of eliminating poverty in Asia by 2015.

2. Developing Asia includes China, India, Indonesia, South Korea, Taiwan, Malaysia, Philippines, Thailand, and Singapore.

3. Draft background paper for Ministerial/Industry Panel on Clean and Sustainable Energy Development at the APEC Ministerial, May 11, 2000.

4. Readers are referred to the *International Energy Outlook 2001* (*IEO2001*), published in March 2001, or the Internet website (http:// http://www.eia.doe.gov/oiaf/ieo/index. html) for complete details on the EIA forecasts and methodology.

5. See Appendix to this chapter. A full description of WEPS is provided in a model documentation report: Energy Information Administration, *World Energy Projection System Model Documentation*, DOE/EIA-M050 (97), Washington, DC, September 1997.

6. United States Geological Survey, June 2001.

7. Industrialized Asia includes Australia, Japan, and New Zealand.

8. Energy Information Administration, *International Energy Outlook 2001* (Washington, DC, March 2001).

9. "China US$3bn Changbei Project Moves Ahead," *Financial Times International Gas Report*, vol. 394 (March 17, 2000): 2-3; and "What's New Around the World," *World Gas Intelligence* vol. 11 (June 16, 2000):11

10. Energy Information Administration, AEO2001 National Energy Modeling System run AEO2001. D101699A (Washington, DC, October 2000).

11. International Energy Agency, *Coal Information 2000* (Paris, August 2000), Table 4.2.

12. Energy Information Administration, *International Energy Outlook 2001* (Washington, DC, March 2001).

13. J. Pomfret, "China's Giant Dam Faces Huge Problems," *Washington Post* (January 7, 2001): A1.

14. APEC's Energy Regulator's Forum, Electricity Regulatory Arrangements, "Summary Submission: China," Department of Agriculture, Fisheries and Forestry, Australia (http://dpie.gov.au/resources).

15. "China Includes Renewables in Energy Blueprint, Receives GEF Grant for Wind Power Projects," *Wind Energy Weekly*, vol. 19, no. 922 (November 17, 2000).

16. "Chinese Official Sentenced to Death for Three Gorges Corruption," Muzi.com News, March 10, 2000 (www.muzi.com).

17. "Nam Theun 2 MOU Signed," Financial Times, *Power in Asia*, no. 304 (June 12, 2000):11.

18. "EVN Studies Hydro Scheme," Financial Times, *Power in Asia*, no 310 (September 5, 2000).

19. Standard & Poor's DRI, World Energy Service, *Asia/Pacific Outlook* (Lexington, MA, 2000): 241.

20. Republic of the Philippines, Department of Energy, *Philippine Energy Plan 1999-2008* (Manila, Philippines, 2000).

21. Includes Kazakhstan, Kyrgyzstan, Tajikistan, Turkmenistan, Uzbekistan and Xinjiang, China. While Xinjiang is politically part of the People's Republic of China, geographically it is part of the region known by social scientists as Central Asia.

22. Shakarim F. Zhanseitov and Madenyat A. Asanov, "Kazakhstan's Mineral Raw Materials Industry and its Potential," in James P. Dorian, Pavel A. Minakir, and Vitaly T. Borisovich (eds) *CIS Energy and Minerals Development: Prospects, Problems, and Opportunities for International Cooperation* (Dordrecht, The Netherlands: Kluwer Academic Publishers, 1993), 388.

23. Energy Information Administration, "Kazakhstan," Country Analysis Brief (Washington, DC, April 2000) 10.

24. Ibid.

25. Ibid.

26. Interfax News Agency, May 4, 2000, "Oil, Gas Wealth of Uzbekistan Estimated at $1 Trillion," Tashkent, Uzbekistan.

27. Sun Shu and Sun Yiyun, "The Study and Development of Mineral and Energy Resources in China," Chapter 8 in James P. Dorian and David G. Fridley (eds). *China's Energy and Mineral Industries: Current Perspectives* (Boulder, CO: Westview Press, 1988): 99-104.

28. Ibid.

29. Current reserve estimates are in the range of 10 billion to 20 billion tons of oil.

30. Zhanseitov and Asanov, op. cit.

31. Qiu Da Xiong, "Central Asia Regional Economic Cooperation: Energy in Xinjiang, China," unpublished draft (May 1997): 2.

32. Asian Development Bank, "Kazakhstan: Country Operational Strategy" (Manila: Asian Development Bank, 1996): 13.

33. The northern half of Kazakhstan is part of the Russian regional electricity network.

34. Paul S. Triolo and Christopher Hegadorn, "China's Wild West: A Wealth of Natural Resources Has Made Xinjiang a Bustling New Frontier," in *The China Business Review* (March-April 1996).

35. *International Power Generation*, vol. 24, no. 3 (April 2001):12-14.

36. Asian Development Bank, *Regional Economic Cooperation in Central Asia* (Manila: Asian Development Bank, 1988), 354; and Ben-Hur Salcedo, James P. Dorian, Maurice H. Kaya, and John Tantlinger, "Restructuring of the Philippines Electric Power Industry and Future Development," *ASEAN Energy Bulletin*, vol. 4, no. 4, published by the ASEAN Centre for Energy, Jakarta, Indonesia (December 2000).

Chapter 3

1. See Table 3.1 for a complete list of countries in Asia. The definition conforms to that used by the US Department of Energy's Energy Information Administration.

2. Energy Intelligence Group, *Oil Market Intelligence* database, by subscription, July 2001.

3. Based on authors' projections. For a more detailed forecast see *World Energy Outlook*, International Energy Agency (IEA), Paris, France (1998 and 2000).

4. See Ronald Soligo and Amy M. Jaffe. "China's Growing Energy Dependence: The Costs and Policy Implications of Supply Alternatives," Working Paper (Houston, TX: James A. Baker III Institute for Public Policy, Rice University, 1999).

5. Calculation made using data from IEA *Energy Balances of Non-OECD Countries, 1971-1999*. GDP figures are in 1995 PPP$.

6. See Kenneth B. Medlock III and Ronald Soligo, "Economic Development and End-Use Energy Demand," *Energy Journal* vol. 22, no. 2 (April 2001).

7. Ibid.

8. This calculation is made using the results derived in Medlock and Soligo (2001). Specifically, they show the income elasticity of energy demand to be a decreasing function of income per capita. Thus, given any level of per capita income, a corresponding elasticity can be calculated. Note that the formula in that paper is contingent on GDP per capita denominated in 1985 PPP$, whereas the GDP per capita values quoted here are denominated in 1995 PPP$. Therefore, a conversion must be made prior to calculation.

9. Medlock and Soligo (2001), op cit.

10. See EIA *Country Analysis Briefs*, EIA *International Energy Annual 2002*, and IEA *Energy Balances of Non-OECD Countries, 1971-1999*.

11. When the Protocol was originally negotiated at the meetings in Kyoto, Japan in 1998, it was signed by the then Vice President Al Gore, bringing the US into the fold. Since then, however, Congressional Acts such as the Bird-Hagel Resolution, a 97-0 vote not to participate, and public criticism of the Protocol by President George W. Bush and

others have shifted US policy in favor of adopting an alternative approach, although none has been outlined to date.

12. Peter Hartley, Kenneth B. Medlock III and Michael Warby, "First Thing First—Economic Development and Global Warming," Working Paper (Houston, TX: James A. Baker III Institute for Public Policy, Rice Unversity, 1999). See: www.bakerinstitute.org.

13. EIA, *International Energy Annual, 2002*.

14. Japan Access Information Service, subscription database, Washington DC.

15. See Xiaojie Xu, "The Gas Dragon's Rise: Chinese Natural Gas Strategy and Import Patterns," Working paper (Houston, TX: James A. Baker III Institute for Public Policy, Rice University, 1999). See: www.bakerinstitute.org.

16. India, *Country Analysis Brief* (www.eia.doe.gov/emeu/cabs/india).

17. See Energy Intelligence Group, *Oil Market Intelligence*, "Asia Coming to Life"; see also *World Gas Intelligence*, "Market Insight: TEPCO Buys Spot," October 30, 2002, available by subscription (www.energyintel.com).

18. Kenneth B. Medlock III and Ronald Soligo, "Japanese Energy Demand to 2015," Working Paper (Houston, TX: James A. Baker III Institute for Public Policy, Rice University, 2000.

19. Medlock and Soligo (2001), op. cit.

20. Medlock and Soligo (2001), op. cit.

21. For more detail on the estimation procedure see Medlock and Soligo (2001), op. cit. The adjustment is done by calculating a fixed effect as a percentage deviation from the sample average fixed effect in Medlock and Soligo. The percentage deviation is calculated as the percentage deviation of actual Asian TFC from the predicted values for TFC using the 'Sample Average' curve at the Asian per capita income.

22. *Petroleum Intelligence Weekly*, Oil Market Intelligence database 2001.

23. Ibid.

24. See, for example, James Hamilton, "Oil and the Macroeconomy since World War II," *Journal of Political Economy*, vol. 91, no. 2 (1983): 228-48. Also Peter Ferderer, "Oil Price Volatility and the Macroeconomy," *The Journal of Macroeconomics*, vol. 18, no.1 (Winter 1996): 1-26.

25. See Weiyu Gao, Kenneth B. Medlock III and Robin Sickles, "The Effect of Oil Price Volatility on Productivity and Technical Change," Working Paper (Houston, TX: Rice University, 1999).

26. See Kenneth B. Medlock III and Ronald Soligo, "The Composition and Growth in Energy Demand in China," Working Paper (Houston, TX: James A. Baker III Institute for Public Policy, Rice University, 1999).

27. See IEA *World Energy Outlook*, Paris (1998).

28. See The Royal Institute of International Affairs. "Northeast Asian Energy in a Global Context," London (1996), 11.

29. See Julie A. MacDonald and S. Enders Wimbush. *Energy Strategies and Military Strategies in Asia* (McLean, VA: Hicks & Associates, 1999), 9-15.

30. Authors' own calculations.

31. Amy M. Jaffe and Ronald Soligo (1999), op. cit.

32. See Steven Lewis, "Privatizing China's State-Owned Oil Companies" Working paper (Houston, TX: James A. Baker III Institute for Public Policy, Rice University, 1999). See: www.bakerinstitute.org.

33. *Petroleum Argus Newsletter*, June 18, 2001, 10.

34. Ronald Soligo and Amy M. Jaffe, "China's Growing Energy Dependence: The Costs and Policy Implications of Supply Alternatives," Working Paper (Houston, TX: James A. Baker III Institute for Public Policy, Rice University, 1999).

35. EIA, op. cit.

36. Robert Manning, *The Asian Energy Factor: Myths and Dilemmas of Energy, Security, and the Pacific Future* (New York, NY: Palgrave, October 2000).

37. Ibid.

38. See "Special Report: Japan and the Middle East," *Middle East Economic Digest* (1997).

39. *Petroleum Argus*, June 18, 2001, 4.

40. Author's interviews with officials from CNPC.

41. *Petroleum Intelligence Weekly*, various issues.

42. See Gaye Christoffersen, "China's Intentions for Russian and Central Asian Oil and Gas." NBR Analysis vol. 9, no. 2, March 1998 (Seattle, WA: National Bureau of Asian Research).

43. See Soligo and Jaffe (1999), op. cit.

44. *Petroleum Intelligence Weekly*, "China's CNPC Leaps on to Global Oil Production Stage," June 9, 1997, 3.

45. See Gaye Christoffersen (1998), op. cit.

46. See *World Gas Intelligence*, "Russia to China Race," August 22, 2001, vol. XII, no. 24, 1.

47. See "Energy Security and Development in Northeast Asia: Prospects for Cooperative Policies," Report of the Workshop held by the Economic Research Institute for Northeast Asia (ERINA), in Nigata, Japan, December 17-19, 1999.

48. Ibid.

49. See *Petroleum Intelligence Weekly*. "Russia Reaches for Chinese Oil and Gas Outlets," vol. XL, no. 30, (July 23, 2001): 4.

50. See "East Asia: a New Market for Russian Gas," *Petroleum Economist* (September 1996): 60-62.

[365]

51. See Alan Troner, "Russian Far East: The Economics and Competitive Impact of Least-Cost Gas Imports," Working Paper (Houston, TX: James A. Baker III Institute for Public Policy, 1999). See: www.bakerinstitute.org.

52. Ibid.

53. See Matthew Sagers, Planecon Consulting Presentation to the Baker Institute Workshop of Northeast Asian Energy Cooperation, Houston, Texas, December 14-15, 1999. For more details, see Alan Troner, "Japan and the Russian Far East: The Economics and Competitive Impact of Least Cost Gas Imports." Baker Institute working paper, May 2000.

54. *New York Times*, July 16, 2001, 1.

55. See Amy Myers Jaffe and Robert Manning, "Russia, Energy and the West." *Survival*, vol. 43, no. 2 (Summer 2001): 133-152.

56. See Vladimir Ivanov, "Prospects for Russia's Energy Diplomacy in Northeast Asia," Working paper no. 15, ERINA (1999).

57. For more detailed discussion of the future threats that could bring these burden sharing issues to the fore, read Jaffe and Manning (2001), op. cit.

58. See Amy Myers Jaffe and Robert Manning, "The Shocks of a World of Cheap Oil" *Foreign Affairs*, vol. 79, no. 1 (January/February 2000): 16-29.

59. See "Oil Piracy Poses Growing Menace to Tanker Traffic in South China Sea," *Oil and Gas Journal*, October 18, 1999.

60. For more detailed discussion, see John Noer and David Gregory, *Chokepoints: Maritime Economic Concerns in Southeast Asia* (Washington, DC: National Defense University Press, 1996).

Chapter 4

1. For the purposes of this paper, Asia is taken to include the region bounded by Russia in the north, Japan in the east, Indonesia in the south, and the Caspian Sea in the west. It specifically excludes the Middle East.

2. International Energy Agency, *World Energy Outlook 2000* (Paris: OECD/IEA, 2000).

3. Dieter Helm, John Kay and David Thompson, "Energy Policy and the Role of the State in the Market for Energy," *Fiscal Studies* vol. 9, no. 1 (February 1988): 41-61. Paul Stevens, "Energy Privatization: Sensitivities and Realities," *The Journal of Energy and Development* vol. 23, no.1 (1998): 1-14.

4. Helm et al., op cit. See also Colin Robinson, "The Case for an Energy Policy," in *Energy Policy: Errors, Illusions and Market Realities*, IEA Occasional Paper No. 90 (London: Institute of Economic Affairs, 1993): 50-62. Also Mark Jaccard, "Oscillating Currents: The Changing Rationale for Government Intervention in the Electricity Industry," *Energy Policy* vol. 23, no. 7 (1995): 579-592.

5. Colin Robinson (1993), op. cit.

6. Dieter Helm et al., op. cit.; Colin Robinson (1993), op. cit.; and Mark Jaccard, op. cit.

7. David M. Newberry, "The Restructuring of UK Energy Industries: What Have We Learned?" in Gordon MacKerron and Peter Pearson (eds) *The UK Energy Experience: A Model or a Warning?* (London: Imperial College Press, 1996): 1-30.

8. Dieter Helm et al., op. cit.; Colin Robinson (1993), op. cit.

9. F. A. Hay, *The Constitution of Liberty* (London: Routledge & Kegan Paul, 1960). Milton Friedman, *Capitalism and Freedom* (Chicago: University of Chicago Press, 1962).

10. V. Wright, "Industrial Privatization in Western Europe: Pressures, Problems and Paradoxes," in V. Wright (ed) *Privatization in Western Europe: Pressures, Problems and Paradoxes* (London: Pinter, 1994): 1-43. Also J. Ernst, *Whose Utility?* (Buckingham: Open University Press, 1994).

11. Paul Stevens, "The Practical Record and Prospects of Privatization Programs in the Arab World," in T. Niblock and E. Murphy (eds) *Economic and Political Liberalization in the Middle East* (London: British Academy Press, 1993): 114-131; Jozef M. von Brabant, "On the Economics of Property Rights and Privatization in Transitional Economies," in Paul Cook and Colin Kirpatrick (eds) *Privatization Policy and Performance: International Perspectives* (New York, NY: Prentice Hall, 1995): 48-83; Gerd Swartz, "Privatization in Eastern Europe: Experience and Preliminary Policy Lessons," in Paul Cook and Colin Kirpatrick (eds) *Privatization Policy and Performance: International Perspectives* (New York, NY: Prentice Hall, 1995): 31-47.

12. Colin Robinson, "Privatizing the Energy Industries," in C. Veljanovski (ed.) *Privatization and Competition—A Market Prospectus* (London: Institute of Economic Affairs, 1988): 113-128; David N. Newberry, op. cit.; Matthew Bishop, John Kay and Colin Mayer, "Introduction: Privatization in Performance," in Bishop, Kay and Mayer (eds) *Privatization and Economic Performance* (Oxford: Oxford University Press, 1994): 1-14.

13. N. Van der Walle, "Privatization in Developing Countries: A Review of the Issues," *World Development* vol. 17, no. 5 (1989): 601-615.

14. John Vickers and George Yarrow, *Privatization: An Economic Analysis* (Cambridge, MA: MIT Press, 1988).

15. V. Wright, op. cit.

16. Colin Robinson, *Regulation as a Means of Introducing Competition* (Guildford: Surrey Energy Economics Centre, 1995); N. Van der Walle, op. cit., and Bishop et al., op. cit.

17. V. Wright, op. cit.

18. H. Bienen and J. Waterbury, "The Political Economy of Privatization in Developing Countries," *World Development* vol. 17, no. 5 (1989): 617-32.

19. John Besant-Jones, "Lessons from UK Electricity Reforms for Developing Countries," in Gordon MacKerron and Peter Pearson (eds) *The UK Energy*

Experience: A Model or a Warning? (London: Imperial College Press, 1996): 479-483.

20. "California's Power Crisis. How to Keep the Fans Turning," *The Economist*, July 21, 2001: 46-47. "Brazil Unplugged," *The Financial Times*, June 6, 2001, 20.

21. Colin Robinson (1993), op. cit.

22. Gordon MacKerron and Jim Watson, "The Winners and Losers so Far," in John Surrey (ed) *The British Electricity Experiment: Privatization: The Record, the Issues, the Lessons* (London: Earthscan Publications, 1996): 185-212. Fereidoon P. Sioshansi, "Sobering Realities of Liberalizing Electricity Markets," *International Association of Energy Economists Newsletter* (Third Quarter, 2002): 12-15.

23. Catherine Waddams Price, "Interaction of Regulation and Competition in the Developing UK Gas Market," in Gordon MacKerron and Peter Pearson (eds) *The UK Energy Experience: A Model or a Warning?* (London: Imperial College Press, 1996): 41-50.

24. R. Frydman, A. Rapaczynski, J.S. Earle et al., *The Privatization Process in Central Europe* (London: Central European Press, 1993).

25. Ibrahim Shihata, "Good Governance and the Role of Law in Economic Development," in A. Siedman, R. B. Seidman and T. Waelde (eds) *Making Development Work: Legislative Reform for Institutional Transformation and Good Governance* (London: Kluwer Law International, 1999): xvii-xxiv. Christian von Hirschhausen and Thomas W. Waelde, "The End of Transition: An Institutional Interpretation of Energy Sector Reform in Eastern Europe and the CIS," *MOCT-MOST*, vol. 11 (2001): 91-108.

26. Gordon MacKerron, "What Can We Learn from the British Nuclear Power Experience?" in Gordon MacKerron and Peter Pearson (eds) *The UK Energy Experience: A Model or a Warning?* (London: Imperial College Press, 1996): 247-257. Also "Nuclear Industry: Fallout," *The Economist*, September 4, 2002, 29-30.

27. Catherine Waddams Price, op. cit.

28. J. D. Simpson, "The Transformation of National Oil Companies," in *The Guide to World Energy Privatization* (London: *Petroleum Economist*, 1995): 14-19.

29. Robert Pritchard, and Philip Andrews-Speed, "Eight Principles of Electricity Reform, *International Energy Law and Taxation Review* no. 1 (2001): 11-17.

30. Robert Pritchard and Philip Andrews-Speed, op. cit.

31. George Ndi and Leon Moller, "Restructuring or Privatization? State Petroleum Enterprises and the Global Economic Adjustment Process," in Thomas Walde and George Ndi (eds) *International Oil and Gas Investment, Moving Eastward?* (London: Graham and Trotman, 1994): 71-86.

32. C. D. Foster, *Privatization, Public Ownership and the Regulation of Natural Monopoly* (Oxford: Blackwell, 1992); Colin Robinson, *Regulation as a Means of Introducing Competition* (Guildford: Surrey Energy Economics Centre, 1995); Robert Pritchard and Philip Andrews-Speed, op. cit.

33. C. D. Foster, op. cit.

34. Jonathan Stern, "Electricity and Telecommunications Regulatory Institutions in Small and Developing Countries," *Utilities Policy,* vol. 9 (2000): 131-157; Matthew Bishop, John Kay and Colin Mayer, "Introduction," in Bishop, Kay and Mayer (eds) *The Regulatory Challenge* (Oxford: Oxford University Press, 1995): 1-17. See also Dieter Helm, "British Utility Regulation: Theory, Practice and Reform," in Helm (ed.) *British Utility Regulation: Principles, Experience and Reform* (Oxford: The Oxera Press, 1995): 41-71; Deepak Sharma, "Australian Electricity Reform: A Regulatory Quagmire," *International Association of Energy Economists Newsletter* (Second Quarter, 2002): 22-26.

35. British Petroleum, *BP Statistical Review of World Energy 1997* (London: British Petroleum, 1997)

36. Jonathan Sinton and David Fridley, "What Goes Up: Recent Trends in China's Energy Consumption," *Energy Policy* vol. 28, no. 10 (2000).

37. Ibid.

38. International Energy Agency, op. cit.; Kenneth B. Medlock III and Ronald Soligo, "The Composition and Gowth of Energy Demand in China," in *China and Long-Range Asia Energy Security: An Analysis of the Political, Economic and Technological Factors* (Houston, TX: James Baker III Institute for Public Policy, Rice University, 1999). Also Philip Andrews-Speed, Xuanli Liao and Roland Dannreuther, "The Strategic Impact of China's Energy Needs," *Adelphi Paper 346* (London: International Institute for Strategic Studies, 2002).

39. Kang Wu, "Fossil Energy Consumption and Supply Security in Northeast Asia*." Policy Paper 36* (La Jolla, CA: University of California Institute on Global Conflict and Cooperation, 1998). Also Fengqi Zhou and Dadi Zhou, *Medium and Long Term Energy Strategies for China* (Beijing: China Planning Publishing House, 1999).

40. Kenneth B. Medlock III and Ronald Soligo, op. cit.; Asia Pacific Energy Research Centre, *Emergency Oil Stocks and Energy Security in the APEC Region* (Tokyo: Asia Pacific Energy Research Centre, 2000); International Energy Agency, op. cit; Philip Andrews-Speed, Xuanli Liao and Roland Dannreuther, op. cit.

41. Erica Strecker Downs, *China's Quest for Energy Security*, RAND Report MR-1244-AF (2000); International Energy Agency, op. cit.; Philip Andrews-Speed, Xuanli Liao and Roland Dannreuther, op. cit.

42. Ministry of Energy, *Energy in China 1992* (Beijing: Ministry of Energy, 1992).

43. State Planning Commission, *1995 Energy Report of China* (Beijing: State Planning Commission, 1995)

44. State Development Planning Commission, *Energy Development Plan of the Tenth Five-Year Scheme (2001-2005) of National Social and Economic Development* (Beijing: State Development Planning Commission, 2001).

45. Philip Andrews-Speed et al., *Energy Policy and Structure in China*, CEPMLP Paper No. CP3/99 (Dundee: Centre for Energy, Petroleum and Mineral Law and Policy, 1999); Fengqi Zhou and Dadi Zhou, op. cit.

46. At this time central and local government coal mines account for only about 60% of annual production. In contrast, the state institutions in the other energy industries produced 80-90% of domestic output.

47. Philip Andrews-Speed, Stephen Dow and Zhiguo Gao, "An Evaluation of the Ongoing Reforms to China's Government and State Sector: The Case of the Energy Industry," *Journal of Contemporary China* vol. 9, no. 23 (2000): 5-20.

48. China Star was taken over by Sinopec in 1999.

49. Philip Andrews-Speed, "Reform of China's Energy Sector: Slow Progress to an Uncertain Goal," in Sarah Cook, Shujie Yao and Juzhong Zhuang (eds) *China's Transitional Economy* (London: Macmillan, 2000): 111-130.

50. "China's Oil Price Reforms. A Major Step in Deregulating its Petroleum Sector," *Oil and Gas Journal* August 10 (1998): 46-48.

51. Ibid.

52. Philip Andrews-Speed, "Why is China's Onshore Acreage Proving to be Unattractive to Foreign Oil Companies?" *Oil and Gas Law and Taxation Review* no. 3 (1996): 124-126.

53. Philip Andrews-Speed, "China's Power Industry: Heading for Reform," *Power Economics* (September 2000): 18-20.

54. See Mehmet Ogutcu, "China's Energy Future and Global Implications," in W. Draughen and R. Ash (eds), *China's Economic Security* (Richmond, VA: Curzon Press, 1999): 84-141; See also Philip Andrews-Speed, Xuanli Liao and Roland Dannreuther, op. cit.

55. See for example, Weidou Ni and Nien Dak Sze, "Energy Supply and Development in China," in Michael B. McElroy, Chris P. Nielsen and Peter Lydon (eds) *Energizing China: Reconciling Environmental Protection and Economic Growth* (Cambridge, MA: Harvard University Press, 1998): 67-117; Nobuhiro Horii and Shuhua Gu (eds), *Transformation of China's Energy Industries in Market Transition and its Prospects* (Chiba, Japan: Institute of Developing Economies, 2001).

56. Philip Andrews-Speed, Stephen Dow and Zhiguo Gao op. cit.; Philip Andrews-Speed and Stephen Dow, "Reform of China's Electric Power Industry: Challenges Facing the Government," *Energy Policy* no. 28 (2000): 335-347. See also Yi-chong Xu, *Powering China: Reforming the Electric Power Industry in China* (Dartmouth: Ashgate Press, 2002).

57. Philip Andrews-Speed, Stephen Dow and Zhiguo Gao op. cit.

58. Philip Andrews-Speed et al. (1999), op. cit.; Philip Andrews-Speed, "China's Energy Policy in Transition: Pressures and Constraints," *Journal of Energy Literature* vol. VII, no.2 (2001): 3-34.

59. Jonathan Stern, op. cit.; Philip Andrews-Speed, Stephen Dow and Zhiguo Gao op. cit.

60. Philip Andrews-Speed, Stephen Dow and Minying Yang, "Regulating Energy in Federal Transition Economies: The Case of China," in Gordon MacKerron and Peter Pearson (eds) *The International Energy Experience. Markets, Regulation and Environment* (London: Imperial College Press, 2000): 91-102; Also Xiaoyang Ma and Leonard Ortalano, *Environmental Regulation in China. Institutions, Enforcement and Compliance* (Lanham, MD: Rowman & Littlefield, 2000)

61. See for example, *World Energy Council*, Electricity Market Design and Creation in Asia Pacific (London, World Energy Council, 2001); Also Reza Fathollahzadeh and

Deepak Sharma, "Rationale Behind Electricity Industry Reform in the ASEAN: A Review," in *International Association of Energy Economists*, Annual Conference, June 2002, Aberdeen; Fereidoon P. Sioshansi, op. cit.; See also Noureddine Berrah, Ranjit Lamech and Jianping Zhao, "Fostering Competition in China's Power Markets" *World Bank Discussion Paper* no. 416 (Washington, DC: World Bank, 2001); World Bank and Institute of Economic System and Management, "Modernizing China's Oil and Gas Sector: Structure Reform and Regulation" (Beijing: Institute of Economic System and Management, 2001).

Chapter 5

1. British Petroleum Company, *Statistical Review of World Energy June 2001* (London: BP, 2001), Electronic version, workbook "bp_global_stats.XLS" (www.bp.com); United States Department of Energy, Energy Information Administration (Washington, DC: USDOE/EIA, 2001) International energy figures from http://www.eia.doe.gov/ emeu/iea/wecbtu.html. Also D.F. Von Hippel and P. Hayes (Berkeley, CA: Nautilus Institute, 1997), *Demand for and Supply of Electricity and other Fuels in the Democratic People's Republic of Korea (DPRK): Results and Ramifications for 1990 through 2005*. Nautilus Institute report prepared for the Northeast Asia Economic Forum/East-West Center. A summary of this report is available at http://www. nautilus.org/papers/energy/dvh_hayesscenarios.pdf.; Russian Far East data taken largely from Victor D. Kalashnikov, *Electric Power Industry of the Russian Far East: Status and Prerequisites for Cooperation in North-East Asia* (Honolulu, HI: East-West Center, 1997). Draft Report prepared for the Working Group Meeting on "Comparisons of the Electricity Industry in China, North Korea and the Russian Far East," organized by the East-West Center, Honolulu, Hawaii, July 28-29, 1997.

2. Population figures used for these calculations are from USDOE Energy Information Administration International data file "table1.XLS" downloaded from http://www. eia.doe.gov/emeu/iea/wecbtu.html. Data in Table 5.1 and elsewhere in this overview section update information found in D.F. Von Hippel, *Global Dimensions of Energy Growth Projections in Northeast Asia* (Berkeley, CA: Nautilus Institute, 1996). Prepared for the Nautilus Institute Energy Security and the Environment in Northeast Asia (ESENA) project.

3. Lawrence Berkeley National Laboratory, *China Energy Databook* (Berkeley, CA: LBNL, 2001), CD-ROM edition v. 5.0, May 2001. Data in Figure 5.1 are from Table 4B.1.

4. Lawrence Berkeley National Laboratory, *China Energy Databook* (Berkeley, CA: LBNL, 2001), CD-ROM edition v. 5.0, May 2001. Table 2B.11.

5. Lawrence Berkeley National Laboratory, *China Energy Databook*, (Berkeley, CA, USA: LBNL, 2001), CD-ROM edition v. 5.0, May 2001. Table 7A.1.1.

6. Primary energy counts all fuel use, including conversion and transmission/distribution losses. Commercial energy excludes, for the most part, use of biomass fuels such as firewood and crop wastes.

7. The summary data and text presented here are adapted from D.F. Von Hippel and P. Hayes (Berkeley, CA: Nautilus Institute, 1997), *Demand for and Supply of Electricity and other Fuels in the Democratic People's Republic of Korea (DPRK): Results and Ramifications for 1990 through 2005*. Nautilus Institute report prepared for the Northeast Asia Economic Forum/East-West Center. A summary is available at http://www.nautilus.org/papers/energy/dvh_hayesscenarios.pdf.

8. See D. Von Hippel and T. Savage, *The DPRK Energy Sector: Estimated Year 2000 Energy Balance and Suggested Approaches to Sectoral Redevelopment*, a Nautilus Institute report prepared for the Korea Energy Economics Institute, and revised in March 2003 (Berkeley, CA: Nautilus Institute, 2003)

9. Korea Energy Economics Institute, *Yearbook of Energy Statistics, 1991* (Seoul, ROK: KEEI, 1991).

10. One terawatt-hour is equal to 3600 terajoules, 3.6 million gigajoules, or one billion kilowatt-hours (kWh).

11. Data from Statistics Bureau and Statistics Center, Ministry of Public Management, Home Affairs, Posts and Telecommunications in Japan, *Japan Statistical Yearbook 2001* (Tokyo: Statistics Bureau and Statistics Center, 2001). Extracted from files b0915000.XLS and b0916000.XLS (http://www.stat.go.jp/english/1431.htm).

12. Energy Data from Statistics Bureau and Statistics Center, Ministry of Public Management, Home Affairs, Posts and Telecommunications in Japan, *Japan in Figures 2001* (Tokyo: Statistics Bureau and Statistics Center, 2000), Data from workbook 1636.XLS (http://www.stat.go.jp/english/16.htm).

13. Data from Statistics Bureau and Statistics Center, Ministry of Public Management, Home Affairs, Posts and Telecommunications in Japan, *Japan Statistical Yearbook 2001* (Tokyo: Statistics Bureau and Statistics Center, 2001). Extracted from files b0915000.XLS and b0916000.XLS (http://www.stat.go.jp/english/1431.htm).

14. British Petroleum Company data taken from spreadsheet "OIL-INTER-AREA MOVEMENTS" in workbook "BP_GLOBAL_STATS.XLS," Inter-Area Movements [of oil] 2000, as obtained from the British Petroleum Company (BP) website: www.bp.com (London: BP, 2001).

15. Energy Data from Statistics Bureau and Statistics Center, Ministry of Public Management, Home Affairs, Posts and Telecommunications in Japan, *Japan in Figures 2001* (Tokyo: Statistics Bureau and Statistics Center, 2000). Data from workbook 1636.XLS (http://www.stat.go.jp/english/16.htm).

16. Data from Statistics Bureau and Statistics Center, Ministry of Public Management, Home Affairs, Posts, and Telecommunications in Japan, *Japan Statistical Yearbook 2001* (Tokyo: Statistics Bureau and Statistics Center, 2001). Extracted from files b0915000.XLS and b0916000.XLS (http://www.stat.go.jp/english/1431.htm).

17. British Petroleum Company data from spreadsheet "Gas-Trade Movements LNG" in workbook "BP_GLOBAL_STATS.XLS," Natural Gas: Trade Movements 2000–LNG," as obtained from the British Petroleum Company (BP) website: www.bp.com (London: BP, 2001).

18. Population and energy data used for these calculations are from USDOE Energy Information Administration International data files "tableb1.XLS" and "tablee1.XLS" (http://www.eia.doe.gov/emeu/iea/wecbtu.html).

19. Asian Development Bank (ADB), the Global Environment Facility, and the United Nations Development Programme (Manila, Philippines: Asian Development Bank, 1998), *Asia Least-Cost Greenhouse Gas Abatement Strategy: Mongolia* (Manila: ADB, October 1998). Data shown are from Table 3-5, page 38.

20. Energy data used for these calculations are from USDOE Energy Information Administration International data files "tableb1.XLS" and "tablee1.XLS" (http://www.eia.doe.gov/emeu/iea/wecbtu.html). "Others" denotes the difference between total energy figures and the total of coal and petroleum products use.

21. Korea National Statistical Office, *2001 Korea in Figures* (Seoul: National Statistics Office, 2001), from http://www.nso.go.kr/eng/info/e-figures.htm.

22. Asia Pacific Energy Research Center, *Republic of Korea—Energy Overview* (Tokyo: APERC, 2000), Downloaded from the APERC web site as "Korea.pdf."

23. Most of the energy data provided in this section are drawn from Korea National Statistical Office databases from http://www.nso.go.kr/cgi-bin.

24. Data for this figure from the Korean Electric Power Company (KEPCO), Seoul, 2001. (http://www.kepco.co.kr/en/static.html).

25. Quantitative data on the energy sector in the Russian Far East are very difficult to obtain for the period since 1990 and the data shown should be considered rough estimates only.

26. Victor D. Kalashnikov, *Electric Power Industry of the Russian Far East: Status and Prerequisites for Cooperation in North-East Asia* (Honolulu, HI: East-West Center, 1997). Khabarovsk Economic Research Institute Far Eastern Branch of Russian Academy of Sciences, draft report prepared for the Working Group Meeting on "Comparisons of the Electricity Industry in China, North Korea and the Russian Far East," organized by the East-West Center, Honolulu, Hawaii, July 28-29, 1997.

27. Victor D. Kalashnikov, *National Energy Futures Analysis and Energy Security Perspectives in the Russian Far East.* Khabarovsk Economic Research Institute, Far Eastern Branch of Russian Academy of Sciences, paper prepared for The Nautilus Institute East Asia Energy Futures Project, June 2000.

28. The scenario work described here builds on the analysis presented in D.F. Von Hippel, *Modeling of Clean-Coal Scenarios for China: Progress Report and Initial Results* (Berkeley, CA: Nautilus Institute, October 1999). Nautilus Institute Report available at http://www.nautilus.org/energy/eaef/DVH_cc_PAPER.PDF. In collaboration with teams from China and from other countries of the region in Nautilus Institute's "East Asia Energy Futures" project, Nautilus staff will be involved in preparing updated energy sector models for the countries of Northeast Asia. The China energy scenarios work presented in this paper are initial findings based on research done for D.F. Von Hippel, P. Hayes and M. Nakata, *Relative Costs and Benefits of Reference Case and Alternative Energy Scenarios for China: 1998 to 2020* (Nautilus Institute Report, 2003, in preparation).

29. The Long-range Energy Alternatives Planning (LEAP) energy and environmental planning software tool, developed by the Stockholm Environment Institute (SEI), Boston Center, Massachusetts, was used as the modeling framework for the China, DPRK and Japan scenario analyses described in this paper. See www.leap2000.org for additional information about the LEAP software and related programs.

30. Both the BAU and Alternative cases include increases in domestic Chinese crude oil production, natural gas production, and oil refining capacity (year 2020 to year 1998 capacity ratios of 1.4, 2.4, and 1.6, respectively), but these increases are much less than sufficient to keep up with demand for crude oil, gas and oil products.

31. The work referred to is documented in D.F. Von Hippel and P. Hayes, *Demand for and Supply of Electricity and other Fuels in the Democratic People's Republic of Korea (DPRK): Results and Ramifications for 1990 through 2005* (Berkeley, CA: Nautilus Institute, 1997). This Nautilus Institute report was prepared for the Northeast Asia Economic Forum/East-West Center. The illustrative energy scenarios in the DPRK for 2000 to 2010 shown here have been prepared by simply assuming 1996 estimates prepared for the 1997 work hold (roughly) for 2000, and that previously prepared scenario estimates for the years 2000 and 2005 (also drawn up in 1997) are now reasonable guesses for the years 2005 and 2010, respectively.

32. The Japan energy scenarios work summarized briefly here is described in more detail in T. Suzuki, D. F. Von Hippel, K. Wilkening and J. Nickum, *Pacific Asian Regional Energy Security: Frameworks for Analysis and Japan Case Study* (Berkeley, CA: Nautilus Institute, 1998). A Synthesis Report prepared for Phase I of the Pacific Asian Regional Energy Security (PARES) Project. This report and related publications are available from the website of Nautilus Institute, Berkeley, California (http://www.nautilus.org/pares/PARES_Synthesis_Report.PDF).

33. Energy services are the services that fuel use provides. Examples are the production of a tonne of steel, the cooking of a meal, or the transporting of a passenger for one kilometer. The same energy service can usually be provided using different types and amounts of fuel, depending on the technology used. As a result, there are often opportunities to modify the energy security impacts of providing energy services (for example, by reducing the use of key fuels, or reducing the environmental impacts of energy services) without reducing the actual amount of energy services provided.

34. These Microsoft Excel™ based spreadsheets, supplied by Lee Schipper and Michael Ting of Lawrence Berkeley National Laboratory, Berkeley, California, include data complied from a collection of Japanese statistical publications and unpublished information from energy researchers in Japan.

35. Note that the same set of future fuel prices was used in evaluating the costs and benefits of both scenarios.

36. Asian Development Bank (ADB), the Global Environment Facility, and the United Nations Development Programme (Manila, Philippines: Asian Development Bank, 1998), *Asia Least-Cost Greenhouse Gas Abatement Strategy: Mongolia* (ADB, October 1998). Data presented from the Mongolia ALGAS report, pages 46-47.

37. In-Gang Na, Yongduk Pak, Tae Heon Kim, Do Young Choi, *Mid-Term Energy Outlook, 2001-2005* (Seoul: Korea Energy Economics Institute, 2001). Also document dated October 2001 in Korean, with title roughly translated as *Korean

Energy to 2030, downloaded from www.keei.re.kr (Seoul: Korea Energy Economics Institute, 1994).

38. Tables 5.9 and 5.10 are taken from In-Gang Na, Yongduk Pak, Tae Heon Kim, Do Young Choi, *Mid-Term Energy Outlook, 2000-2005* (Seoul: Korea Energy Economics Institute, 2001), document dated October 2001 downloaded from www.keei.re.kr.

39. Victor D. Kalashnikov, *National Energy Futures Analysis and Energy Security Perspectives in the Russian Far East*, Khabarovsk Economic Research Institute, Far Eastern Branch of Russian Academy of Sciences. Paper prepared for The Nautilus Institute East Asia Energy Futures Project, June 2000.

40. Some of the text and data presented here were first compiled in D. Von Hippel, *Technological Alternatives to Reduce Acid Gas and Related Emissions from Energy-Sector Activities in Northeast Asia* (Berkeley, CA: Nautilus Institute, 1996). Prepared for the Nautilus Institute Energy Security and the Environment in Northeast Asia (ESENA) project.

41. P. Hayes and L. Zarsky, "Acid Rain in a Regional Context" in Science and Technology Policy Institute and the United Nations University's Joint Seminar on "The Role of Science and Technology in Promoting Environmentally Sustainable Development," Science and Technology Policy Institute and The United Nations University, Seoul, Republic of Korea, June 1995.

42. J. Hamburger, *China's Energy and Environment in the Roaring Nineties: A Policy Primer* (Washington, DC: Pacific Northwest Laboratories, 1995). Prepared for the United States Environmental Protection Agency and the United States Department of Energy by Pacific Northwest Laboratories Advanced International Studies Unit, Washington, DC, 1995.

43. "pH" is a measure of the acidity (hydrogen ion concentration) in a substance. The pH scale runs from 1 to 14, with 1 being very acid, 7 being neutral (the pH of pure water), and 14 being very alkaline. As the pH scale is a logarithmic one, the acidity of a sample with pH 3 (for example), is ten times that of a sample with a pH of 4. A normal pH for rainwater is about 5.6.

44. Figures in this table were drawn from Hayes and Zarsky (1995) and from a table provided by David Streets of Argonne National Laboratory. Both sources used results from the RAINS-Asia project. See P. Hayes and L. Zarsky, "Acid Rain in a Regional Context," in Science and Technology Policy Institute and the United Nations University's Joint Seminar on "The Role of Science and Technology in Promoting Environmentally Sustainable Development" (Seoul, ROK: Science and Technology Policy Institute and the United Nations University, June 1995).

45. "Area sources" denotes emissions of sulfur oxides from sources other than power plants, large industrial facilities, and other "large point sources."

46. Large point sources, as defined for the RAINS-Asia model, are identified large fossil-fuel-fired power plants and industrial sources that have electricity generation capacity of greater than 500 MW, have fuel input capacity of greater than 1500 MW (thermal), produce greater than 20,000 tonnes of SO_x per year, or produce greater than 5000 tonnes of NO_x per year.

47. Hayes and Zarsky, op. cit.

48. The sensitivity of soils to acidification does not, of course, relay the complete picture of where acid precipitation could cause the most damage. Vegetation types, topography, and land use also play important roles. For example, areas with soil types that are most sensitive to acidification may not (and often do not) have vegetation that is similarly at risk.

49. Some of the text and data presented here were first compiled in D.F. Von Hippel, *Global Dimensions of Energy Growth Projections in Northeast Asia* (Berkeley, CA: Nautilus Institute, 1996). Prepared for the Nautilus Institute Energy Security and the Environment in Northeast Asia (ESENA) project.

50. Intergovernmental Panel on Climate Change (IPCC), *Climate Change 1995: The Science of Climate Change,* Contribution of Working Group I to the Second Assessment Report of the Intergovernmental Panel on Climate Change (New York, NY: Cambridge University Press, 1996).

51. K. Fujime, "Long-Term Energy Supply/Demand Outlook for Asia APEC Nations," *Energy in Japan* (January 1996).

52. F. Fesharaki, A.L. Clark and D. Intarapravich (eds) in *Pacific Energy Outlook: Strategies and Policy Imperatives to 2010* (Honolulu, HI: East-West Center Program on Resources: Energy and Minerals, March 1995).

53. Most of the tanker traffic headed for the region will need to pass through the straits that lie between Malaysia/Singapore and Indonesia. Tankers headed for Southern and Eastern China, the Koreas, and Japan usually pass through the Formosa or Luzon Straits, the East China Sea, and often the Korea Strait to service tanker terminals on the east coasts of South Korea and Japan. See M.J. Valencia, "Northeast Asian Marine Environmental Quality and Living Resources: Transnational Issues for Sustainable Development," in *The Role of Science and Technology in Promoting Environmentally Sustainable Development*, Proceedings of the Joint Seminar by the Science and Technology Policy Institute and the United Nations University, Seoul, June 13-15, 1995.

54. M.J. Valencia, and J. P. Dorian, "Multilateral Cooperation in Northeast Asia's Energy Sector: Possibilities and Problems," prepared for the *Energy Workshop of Northeast Asia Cooperation Dialogue V*, sponsored by the Institute of Foreign Affairs and National Security, Seoul, September 11-12, 1996.

55. D. F. Von Hippel and Peter Hayes, *Modernizing the US-DPRK Agreed Framework: The Energy Imperative* (Berkeley, CA: Nautilus Institute, 2001). Nautilus Institute Report, February 2001 (http://www.nautilus.org/papers/energy/ ModernizingAF.pdf).

Chapter 7

1. EIA, *China Country Analysis Brief,* 2002, and IEA, *Energy Balances of Non-OECD Countries, 1971-1999* (2001 edition).

2. Kenneth B. Medlock III and Ronald Soligo, "Economic Development and End-Use Energy Demand," *Energy Journal,* vol. 22, no. 2 (2001).

3. See, for example, Simon Kuznets, *Economic Growth of Nations: Total Output and Production Structure* (Cambridge MA: The Belnapp Press of Harvard University Press, 1971). Also Hollis B. Chenery and Moshe Syrquin, *Patterns of Development, 1950-1970* (London: Oxford University Press, 1975).

4. See, for example, Joyce Dargay and Dermot Gately, "Vehicle Ownership to 2015: Implications for Energy Use and Emissions," *Energy Policy* vol. 25 (1997). Also Kenneth B. Medlock III and Ronald Soligo, "Automobile Ownership and Economic Development—Forecasting Motor Vehicle Stocks to 2015," *Journal of Transport Economics and Policy*, vol. 36, part 2 (2002).

5. Medlock and Soligo (2002), op. cit.

6. See Medlock and Soligo (2002), op. cit., for more on this issue.

7. TFC is differentiated from TPES in energy balances by transmission and conversion losses. Hence, TPES will typically be larger than TFC by some efficiency factor.

8. Note there is no restriction placed on the sign of β_1 or β_2. So the data must bear out the hypothesis of declining elasticity. See Medlock and Soligo (2001), op. cit., for more detail.

9. Medlock and Soligo (2001), op. cit.

10. 'Other' refers to the agricultural and chemical industries. The relative sizes of these industries are typically small when compared to the industrial sector.

11. IEA, *Energy Balances of Non-OECD Countries, 1971-1999* (2001 edition).

12. Another potential explanation lies in data reliability. In particular the accuracy of GDP figures as well as energy use estimates, has been called into question by multiple analysts.

13. The data set from Medlock and Soligo (2001) op. cit., was updated through 1999 for this analysis.

14. Dargay and Gately (1997), op. cit., project a stock of about 40 vehicles per thousand people by 2020.

15. Interestingly, it is worth noting that at per capita GDP similar to that currently in the US, energy intensity for China is predicted to be similar to current energy intensity in the US. The same cannot be said of the other developing countries in the sample.

16. An example of this can be seen in cellular phone/wireless technology. The absence of land-line infrastructure has encouraged the adoption of newer technologies, virtually skipping an entire phase of communications development.

17. The underlying assumption to generate the 8.7 percent natural gas share in total energy is that the share of natural gas in each end-use sector increases. In particular, the natural gas share increases from 2.3 percent in 1999 to 8.0 percent in 2020 in the residential and commercial sector, from 0.4 percent in 1999 to 1.5 percent in 2020 in the transportation sector, and from 3.4 percent in 1999 to 12.0 percent in 2020 in the industrial sector.

18. EIA, *China Country Analysis Briefs*, 2002.

19. Christoffersen, Gaye. "China's Intentions for Russian and Central Asian Oil and Gas." NBR Analysis vol. 9, no. 2 (Seattle, WA: National Bureau of Asian Research, March 1998).

20. Petroleum Argus Newsletter, June 18, 2001, 10.

21. See Steven W. Lewis, "Privatizing China's State-Owned Oil Companies" (Houston, TX: James A. Baker III Institute for Public Policy, Rice University, 1999).

22. "Russia to China Race," *World Gas Intelligence*, August 22, 2001, vol. XII, no. 24, and "Russia Reaches for Chinese Oil and Gas Outlets," *Petroleum Intelligence Weekly*, July 23, 2001, vol. XL, no. 30.

23. See Amy M. Jaffe and Ronald Soligo, "A Note on Saudi Arabian Price Discrimination," *The Energy Journal* vol. 21, no. 1 (2000).

24. Ronald Soligo and Amy M. Jaffe, "China's Growing Energy Dependence: The Costs and Policy Implications of Supply Alternatives," Working paper (Houston, TX: James A. Baker III Institute for Public Policy, Rice University, 1999). See: www.bakerinstitute.org.

25. See Christoffersen (1998), op. cit.

26. "China's CNPC Leaps on to Global Oil Production Stage," *Petroleum Intelligence Weekly*, vol. xxxvi, no. 23, June 9, 1997, 3.

27. See Christoffersen (1998), op. cit.

28. Ibid.

Chapter 8

1. This refers to the proportion of electricity lost in the process of transmission and distribution of electricity to consumers, including losses due to pilferage. It is expressed as a percentage of electricity generated.

2. Since 75% of coal produced in India is coming from mechanized open cast mines, there is a pronounced degree of contamination, which lowers the quality of coal being supplied to the power plants. Moreover, there are very few power plants (except some pit-head super thermal power plants) getting coal from a single dedicated source. Multiplicity of supply sources adds to the problem of inconsistency in the quality of coal. At least half of the operating power stations are receiving coal from more than one mine. As a result, they are getting coal of differing quality and size. In the absence of proper blending facilities, it is not operationally feasible for the power plants to homogenize the feed coal. Additionally, as per the mandate of the Ministry of Environment and Forests, the use of beneficiated coal (with less than 34% ash) is stipulated for all power plants located more than 1000 km away from the coal sources and also for those located in urban and environmentally sensitive locations. Thus, the total tonnage of coal that would need to be beneficiated is really huge and has led to the increase in the total washing capacity for thermal coal.

Concluding Observations

1. This refers to the Neutral Zone between Saudi Arabia and Kuwait in which access to resources is shared.

2. The recent emergence of the "Dubai-Oman" contract may improve the efficiency of the market.

Bibliography

Amin, Mohamad Farid bin Mohamad. "Opportunities and Challenges Towards the Realization of the Trans-ASEAN Gas Pipeline Infrastructure" (http://www.ascope.com.my).

Andrews-Speed, Philip and Stephen Dow. "Reform of China's Electric Power Industry: Challenges Facing the Government." *Energy Policy* vol. 5, no. 28 (2000).

Andrews-Speed, Philip et al. *Energy Policy and Structure in China*, CEPMLP Paper No. CP3/99 (Dundee: Centre for Energy, Petroleum and Mineral Law and Policy, 1999).

Andrews-Speed, Philip, Stephen Dow and Minying Yang. "Regulating Energy in Federal Transition Economies: The Case of China," in Gordon MacKerron and Peter Pearson (eds) *The International Energy Experience: Markets, Regulation and Environment* (London: Imperial College Press, 2000).

Andrews-Speed, Philip, Stephen Dow and Zhiguo Gao. "An Evaluation of the Ongoing Reforms to China's Government and State Sector: The Case of the Energy Industry." *Journal of Contemporary China* vol. 9, no. 23 (2000).

Andrews-Speed, Philip, Xuanli Liao and Roland Dannreuther. "The Strategic Impact of China's Energy Needs." *Adelphi Paper* 346 (London: International Institute for Strategic Studies, 2002).

Andrews-Speed, Philip. "China's Energy Policy in Transition: Pressures and Constraints." *Journal of Energy Literature* vol. VII, no. 2 (2001).

Andrews-Speed, Philip. "China's Power Industry: Heading for Reform." *Power Economics* (September 2000).

Andrews-Speed, Philip. "Reform of China's Energy Sector: Slow Progress to an Uncertain Goal," in Sarah Cook, Shujie Yao and Juzhong Zhuang (eds) *China's Transitional Economy* (London: Macmillan, 2000).

Andrews-Speed, Philip. "Why is China's Onshore Acreage Proving to be Unattractive to Foreign Oil Companies?" *Oil and Gas Law and Taxation Review* no. 3 (1996).

APERC. APEC Energy Demand and Supply Outlook Energy Balance Tables (Tokyo, APERC, 1998).

APERC. *Energy Supply Infrastructure Development* (Tokyo, APERC, 2001).

APERC. *Power Interconnection in the APEC Region: Current Status and Future Potentials* (Tokyo, APERC, 2000).

APERC-a. *APEC Energy Review* (Tokyo, APERC, 2002).

APERC-b. *APEC Energy Demand and Supply Outlook* (Tokyo, APERC, 2002).

APERC. *Republic of Korea—Energy Overview* (Tokyo: APERC, 2000). "Korea.pdf," APERC website.

APERC. *Emergency Oil Stocks and Energy Security in the APEC Region* (Tokyo: Asia Pacific Energy Research Centre, 2000).

Asian Development Bank (ADB), Global Environment Facility, and the United Nations Development Program (Manila, Philippines: Asian Development Bank, 1998). *Asia Least-Cost Greenhouse Gas Abatement Strategy: Mongolia* (Manila: ADB, October 1998).

Background Note for Annual Renewable Energy Conference on "Policy Perspectives: 2000-2012," 23-24, New Delhi, 2000.

Ben-Hur Salcedo, James P. Dorian, Maurice H. Kaya and John Tantlinger. "Restructuring of the Philippines Electric Power Industry and Future Development," *ASEAN Energy Bulletin*, vol. 4, no. 4 (Jakarta: ASEAN Centre for Energy, December 2000).

Berrah, Noureddine, Ranjit Lamech and Jianping Zhao. "Fostering Competition in China's Power Markets." *World Bank Discussion Paper* no. 416 (Washington DC: World Bank, 2001).

Besant-Jones, John. "Lessons from UK Electricity Reforms for Developing Countries," in Gordon MacKerron and Peter Pearson (eds) *The UK Energy Experience: A Model or a Warning?* (London: Imperial College Press, 1996).

Bienen, H. and J. Waterbury. "The Political Economy of Privatization in Developing Countries." *World Development* vol.17, no. 5 (1989).

Bishop, Matthew, John Kay and Colin Mayer. "Introduction," in Bishop, Kay and Mayer (eds) *The Regulatory Challenge* (Oxford: Oxford University Press, 1995).

Bishop, Matthew, John Kay and Colin Mayer. "Introduction: Privatization in Performance," in Bishop, Kay and Mayer (eds), *Privatization and Economic Performance* (Oxford: Oxford University Press, 1994).

BP Statistical Review of World Energy for various years.

British Petroleum Company *Statistical Review of World Energy June 2001*. Electronic version, workbook "bp_global_stats.XLS" (www.bp.com).

British Petroleum Company. Data from spreadsheet "Gas—Trade Movements LNG" in workbook BP_GLOBAL_STATS.XLS," "Natural Gas: Trade Movements 2000—LNG," British Petroleum Company web site: www.bp.com. (London: BP, 2001).

British Petroleum Company. Data from spreadsheet "OIL-INTER-AREA MOVEMENTS" in workbook BP_GLOBAL_STATS.XLS," Inter-Area Movements [of oil] 2000, British Petroleum Company web site: www.bp.com (London: BP, 2001).

British Petroleum Company. *BP Statistical Review of World Energy, 2002*.

Central Electricity Authority. Report of the Working Group on Power for the Tenth Plan, 2002.

Chenery, Hollis B. and Moshe Syrquin. *Patterns of Development, 1950-1970* (London: Oxford University Press, 1975).

Chonglertvanichkul, Prutichai. "The Electricity Interconnection of the Greater Mekong Sub-Region." Paper presented at the APERC Annual Conference 2000, Tokyo, Japan.

Christoffersen, Gaye. "China's Intentions for Russian and Central Asian Oil and Gas." NBR Analysis vol. 9, no. 2 (Seattle, WA: National Bureau of Asian Research, March 1998).

Dargay, Joyce and Dermot Gately. "Vehicle Ownership to 2015: Implications for Energy Use and Emissions." *Energy Policy* vol. 25 (1997).

Dorian, James P. *Oil and Gas in Central Asia and Northwest China.* (London: The CWC Group, 2001):176.

Downs, Erica Strecker. *China's Quest for Energy Security.* RAND Report MR-1244-AF (2000).

Energy Argus -a. "Asia Gas and Power," vol. 3, no. 12, July 2, 2003.

Energy Argus -b. "Asia Gas and Power," vol. 3, no. 11, June 18, 2003.

Energy Argus -c. "Asia Gas and Power," vol. 3, no. 11, May 18, 2003.

Energy Argus. "Asia Gas and Power," vol. 1, no. 2, December 5, 2001.

Energy Information Administration. *International Energy Outlook 2002*, US Department of Energy, Washington, DC, 2002 (http:/www.eia.doe.gov).

Energy Information Administration. *International Energy Annual 2002.* US Department of Energy, Washington, DC, 2002 (http:/www.eia.doe.gov).

Energy Information Administration. *International Energy Outlook 2001.* Washington, D.C: United States Department of Energy, 2001 (http:/www.eia.doe.gov).

Ernst, J. *Whose Utility?* (Buckingham: Open University Press, 1994).

Fathollahzadeh, Reza and Deepak Sharma. "Rationale Behind Electricity Industry Reform in the ASEAN: A Review," in International Association of Energy Economists, Annual Conference, June 2002, Aberdeen.

Ferderer, Peter (1996). "Oil Price Volatility and the Macroeconomy." *The Journal of Macroeconomics.* vol.18, no.1 (Winter 1996): 1-26.

Fesharaki, Fereidun, A.L. Clark and D. Intarapravich (eds) *Pacific Energy Outlook: Strategies and Policy Imperatives to 2010* (Honolulu, HI: East-West Center Program on Resources: Energy and Minerals, March 1995).

Fesharaki, Fereidun. "China Oil Price Reforms a Major Step in Deregulation of its Petroleum Sector." *Oil and Gas Journal*, vol. 96, no. 32 (August 10, 1998).

Fesharaki, Fereidun. "Promoting Energy Security in APEC through Improved International Market Operations" (Honolulu, HI: East-West Center, 1998).

Foster, C.D. *Privatization, Public Ownership and the Regulation of Natural Monopoly* (Oxford: Blackwell, 1992).

Friedman, Milton. *Capitalism and Freedom* (Chicago: University of Chicago Press, 1962).

Frydman, R., A. Rapaczynski, J.S. Earle et al. *The Privatization Process in Central Europe* (London: Central European Press, 1993).

Fujime, K. "Long-Term Energy Supply/Demand Outlook for Asia APEC Nations." *Energy in Japan*, Bimonthly Report No. 137 (January 1996).

Gao, Weiyu, Kenneth B. Medlock III and Robin Sickles. "The Effect of Oil Price Volatility on Productivity and Technical Change." Working Paper (Houston, TX: Rice University, 1999).

Government of India. Annual Report, Ministry of Non-Conventional Energy Sources, 2001-2002.

Government of India. Economic Survey, 2001-2002.

Government of India. Indian Petroleum and Natural Gas Statistics, Ministry of Petroleum and Natural Gas, 2001-2002.

Government of India, Planning Commission. R. Sengupta (ed.) *Integrated Energy Model and the Planning for the Long Run Supply of Electricity in India* (1989).

Government of India. Report of the Sub-Group on Refining for the Tenth Plan, Ministry of Petroleum and Natural Gas, 2001.

Government of India. Provisional Census, 2001.

Government of India. *Hydro Carbon Vision 2025*. Sub-Group on Development of Refining, Marketing, Transportation and Infrastructure Requirements Based on Demand and Supply Projections, 1999.

Hamburger, J. *China's Energy and Environment in the Roaring Nineties: A Policy Primer* (Washington DC: Pacific Northwest Laboratories, 1995). Prepared for the United States Environmental Protection Agency (EPA) and the United States Department of Energy (DOE) by Pacific Northwest Laboratories Advanced International Studies Unit, Washington D.C, 1995.

Hamilton, James. "Oil and the Macroeconomy since World War II." *Journal of Political Economy*, vol. 91, no. 2 (1983): 228-48.

Hartley, Peter, Kenneth B. Medlock III and Michael Warby. "First Things First—Economic Development and Global Warming." Working paper (Houston, TX: James A. Baker III Institute for Public Policy, Rice University, 1999). www.bakerinstitute.org.

Hay, F.A. *The Constitution of Liberty* (London: Routledge and Kegan Paul, 1960).

Hayes, P. and L. Zarsky. "Acid Rain in a Regional Context" in Science and Technology Policy Institute and the United Nations University's Joint Seminar on "The Role of Science and Technology in Promoting Environmentally Sustainable Development" (Seoul, ROK: Science and Technology Policy Institute and the United Nations University, June 1995.

Heads of ASEAN Power Utilities/Authorities. Report of the 16th Meeting, April 25-28, 2000.

Helm, Dieter, John Kay and David Thompson. "Energy Policy and the Role of the State in the Market for Energy." *Fiscal Studies* vol. 9, no.1 (February 1988).

Helm, Dieter. "British Utility Regulation: Theory, Practice and Reform," in Helm (ed) *British Utility Regulation: Principles, Experience and Reform* (Oxford: The Oxera Press, 1995).

Horii, Nobuhiro and Shuhua Gu (eds) *Transformation of China's Energy Industries in Market Transition and its Prospects* (Chiba, Japan: Institute of Developing Economies, 2001).

Horsnell, Paul. *Oil in Asia: Markets, Trading, Refining and Deregulation* (London: Oxford University Press, 1997).

Hsiao, Cheng. *Analysis of Panel Data* (Cambridge University Press, 1986).

Hunst, S. and G. Shuttleworth, *Competition and Choice of Electricity* (John Wiley & Sons, 1996).

Ibrahim, Hassan. "Policy Instruments for New and Renewable Energy in Malaysia." *ASEAN Energy Bulletin*, vol. 6, no. 2 (2002).

Intergovernmental Panel on Climate Change (IPCC). *Climate Change 1995: The Science of Climate Change*, Contribution of Working Group I to the Second Assessment Report of the Intergovernmental Panel on Climate Change (New York, NY: Cambridge University Press/IPCC, 1996).

International Energy Agency. *International Coal Trade—The Evolution of a Global Market* (Paris: OECD/IEA, 1997).

International Energy Agency. *Natural Gas Pricing in Competitive Markets* (Paris: OECD/IEA, 1998).

International Energy Agency. *World Energy Outlook 2000* (Paris: OECD/IEA, 2000).

International Energy Agency. *World Energy Outlook 1998* (Paris: OECD/IEA, 1998).

Ishiguro, Masayasu and Takamasa Akiyama. "Energy Demand in Five Major Asian Developing Countries." *World Bank Discussion Papers* No. 277 (1995).

Ivanov, Vladimir. "Prospects for Russia's Energy Diplomacy in Northeast Asia," Working paper no.15, The Economic Research Institute for Northeast Asia (ERINA), Nigata, Japan, 1999 (www.nira.go.jp).

Jaccard, Mark. "Oscillating Currents: The Changing Rationale for Government Intervention in the Electricity Industry." *Energy Policy* vol. 23, no.7 (1995).

Jaffe, Amy M. and Ronald Soligo. "A Note on Saudi Arabian Price Discrimination." *The Energy Journal* vol. 21, no. 1 (2000).

Jaffe, Amy M. and Robert Manning. "Russia, Energy and the West." *Survival* vol. 43, no. 2 (Summer 2001): 133-152.

Jaffe, Amy M. and Robert Manning. "The Shocks of a World of Cheap Oil" *Foreign Affairs*, vol. 79, no. 1 (January/February 2000):16-29.

Jirapraditkul, Viraphol. "Policy Instruments for Renewable Energy Applications in Thailand." *ASEAN Energy Bulletin*, vol. 6, no. 2 (2002).

Kalashnikov, Victor D. *Electric Power Industry of the Russian Far East: Status and Prerequisites for Cooperation in North-East Asia*. Khabarovsk Economic Research Institute, Far Eastern Branch of Russian Academy of Sciences (Honolulu, HI: East-West Center, 1997).

Kalashnikov, Victor D. *National Energy Futures Analysis and Energy Security Perspectives in the Russian Far East*. Khabarovsk Economic Research Institute, Far Eastern Branch of Russian Academy of Sciences. Paper prepared for The Nautilus Institute, East Asia Energy Futures Project, June 2000.

Korea Energy Economics Institute. *Yearbook of Energy Statistics, 1991* (Seoul: KEEI, 1991).

Korea National Statistical Office databases (http://www.nso.go.kr/cgi-bin).

[383]

Korea National Statistical Office. *2001 Korea in Figures* (Seoul, ROK: National Statistics Office, 2001). http://www.nso.go.kr/eng/info/e-figures.htm.

Korean Electric Power Company (KEPCO) Seoul, Republic of Korea, 2001 (http://www.kepco. co.kr/en/static.html).

Korea Energy Economics Institute (KEEI). *Korean Energy to 2030* (in Korean) Seoul, Republic of Korea, 1994 (www.keei.re.kr).

Kuznets, Simon. *Economic Growth of Nations: Total Output and Production Structure* (Cambridge, MA: The Belnapp Press of Harvard University Press, 1971).

Langcake, Peter. "Getting a Clear View: Strategic Perspectives for Renewable Energy Companies." *Renewable Energy World* vol. 6, no. 2 (March-April 2003).

Laszlo, Lovei. "The Single-Buyer Model" (http://rru.worldbank.org/viewpoint/HTMLNotes/ 225/225Lovei-1211.pdf).

Lawrence Berkeley National Laboratory. *China Energy Databook*, CD-ROM edition v. 5.0, May 2001 (Berkeley, CA: LBNL, 2001).

Lefevre, Thierry and Romeo Pacudan. *Coal and Natural Gas Competition in APEC Economies* (Bangkok: Asian Institute of Technology, 1999).

Lewis, Steven. "Privatizing China's State-Owned Oil Companies." (Houston, TX: James A. Baker III Institute for Public Policy, Rice University, 1999).

Ma, Xiaoyang and Leonard Ortalano. *Environmental Regulation in China: Institutions, Enforcement and Compliance* (Lanham, MD: Rowman and Littlefield, 2000)

MacDonald, Julie A. and S. Enders Wimbush. *Energy Strategies and Military Strategies in Asia* (McLean, VA: Hicks & Associates, 1999), 9-15.

MacKerron, Gordon and Jim Watson. "The Winners and Losers so Far," in John Surrey (ed.) *The British Electricity Experiment—Privatization: The Record, the Issues, the Lessons* (London: Earthscan Publications, 1996).

MacKerron, Gordon. "What Can we Learn from the British Nuclear Power Experience?" in Gordon MacKerron and Peter Pearson (eds) *The UK Energy Experience: A Model or a Warning?* (London: Imperial College Press, 1996).

Mahmood, Dato' Tengku. "Opportunities and Challenges Towards the Realization of the ASEAN Power Grid" (http://www.ascope.com.my).

Mahoney, Nicholas. "Renewable Energy Market Overview 2000." *Renewable Energy World*, vol 4, no. 1 (January–February 2001).

Manning, Robert. *The Asian Energy Factor: Myths and Dilemmas of Energy, Security, and the Pacific Future* (New York, NY: Palgrave, 2000).

Medlock III, Kenneth B. and Ronald Soligo. "Economic Development and End-Use Energy Demand," *Energy Journal* vol. 22, no. 2 (April 2001).

Medlock III, Kenneth B. and Ronald Soligo. "Automobile Ownership and Economic Development—Forecasting Motor Vehicle Stocks to 2015," *Journal of Transport Economics and Policy* vol. 36, part 2 (2002).

Medlock III, Kenneth B. and Ronald Soligo. "Japanese Energy Demand to 2015," Working Paper (Houston, TX: James A. Baker III Institute for Public Policy, Rice University, 2000).

Medlock III, Kenneth B. and Ronald Soligo. "The Composition and Growth in Energy Supply in China," Working Paper (Houston, TX: James A. Baker III Institute for Public Policy, Rice University, 1999).

Medlock III, Kenneth B. and Ronald Soligo. "The Composition and Growth of Energy Demand in China," in *China and Long-Range Asia Energy Security: An Analysis of the Political, Economic and Technological Factors* (Houston, TX: James Baker III Institute for Public Policy, Rice University, 1999).

Medlock III, Kenneth B. and Ronald Soligo. "Japanese Energy Demand to 2015." Working Paper (Houston, TX: James A. Baker III Institute for Public Policy, Rice University, Houston, Texas (2000).

Middle East Economic Digest. "Special Report: Japan and the Middle East." November 28, 1997.

Ministry of Energy. *Energy in China 1992* (Beijing: Ministry of Energy, 1992).

Na, In-Gang, Yongduk Pak, Tae Heon Kim, Do Young Choi. *Mid-Term Energy Outlook, 2001-2005* (Seoul, ROK: Korea Energy Economics Institute, 2001).

Ndi, George and Leon Moller. "Restructuring or Privatization? State Petroleum Enterprises and the Global Economic Adjustment Process," in Thomas Walde and George Ndi (eds) *International Oil and Gas Investment, Moving Eastward?* (London: Graham & Trotman, 1994).

Newberry, David M. "The Restructuring of UK Energy Industries: What have we Learned?" in Gordon MacKerron and Peter Pearson (eds) *The UK Energy Experience: A Model or a Warning?* (London: Imperial College Press, 1996).

Ni, Weidou and Nien Dak Sze. "Energy Supply and Development in China," in Michael B. McElroy, Chris P. Nielsen and Peter Lydon (eds) *Energizing China: Reconciling Environmental Protection and Economic Growth* (Cambridge, MA: Harvard University Press, 1998).

Noer, John and David Gregory. *Chokepoints: Maritime Economic Concerns in Southeast Asia* (Washington, DC: National Defense University Press, 1996).

Ogutcu, Mehmet. "China's Energy Future and Global Implications," in W. Draughen and R. Ash (eds), *China's Economic Security* (Richmond,VA: Curzon Press, 1999).

Oil and Gas Journal. "Oil Piracy Poses Growing Menace to Tanker Traffic in South China Sea." October 18, 1999.

Pacudan, Romeo. "Natural Gas Pricing Policies in Asia." *Natural Resources Forum*, vol. 22, no. 1 (1998): 27-36.

Pacudan, Romeo. "Post-Crisis Asia: Time for Reform?" *Asia Energy Infrastructure*, vol 2, no. 3 (September, 2000).

Pacudan, Romeo-a. "Grid-based Renewable Energy Promotion in Southeast Asia: Case of the Philippines and Thailand." The International Renewable Energy Conference, Sonderborg, Denmark (September 17-19, 2003).

Pacudan, Romeo-b. "NRE Opportunities in Vietnam." A report submitted to the Regional Institute for Environmental Technology (RIET) for the EU-funded project "Stimulating EU-Indochina New and Renewable Energy (NRE) Projects Through Private Sector Participation in Economic Cooperation and Foreign Direct Investment (FDI) Initiatives" (August 2003).

Petroleum Argus Newsletter, June 18, 2001.

Petroleum Economist. "East Asia: A New Market for Russian Gas" (September 1996): 60-62.

Petroleum Intelligence Weekly, "China's CNPC Leaps on to Global Oil Production Stage," vol. xxxvi, no. 23 (June 9, 1997).

Petroleum Intelligence Weekly. "Russia Reaches for Chinese Oil and Gas Outlets," vol. XL, no. 30 (July 23, 2001).

Petroleum Intelligence Weekly. "Asian Demand Flat, and May Get Worse." vol. XL, no. 31 (July 30, 2001).

Petroleum Intelligence Weekly. "Russia to China Race, World Gas Intelligence." vol. XII, no. 24 (August 22, 2001).

Pritchard, Robert and Philip Andrews-Speed, "Eight Principles of Electricity Reform," *International Energy Law and Taxation Review* no. 1 (2001).

Robinson, Colin. "Privatizing the Energy Industries," in C. Veljanovski (ed.) *Privatization and Competition—A Market Prospectus* (London: Institute of Economic Affairs, 1988).

Robinson, Colin. "The Case for an Energy Policy," in *Energy Policy: Errors, Illusions and Market Realities.* IEA Occasional Paper no. 90 (London: Institute of Economic Affairs, 1993).

Robinson, Colin. *Regulation as a Means of Introducing Competition* (Guildford: Surrey Energy Economics Centre, 1995).

Sagers, Matthew. Planecon Consulting presentation to the Baker Institute Workshop of Northeast Asian Energy Cooperation, Houston., Texas, December 14-15, 1999.

Sankey, Paul and Gavin Thompson. "Asia-Pacific Energy Markets Service." Wood/Mackenzie Asia Pacific Energy Consulting, January 1999.

Sharma, Deepak. "Australian Electricity Reform: A Regulatory Quagmire," *International Association of Energy Economists Newsletter* (Second Quarter 2002).

Shihata, Ibrahim. "Good Governance and the Role of Law in Economic Development," in A. Siedman, R. B. Seidman and T. Waelde (eds) *Making Development Work: Legislative Reform for Institutional Transformation and Good Governance* (London: Kluwer Law International, 1999).

Simpson, J.D. "The Transformation of National Oil Companies" in *The Guide to World Energy Privatization* (London: Petroleum Economist, 1995).

Sims, Ralph. "A Kind of Evolution—Latest IPPC Report Identifies a Major Role of Renewables." *Renewable Energy World,* vol. 4, no. 3 (May–June 2001).

Sinton, Jonathan and David Fridley. "What Goes Up: Recent Trends in China's Energy Consumption." *Energy Policy* vol. 28, no. 10 (2000).

Sioshansi, Fereidoon P. "Sobering Realities of Liberalizing Electricity Markets." *International Association of Energy Economists Newsletter* (Third Quarter, 2002).

Soligo, Ronald and Amy M. Jaffe. "Caspian Pipelines: Pipe Dream or Reality?" in Amy M. Jaffe, Yelena Kalyuzhnova, Dov Lynch and Robin Sickles (eds) *Energy in the Caspian Region: Present and Future* (New York, NY: Palgrave, 2002).

Soligo, Ronald and Amy M. Jaffe. "China's Growing Energy Dependence: The Costs and Policy Implications of Supply Alternatives" (Houston, TX: James A. Baker III Institute for Public Policy, Rice University, 1999).

Soligo, Ronald and Amy M. Jaffe. "The Economics of Pipeline Routes: The Conundrum of Oil Exports From the Caspian Basin," Working Paper (Houston, TX: James A. Baker III Institute for Public Policy, Rice University, Houston, Texas, 1998).

State Development Planning Commission. *Energy Development Plan of the Tenth Five-Year Scheme (2001-2005) of National Social and Economic Development* (Beijing: State Development Planning Commission, 2001).

State Planning Commission. *1995 Energy Report of China* (Beijing: State Planning Commission, 1995)

Statistics Bureau and Statistics Center, Ministry of Public Management, Home Affairs, Posts and Telecommunications, Japan. *Japan Statistical Yearbook 2001* (Tokyo, Japan: Statistics Bureau and Statistics Center, 2001). http://www.stat.go.jp/english/1431.htm. Files b0915000.XLS and b0916000.XLS.

Statistics Bureau and Statistics Center, Ministry of Public Management, Home Affairs, Posts, and Telecommunications, Japan. *Japan in Figures 2001* (Tokyo, Japan: Statistics Bureau and Statistics Center, 2000). Data from workbook 1636.XLS (http://www.stat.go.jp/english/16.htm).

Stern, Jonathan. "Electricity and Telecommunications Regulatory Institutions in Small and Developing Countries." *Utilities Policy*, vol. 9, no. 3 (2000).

Stevens, Paul. "Energy Privatization: Sensitivities and Realities." *The Journal of Energy and Development* vol. 23, no. 1 (1998).

Stevens, Paul. "The Practical Record and Prospects of Privatization Program in the Arab World," in T. Niblock and E. Murphy (eds) *Economic and Political Liberalization in the Middle East* (London: British Academy Press, 1993).

Suzuki, T., D. F. Von Hippel, K. Wilkening and J. Nickum. *Pacific Asian Regional Energy Security: Frameworks for Analysis and Japan Case Study.* Synthesis Report for Phase I of the Pacific Asian Regional Energy Security (PARES) Project (Berkeley, CA: Nautilus Institute, 1998).

Swartz, Gerd. "Privatization in Eastern Europe: Experience and Preliminary Policy Lessons," in Paul Cook and Colin Kirpatrick (eds) *Privatization Policy and Performance: International Perspectives* (New York, NY: Prentice Hall, 1995).

The Energy and Resources Institute (TERI). Report on Energy Loss Estimation in Uttar Pradesh (Meerut Zone), 1998.

The Energy and Resources Institute (TERI). *Tata Energy Data Directory and Yearbook* (TEDDY) 2000/2001.

The Energy and Resources Institute (TERI) *Handbook on Energy Management and Audit* (TERI, 2000).

The Economic Research Institute for Northeast Asia. "Energy Security and Development in Northeast Asia: Prospects for Cooperative Policies." Report of the Workshop held in Nigata, Japan, December 17-19, 1999.

The Royal Institute of International Affairs. "Northeast Asian Energy in a Global Context" (London: RIIA, 1996) www.riia.org.

Tjaroko, Tjarinto, Maritess Cabrera and Thierry Lefevre. "Policy Instruments to Promote RE Projects Interconnected to National Grids." *GrIPP-Net News*, vol 2, no. 4 (August 2003).

Troner, Alan. "Japan and the Russian Far East: The Economics and Competitive Impact of Least-Cost Gas Imports." Working paper (Houston, TX: James A. Baker Institute for Public Policy, 1999). www.bakerinstitute.org.

Troner, Alan. "Russian Far East Natural Gas." *Oil and Gas Journal* vol. 99, no. 10 (March 5, 2001).

United Nations Development Program (UNDP). World Energy Assessment, 2000.

United States Department of Energy (DOE). EIA, Washington, DC, USDOE/EIA, 2001 (http://www.eia.doe.gov/emeu/iea/wecbtu.html).

United States Department of Energy (DOE). EIA, International data files "tableb1.XLS" and "tablee1.XLS" (http://www.eia.doe.gov/emeu/iea/wecbtu.html).

Valencia, M.J. "Northeast Asian Marine Environmental Quality and Living Resources: Transnational Issues for Sustainable Development," in *The Role of Science and Technology in Promoting Environmentally Sustainable Development,* Proceedings of the Science and Technology Policy Institute and United Nations University Joint Seminar, Seoul, June 13-15, 1995.

Valencia, M.J. and J.P. Dorian. "Multilateral Cooperation in Northeast Asia's Energy Sector: Possibilities and Problems." Prepared for Energy Workshop of Northeast Asia Cooperation Dialogue V, Institute of Foreign Affairs and National Security, Seoul, September 11-12, 1996.

Van der Walle, N. "Privatization in Developing Countries: A Review of the Issues." *World Development* vol. 17, no. 5 (1989).

Vickers, John and George Yarrow. *Privatization: An Economic Analysis* (Cambridge, MA: MIT Press, 1988).

Von Brabant, Jozef M. "On the Economics of Property Rights and Privatization in Transitional Economies," in Paul Cook and Colin Kirpatrick (eds) *Privatization Policy and Performance: International Perspectives* (New York, NY: Prentice Hall, 1995).

Von Hippel D.F. and P. Hayes. *Demand for and Supply of Electricity and Other Fuels in the Democratic People's Republic of Korea: Results and Ramifications for 1990 through 2005* (Berkeley, CA: Nautilus Institute, 1997). http://www.nautilus.org/papers/ energy/ dvh_hayesscenarios.pdf.

Von Hippel, D. F. and Peter Hayes. *Modernizing the US-DPRK Agreed Framework: The Energy Imperative* (Berkeley, CA: Nautilus Institute Report, February 2001) http://www.nautilus.org/papers/energy/ModernizingAF .pdf.

Von Hippel, D. F. *Technological Alternatives to Reduce Acid Gas and Related Emissions from Energy-Sector Activities in Northeast Asia* (Berkeley, CA: Nautilus Institute, 1996). Prepared for the Nautilus Institute Energy Security and the Environment in Northeast Asia (ESENA) project.

Von Hippel, D.F. *Modeling of Clean-Coal Scenarios for China: Progress Report and Initial Results* (Berkeley, CA: Nautilus Institute, 1999) http://www.nautilus.org/energy/eaef/DVH_cc_PAPER.PDF.

Von Hippel, D.F. *Global Dimensions of Energy Growth Projections in Northeast Asia* Prepared for the Nautilus Institute Energy Security and the Environment in Northeast Asia (ESENA) project (Berkeley, CA: Nautilus Institute, 1996).

Von Hippel, D.F., P. Hayes and M. Nakata. *Relative Costs and Benefits of Reference Case and Alternative Energy Scenarios for China: 1998 to 2020* (Nautilus Institute Report, 2002).

Von Hirschhausen, Christian and Thomas W. Waelde. "The End of Transition: An Institutional Interpretation of Energy Sector Reform in Eastern Europe and the CIS." MOCT-MOST, vol. 11 (2001).

Waddams-Price, Catherine. "Interaction of Regulation and Competition in the Developing UK Gas Market," in Gordon MacKerron and Peter Pearson (eds) *The UK Energy Experience: A Model or a Warning?* (London: Imperial College Press, 1996).

World Bank and Institute of Economic System and Management. *Modernizing China's Oil and Gas Sector: Structure Reform and Regulation* (Beijing: Institute of Economic System and Management, 2001).

World Development Report 1999/2000 (New York, NY: Oxford University Press).

World Energy Council. *Electricity Market Design and Creation in Asia Pacific* (London: World Energy Council, 2001).

Wright, V. "Industrial Privatization in Western Europe: Pressures, Problems and Paradoxes," in V. Wright (ed.) *Privatization in Western Europe: Pressures, Problems and Paradoxes* (London: Pinter, 1994).

Wu, Kang. *Fossil Energy Consumption and Supply Security in Northeast Asia.* Policy Paper 36 (La Jolla, CA: University of California Institute on Global Conflict and Cooperation, 1998).

Xu, Xiaojie. "The Gas Dragon's Rise: Chinese Natural Gas Strategy and Import Patterns." Working paper (Houston, TX: James A. Baker III Institute for Public Policy, Rice University, 1999). www.bakerinstitute.org.

Xu, Yi-chong. *Powering China. Reforming the Electric Power Industry in China* (Dartmouth: Ashgate Press, 2002).

Zhou, Fengqi and Dadi Zhou. *Medium and Long Term Energy Strategies for China* (Beijing: China Planning Publishing House, 1999).

INDEX

A

accountability 103
acid rain
    and coal 36
    nuclear solution 125
    overview 226–29
Agip 297
agriculture
    and pollution 229
    share of GDP 277
air pollution
    and coal 93
    nuclear solution 125
    trans-boundary 62
    vs rest of world 122
ALGAS (Asia Least-Cost
    Greenhouse Gas Abatement
    Strategy) projection 219–21
alternative energy
    and energy security 122
    and environmental issues 122
    new technologies 46–47, 132,
      197, 236
    see also renewable energy
Amoco 72, 297
"arms race" 47, 50, 51
Arroyo, Gloria 100
ASEAN (Association of South East
    Asian Nations) 6, 30
    Vision 2020 249, 259
Asia-Pacific Economic Cooperation
    (APEC) forum 6
Asia-Pacific region
    LNG trade 71
    oil
      imports 21, 31, 36, 67, 135
      production 38
    population 57
    primary energy consumption 120
Asian Development Bank (ADB) 219
Australasia 67

Australia
    coal
      exports 75
      reserves 37
    electricity 82
    gas consumption 15
    oil consumption 67
automobiles *see* vehicles

B

Baker Institute, Rice University 46
banking reform 61
biomass 82, 186
BP (British Petroleum) 72, 137, 297
Brazil 152
brownouts 33
Brunei 37

C

Calder, Ken 45
capital markets 232
carbon emissions
    as Asian problem 122–24
    by source (Asia/World) 124
    and demand growth 62
    and fossil fuels 63, 107
    and NE Asia 226, 229–30
    Asian share of world's output
      122–23
Chalabi, Fadhil 40
Chemical Weapons Convention
    (CWC) 48
Chevron 297
China
    coal
      consumption 32, 119, 183,
        276, 284–85
      exports 246–47, 276
      production 156, 158
      reserves 36, 119, 156, 183

electricity
    consumption 33, 34–35, 57,
        75–76, 257
    generation 73, 77–78, 80
    reforms 78, 166–67, 266, 268
end-use energy
    commercial energy
        consumption 156, 183
    demand by sector 283
    demand growth scenarios
        285–91
    efficiency of usage 158
energy industry
    evolving policy 160–61
    forward challenges 168–70,
        174–76
    government structure 162–64
    refining industry 305–07, 308
energy intensity 157, 284, 291
future demand/supply scenarios
    203–05
    coal demand 206–07
    demand by sector 205, 206
    electricity generation 208–09
    oil/oil products imports
        207–08
gas
    consumption 22, 276, 294–
        95, 300
    development of industry 72,
        160
    LNG imports 72
    production 184, 298
    reserves 37, 72, 183
infrastructure deficiencies 174
investment
    by foreigners 105, 137, 167–
        68, 297
    outwards 42, 43–44, 135–
        37, 307–08
liberalization 5, 170–76, 289, 304
nuclear energy 125, 156
oil
    consumption 22, 32–33, 64,
        276, 291–93

    effect of rational pricing
        164–65
    imports 35–36, 136, 231,
        276, 300
    production 38, 66, 69, 184,
        295–97, 299–300
    reserves 183
petroleum industry 164–66
population 183, 275
primary energy
    composition by source 284–85
    consumption by fuel 157,
        183–84
    supply options 300–304
    supply vs demand 156, 157
renewable energy 80–82, 120,
    156, 256
transport sector 35, 65, 282–85,
    288, 291–93
China National Oil Development
    Corporation (CNODC) 91, 297
Chinese National Offshore Oil
    Corporation (CNOOC) 72, 297
Chinese National Petroleum
    Corporation (CNPC) 11, 42, 136–
    37, 307–08
Chinese National Star Petroleum
    Corporation (CNSPC) 11
Chinese Taipei 252, 256, 268
Christofferson, Gaye 308
clean fuel policies 124, 125, 183
climate change 229
climate stabilization 230
coal
    consumption 32, 73, 76, 119–
        20, 129
    exports 247
    imports 247, 252
    industry development 252
    inefficiency of 185
    pollution 36, 93, 123, 183–84, 227
    price trends 251
    reduction of use 132, 183
    reserves 36, 37, 55, 119

see also under individual
   countries
coal bed methane (CBM) 95
Combined Cycle Gas Turbine
   (CCGT) generation 6
Comprehensive Test Ban Treaty
   (CTBT) 48
consumer goods 278
consumer revolution 35
consumption of energy
   Asian energy mix 32
   by Asian country (2000) 117
   by type 119–27
   developed vs developing Asia
     117–19
   fuels by country/type 181–82
   imports 114, 121–22, 127–34, 159
   overall growth 57, 61–62, 63, 107
   per capita 32–33, 118
   production shortfall 121–22, 129
   vs economic growth 33, 85,
     113, 277–82
   vs income 278–81
   vs rest of world 3, 25, 113
   worldwide by region 107, 116
   see also under countries and
     individual fuels
corporatization *see* privatization
crop waste 186
cross-border trade 249–50
   LNG facilities for 125
   as means of securing supplies 136
   natural gas trade 249–50

D
demand
   as conflict driver 45–50
   distribution shifts 36
   influences on growth 33–35
   potential demand per capita 128
   see also consumption of energy
democracy 150
Deng Xiao-peng 25
devaluation 29
developed (industrialized) Asia

gas consumption 71
low growth rates 60
oil consumption 32, 66–67
per capita energy use 32
renewable energy 81
developing Asia
   economic growth 115–16
   electricity consumption 75
   evolving energy intensity 33
   gas consumption 61, 70
   oil consumption 65–66
   population 115, 116
   renewable energy 80
diversification
   and energy security 105–06, 115
   and environmental issues 122
domestic appliances 34

E
e-commerce 107
economic growth
   Asia vs world 115
   developing Asia 59, 61, 65, 115
   and oil prices 130, 131
   share of world output 116
   and structure of consumption
     278–80
   and structure of production
     277–78
   vs energy demand 33, 85, 113,
     277–82
economic reforms *see* liberalization;
   privatization
economy
   continuing vulnerabilities 29
   debt overhang 30
   industrialization phase 63
   mid-1997 crisis 26, 28–29, 75, 130
   recovery prospects 30–31
education 61
efficiency savings 13
electricity
   competition 75
   consumption 25, 61–62, 75–76,
     242–43

generation
  coal 75, 76–78, 92, 252
  fuel price impact 250, 252
  natural gas 37, 69, 76, 93
  nuclear energy 22, 76, 82
  renewables 76, 78–82, 93
grids
  interconnection 256–62
  international 141–42
  regional 78, 94, 262
shortages 78, 93–94, 95, 152
see also under individual
  countries
electricity industry
  reforms 75, 96–101, 146, 262–63
    current status 265–68
    privatization 264
    regulation 265
    unbundling assets 263–64
    and world prices 269–70
  structure and ownership 267
emissions
  carbon dioxide (CO$_2$) see carbon
    emissions
  greenhouse gases 32, 57, 181,
    226, 257
end-use efficiency 157, 158, 168–69
energy
  status within society 147–48
  structural trends 101–07
  trends in overall use 115–19
"energy diplomacy" 139
energy efficiency
  and demand 8, 39, 63
  environmental issues 236
  low levels of 131
Energy Information Administration
  (EIA) 3, 4, 31, 63–64, 75, 107
energy intensity
  and development 33
  and income 277–78, 281
  and industrialization 63, 278
  and liberalization 284
energy markets
  Asian impact on 25, 55, 59, 130

international nature of 6, 22–23,
    140
  NE Asian impact on 181
  use of e-commerce 107
energy policy
  liberalization see liberalization
  see also under governments
energy security
  and alternative energy 122
  energy conflict fears 23–25, 27–
    28, 114–15
  and the environment 115
  fears about China 45–50
  fears about Middle East 44
  and globalization 23–24, 48–49
  military protection options 344–45
  and shortage fears 144–45
energy use
  by type 119–27
  and economic reforms 132
  and energy efficiency 8, 39, 63,
    131, 236
  vs available resources 119
Eni 297
Enron 72
environmental concerns
  advantages of natural gas 6, 63,
    124, 253
  clean fuel policies 124, 125,
    183, 252
  climate change 229
  competition for capital 232
  and energy efficiency 236
  and LPG vehicles 197
  marine environment 231
  and nuclear energy 124
  and public opinion 36, 132
  renewable energy see renewable
    energy
Europe
  coal consumption 73
  energy consumption 3
European Union (EU) 3
exploration
  improvements in 69

joint ventures 42–43
lack of new finds 38
Exxon 43, 137, 297, 307

F
fertilizers 89
financial markets
impact of NE Asia 181
weaknesses in 29–30
Former Soviet Central Asia
alternative energy 95–97
electricity 93–95
energy overview 82–89
major oil fields 84
obstacles to progress 56, 83–85,
92–93
pollution problems 93
reserves 83, 85–88
Former Soviet Union (FSU)
coal consumption 73
gas reserves 72
fossil fuels
Asian share of world supplies 129
growing use of 21, 63, 181
as main energy source 21, 62,
63, 107
and pollution 62, 63, 107, 229–31
"four transitions" 5–6
fuel mix 8–9
fuel cell vehicles 46–47, 132, 293
fuel oil 67

G
gas
consumption 32, 71, 119–20,
124, 129
environmental gains 6, 63, 124,
253
growth forecasts 15–17, 37–38,
69–70
and international companies 344
liberalization effect 343–44
reserves 71–72
underutilization reasons 15,
124–25

see also LNG; LPG: *see also*
under individual countries
gas condensate 89
gas market
effect of Chinese demand 276
exports 37, 247–48
grid interconnection 247–50
gasoline
and automobiles 131
price rise 67
Gazprom 137
GDP (Gross Domestic Product)
and developing Asia 59, 61
GDP growth and oil demand 130
GDP per capita vs demand 35,
117–19, 127–28
growth rate, overall 25, 58–59
newly industrialized economies 60
per capita comparisons 117
General Agreement on Tariffs and
Trade (GATT) 4
geopolitics
Asia-Middle East energy nexus
39–52, 135
Asian-Russian alliances 139
cooperation
international 236–38
regional 140–42, 234
"energy diplomacy" gains 139
new political/economic ties 115,
137–42
possible East-West energy
rivalry 113
Sino-Middle East relationship
47–48
geothermal power 82, 95, 96
Global Environment Facility 219
Global Environmental Fund (GEF) 81
global warming 36, 122
globalization 21, 22–23, 102–03
governments
attitude to reform 145–46, 176
clean fuel policies 124, 125, 183
energy control 22, 145, 147–48,
176, 342

problems of 148–50, 176
liberalization *see* liberalization
renewable energy policies 255–56
Greater China 35
Greater Mekong Sub-region (GMS)
259
greenhouse gas (GHG) emissions
Asia as leading source 32, 57
and climate change 226
as global problem 181
and Kyoto Protocol 122, 252, 257
grids
effect of energy prices 261–62
electricity 78, 94
interconnection 256–61
hydropower 142
natural gas 141, 247–50, 253–54
oil 141
Gulf (Arabian) defense
burden-sharing issues 52, 140
as US responsibility 49, 50–52,
140, 309
see also Middle East
Gulf War, 1990–91 48, 51, 141

H
Hashimoto, Ryutaro 43
Horsnell, Paul 38
human labor 186
Huntington, Samuel 23
Huskey Oil 297
hybrid engines 82, 132
hydropower
consumption 32, 79–80, 120
environment 124
potential 246
projects 77–78, 80–82
water shortages 95

I
import dependence 121–22, 129–
34, 144
income
and automobiles 34, 131, 204,
278–80

and consumer goods 278–79
current per capita levels 116–17
and energy intensity 277–78, 281
and new middle classes 22, 33,
34, 35
vs electricity demand 75–76
vs energy demand 118–19,
127–28, 184, 278–81
India
biomass fuel 323–24
carbon emissions 123
coal
consumption 32, 73–74,
313, 317
imports 331–32
production 319, 331
reserves 36, 322, 331
coal bed methane (CBM) 324, 335
economic reforms 332–34
electricity
consumption 33, 78, 315
forecast growth 78
generation 74, 78, 324–28
grid plans 327
reforms 328–30
energy efficiency 131, 338–40
energy intensity 312, 338
gas
consumption 22, 317–18
demand forecast 70
and environment 333
import options 320
marketing 335
liberalization 5, 11–12, 313–14
naval plans 49
nuclear energy 318
oil consumption 22, 36, 66, 317
imports 5, 316, 335
per capita 315
projections 36, 66, 333
vs overall energy 333
oil pipelines 334–35
oil/gas exploration 322
oilfield investment 135–36
overall energy

commercial energy 311, 313
current/projected mix 317
elasticity by type 313–14
government ministries 318–19
household sector 313
per capita 314
vs GDP 312
prices 332, 334
renewable energy 318, 321–24,
335–38
transport sector 320–21, 338
Indonesia
coal
production 74, 246–47
reserves 37
electricity industry 266
energy use vs availability 119
gas
consumption 15
production 37, 119
reserves 72, 119, 138
oil
production 69, 119
reserves 119
renewable energy 255
industrial pollution 36, 62
industrialization
and energy intensity 63, 278
industrialization phase 63
process of 281
information technology 30
infrastructure
cost of 24
deficiencies in 83–84, 174
investment in 71, 125, 253
requirements 62, 69
International Energy Agency (IEA)
7, 16, 64, 135, 141
International Energy Outlook 7, 64,
69, 74, 107, 113, 286, 291–92
International Monetary Fund (IMF) 29
internationalization 101, 341–45
investment
Asia-Russia ventures 43–44

Asian-Middle East projects 41–
43, 135–36
by foreigners 103–05, 137, 146
cross-border trend 136
energy vs social investments 232
and globalization 103
NE Asia capital requirement 232
private participation 97, 99–100
privatization *see* privatization
Iran
nuclear ambitions 48
oilfield investment 42, 135
revolution disruption 49
Iran-Iraq war 47
Iraq 42
Israel 48

J
Japan
coal
consumption 75, 246–47
production 192–93
economy 21, 29, 30
electricity
consumption 76
generation 250, 252–3 (*see
also below* nuclear energy)
reforms 250, 268
energy, overall
end-use demand by
sector/fuel 190–92
primary energy demand by
fuel 191–92
primary energy supply 192–93
future energy demand/supply
scenarios 212–18
demand by sector 215
end-use demand by fuel type
214
growth rates by sector 215–16
primary fuel supplies by type
216–17
relative costs of scenarios 218
gas
consumption 15, 37, 70

LNG imports 37, 71, 193,
    246–47
production 193
liberalization of energy 10–11, 71
nuclear energy 82, 125–27, 193
    FBR reactors 252–53
    non-nuclear scenario 127, 132
    public opposition 126, 233,
        257
oil
    consumption 35, 66–67
    imports 192
    refining industry 343
oilfield investment 42–43, 135
pollution 228
renewable energy 82, 256
Japan National Oil Corporation
    (JNOC) 91
Ji Guoxing 49
Jiang Zemin 39, 41–42, 137, 301

K
Kasanov, Mikhail 137
Kazakhstan
    alternative energy 95–96
    coal
        production 91
        reserves 83, 91
    electricity 93–94, 104
    gas
        pipeline investment 104
        production 87
        reserves 87
    inward investment 104, 137
    oil
        prices 92
        production 85, 86
        reserves 83, 85–86
    refineries 86
Kemp, Geoffrey 51
Koizumi, Junichiro 126
Korea
    electricity
        nuclear generation 8
        reforms 8–9, 268

financial weaknesses 29–30
    gas consumption 15
    refining industry 343
    see also North Korea; South
        Korea
Korea Energy Economics Institute
    (KEEI) 221
Kuwait 140, 342
Kyoto Protocol 122, 252, 257
Kyrgyzstan
    coal production 93
    hydropower 83, 95
    oil production 89

L
liberalization
    and energy intensity 284
    fundamentals of 147–55
    government reluctance 145–46
    major reforms within 143
    overview 9–11
    reasons for 150–52, 241–42
    requirements for success 154–55
    risks of 152–54
Libya 42
Liu Huaqing 49
LNG (liquefied natural gas)
    cost of projects 125
    growth forecast 37
    imports 233–34, 247
    infrastructure investment 71,
        125, 248, 253, 299
    price trends 71, 251
    regional trade 55
LPG (liquefied petroleum gas) 132,
    197
Lukman, Rilwanu 41

M
Malaysia
    electricity industry 266, 268
    gas
        consumption 15

LNG trade 37, 70–71
  reserves 72
oil production 69
oilfield investment 135
renewable energy 255
marine environment 231
market economics 3–4, 5
markets, liberalization of 8–9
"megacities" 62
methane 229
middle classes 22, 33, 34, 35
middle distillates 67
Middle East
  Asia-Middle East energy nexus
    39–52, 135
  foreign investment in 42
  future oil output requirement 61
  growing Asian oil/gas
    dependence on 21, 39–41, 61,
    135, 140, 231
  growing capital flows into 44
  NE Asia cooperation benefits
    238–39
  reserves 61
  see also Gulf, Arabian
military weapons
  Chinese arms supplies 45, 47, 48
  Chinese military plans 47, 49–50
  Indian naval plans 49–50
  potential arms race 47, 50, 51
Missile Technology Control Regime
  (MTCR) 48
Mobil 137
Mongolia
  commercial fuel use by sector
    193–94
  fuel supply 194
  future energy use projections
    219–21
    final demand by fuel 219
    final demand by sector 220
    fuel supply estimates 220

infrastructure hosting 235
primary energy trends 195

N
National Iranian Oil Company 136
nationalism 171
natural gas see gas
Nautilus Institute 185, 186
New Zealand 82
NIEs (newly industrialized
  economies) 60
nitrogen oxides 62, 124, 227, 228
"non-fuel" oils 197
Non-Proliferation Treaty (NPT) 48
North America
  energy consumption 3
  oil production 69
  see also United States
North American Free Trade Area
  (NAFTA) 3
North Korea (DPRK)
  coal
    consumption 185, 186
    reserves 188
  electricity 187, 188–89
  energy, overall
    demand (by fuel and sector)
      185–87
    reduction in usage 185–86
    supply 185, 188–90
  energy-sector problems 187–88
  fuel inefficiency 185
  future energy demand/supply
    scenarios 209–12
    final energy by fuel type 210
    final energy by sector 211
    primary energy by fuel 211–12
  historic economic ties 235
  pollution 229
Northeast Asia 202–03
  capital investment requirement
    232
  China as energy driver 183
  commercial fuel consumption
    181–82

electricity demand 242–43
electricity generation 242–43
  by country/fuel 244–45
  natural gas 247, 253
environmental effects of energy
  use 226–31
  acid rain 226–29
  emissions of acid gases 228
  fossil fuel growth scenarios
    230–31
  global climate change 229–31
  global marine pollution 231
  impact-reducing measures 236
  share of world carbon
    emissions 229–30
  gas supplies 253–54
  impact on energy markets 181
  international cooperation
    benefits 236–38
  nuclear energy 244
  renewable energy policies 256
  reserves 245–46
Northeast Asian Power Grid Ring
  (proposed) 257–59
nuclear power
  as clean fuel 124, 125
  consumption 22, 76, 121
  limiting factors 36, 125–27,
    132, 233

O
offshore oil 297
oil
  consumption
    effect of economic crisis
      25–26, 28
    projections 21, 46–47, 65,
      114, 131–32
    and transport 22, 38, 65, 66,
      131, 182
    vs rest of world 31, 32, 55, 129
    worldwide 64, 68
  exports 38
  imports

    dependence on Middle East
      21, 39–41, 61, 135, 140, 231
    growth of 31, 114, 121–22,
      231
    limited international companies'
      role 343
    production 38, 39, 69, 133
    reserves 38–39, 69
    supply vs demand 158
oil markets
  Asia as driver 21
  effect of Chinese demand 276
  global nature of 23, 40
  OPEC share 67
  and transport costs 40
oil prices
  and Asian demand 130, 131
  and currency swings 29
  and electricity supply 250
  global linkage of 250
  limitation of competition 343
  mid-1980s fall 46
  price trends 251
  price-maintenance cutbacks in
    1980s 39
  rise in 2000 64, 78
oil recovery 13–14
Organization for Economic
  Cooperation and Development
  (OECD) 4
Organization of Petroleum
  Exporting Countries (OPEC)
  Asia as main market 41
  Asian downstream investment
    41–43
  overall exports 67–68
  potential capital flow 44

P
Pacific Rim 64
particle emission 62, 93
Pearl Harbor 45
petrochemicals 89
petroleum products

demand growth by type 67
retailing competition 146
Petron 43, 136
Petronas 42, 135, 137
Philippines
electricity
consumption 56
generation 82, 252
restructuring 56, 97–101,
266, 268
foreign investment 105
renewable energy 82, 255
photovoltaic power 82
pipelines
gas 37, 137, 247–50, 344
interconnection projects
247–50
"West-East" pipeline 16, 37
international investment 72,
137–38, 298
oil 137–38, 301–02, 344
politics *see also* geopolitics
pollution
and agriculture 229
international opposition 123–24
as regional issue 227–28
see also individual types: *see
also under* coal; fossil fuel;
environmental issues
population
Asian vs world 62, 115, 128
China 183, 275
and demand growth 62, 118–19,
128
developing Asia vs world (2000)
61, 116
growth projection 62
Russian Far East (RFE) 200
South Korea (ROK) 195
United States 275
"post-industrial" phase 278
prices
coal 250–51
as diversification driver 78
effect of rational pricing 132

effect on renewable energy 254
LNG trends 71, 251
oil *see* oil prices
oil product differentials 67
and reforms 269–70
subsidization by state 145
privatization
main reasons for 149–50, 241–42
opportunities within 104
process of 102, 264
resistance to 77
undesirable outcomes 153

R
rational pricing 132
refineries
and crude types 45, 159
major centers 39
Middle East investment 136
oil sources 39
and petroleum demand 67
renewable energy
comparative costs 254
consumption 79–82
and environmental concerns 63,
122
government policies 255–56
growth projections 76, 78–79
reasons for using 254
see also individual forms of
energy
Republic of Korea (ROK) *see* South
Korea
reserves
coal 55, 246
gas
East Asia 246
worldwide 71–72
oil 38, 69, 246
see also under individual
countries
Riyadh 44
Royal Dutch/Shell 43, 72
Russia
distance from markets 138

impact of exports 235–36
as source of Asian oil/gas 137–39
trade with China 137–38, 301
Russia Petroleum 137
Russian Far East (RFE)
    consumption vs imports 201
    energy demand 200, 201
    energy supply 200–201
    future energy use projections
        224–25
        demand by fuel 224–25
        demand by sector 225–26
    gas reserves 37
    population 200
    resources 138–39, 200–202, 234

S
Saudi Aramco 43, 136, 307
Saudia Arabia 39, 41–42, 45
Sea Lanes of Communication
    (SLOC) 49
self-sufficiency 106–07
Shell 72, 137, 297
Silk Road Petroleum 135
Singapore
    electricity reform 265, 268
    and recession 21
    as refining center 67, 135
skills shortages 173–74
social equity 155
socialism 171
solar power 82, 95–96
sour crude 159
South Asia 60–61
South China Sea 45
South Korea (ROK)
    coal consumption 74, 197, 198,
        246–47
    electricity
        consumption 198, 199, 257
        generation 74, 199, 252
        industry structure 266
    energy, overall
        demand by fuel 196–98
        growth pattern 33–34

        supply by fuel 198
    fuel imports 199
    future energy use projections
        221–24
        final fuels demand/by fuel
            type 223
        final fuels demand/by sector
            223
        long-range forecast 223–24
        primary energy demand
            221–22
    gas consumption
        LNG 37, 247
        LPG 197
        "town gas" 198
    GDP growth 196
    nuclear power 125–26, 252
    oil consumption 33–34, 66
        fuel oils 197, 198
    pollution 228–29
    population 195
    renewable energy 256
    transport 34
Southeast Asia
    economic growth 60
    electricity demand 242–43
    electricity generation 242–43
        by country/fuel 244–45
        natural gas 247, 253
    oil consumption 36
    renewable energy policies 255–56
    reserves 245–46
Southeast Asia Power
  Interconnection project 257, 259–61
Southern China 132
Southwest Asia 4
Ssangyong Oil Refining 43, 136
structural trends, energy 101–08
subsidization of prices 145
Sudan 42
sulfur oxides 52, 124, 227, 228
sustainability 63
sweet crude 45
synthetic oil 91–92

T
Taiwan 37, 74, 247, 266

Tajikistan 89, 105
technology
    efficiency savings 13, 281
    increasing role 24
    new automobile technologies
        46–47, 132, 197, 236
    oil recovery 13–14
Tenaga Nasional Berhad (TNB) 266
Texaco 297
Thailand 34, 252
    automobile purchases 34
    coal consumption 252
    electricity
        generation 252
        reforms 266, 268
    financial problems 29
    pollution control 252
    renewable energy 255
Tokyo Electric Power Company
  (TEPCO) 126–27
"town gas" 198
Tractebel 104
transport sector 38, 66, 131
    see also vehicles
transportation of oil/gas
    inadequacy of 83–84, 88, 89–
        90, 92–93
    markets determined by costs of
        140
    sea-lanes
        disruption study 50–51
        effect of increased shipping
            226
        fears of disruption 45–50
        possible security cooperation
            49, 142
    see also grids; pipelines
Turkmenistan
    foreign investment 104–05
    gas
        production 88
        reserves 83, 88

U
United Kingdom 153–54
United Nations Development
  Program 219

United States
    1960–1977 growth in oil imports
      46
    coal consumption 73, 156
    energy, overall
        diversification 106
        self-sufficiency 106
        shortages 78, 152, 153
    gas consumption 22
    as guardian of Gulf stability 49,
      50–52, 140, 309
    high CO_2 emissions 63
    oil consumption 21, 22, 114
    oil-saving auto technologies
      132
    oil/gas supplies from Western
      Hemisphere 40, 140
    overall energy consumption 32, 65
    population 275
    primary energy supply 275
    real GDP 275
    reduction in Gulf oil imports 40,
      140
uranium 125–26, 253
urbanization 62
US Center for Naval Analysis
  (CNA) 50, 51
US Department of Energy (DOE) 31
Uzbekistan
    electricity 93–94
    foreign investment 105
    gas reserves 83
    oil production 88
    resources 88–89

V
vehicles
    automobile growth vs income
      34, 131, 204, 278–80
    new technologies 46–47, 132,
      197, 236
    nitrous oxide pollution 227
    and oil demand 22, 38, 65, 66,
      131, 182
    registrations by country 279–80
Vietnam 256

W
water shortages 95
wind power 82, 95–96
wood 186
workforce 61
World Bank 81
World Energy Outlook 7, 16, 64
World Energy Projection System
 (WEPS) 64, 109–10
World Health Organization (WHO)
 62, 122
World Trade Organization (WTO) 4

X
Xinjiang

alternative energy 96
coal
 production 91
 reserves 83, 91, 92
and foreign investment 105
oil
 production 89–90, 91
 reserves 90

Y
Yamani, Ahmed Zaki 41
Yergin, Daniel 24

Z
Zhang Zhigang 299